Licensing and Access to Content in the European Union

Copyright is territorial, but the same cannot be said of the Internet, whose borderless nature has changed the way we consume copyright-protected material. Nevertheless, territorial segmentation of online content remains a reality in the 28 Member States of the European Union. Licensing and access practices do not reflect this digital reality, in which end users demand ubiquitous access to content. For this reason, the territorial nature of copyright and traditional business models based on national exploitation prevents the completion of the Digital Single Market. Sebastian Felix Schwemer provides a unique analysis of the dynamic licensing and access arrangements for audiovisual works and music and shows how they are being addressed by sector regulation and competition law in the Digital Single Market. His analysis, which includes case law of the Court of Justice, the Commission's competition proceedings and various legislative tools, reveals the overlapping nature of legislative and non-legislative regulatory solutions.

Sebastian Felix Schwemer is an industrial postdoctoral researcher at the Centre for Information and Innovation Law (CIIR) at the University of Copenhagen. His research interests are at the intersection of regulation, technology and society, and he frequently speaks on related issues.

T0371063

Cambridge Intellectual Property and Information Law

As its economic potential has rapidly expanded, intellectual property has become a subject of front-rank legal importance. Cambridge Intellectual Property and Information Law is a series of monograph studies of major current issues in intellectual property. Each volume contains a mix of international, European, comparative and national law, making this a highly significant series for practitioners, judges and academic researchers in many countries.

Series Editors

Lionel Bently,
Herchel Smith Professor of Intellectual Property Law, University of Cambridge

Graeme Dinwoodie,
Professor of Intellectual Property and Information Technology Law, University of Oxford

Advisory Editors

William R. Cornish, Emeritus Herchel Smith Professor of Intellectual Property Law, University of Cambridge

François Dessemontet, Professor of Law, University of Lausanne

Jane C. Ginsburg, Morton L. Janklow Professor of Literary and Artistic Property Law, Columbia Law School

Paul Goldstein, Professor of Law, Stanford University

The Rt Hon. Sir Robin Jacob, Hugh Laddie Professor of Intellectual Property, University College London

Ansgar Ohly, Professor of Intellectual Property Law, Ludwig-Maximilian University of Munich

A list of books in the series can be found at the end of this volume.

Licensing and Access to Content in the European Union

Regulation between Copyright and Competition Law

Sebastian Felix Schwemer

University of Copenhagen, Faculty of Law

CAMBRIDGE
UNIVERSITY PRESS

University Printing House, Cambridge CB2 8BS, United Kingdom

One Liberty Plaza, 20th Floor, New York, NY 10006, USA

477 Williamstown Road, Port Melbourne, VIC 3207, Australia

314-321, 3rd Floor, Plot 3, Splendor Forum, Jasola District Centre, New Delhi - 110025, India

103 Penang Road, #05-06/07, Visioncrest Commercial, Singapore 238467

Cambridge University Press is part of the University of Cambridge.

It furthers the University's mission by disseminating knowledge in the pursuit of education, learning and research at the highest international levels of excellence.

www.cambridge.org
Information on this title: www.cambridge.org/9781108468893
DOI: 10.1017/9781108653213

First published 2019
First paperback edition 2022

A catalogue record for this publication is available from the British Library

Library of Congress Cataloging in Publication data
Names: Schwemer, Sebastian Felix.
Title: Licensing and access to content in the European Union : regulation between copyright and competition law / Sebastian Felix Schwemer, University of Copenhagen, Faculty of Law.
Description: Cambridge, United Kingdom ; New York, NY, USA : Cambridge University Press, 2019. | Series: Cambridge intellectual property and information law | Based on author's thesis (doctoral – Kobenhavns universitet. Juridiske fakultet, 2016) issued under title: Digital Content Licensing : Licensing and access arrangements between competition law and sector-regulation. | Includes bibliographical references and index.
Identifiers: LCCN 2018042043 | ISBN 9781108475778 (hardback)
Subjects: LCSH: Digital media – Law and legislation – European Union countries. | Copyright licenses – European Union countries. | Antitrust law – European Union countries. | BISAC: LAW / Intellectual Property / General.
Classification: LCC KJE2655.79 .S39 2019 | DDC 346.2404/82–dc23
LC record available at https://lccn.loc.gov/2018042043

ISBN 978-1-108-47577-8 Hardback
ISBN 978-1-108-46889-3 Paperback

Contents

Figures and Tables

Figures

Table

Preface

Copyright is territorial. But is the Internet? The Internet has changed the way in which we consume copyright-protected material. Yet, territorial segmentation of online content is a reality in the 28 European Union Member States. Licensing and access practices do not reflect the digital reality, in which end users demand ubiquitous access. The territorial nature of copyright, and business models traditionally based on national exploitation, collide with the borderless nature of the Internet. This is recognised by EU policymakers as hampering the development of new business models as well as the goal of the European lawmaker to complete the Digital Single Market (DSM).

National and European authorities and legislators have created a host of – often industry- and sometimes business model-specific – initiatives, proposals and rules in order to facilitate the DSM and reconcile it with the territorial nature of copyright and its business practices, in part accompanying, refining or codifying industry-led solutions. In this, despite the novel nature of Internet uses and business models, traditional stress field, competition law and policy and copyright overlap and interfere.

This book probes the different regulatory (legislative and non-legislative) initiatives that support the facilitation of multi-territorial licensing and cross-border access to online content. It investigates the regulation of two online markets that have recently been subject to scrutiny by the EU institutions: the audiovisual and music sectors. Both are addressed by *ex ante* sector-specific legislation and *ex post* control under competition law. Based on these case studies, the book argues that the interplay between harmonisation efforts and competition proceedings has been helpful in mitigating the effects of licences, thereby enabling cross-border dissemination.

The book, however, reveals that this interplay has not always been coherent. The author argues that more coherent measures are necessary in order to reduce frictions in licensing arrangements and to enable cross-border access across the EU. Furthermore, the book suggests that the regulatory interventions to date may have been driven more by a competition and subsidiary harmonisation agenda than by a focus on consumers and innovative service providers.

Acknowledgements

This book is based on the research that I have performed in the course of my PhD dissertation at the Centre for Information and Innovation Law (CIIR) at the Faculty of Law, University of Copenhagen, from 2013 to 2016.

I am indebted to my supervisor, Professor Thomas Riis: not only did he patiently support me with valuable critique; he also helped me to navigate, with the right amount of steering in stimulating discussions. My thanks also go to Professor Bernt Hugenholtz for being willing to provide his supportive critique before I submitted my dissertation. This book project has also benefited greatly from valuable comments and thoughtful discussion with my assessment committee during my PhD defence in December 2016: Professor Morten Rosenmeier, Associate Professor Lucie Guibault and Professor Ole-Andreas Rognstad.

My thanks go to my colleagues at the CIIR at the University of Copenhagen for providing a stimulating and warm environment. A final word to my family and friends: I am grateful for your patience, understanding and support. Without this, my endeavour would have been a much less worthwhile journey.

Abbreviations

AG	Advocate General
AVMSD	Audiovisual Media Services Directive
BGH	Bundesgerichtshof (German Federal Supreme Court)
BIEM	Bureau International de l'Edition Mecanique
BR	Better Regulation
CIIR	Centre for Information and Innovation Law
CISAC	International Confederation of Societies of Authors and Composers
CJEU	Court of Justice (European Union) (formerly European Court of Justice (ECJ))
CMO	collective management organisations
CRM	collective rights management
DG	Directorate-General of the European Commission
DG MARKT	Directorate-General for Internal Market
DG COMP	Directorate-General for Competition
DSM	Digital Single Market
DSMS	Digital Single Market Strategy of the European Commission
DSP	digital service provider
EEA	European Economic Area
ECL	Extended collective licensing
EP	European Parliament
EU	European Union
EULA	End user licensing agreements
FAPL	Football Association Premier League Ltd
IA	impact assessment
IME	independent management organisation
MEP	Member of the European Parliament
MS	Member State(s)
MTL	multi-territorial licensing
NIE	new institutional economics
OJ	*Official Journal*

OLG	Oberlandesgericht (German District Court)
RRA	reciprocal representation agreement
SO	statement of objections
SVOD	Subscription video-on-demand service(s)
TEU	Treaty on European Union
TFEU	Treaty on the Functioning of the European Union
TPM	technological protection measures
TRIPS	Agreement on Trade-Related Aspects of Intellectual Property Rights
UrhG	Urheberrechtsgesetz (German Copyright Act)
WCT	WIPO Copyright Treaty
WIPO	World Intellectual Property Organization
WPPT	WPO Performances and Phonograms Treaty

Table of Cases

General Court

Commission

Table of Legislation

and amending Regulations (EC) No 2006/2004 and (EU) 2017/2394 and Directive 2009/22/EC [2018] OJ L601 (Geo-blocking Regulation), 5, 26, 180, 201–209, 213, 216, 226, 227, 229, 255

Denmark

Lov om kollektiv forvaltning af ophavsret (Lov nr 321 af 05/04/2016), 137, 139, 263

Germany

Verwertungsgesellschaftengesetz vom 24. Mai 2016 (BGBl. I S. 1190), das zuletzt durch Artikel 14 des Gesetzes vom 17. Juli 2017 (BGBl. I S. 2541) geändert worden ist, 137, 140, 142

Sweden

Lag (2016:977) om kollektiv förvaltning av upphovsrätt (Svensk författningssamling (SFS); Number: SFS 2016:977, 2016–11-10), 137

1 Introduction

1.1 Background

Endeavours exploring aspects of digitalisation and law often start with a generic analysis of the multiple transformational effects that the Internet has had on our information society and how the law needs to adapt in one way or another.[1] Let me skip this part – for now – and start by posing the following question: Copyright is territorial. But is the Internet?

Country-code top-level domain names, like '.de' or '.se', provide a somewhat natural geographical delineation of the Internet. But the answer, in technological terms, is 'no'. Yet, the traditional practice of national exploitation of content by its rights holders has continued through the first two decades of the twenty-first century. This delineation, it seems, is at odds with the technological possibilities of the Internet, and even more so with the digital pendant to the internal market, the Digital Single Market, whose completion is the main harmonisation goal of the European Commission in the digital sphere.[2] So, in ten or fifteen years from now, will we still see this territorial delineation of content on the Internet? My hope is that the answer is again likely to be 'no'. What, then, stands between us, in a digital content world consisting of twenty-eight national markets and twenty-four official languages, and this vision of a common European market for online content for the more than 500 million citizens?

The starting point is relatively clear, and so is the goal: from a European Union (EU) regulatory perspective, a Digital Single Market instead of twenty-eight national markets – and, from a right holder's perspective, preserving the exploitation of national markets. But everything in between is complex. This makes for a fascinating topic with intriguing

---

[1] The same can be observed in the documents on digital copyright by the European legislator: see, e.g., E. Rosati, 'The Digital Single Market Strategy: Too many (strategic?) omissions' (*IPKat*, 7 May 2015), 40: http://ipkitten.blogspot.dk/2015/05/the-digital-single-market-strategy-too.html
[2] See Commission, 'Digital Single Market' (*European Commission*, 25 February 2016): https://ec.europa.eu/digital-single-market/digital-single-market

questions, devoting closer scrutiny to the regulatory framework surrounding content licensing on the Internet.

Let us turn back to the transformational effects of the Internet. The dissemination of copyright-protected content has undergone extensive developments. In recent years, digital technologies have fostered the emergence of new legal and illegal distribution channels for musical and film works, and have challenged traditional business models. According to a study performed in 2014, close to 70 per cent of EU citizens 'download or stream films for free, whether legally or illegally'.[3] Online streaming has become the dominant form of consumption, but there exist only relatively few pan-European music- or film-streaming platforms.[4]

Cross-border activities are becoming more prevalent, too: in a 2015 Eurobarometer survey[5] of 26,000 EU citizens on cross-border access to online content, 3 per cent of the participants indicated having a paid subscription for an online service and having tried to access it in a cross-border situation. Some 5 per cent of participants had, within the preceding twelve months, tried to access audiovisual content (films, TV series, etc.) via an online service that was intended for users of a different Member State. As many as 27 per cent of citizens are interested in accessing audiovisual content or music transmitted from their home country while temporarily abroad.[6] Despite the cultural and industrial fragmentation of the EU audiovisual sector,[7] 19 per cent of citizens are

[3] See Commission, 'Lack of choice driving demand for film downloads' (Press release) IP/14/120, Brussels, 6 February 2014.

[4] According to the EU Commission, more than 2,500 on-demand audiovisual services were available in the EU at the end of 2014 (Commission, 'A Digital Single Market Strategy for Europe – Analysis and Evidence Accompanying the document Communication from the Commission to the European Parliament, the Council, the European Economic and Social Committee and the Committee of the Regions' (Commission Staff Working Document) SWD(2015) 100 final, Brussels, 6 May 2015, 26). This compares with estimates of 700 on-demand and catch-up services in 2010 (KEA European Affairs and Mines ParisTech, *Multi-Territory Licensing of Audiovisual Works in the European Union* (Final Report prepared for the European Commission, DG Information Society and Media 2010), 2).

[5] Commission, 'Cross-border Access to Online Content, Report' (2015) Flash Eurobarometer, 411, TNS Political & Social.

[6] Commission, 'A Digital Single Market Strategy for Europe – Analysis and Evidence Accompanying the document Communication from the Commission to the European Parliament, the Council, the European Economic and Social Committee and the Committee of the Regions', 26.

[7] KEA European Affairs and Mines ParisTech, 3. The European Parliament notes that heterogeneous cultural and linguistic diversity 'should be considered a benefit rather than an obstacle to the single market': see European Parliament, 'Report on the implementation of Directive 2001/29/EC of the European Parliament and of the Council of 22 May 2001 on the harmonisation of certain aspects of copyright and related rights in the information society (2014/2256(INI))' – Committee on Legal Affairs, Rapporteur: Julia Reda, 24 June 2015, PE 546.580v03-00, A8-0209/2015, Recital 9.

interested in watching or listening to content from other EU countries.[8] These numbers are likely to have continued to grow. The need to create a 'seamless global digital marketplace' is also acknowledged by the World Intellectual Property Organization (WIPO) Director General Francis Gurry.[9]

The market reality looks different, though.[10] In 2012, the European Commission urged the industry 'to deliver innovative solutions for greater access to online content'.[11] According to findings published in March 2016 based on replies of more than 1,400 companies, however, 77 per cent of subscription-based and 82 per cent of publicly funded business models apply geo-blocking.[12] In respect of collective management, Commissioner Michel Barnier commented that many collective management organisations (CMOs) have not been able to meet the challenges, 'resulting in fewer online music services available to consumers'.[13] Towards this reality, in May 2015, the European Parliament urged 'the Commission (. . .) to propose adequate solutions for better cross-border accessibility of services and copyright content for consumers'.[14]

---

[8] Commission, 'A Digital Single Market Strategy for Europe – Analysis and Evidence Accompanying the document Communication from the Commission to the European Parliament, the Council, the European Economic and Social Committee and the Committee of the Regions', 26.

[9] WIPO Director General Francis Gurry, '2013 Address by the Director General', *WIPO Assemblies* – September 23 to October 2, 2013: www.wipo.int/about-wipo/en/dgo/spee ches/a_51_dg_speech.html

[10] Kalimo et al., for example, remark '[i]t seems puzzling that still in the year 2015, not all of the involved stakeholders seem convinced that the commercial possibilities of digitalization surpass what is possible with traditional distribution channels'. H. Kalimo, K. Olkkonen and J. Vaario, 'EU Intellectual Property Rights Law – Driving Innovation or Stifling the Digital Single Market?' in H. Kalimo and M. S. Jansson (eds.), *EU Economic Law in a Time of Crisis* (Edward Elgar, 2016), p. 157.

[11] Commission, 'Copyright: Commission urges industry to deliver innovative solutions for greater access to online content' (Press release) IP/12/1394, Brussels, 18 December 2012. See also economic studies by M. Batikas, E. Gomez-Herrera and B. Martens, 'Geographic Fragmentation in the EU Market for e-Books: The case of Amazon', Institute for Prospective Technological Studies, Digital Economy Working Paper [2015], 2015/13; L. Aguiar and J. Waldfogel, 'Streaming Reaches Flood Stage: Does Spotify Stimulate or Depress Music Sales?' (2015) NBER Working Paper Series, Working Paper 21653: www.nber.org/papers/w21653; E. Gomez-Herrera and B. Martens, 'Language, Copyright and Geographic Segmentation in the EU Digital Single Market for Music and Films', Digital Economy Working Paper (2015), 2015–4.

[12] See Commission, 'Geo-blocking practices in e-commerce; Issues paper presenting initial findings of the e-commerce sector inquiry conducted by the Directorate-General for Competition' (Commission Staff Working Document) SWD(2016) 70 final, Brussels, 18 March 2016, paras. 135–136.

[13] Commission, 'Commissioner Michel Barnier welcomes the trilogue agreement on collective rights management' (Press release) MEMO/13/955, Brussels, 5 November 2013.

[14] European Parliament, 'Report on the implementation of Directive 2001/29/EC of the European Parliament and of the Council of 22 May 2001 on the harmonisation of certain

This book deals with access to online content and the challenges of licensing copyright-protected works on the Internet: an area in which the territorial nature of copyright[15] and its traditionally national exploitation collide, given the borderless nature of the Internet.[16] Whereas the territorial exploitation of copyright in the EU is not a novel phenomenon, its associated challenges have been exacerbated. In the information society, consumers' demand for ubiquitous access (cross-border, portable, full-repertoire) to copyright-protected works has emerged. In copyright-heavy industries like the music and film business, online content service providers such as Spotify, iTunes, Netflix, Amazon and the like cannot develop business models without heavy involvement from the respective rights holders. It appears that traditional licensing mechanisms and arrangements, however, have not been able to facilitate rights clearance smoothly in the changed environment.

National and European authorities and legislators have created a host of – often industry- and sometimes business model-specific– initiatives, proposals and rules in order to facilitate a Digital Single Market – in part accompanying, refining or codifying industry-led solutions. The territorial delineation of markets along national borders, which has historically found support in EU courts' practice, has been challenged by the courts and the European legislator (specifically, the EU Commission as legislative initiator), who emphasises different policy goals with the aim of introducing more competition and ultimately making more content accessible for consumers – without abandoning the exclusive and territorial nature of rights, though. This is supported by the political goal of increased market integration, notably around (entertainment) content. But how are we to solve the problems of cross-border access to content and its licensing in order to enable the Digital Single Market while maintaining the incentive function of copyright? In this stress field, 'geo-blocking', 'cross-border portability' and 'multi-territorial licensing' come together. In this, despite the novel nature of Internet exploitation and business models, traditional

---

aspects of copyright and related rights in the information society (2014/2256(INI))', Recital 9.

[15] See Art. 5 of Berne Convention for the Protection of Literary and Artistic Works (Paris Act of 24 July 1971), as amended on 28 September 1979 and the ten EU Directives relating to copyright and related rights. See also Section 2.2.

[16] Or, as the EU legislator puts it in the context of music: 'While the internet knows no borders, the online market for music services in the Union is still fragmented, and a digital single market has not yet been fully achieved' (Recital 38 of Directive 2014/26/EU of the European Parliament and of the Council of 26 February 2014 on collective management of copyright and related rights and multi-territorial licensing of rights in musical works for online use in the internal market [2014] OJ L84/72).

stress fields, competition law and policy and copyright overlap and interfere with another.

1.2   Scope of This Book

This book, studies two phenomena: first, the licensing of – which is ultimately linked to access to – copyright-protected works on the Internet in cross-border situations. This concept of access can be looked at from at least two different viewpoints, which represents two interrelated sides of the same coin: on the one side, consumers who have access to works, and, on the other side, rights holders who make works accessible. Secondly, there is the interplay between regulatory initiatives to support cross-border access to copyrighted material. This translates into the following guiding questions, which this book will address:

What is the regulatory framework for licensing of – and, related to this – access to online music and audiovisual content in cross-border situations?

How do the different regulatory frameworks interact, what inconsistencies emerge and how could these be resolved?

This book contains expository elements, which centre on investigating the legal framework and functioning of the system of cross-border licensing and access arrangements. Given the complexity of the subject matter, the current practices in the market for collective licensing of online music are analysed and the territorial practices towards consumers, as well as in licensing agreements regarding audiovisual works, are laid out. As regards the regulatory environment, both proceedings under the general competition rules (i.e. *ex post* control by the European Commission in its function as competition authority as well as the courts[17]) and sector-specific regulation (i.e. *ex ante* legislative measures[18]) are examined.

Secondly, this book assesses how these regulatory frameworks interact. Different forms of regulation might be based on different rationales, such as competition, internal market or harmonisation considerations. But how does this interplay unfold, and to what effect? In other words, the

---

[17] Such as CISAC proceedings; Joined Cases C–403/08 and C–429/08, *Football Association Premier League Ltd and Others* v. *QC Leisure and Others* [2011] ECR I–9159–9245, ECLI: EU:C:2011:631; as well as the Commission's pay-TV investigation.

[18] Such as Directive 2014/26/EU, Regulation (EU) 2017/1128 of the European Parliament and of the Council of 14 June 2017 on cross-border portability of online content services in the internal market [2017] OJ L168; Regulation (EU) 2018/302 of the European Parliament and of the Council of 28 February 2018 on addressing unjustified geo-blocking and other forms of discrimination based on customers' nationality, place of residence or place of establishment within the internal market and amending Regulations (EC) No 2006/2004 and (EU) 2017/2394 and Directive 2009/22/EC [2018] OJ L60I.

guiding questions here are what the relationship between competition law and (legislative) measures directed towards the facilitation of content licensing is, and how the EU's complementing competition and copyright-related sector-regulation routes interact and whether they support each other in achieving their goals (i.e. in overcoming licensing issues based on territoriality). In this context, the book first analyses the different arrangements and regulatory models. In order to identify potential inconsistencies in the regulatory framework, it examines the interplay between the different forms of regulatory initiatives – namely, state-induced, on the one hand, and market developments, i.e. private regulation, on the other. What is regulation, and are licensing structures regulatory instruments that help to shape the market, or are they to be seen as products of regulatory intervention? From these insights, normative considerations are derived as to whether the chosen routes reflect on the goal of EU-wide access, to what extent this has been achieved, and how some of the identified conflicts could be resolved – leading to a more coherent framework for online licensing for EU-wide purposes.

First, however, there exist several key concepts and notions that need to be refined. The scope of this book can be defined along three dimensions: (1) subject matter, (2) legal areas and (3) geographical focus.

Territorial restrictions on content are not a novel challenge, and there have been comparable issues with more traditional forms of exploitation, which are thematically connected to or comparable to those under scrutiny in this work. I have chosen not to follow a traditional past-present-future narrative, though. Instead, this book investigates the provision of so-called 'interactive on-demand services', which means that consumers can actively choose the musical or audiovisual work and the time of consumption (non-linear).[19] This limitation does not preclude drawing on learning from past experiences in different arrangements, where relevant. An exhaustive account and comparison of the different forms of consumption, however, would go far beyond the objective of this book. Other forms of consumption, for example downloads or even physical copies, may involve different arrangements and rights. Additionally, as mentioned above, interactive on-demand streaming has become the prevailing form of consumption of content in most EU Member States, with online service providers such as Spotify, Apple Music, YouTube, Netflix or online libraries of private and public TV channels. In this 'age of access'

---

[19] As opposed to linear services, where the content is not at the consumer's individual request. See also definition in Art. 1(1)(g) of Directive 2010/13/EU of the European Parliament and of the Council of 10 March 2010 on the coordination of certain provisions laid down by law, regulation or administrative action in Member States concerning the provision of audiovisual media services [2010] OJ L95/1.

(Hilty and Köklu), issues of cross-border access have been exacerbated. Thus, streaming is increasingly in the cross-hairs of – otherwise technological neutral – regulatory intervention. Given the multiple differences of commercial services to public broadcasting or cultural heritage institutions, the book will only selectively look over the fence towards these services.

Thematically, this study looks at two different, yet related, industry verticals and forms of online content: audiovisual works and musical works. In the following chapters I first look at the licensor–licensee relationship between online music service providers and CMOs.[20] Secondly, I look at the licensing and contractual relationship between rights holders, online service providers and consumers[21] regarding cross-border access to audiovisual works. This correlates roughly with the differentiation of market participants in a copyright market by Watt, who distinguishes rights holders, commercial users and consumers.[22] But is this an endeavour to compare apples with apples, or apples with oranges? I argue that juxtaposing these two forms of online content is beneficial for several reasons: first, the licensing of interactive on-demand streaming and access to these services has come into the cross-hairs of regulatory activity, which makes them worthwhile studying.[23] Secondly, whereas they invoke fairly similar rights, the

---

[20] A word on the notion of collective management of rights and its organisations: in earlier economic and legal scholarship such arrangements have often been referred to as 'collecting societies'. Other notions used include rights management organisations (CRMOs), Collective Rights Organisations (CROs), joint copyright management (C. Handke, 'Collective Administration' in R. Watt (ed.), *Handbook on the Economics of Copyright* (Edward Elgar 2014)) or, sometimes, more broadly, intellectual property rights (IPR) exchange institutions (R. P. Merges, 'Contracting into Liability Rules: Intellectual Property Rights and Collective Rights Organizations', *California Law Review*, 84 (1996), 1293), private intellectual property rights organisations (Posner, 'Transaction Costs and Antitrust Concerns'), or intellectual property clearinghouses. For the sake of conformity, I have chosen to refer to these organisations throughout this book as collective management organisations (CMOs). This imposed unitary terminology is to be employed with care, though. Concepts may already exist (as is the case here) and similar terms may be used by different theories for different concepts. See also P. te Hacken, 'Terms and Specialized Vocabulary. Taming the Prototype' in H. J. Kockaert and F. Steurs (eds.), *Handbook of Terminology*, vol. 1 (Jon Bejamins Publishing Co., 2015), p. 4.

[21] Whereas consumers play a key role, e.g., in Regulation (EU) 2017/1128, the regulatory focus in music has been on the horizontal relationship between CMOs and the vertical licensing relationship between rights holders and online service providers.

[22] R. Watt, *Copyright and Economic Theory: Friends or Foes?* (2000), 8.

[23] Van Gestel and Micklitz accuse legal researchers of 'herd behaviour' regarding scholarly work on policy, where 'researchers choose to follow "hot topics" and trends' (R. van Gestel and H.-W. Micklitz, 'Revitalizing Doctrinal Legal Research in Europe: What About Methodology?' in U. Neergaard, R. Nielsen and L. Roseberry (eds.), *European Legal Method – Paradoxes and Revitalisation* (DJØF Publishing, 2011),

situation regarding rights holders and their organisation, as well as the licensing relationship, look quite different for the respective subject matters. Still, some important insights might be gained by opposing these two: economists Liebowitz and Watt have noted that developments in the music industry are seen as 'a likely harbinger of most forms of entertainment, such as movies, computer software, videogames and the like'.[24] In both verticals, streaming is becoming the predominant form of consumption, and in both cases territorial delineation constitutes a prime hurdle towards the establishment of a Digital Single Market. At the same time, rights clearance for online music and audiovisual streaming respectively differ significantly, and solutions may not be 'one size fits all'.

Related to this, another dimension of comparing these two forms is how the concepts 'multi-territorial licensing' and 'cross-border access' are related. This will be explored in depth in Chapter 2. The debates in online music have been dominated by 'cross-border' and 'multi-territorial' notions, whereas the more recent debates regarding audiovisual content have been dominated by the notions of 'cross-border portability' and 'geo-blocking'. Whereas these notions are often used to describe similar phenomena, it is necessary to refine them: 'geo-blocking' refers to the use of technologies to limit the accessibility of a content service to certain geographical areas.[25] From a 'copyright-related perspective', this technical practice can be used to limit access to online content services to areas 'where the content owners have licensed the

---

pp. 38–41). At first glance, my research also falls into this trap of 'pre-programmed research' – seduced by a hot topic – whereas are territorial access restrictions just a luxury problem involving EU officials who are missing access to their favourite TV shows from back home? For example, Commissioner for Competition, Margrethe Vestager, noted in a speech: 'I, for one, cannot understand why I can watch my favourite Danish channels on my tablet in Copenhagen – a service I paid for – but I can't when I am in Brussels. Or why I can buy a film on DVD back home and watch it abroad, but I cannot do the same online.': see Commissioner for Competition, Margrethe Vestager, 'Competition policy for the Digital Single Market: Focus on e-commerce' (Bundeskartellamt International Conference on Competition, Berlin, 26 March 2015): http://europa.eu/rapid/press-rele ase_SPEECH-15-4704_en.htm. However, as is noted above, consumer behaviour has shifted and has put the regulatory framework under pressure. Underneath lie many issues that regard the transition of the legal framework in the new reality, which can justify such research endeavour.

[24] S. J. Liebowitz and R. Watt, 'How to Best Ensure Remuneration for Creators in the Market for Music? Copyright and its Alternatives', *Journal of Economic Surveys*, 20 (2006), 513, 514.

[25] See, e.g., P. Ibáñez Colomo, 'Copyright Licensing and the EU Digital Single Market Strategy', LSE Law, Society and Economy Working Papers 19/2015 (2015), 2: http:// ssrn.com/abstract=2697178; M. Trimble, 'The Territoriality Referendum', *World Intellectual Property Organization Journal* [2014], 89, 90.

commercial exploitation of their work'.[26] Cross-border portability, on the other hand, refers to the possibility of a consumer's accessing the content of its service provider from its resident Member State, while being temporarily present in another Member State. The European legislator defines a 'multi-territorial licence' in Article 3(m) of Directive 2014/26/EU tautologically, as a licence that covers the territory of more than one Member State.[27] When taking cross-border licensing as starting point, this can refer to two situations: the licensing of foreign content and licensing domestic content abroad. Suffice it for this section to state that, ultimately, both forms impact on the availability of content for consumers, but with different tools in the downstream relationship. Thus, on a broader level, the concepts can also be seen as two sides of the same coin.

Besides licensing, i.e. copyright-exertion related motives, there exist a variety of other legal and commercial aspects that might hinder the cross-border accessibility of content. These can be common to all online activities (e.g., VAT regime, consumer protection, business decisions) or specific to online content (e.g., release windows, piracy).[28] These causes are outside the scope of this book. Closely related to the study of licensing and access to copyright-protected works is the lack of legitimate access to content and its relation to piracy.[29] This theme has been subject to substantial academic research by both legal scholars and economists.[30]

---

[26] G. Mazziotti, 'Is Geo-blocking a Real Cause for Concern?', *European Intellectual Property Review*, 38 (2016), 365.

[27] Correspondingly, in Art. 1(d) of Commission Recommendation 2005/737/EC of 18 May 2005 on collective cross-border management of copyright and related rights for legitimate online music services [2005] OJ L276/54.

[28] See, e.g., Commission, 'A Digital Single Market Strategy for Europe – Analysis and Evidence Accompanying the document Communication from the Commission to the European Parliament, the Council, the European Economic and Social Committee and the Committee of the Regions', 28.

[29] See, e.g., Recital 40 of Directive 2014/26/EU, in which the European legislator expresses its expectation that the development of legal music streaming services contributes to the fight against piracy.

[30] Thomes, for example, studies the link between piracy and streaming services and finds 'that an increase in copyright enforcement shifts rents from consumers to the monopolistic provider, and moreover that a maximal punishment for piracy will be welfare-maximizing' (T. P. Thomes, 'An economic analysis of online streaming: How the music industry can generate revenues from cloud computing', ZEW-Centre for European Economic Research, Discussion Paper No. 11-039 (2011): http://ftp.zew.de/pub/zew-docs/dp/dp11039.pdf). Danaher and Waldfogel look at the audiovisual sector in the United States and suggest that 'delayed legal availability of the content abroad may drive the losses to piracy' (B. Danaher and J. Waldfogel, 'Reel Piracy: The Effect of Online Film Piracy on International Box Office Sales', University of Minnesota and NBER (2012): http://ssrn.com/abstract=1986299). Barker suggests that 'P2P downloads have a strong negative effect on legitimate music purchases' (G. R. Barker, 'Assessing the Economic Impact of Copyright Law: Evidence of the Effect of Free

Again, this book takes its starting point exclusively as construing the arrangements around access to content, which is why endeavours regarding piracy- and enforcement-related questions lie outside the scope of this work.

The theme of this book – licensing of and cross-border access to content – touches upon different fields of law, such as copyright law, contract law, competition law and rights of associations, as well as EU law and fundamental freedoms. There exists a plurality of intersections between these different legal domains and their equivalents in economic research and other disciplines. The focus of this book is on copyright and competition law. Within the broader copyright framework, the focus is on arrangements around the exercise of rights. Thus, the aim of this book is to address not the substantive norms of copyright, but the clearance of those rights. Therefore, I will not go into the relevant rights harmonised by the InfoSoc Directive[31] and the respective exceptions and limitations, or the intriguing questions around exhaustion in the digital landscape. Whereas it covers contractual arrangements, contract law as such is not part of this book. Also, licensing arrangements regarding orphan works[32] and for creative uses such as remixes are outside the scope of this work.

Finally, the geographical focus of this work is at the EU level. Cross-border licensing is inherently of an international dimension and has moved into the focus of EU legislative initiatives in order to enable a European Digital Single Market. Whereas copyright legislation is national and whereas I will not cover issues of national implementation, at times, I will resort to national samples as supportive or anecdotal evidence, when needed as examples or for rendering the situation more precisely.[33] As the reader will discover, some of the European (regulatory and market) developments can also be construed in a United States–

Music Downloads on the Purchase of Music CDs'. Centre for Law and Economics, ANU College of Law Working Paper No. 2 (2012)). For a comprehensive overview of the earlier literature, see also M. Peitz and P. Waelbroeck, 'An Economist's Guide to Digital Music', CESifo Working Paper No. 1333 (2004): cesifo.oxfordjournals.org/content/51/2-3/359.full.pdf

[31] Directive 2001/29/EC of the European Parliament and of the Council of 22 May 2001 on the harmonisation of certain aspects of copyright and related rights in the information society [2001] OJ L167/10 (InfoSoc Directive).

[32] Directive 2012/28/EU of the European Parliament and of the Council of 25 October 2012 on certain permitted uses of orphan works [2012] OJ L299/5. See also Commission, 'Proposal for a Directive of the European Parliament and of the Council on copyright in the Digital Single Market' COM/2016/0593 final – 2016/0280 (COD), Brussels, 14.9.2016 (Orphan Works Directive).

[33] For example, the incorporation of EU rules into national law in Germany, the United Kingdom and the Scandinavian countries. The selection is largely guided by the author's knowledge of languages and does not follow a specific methodology.

American context.[34] At times, it is therefore useful to look over the European fence to construe developments in a broader context.

1.3   Towards a Digital Single Market

The establishment of the internal market – or the single market as it is referred by EU policymaking[35] – has been the leading political and legislative priority in recent decades at the EU level. It is a prime objective of the EU, as set out in Article 3(3) of the Treaty on European Union (TEU), which confers a legislative obligation on the Union established in Article 26 of the Treaty on the Functioning of the European Union (TFEU) to create an internal market 'without internal frontiers in which the free movement of goods, persons, services and capital (...)'. Thereby the European legislator can rely on a variety of legal tools, ranging from non-binding soft law to Directives or Regulations.[36] If one takes harmonisation of the twenty-eight current and different regimes as reference point, much has been achieved by the four fundamental freedoms, implemented by various harmonising Directives and Regulations in the different policy fields, and their interpretation by the courts.

As regards copyright and related rights, between 1991 and 2018, several Directives have been adopted to harmonise aspects of national laws.[37] When the first copyright-related Directive[38] entered into force in 1991, harmonisation efforts had to accommodate just twelve Member States, compared with twenty-eight today. Notably, collective

---

[34] Whereas licensing and access arrangements, and notably CMOs, look different, today's content industry is heavily influenced by North American rights holders and service providers.

[35] Notably, this notion is used by the European Commission, not the Treaties; the Treaty of Rome from 25 March 1957 and the Maastricht Treaty on European Union (92/C 191/01) refer to the 'common market'. With the Lisbon Treaty the notion 'internal market' was introduced: see also Art. 26(2) TFEU. A nuanced reflection on the different concepts is offered by the Court of Justice, which states: 'The concept of a common market as defined by the Court in a consistent line of decisions involves the elimination of all obstacles to intra-community trade in order to merge the national markets into a single market bringing about conditions as close as possible to those of a genuine internal market'. See Case 15/81, *Gaston Schul Douane Expediteur BV* v. *Inspecteur der Invoerrechten en Accijnzen, Roosendaal* [1982] ECR 1409, ECLI:EU:C:1982:135, para. 33.

[36] Art. 288 TFEU.

[37] For an overview of policy initiatives in the United States and some of the parallel developments, as well as differences, see S. Perlmutter, 'Making Copyright Work for a Global Market: Policy Revision on Both Sides of the Atlantic', *Columbia Journal of Law & the Arts*, 38 (2014), 49.

[38] Council Directive 91/250/EEC of 14 May 1991 on the legal protection of computer programs [1991] OJ L122/42 (repealed).

management of copyright and related rights has been on the legislative agenda of the European Commission for at least twenty years. In 1995, for example, the Commission commented on the regulation of collective rights management in its *Green Paper on Copyright and Related Rights in the Information Society*.[39] As will be seen in the following chapters, though, until the more recent interference by competition authorities and Directive 2014/26/EU on collective management of copyright and related rights and multi-territorial licensing of rights in musical works for online use in the internal market, collective management has been anything but a level playing field and remained largely unaddressed.

More recently, the establishment of a 'Digital Single Market' has joined the EU policy goals. By definition, territorially segmented digital markets are at odds with a Digital Single Market without internal frontiers. In its *Communication on content in the Digital Single Market* of 2012, the previous Commission laid out its two parallel tracks of action, which ensure an effective single market in the area of copyright.[40] These two trajectories consist of: (1) the 'on-going effort to review and to modernise the EU copyright legislative framework' and (2) the facilitation of 'practical industry-led solutions' to issues on which rapid progress was deemed necessary and possible.[41] Also, the assessment of the existing copyright framework and its fitness in the digital setting have been topical for some time. In 2014, for example, the seventeen-year-old InfoSoc Directive, with its framework based on the minimal protection approach, was placed under review by the European institutions. Under the previous Commission, also, a major, general consultation on copyright was conducted from December 2013 to March 2014,[42] following the 'Licenes for Europe' stakeholder initiative and the EU Commission's *Communication on content in the Digital Single Market*. The consultation contemplates that '[d]espite progress, there are continued problems with the cross-border provision of, and access to, services. These problems are most obvious to consumers wanting to access services that are made available in Member States other than the one in which they live'.[43]

---

[39] Commission, 'Green Paper on Copyright and Related Rights in the Information Society' COM(95) 382 final, Brussels, 19 July 1995, 69ff.

[40] Commission, 'Content in the Digital Single Market' (Communication) COM(2012) 789 final, 2.

[41] Ibid., 2–3.

[42] Commission, 'Public Consultation on the review of the EU copyright rules' (23 July 2014): http://ec.europa.eu/internal_market/consultations/2013/copyright-rules/index_en.htm. The deadline was extended by one month.

[43] Commission, 'Public Consultation on the review of the EU copyright rules' (2013), 7: http://ec.europa.eu/internal_market/consultations/2013/copyright-rules/docs/consultation-document_en.pdf

The consultation resulted in more than 9,500 replies, with roughly 59 per cent of respondents being consumers and roughly 25 per cent authors or performers.[44] The prominently featured first question asked: 'Why is it not possible to access many online content services from anywhere in Europe?'[45]

In a leaked draft of the White Paper *A Copyright Policy for Creativity and Innovation in the European Union* from June 2014, the European Commission considered cross-border dissemination of creative content in the single market and effective tools for a functioning marketplace and value-chain as two of the three main areas for review. Here, the Commission considered that obstacles of ubiquitous cross-border access 'can derive from both issues related to the definition and to the exercise of rights'.[46] In the internal draft, it continues both to consider the definition of the act of making available on the Internet, in suggesting that this could be done by introducing a country of origin principle or localisation of the act in Member States towards which the activity is directed, and the introduction of a single unitary copyright title, notably as a substitute for the current system of national copyright titles.[47] As regards the exercise of rights, the internal draft suggests that 'addressing restrictions of cross-border access to content resulting from purely contractual arrangements could be envisaged'.[48] Notably, that is an aspect that has found its way forward in the form of the Portability Regulation under the current Commission.

The updated *Digital Single Market Strategy for Europe*, dating from 6 May 2015,[49] too, focused on 'Better online access for consumers and businesses across Europe'. However, compared with the previous Commission's Digital Single Marketplace roadmap, multi-territorial licensing and cross-border access were featured less prominently. It proposed 'Better access to digital content – A modern, more European copyright framework', in which it focuses on 'unjustified' geo-blocking and specifically announced the making of a legislative proposal to address the cross-border portability.[50]

---

[44] See Commission, 'Public Consultation on the review of the EU copyright rules'. The high volume of responses was caused by several popular initiatives such as Fix Copyright! and Creators for Europe and Copywrongs.eu. See E. Rosati, 'BREAKING: Report on responses to Public Consultation on EU copyright now available' (*IP Kat*, 23 July 2014): http://ipkitten.blogspot.dk/2014/07/breaking-report-on-responses-to-public.html

[45] Commission, 'Public Consultation on the review of the EU copyright rules', 7.

[46] Commission, 'A Copyright Policy for Creativity and Innovation in the European Union' (2014) White Paper, Internal Draft, 6, made available via: http://ipkitten.blogspot.dk/2014/06/super-kat-exclusive-heres-commissions.html

[47] Ibid.   [48] Ibid., 7.

[49] Commission, 'A Digital Single Market Strategy for Europe' (Communication) COM (2015) 192 final.

[50] Ibid., 7–8. See also Mazziotti, 'Is geo-blocking a real cause for concern?', 365.

Some of these thoughts from the White Paper have been adapted in the European Commission's follow-up on copyright in its Communication *Towards a Modern, More European Copyright framework*,[51] which was published concurrently with the proposal for the Portability Regulation on 9 December 2015. The Commission reflected that

[t]he ultimate objective of full cross-border access for all types of content across Europe needs to be balanced with the readiness of markets to respond rapidly to legal and policy changes and the need to ensure viable financing models for those who are primarily responsible for content creation.[52]

Therefore, the Commission proposed 'a gradual approach to removing obstacles to cross-border access to content and to "the circulation of works"'.[53] Ultimately, however, this incremental approach is expected to lead to the realisation of the single market. In recalling the difficulties and long lead-times that have accompanied the harmonisation of trademark and patent law, the Commission states that the complexities of a full harmonisation of copyright in the EU 'cannot be a reason to relinquish this vision as a long-term target'.[54] In order to ensure wider access to content across the EU, besides its proposal on content portability, the Commission considered legislative proposals in three areas, for adoption in spring 2016:

- Enhancing cross-border distribution of television and radio programmes online in the light of the results of the review of the Satellite and Cable Directive;
- Supporting right holders and distributors to reach agreement on licences that allow for cross-border access to content, including catering for cross-border requests from other Member States, for the benefit of both European citizens and stakeholders in the audiovisual chain. In this context, the role of mediation, or similar alternative dispute resolution mechanisms, to help the granting of such licences, will be considered;
- Making it easier to digitise out-of-commerce works and make them available, including across the EU.[55]

Notably, the Commission also considers financial and other support measures of public authorities to be vital, referring to, inter alia, the Creative Europe programme.

In a draft version of a Communication on *Online Platforms and the Digital Single Market, Opportunities and Challenges for Europe*, leaked in April 2016, the Commission notes that, in the next copyright package, which was envisioned to be adopted in autumn 2016, it aims at 'ensuring fair allocation of the value generated by the online distribution of

---

[51] Commission, 'Towards a modern, more European copyright framework' (Communication) COM(2015) 626 final.
[52] Ibid., 5.   [53] Ibid.   [54] Ibid., 12.   [55] Ibid., 6.

copyright-protected content by online platforms whose businesses are based on the provision of access to copyright-protected material'.[56] On 14 September 2016, then, the Commission proposed its modernisation of EU copyright rules, consisting of two proposals for Regulations and two Directives.[57]

The European Commission, and especially the former Directorate-General Internal Market and Services (DG MARKT), which was headed by Commissioner Michel Barnier from 2010 to 2014, in 2014 underwent major structural changes[58] that are noteworthy in the context of this book: Unit MARKT D1 (Copyright), which was headed by Maria-Martin Prat, together with the part of Unit MARKT D3 (Fight against counterfeiting and piracy) dealing with copyright enforcement and the part of Unit MARKT D4 (Online and postal services) dealing with online services, were moved to the Directorate-General for Communications Networks, Content and Technology (DG CONNECT), which was headed by Commissioner Günther Oettinger until 2016, who succeeded Neelie Kroes.[59] Furthermore, inter alia, unit EAC E3 (Creative Europe Programme – MEDIA) was relocated to DG CONNECT. In addition, the former Prime Minister of Estonia, Andrus Ansip, served as Vice President for the European Commission and is Commissioner for the Digital Single Market, in that he heads the project team 'A Connected Digital Single Market' consisting of the Commissioners of different Directorates General. The relevant implications of these structural changes are twofold: first, the restructuring led to an upgrading of the digital agenda within the Commission. Secondly, the copyright unit moved closer to the other units working on Internet- and internal

---

[56] Commission, 'Online Platforms and the Digital Single Market, Opportunities and Challenges for Europe' (2016) Communication from the Commission, Draft, 10, made available via: www.politico.eu/wp-content/uploads/2016/04/Platforms-Communication.pdf

[57] E.g., Commission, 'State of the Union 2016: Commission proposes modern EU copyright rules for European culture to flourish and circulate' (Press release), IP/16/3010, Strasbourg, 14 September 2016, Commission, 'Proposal for a Directive of the European Parliament and of the Council on copyright in the Digital Single Market'; see also Commission, 'Proposal for a Regulation of the European Parliament and of the Council laying down rules on the exercise of copyright and related rights applicable to certain online transmissions of broadcasting organisations and retransmissions of television and radio programmes' COM/2016/0594 final – 2016/0284 (COD), Brussels, 14 September 2016.

[58] See Commission, 'The Juncker Commission: A strong and experienced team standing for change' (Press release) IP/14/984, Brussels, 10 September 2014.

[59] The Directorate-General Enterprise and Industry (DG ENTR) merged with the remainder of DG MARKT, hereunder notably Units MARKT D2 (Industrial Property) and the remaining parts of Unit MARKT D3 (Fight against counterfeiting and piracy) under the Directorate General for Internal Market, Industry, Entrepreneurship and SMEs (DG GROWTH).

market-related aspects, while at the same time losing its traditional proximity to the units working on intellectual property related aspects. I will return to these observations in Chapter 6.

1.4   Traditional and New Modes of Governance in the EU

1.4.1   *Analysing the Framework for Licensing and Access*

Much has been, and much could be, written about different concepts and approaches of law-making and how to analyse the recent regulatory developments in this field. Contributing to this discourse is outside the scope of this book. Instead, let me introduce some considerations for this specific endeavour. As noted, this book studies two phenomena: first, the recently introduced regulatory set-up for licensing of and access to copyright protected works (i.e. music and audiovisual works) on the Internet, and secondly the interplay between the different regulatory initiatives. In other words, this book contains both descriptive and normative elements.[60]

In order to understand the licensing regime and access practices, this book investigates the functioning of and the relationship between the recently introduced online licensing framework in relation to multi-territorial licensing and geographical fragmentation. In other words, it finds its starting point in the *de lege lata* situation, i.e. the status quo of the law. Thus, the research first looks at the relevant provisions related to competition law stemming from the TFEU and its application, as well as the relevant provisions relating to copyright found in the relevant Directives and Regulations. For both verticals, music and audiovisual content, the relevant literature is reviewed, and data analysed in terms of competition proceedings, case law, soft law and codifications as well as the contractual arrangements (i.e. standard contracts between CMOs and terms regarding cross-border situations between online service providers and consumers). This book is roughly structured along the line of competition proceedings, on the one side, and other regulatory (legislative) interventions on the other.[61] On a broader note, Posner remarks that the licensing of intellectual property rights presents 'challenging issues (. . .) in which law, economics, finance, business and technology

---

[60] In a similar vein, Cryer et al. differentiate between expository and evaluative scholarship (R. Cryer, T. Hervey and B. Sokhi-Bulley, *Research Methodologies in EU and International Law* (Hart Publishing, 2011), p. 9). Methodologically, the book based on a combination of traditional doctrinal analysis (legal positivism) and 'law in context' analysis (multi-level governance and new institutionalism).

[61] On chosen structure, see also Section 1.5.

are inextricably intertwined'.[62] In order to understand the licensing and access arrangements better, the underlying basic economic rationales also become crucial.[63]

Based on the survey of solutions, I identify how the EU's complementing competition- and copyright-related routes interact and whether they support each other in achieving their policy goals, such as overcoming licensing issues based on territoriality. In order to examine how the legal framework interacts with market developments, in connection with the current law-making approach by the EU Commission, multi-level governance, coined as 'Better Regulation', helps to construe the interplay of the different regulatory arrangements (private, legislative and non-legislative). Based on these considerations, I analyse interactions, identify weaknesses and inconsistencies of the system, and pinpoint solutions that respond to the challenge of mitigating the effect of the fragmented content market, based on twenty-eight versions of copyright law in the EU, on dissemination of content on the Internet.

1.4.2 Different Modes of Regulating

Access to content is governed by licensing agreements, which are subject to contractual freedom. What, then, governs or regulates the underlying (institutional) agreements? From a doctrinal perspective based on a positivist view, *legal* regulation is (implicitly or expressly) sometimes simply understood as a type of *legal* normative instrument. The principal validation of this view stems from the validity of the legal norm.[64] In the absence of specific legislation, the general rules constitute the relevant legal framework. But are these private institutional arrangements and agreements

---

[62] R. A. Posner, 'Transaction Costs and Antitrust Concerns in the Licensing of Intellectual Property', *John Marshall Review of Intellectual Property Law*, 4 (2005), 325.

[63] The combination of law and economics is a research stream that has been applied fruitfully to the analysis of copyright-related questions. While economic theory has proven to be a viable means in law and economics to justify, or to discuss the necessity or the breadth of copyright protection and its collectivised exercise respectively, these themes are not at the centre of attention of the book. Rather, this analysis is based on the existing copyright protection and study of the exercise and exploitation of the rights. For a comprehensive literature review, see, e.g., R. A. Posner, 'Intellectual Property: The Law and Economics Approach', *Journal of Economics Perspectives*, 19 (2005), 57; Liebowitz and Watt, 'How to Best Ensure Remuneration for Creators in the Market for Music?'; R. Towse, C. Handke and P. Stepan, 'The Economics of Copyright Law: A Stocktake of the Literature', *Review of Economic Research on Copyright Issues*, 5 (2008), 1; and Watt, *Copyright and Economic Theory: Friends or Foes?*

[64] Legal positivism is based on the principle that 'all law is created and laid down (...) by human beings and that the validity of a rule of law lies in its formal legal status, not its relation to morality or other external validating factors' (Cryer, Hervey and Sokhi-Bulley, *Research Methodologies in EU and International Law*, p. 37).

(such as licensing agreements or standard contracts) simply the product or the result of regulatory intervention, or can they themselves also be seen as regulatory instruments that shape the market? And what about other regulating factors? In the present field, in which specific legislation has been introduced only recently, proceedings under competition law have been one regulating factor. But, also, 'soft law' instruments and industry initiatives seem to have shaped the arrangements and institutions.

Two issues are at stake here: first, regulation coming from within the traditional law-making arena by traditional institutional actors, but outside traditional legal instruments. Secondly, outside traditional institutional actors, regulation induced by arrangements by private actors.[65] In a traditional legal dogmatic endeavour, neither form would matter.[66] But even the strictest representatives of a traditional positivist view must be inclined to acknowledge that non-legislative measures, such as soft law issued by governmental bodies, are capable of influencing market behaviour. What would be the rationale of non-binding legal instruments, such as Recommendations, which have a firm anchor in the Treaties in the first place, if not exactly that?[67] For the purpose of this book, in any case, in order to construe the existence of the arrangements and uncover inconsistencies in the regulatory framework, it seems necessary to examine the interplay between the different forms of regulatory initiatives, namely state-induced measures on the one hand (in the form of legislative or non-legislative measures), and market developments (i.e. private regulation) on the other.

[65] E.g., Peters notes that: 'From a formal legal perspective, neither type of corporate self- and co-regulation produces ordinary hard (international) law. However, all these shades of hybrid regulation are functionally equivalent to state or inter-state hard law when they do influence behaviour and are complied with.': A. Peters, 'Membership in the Global Constitutional Community' in J. Klabbers, A. Peters and G. Ulfstein (eds.), *The Constitutionalization of International Law* (Oxford University Press, 2009), p. 249.

[66] This is not the place thoroughly to discuss justifications for the different schools of thought. Legal dogmatics, for example, has been criticised as practical jurisprudence, which is uncommon outside European scholar community (A. Peczenik (ed.), *Legal Doctrine and Legal Theory*, vol. 4: Scientia (Springer, 2005), p. 2). Others question the significance of hard law and its exclusive scrutiny in the contemporary phase of European integration (J. Hunt and J. Shaw, 'Fairy Tale of Luxembourg? Reflections on Law and Legal Scholarship in European Integration' in D. Phinnemore and A. Warleigh-Lack (eds.), *Reflections on European Integration, 50 Years of the Treaty of Rome* (Palgrave Macmillan, 2009), p. 3). Schools integrating non-legal sources in their research endeavours based on broader notions of regulation, on the other hand, are criticised that regulation is 'less than law' (J. Black, 'Critical reflections on regulation', Centre for Analysis of Risk and Regulation, London School of Economics and Political Science (2002), 23: eprints.lse.ac.uk/35985). Suffice it to note here that both views have advantages and disadvantages.

[67] The available policy instruments at an EU level are, besides hard, legally binding rules, soft regulation, education and information as well as economic instruments.

This leads me to the notion of 'regulation': in considering more than just the terminology, in the context of this book let us understand 'regulation' conceptually. There seems to be no canon as to what regulation embraces as either concept or terminology.[68] Black notes that the conceptualisation of 'regulation' often depends on the issue on which a scholar is focusing.[69] She further comments that there frequently exists 'an implicit or explicit assumption that the target of regulation is an economic actor'.[70] One conceptual definition understands regulation 'as the means by which the state 'seeks to encourage direct behaviour which it is assumed would not occur without such intervention' and as such should be seen as distinct from the operation of the markets, even though the latter is underpinned by legal rules'.[71]

In this definition, however, the state is the central actor. Others have expanded both the objects of regulation and the subject, i.e. regulators, to other actors (e.g., firms) and other factors (e.g., norms or culture). Black argues that regulation is increasingly 'being seen as "decentred" from the state, and even from the well-recognised forums of self-regulation'.[72] In fact, many streams in legal and economic research address the interplay between different regulatory factors. One renowned approach to construing regulators other than law was coined by Lessig as 'New Chicago School'. There, he identifies four factors (or 'modalities'): law, social norms, markets and architecture.[73] Yet another, related, approach is suggested by Riis as 'user generated law', which I have applied to the field of collective management in previous work related to this research.[74] According to this framework, which builds on von Hippel's theory on user innovation, law that 'accommodates the needs of the knowledge society' is characterised by: (1) flexible norms; (2) with cross-border scope; and (3) which are industry- and subject-specific.[75] In previous work, I revisited the developments in the field with regard to licensing arrangements, and tested whether user-generated law methodology can construe the emerging legal regulatory (based on contracts and laws) and non-regulatory models (based on technology and social norms). I have argued that the development of cross-border online

[68] For an overview of different regulatory concepts, see Black, 'Critical reflections on regulation', 12.
[69] Ibid., 9.   [70] Ibid., 10.   [71] Ibid., 1.   [72] Ibid.
[73] L. Lessig, 'The New Chicago School', *Journal of Legal Studies*, XXVII (1998), 661.
[74] See S. F. Schwemer, 'Emerging models for cross-border online licensing' in T. Riis (ed.), *User Generated Law, Re-Constructing Intellectual Property Law in a Knowledge Society* (Edward Elgar, 2016).
[75] See T. Riis, 'User Generated Law: Re-constructing Intellectual Property Law in a Knowledge Society' in T. Riis (ed.), *User Generated Law, Re-Constructing Intellectual Property Law in a Knowledge Society* (Edward Elgar, 2016), pp. 2–3.

music licensing models, for example, can, to a large extent, be construed as interplay between regulatory activity and private mechanisms.[76] In the case of online music, novel licensing arrangement and entities have emerged: sometimes influenced or accompanied by regulatory action and sometimes not. For the sake of this book, in any event, let us rely on a broad view of 'regulation', which embraces contractual arrangements, industry measures and soft law, as well as competition proceedings and *de lege* regulation in form of hard law, i.e. rule setting by means of legislation and other means that govern the behaviour of the different arrangements.

New Modes of Governance

According to Trubek et al., governance arrangements 'that operate in place of, or along with, the "hard law" that arises from treaties, regulations' are often described under the concept of 'soft law'.[77] There has been a 'growing awareness of the European Commission to use and test regulatory techniques which (. . .) introduce new modes of law-making and enforcement'[78] that has dated back to the 1980s. This development is argued to have led to the

(. . .) far-reaching politicization of law-making and enforcement, politicization here being understood as circumvention or overruling "law" as the decisive means for shaping the European integration process. Traditional legislation became less popular to the advantage of self-regulation, co-regulation and other "new" modes of governance.[79]

---

[76] See Schwemer, 'Emerging models for cross-border online licensing', p. 79.

[77] D. M. Trubek, P. Cottrell and M. Nance, '"Soft Law", "Hard Law" and EU Integration' in G. de Búrca and J. Scott (eds.), *Law and Governance in the EU and the US* (Hart Publishing, 2006), p. 65. However, the notion of soft law is not unproblematic, given its ambiguity (see G. de Búrca and J. Scott, 'New Governance, Law and Constitutionalism' (2006), 5: www.ucl.ac.uk/laws/clge/docs/govlawconst.pdf) and contested as regards non-binding measures (see, e.g., C. Barnard and S. Peers, *European Union Law* (Oxford University Press, 2014), pp. 102–103). Notably, the European Parliament, in its Resolution from 2007 on cross-border collective copyright management refers to the Online Music Recommendation as a 'soft law' approach: see European Parliament, 'Resolution of 13 March 2007 on the Commission Recommendation of 18 October 2005 on collective cross-border management of copyright and related rights for legitimate online music services (2005/737/EC) (2006/2008(INI))' P6_TA(2007)0064 [2006] OJ C301 E/64 at lit C. See also L. Marchegiani, 'Le licenze multiterritoriali per l'uso online di opere musicali nella disciplina comunitaria della gestione collettiva dei diritti d'autore e dei diritti connessi', *Osservatorio del diritto civile e commerciale*, 2 (2013), 293, 297.

[78] van Gestel and Micklitz, 'Revitalizing Doctrinal Legal Research in Europe: What About Methodology?', p. 45.

[79] Ibid., p. 46.

Van Gestel and Micklitz continue that '"integration through law" (...) did not come to an end, but as the dominant paradigm it was replaced by "integration without law"'.[80] This trend towards 'post-regulatory', non-traditional forms of governance and 'democratic experimentalism' has attracted significant scholarly attention.[81] This literature stream has drawn attention to the emerging use of non-legislative forms of regulation by means of soft law and other informal governance instruments in the EU.[82] These new modes of governance raise democratic legitimacy problems, and the question of co-existence between voluntary modes of governance and compulsory regulation.[83] The concept of new governance is not settled.[84] Pierre defines 'governance' as 'sustaining co-ordination and coherence among a wide variety of actors with different purposes and objectives such as political actors and institutions, corporate interests, civil society, and transnational governments'.[85] According to de Búrca and Scott, for example, new governance is 'a construct which has been developed to explain a range of processes and practices that have a normative dimension but do not operate primarily or at all through the formal mechanism of traditional command-and-control-type legal institutions'.[86]

Hunt and Shaw explain that

---

[80] S. Weatherill, 'The Challenge of Better Regulation' in S. Weatherill (ed.), *Better Regulation* (Hart Publishing, 2007), p. 47. This resembles what de Búrca and Scott present as their hybrid thesis: see 'New Governance, Law and Constitutionalism', 9–10.

[81] de Búrca and Scott, 'New Governance, Law and Constitutionalism'; D. Kennedy, 'The Mystery of Global Governance' in J. L. Dunoff and J. P. Trachtman (eds.), *Ruling the World? Constitutionalism, International Law, and Global Governance* (Cambridge University Press, 2009), p. 50.

[82] See W. H. Simon, 'Toyota Jurisprudence: Legal Theory and Rolling Rule Regimes' in G. de Búrca and J. Scott (eds.), *Law and Governance in the EU and the US* (Hart Publishing, 2006); Hunt and Shaw, 'Fairy Tale of Luxembourg?', 98. For an interesting discourse on the distinction between law and 'non-law' and 'presumptive law' in public law, see J. Klabbers, 'Law-making and Constitutionalism' in J. Klabbers, A. Peters and G. Ulfstein (eds.), *The Constitutionalization of International Law* (Oxford University Press, 2009) especially pp. 97ff and 111ff. The concept is also relevant in the United States but 'this development has occurred in a more self-conscious and more closely scrutinised fashion in the EU': see de Búrca and Scott, 'New Governance, Law and Constitutionalism', 2.

[83] van Gestel and Micklitz, 'Revitalizing Doctrinal Legal Research in Europe: What About Methodology?', pp. 47–48. See also de Búrca and Scott, 'New Governance, Law and Constitutionalism'; and Y. Papadopoulos, 'Problems of Democratic Accountability in Network and Multi-Level Governance', *European Law Journal*, 13 (2007), 469.

[84] de Búrca and Scott, 'New Governance, Law and Constitutionalism', 3.

[85] J. Pierre, 'Introduction: Understanding Governance' in J. Pierre (ed.), *Debating Governance* (Oxford University Press, 2000), pp. 3–4.

[86] de Búrca and Scott, 'New Governance, Law and Constitutionalism', 3.

The umbrella term "new governance" covers a range of non-legislative interventions – including soft law, the open method of coordination, (...), the rise of executive power in the EU, seen with the use of comitology and an increasing involvement of agencies.[87]

In defining *new* governance, Walker points towards a 'common starting point (...) in terms of a departure from the Classic Community Method of norm generation and of governance more generally (...)'.[88] Another, more general, starting point refers to the non-legislative, or only marginally legislative, character, which 'comes close to defining new governance as the antithesis of *legal ordering*'.[89] Yet another, more abstract, starting point refers to the 'general properties of new governance, such as participation and power-sharing, multi-level integration, diversity and decentralisation, deliberation, flexibility and revocability of norms, and experimentation and knowledge-creation'.[90] Also, here, however, as Walker sums up, these '"new" properties explicitly or implicitly acquire definition from their contrast with a model of "old" government based on representation, singular authority, centralised command and control, rigidity and stability of norms, and the uniform application of a received regulatory formal'.[91] In this context, de Búrca and Scott note:

New governance processes generally encourage or involve the participation of affected actors (stakeholders) rather than merely representative actors, and emphasize transparency (openness as a means to information-sharing and learning), as well as ongoing evaluation and review.[92]

This brings me to the role of the European Commission, which plays a central role for the topic of this book, both as legislative initiator and as competition authority. Traditionally, a large body of legal research on the EU focuses on the role of the Court of Justice.[93] In this context the so-called 'Better Regulation' approach by the European Commission becomes relevant. In 2001, the EU Commission published its White Paper on 'European Governance',[94] which has been

---

[87] Hunt and Shaw, 'Fairy Tale of Luxembourg?', 98.

[88] N. Walker, 'EU Constitutionalism and New Governance' in G. de Búrca and J. Scott (eds.), *Law and New Governance in the EU and the US* (Hart Publishing, 2006), pp. 21–22, with further references.

[89] Ibid., 22, also de Búrca and Scott, 'New Governance, Law and Constitutionalism', 7.

[90] Walker, 'EU Constitutionalism and New Governance', p. 22, with further references.

[91] Ibid.   [92] de Búrca and Scott, 'New Governance, Law and Constitutionalism', 6.

[93] However, as Hunt and Shaw track, other institutions have also been considered in research endeavours. See Hunt and Shaw, 'Fairy Tale of Luxembourg?', 4; Cryer, Hervey and Sokhi-Bulley, *Research Methodologies in EU and International Law*, p. 17.

[94] Commission, 'European governance – A white paper' (2002) White Paper, COM/2001/0428 final, OJ C 287/1.

marked as a shift in the law-making approach and contains the 'Better Regulation' programme as a key element.[95] The 'Better Regulation' approach was refined in May 2015, when the Better Regulation Agenda was adopted.

According to the Better Regulation Guidelines, 'better regulation' means 'designing EU policies and laws so that they achieve their objectives at minimum cost',[96] while it 'is not about regulating or deregulating'.[97] This approach is deemed 'necessary to ensure that the Union's interventions respect the overarching principles of subsidiary and proportionality'.[98] Better regulation 'consider[s] both regulatory and well-designed non-regulatory means as well as improvements in the implementation and enforcement of existing legislation'.[99] In this iterative approach, close collaboration with stakeholders is key. In this context, a multitude of non-legal factors can influence legal decision making.[100] Stakeholder consultations,[101] for example, can constitute an anchor regarding the initial design of policy interventions and can improve the acceptance of the initiative.[102] This is also underlined, by the interest shown in the public consultation on the review of the EU copyright rules, especially from citizens, as noted by the EU Parliament's Committee of Industry, Research and Energy.[103] However, varying degrees of engagement can be observed: in the public consultation regarding copyright there were more than 8,000 responses, whereas the consultation on the SatCab Directive resulted in little more than 250 responses.[104] Also, the *ex ante* assessment of the impact of regulation is

---

[95] van Gestel and Micklitz, 'Revitalizing Doctrinal Legal Research in Europe: What About Methodology?', p. 47.

[96] Commission, 'Better Regulation Guidelines' (latest edition, 19 May 2015) SWD(2015) 111 final, 5.

[97] Ibid.   [98] Ibid.

[99] Commission, 'Better regulation for better results – An EU Agenda' (Communication) COM(2015) 215 final, 6.

[100] See Peczenik, *Legal Doctrine and Legal Theory*, pp. 14–15, referring inter alia to viewpoints formulated by international organisations, private organisations or civil society.

[101] Stakeholder consultations are a duty under Art. 11 TEU (Consolidated Version of the Treaty on European Union [2010] OJ C831/01).

[102] Commission, 'Synopsis Report on the Responses to the Public Consultation on the Review of the Satellite and Cable Directive', 4 May 2016, 63–64.

[103] European Parliament, 'Opinion of the Committee on Industry, Research and Energy for the Committee on Legal Affairs on the implementation of Directive 2001/29/EC of the European Parliament and of the Council of 22 May 2001 on the harmonisation of certain aspects of copyright and related rights in the information society (2014/2256 (INI))', Committee on Industry, Research and Energy, Rapporteur: José Blanco López, 20 April 2015, Recital 4.

[104] Commission, 'Synopsis Report on the Responses to the Public Consultation on the Review of the Satellite and Cable Directive'.

relatively novel.[105] In the context of this book it is thus interesting to test whether new governance and the 'Better Regulation' approach can construe some of the interplay between both legislative and non-legislative or private mechanisms.[106]

This also informs the choice of sources: in the context of the current and the recently introduced law, preparatory works and reports can serve as a key resource for interpreting the provisions and construing the ideas of the regulator.[107] Explanatory memorandums, which are required to accompany all legislative proposals by the EU Commission, do not form part of the legislative act, but again offer important reflections on the proposal.[108]As described above, this area of the Digital Single Market is addressed by a variety of soft law measures, such as Recommendations, which, despite their non-binding nature, are also regularly recited in judicial proceedings or by the legislator. Finally, other non-binding documents by the EU institutions have been considered. Given the contractual nature of licensing, agreements and other contractual arrangements are central. Generally, the study of these arrangements, however, proves difficult because most agreements are confidential.[109] Thus, the main insights are derived from publicly available information such as the terms of service, other public information from organisations, and information provided in case law or other scholarly reports. The cut-off date for information collection was 30 March 2018.

---

[105] Formal Impact Assessments, for example, have been carried out by the European Commission only since 2003. See F. Chittenden, T. Abler and D. Xiao, 'Impact Assessment in the EU' in S. Weatherill (ed.), *Better Regulation*, vol. 6: *Studies of the Oxford Institute of European and Comparative Law* (Hart Publishing, 2007), p. 284.

[106] And to a certain degree infra- and intra-institutional interplay. The EU Commission, for example, refers to Better Regulation in its Recommendation 2005/737/EC (see Commission, 'Impact Assessment reforming cross-border collective management of copyright and related rights for legitimate online music services' (Commission Staff Working Document) SEC(2005) 1254, Brussels 11 October 2005, 39).

[107] See, e.g., M. Bryde Andersen, *Ret og metode* (Gjellerup, 2002), pp. 144–145.

[108] Impact Assessments (IA), for example, provide an 'ex ante analysis of social economic and environmental impact for a variety of purposes including coordination within the Commission, openness to external stakeholders and transparency in decision-making. (. . .) Finally, IAs explain why action is necessary and the regulatory response is appropriate, or alternatively why no action should be taken'. See Chittenden, Abler and Xiao, 'Impact Assessment in the EU', p. 276.

[109] Other researchers share this obstacle. See G. Mazziotti, 'New Licensing Models for Online Music Services in the European Union: From Collective to Customized Management' Public Law & Legal Theory Working Paper Group 7 Paper Number 11–269, Columbia Law School: http://ssrn.com/abstract=1814264; Rethink Music, 'Fair Music: Transparency and Payment Flows in the Music Industry, Recommendations to Increase Transparency, Reduce Friction, and Promote Fairness in the Music Industry' (2015) Rethink Music, Berklee ICE, Boston, 14: www.rethink-music.com/research/fair-music-transparency-and-payment-flows-in-the-music-industry

1.5   Outline

This book is divided into six chapters. This first chapter consists of an introduction to the topic and the need for cross-border licensing and access solutions for musical and audiovisual works by addressing why territorial segmented markets are problematic in view of the EU's policy goals. It introduces the Digital Single Market and the modes of governance in the EU, of which the lawmaker has made use when addressing cross-border content distribution on the Internet.

Against this backdrop of recent policy developments, Chapter 2 first explores the relationship between cross-border access and multi-territorial licensing. Then it describes the evolution of territorial delineation by author CMOs and the emergence of novel music licensing arrangements, and puts forward essential aspects of the underlying economic rationales and the market context. Finally, it examines territorial practices and licensing arrangements regarding audiovisual works.

Chapter 3 contains a study of how territorial restrictions in access or licensing arrangements have been dealt with from a competition law stance. First, it provides a case study of territorial restrictions of music in the licensor–licensor relationship, which has been dominated by model contracts. Then, it looks at the licensor–licensee relationship regarding territorial restrictions in licensing contracts for audiovisual content.

Chapter 4 looks at how multi-territorial licensing of music has been addressed by the European lawmaker. It analyses the development from voluntary to binding measures in the distinct European setting of harmonisation and market integration. The survey of the community *acquis* concludes with proposed solutions for the licensing of audiovisual content.

Chapter 5 turns towards the recent legislative initiatives regarding multi-territorial access, notably geo-blocking and portability. It also puts these initiatives into the context of preceding consultations on the SatCab Directive and the proposed rules under the copyright package of the European Commission.

Figure 1 provides an overview of the different licensing (and access-related) aspects analysed in Chapters 3 to 5.

The delineation between Chapter 3, on the one hand, and Chapters 4 and 5, on the other, roughly follows the different instruments of regulation – namely competition decisions and judgments (*ex post* control by the European Commission in its function as competition authority as well as the relevant case law of the Court of Justice and the General Court) on the one hand, and the institutional legal framework based on non-binding and binding legal instruments or acts (on *ex ante* the sector-specific

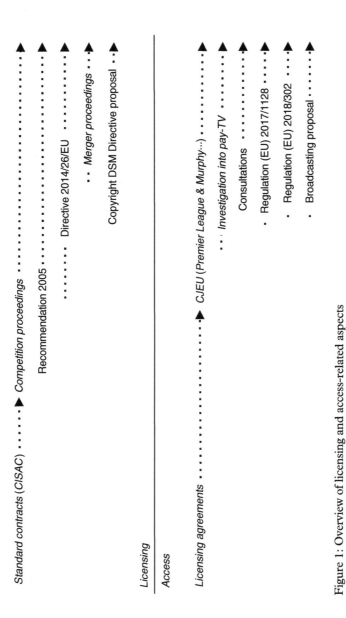

Figure 1: Overview of licensing and access-related aspects

(legislative) initiative of the European Commission) as measures aimed at the harmonisation or promotion of market integration for the Digital Single Market, on the other.[110] Naturally, there exists a certain overlap between proceedings under general competition rules and sector-specific regulation (which may regulate not only behaviour but also competition). Thus, lines might well be more blurred than is provided for in this book's structure.[111]

Finally, Chapter 6 analyses the characteristics of the licensing systems and the EU's sector-regulation/competition approach vis-à-vis private market solutions in order to map overlaps and inconsistencies. The chapter examines the interaction between the legal framework and market developments and discusses how territoriality can be reconciled with borderless access to audiovisual and music content. Chapter 6 concludes with broader considerations on the regulatory patchwork, transferability of findings and suggestions for further research.

---

[110] This delineation is also used by others. See, e.g., R. M. Hilty and T. Li, 'Control Mechanisms for CRM Systems and Competition Law', Max Planck Institute for Innovation and Competition Research Paper No. 16–04 (Max Planck Institute for Innovation and Competition, 2016), 1: http://ssrn.com/abstract=2772482; L. Guibault and S. van Gompel, 'Collective Management in the European Union' in Daniel Gervais (ed.), *Collective Management of Copyright and Related Rights*, 2nd edn. (Kluwer Law International, 2010), p. 149.

[111] The chosen division for the normative analysis serves to provide more clarity when navigating the complex landscape. Instead of the suggested structure, one could also base the analysis on a purely problem-based approach, in which the respective instruments would be jointly assessed under each thematic heading. I find that the chosen delineation for the normative analysis of the different institutional arrangements and regulatory initiatives provides a more useful basis for the discussion that follows, and additionally more clarity than a clean problem-based approach.

2   Market and Economics Context

This chapter puts forward essential aspects of the underlying economic rationales, as well as the market context. The following study reveals the evolution and status quo of multi-territorial licensing and cross-border access, to set the scene for the forthcoming analysis of the legal framework in subsequent chapters.

One important question to address is the following: what is the relationship of multi-territorial licensing and cross-border access to copyright-protected works? After briefly revisiting three underlying core concepts in Section 2.1, I put forward the analytical framework in order to explore the relation of cross-border access and multi-territorial licensing in Section 2.2. I then provide a primer on recent developments as regards access and business models in Section 2.3. In Section 2.4, I turn towards the current arrangements and developments in the market regarding multi-territorial licensing for musical works. Here, the focus is on the institutional arrangements and the licensing relationship between author collective management organisations (CMOs) and licensees (commercial users). Finally, this chapter sketches major differences between the licensing of music and the licensing of audiovisual works.

2.1   Underlying Concepts: Exclusivity, Contractual Freedom and Territoriality

Copyright, just as other intellectual property (IP) rights do, confers, as a property rule, certain exclusive rights to its respective owners. This traditional perspective is enshrined in the Berne Convention as well as European Union (EU) legislation.[1] In reality, however, as Schovsbo underlines, copyright is 'not a monolith based on "property rights" but

---

[1] For example, Art. 9(1) of the Berne Convention on the right of reproduction reads: 'Authors of literary and artistic works protected by this Convention shall have the exclusive right of authorizing the reproduction of these works, in any manner or form.' See also Arts. 2, 3(1) and 4(1) of the Directive on the harmonisation of certain aspects of copyright and related rights in the information society (InfoSoc Directive).

a patch-work of rules and practices based both on property rules and on liability rules'.[2] As a starting point, nevertheless, 'without prior bargaining with the author' the legal entitlement cannot be removed[3] – thus, online service providers need to clear the respective rights with rights holders. These licensing arrangements and practices, which are further explored below, have developed in a highly subject matter-specific way.[4]

However, it is helpful first to provide a primer on copyright licensing more broadly. As regards licensing of IP rights, economists have foremost been occupied with patents, and there is only a relatively small, but growing, body of literature on copyright licensing,[5] which has devoted its attention primarily to the collective administration of rights and their organisations.[6] Strowel and Vanbrabant summarise some key features of copyright licensing: first, it is necessary to differentiate between licence and assignment. Whereas an '[a]ssignment is a transfer of rights in an exclusive and definitive manner', a '[l]icense is the permission to make use of the copyright subject matter under the special terms negotiated by the parties'.[7] Posner simply defines licensing as 'the granting of permission for another person to use your property'.[8] Associated with the identification of the right holder and negotiations are costs that 'are not great in absolute terms, but they are great relative to the value of most copyrighted works'.[9] A high ratio of these transaction costs to the value of the licence 'will often be a formidable barrier to a value-maximizing transaction'.[10]

This relates to the second feature: contractual freedom. Contractual freedom finds its basis in the general private law principle of party autonomy and is considered as being enshrined in the Charter of Fundamental

---

[2] J. Schovsbo, 'The Necessity to collectivize copyright – and dangers thereof' (2010), 10: http://ssrn.com/abstract=1632753

[3] Ibid., with further references.

[4] See also A. Strowel and B. Vanbrabant, 'Copyright Licensing: A European View' in J. de Werra (ed.), *Research Handbook on Intellectual Property Licensing* (Edward Elgar, 2013), p. 30.

[5] See, e.g., R. Watt, 'Licensing of Copyright Works in a Bargaining Model' in Richard Watt (ed.), *Handbook on the Economics of Copyright* (Edward Elgar, 2014), p. 108, with further evidence, or as early as A. Hollander, 'Market Structure and Performance in Intellectual Property', *International Journal of Industrial Organization*, 2 (1984), 199. More recently, however, economists' attention to copyright has grown, as is exemplified by the Society of Economic Research on Copyright Issues (SERCI).

[6] See R. Watt, 'Copyright Collectives: Some Basic Economic Theory' in R. Watt (ed.), *Handbook on the Economics of Copyright* (Edward Elgar, 2014), p. 167.

[7] Strowel and Vanbrabant, 'Copyright licensing: A European view', p. 34.

[8] R. A. Posner, 'Transaction Costs and Antitrust Concerns in the Licensing of Intellectual Property', *John Marshall Review of Intellectual Property Law*, 4 (2005), 325.

[9] Ibid., 326.   [10] Ibid.

Rights of the European Union.[11] According to Strowel and Vanbrabant, '[m]any national laws in Europe have horizontal rules which apply to all contracts, for instance the general rules contained in the civil code, but not many countries have specific rules for intellectual property licensing'.[12] Broadly speaking,

freedom of contract dominates in the copyright field as in other branches of the law where the legislature favours the meeting of private interests as a good way to achieve the public interest.[13]

To a certain extent, this is also reflected in the scope of licences, which are notable for varying greatly.[14]

Now to the third feature: whereas many different aspects of copyright have been harmonised, Hugenholtz noted, more than half a decade ago, that legislative instruments 'have largely ignored the single most important obstacle to the creation of an Internal Market in content-based services: the territorial nature of copyright'.[15] Today, the situation does not look much different. Just as exclusivity is, the principle of territoriality is firmly enshrined in international copyright.[16] Article 5(2) of the Berne Convention reads:

The enjoyment and the exercise of these rights shall not be subject to any formality; such enjoyment and such exercise shall be independent of the existence of protection in the country of origin of the work. Consequently, apart from the provisions of this Convention, the extent of protection, as well as the means of redress afforded to the author to protect his rights, shall be governed exclusively by the laws of the country where protection is claimed.

At the same time, as Torremans remarks, the international legal framework does not use or define the concept of exclusivity.[17] Peukert

---

[11] More specifically, it can be read in Art. 16 of the Charter on freedom to conduct a business, based on the CJEU's case law, notably Case 151/78, *Sukkerfabriken Nykøbing* [1979] ECR 1, ECLI:EU:C:1979:4, para. 19; Case C-240/97, *Kingdom of Spain* v. *Commission of the European Communities* [1999] I-06571, ECLI:EU:C:1999:479, para. 99. See Praesidium of the European Convention, 'Explanations relating to the Charter of Fundamental Rights' (2007/C303/02) [2007] OJ C 303/17, Explanation on Article 16 – Freedom to conduct a business.

[12] Strowel and Vanbrabant, 'Copyright licensing: A European view', p. 47.

[13] Ibid., p. 31.   [14] Ibid., p. 35.

[15] See P. Bernt Hugenholtz, 'Audiovisual Archives across Borders – Dealing with Territorially Restricted Copyright', *IRIS Special* 49, [2010], 49.

[16] P. Torremans, 'Questioning the Principles of Territoriality: The Determination of Territorial Mechanisms of Commercialisation' in P. Torremans (ed.), *Copyright Law, A Handbook of Contemporary Research* (Edward Elgar, 2007), p. 460; G. Mazziotti, 'Is Geo-blocking a Real Cause for Concern?', *European Intellectual Property Review*, 367 (2016), 365, 367; J. Blomqvist, *Primer on International Copyright and Related Rights* (Edward Elgar, 2014), p. 47.

[17] Torremans, 'Questioning the Principles of Territoriality', p. 460.

Exclusivity, Contractual Freedom and Territoriality

comments, in view of the high number of contracting states to the Berne Convention, that 'it is safe to say that objective and subjective territoriality are universally accepted concepts'.[18] Territoriality is also acknowledged in the directives dealing with copyright and related rights, and has been confirmed by the Court of Justice[19] and clarified in Case C-192/04, *Lagardère*:

> At the outset, it must be emphasised that it is clear from its wording and scheme that Directive 92/100 provides for minimal harmonisation regarding rights related to copyright. Thus, it does not purport to detract, in particular, from the *principle of the territoriality of those rights, which is recognised in international law and also in the EC Treaty*. Those rights are therefore of a territorial nature and, moreover, domestic law can only penalise conduct engaged in within national territory.[20]

Thus, some have described the territorial nature as forming part of the 'quasi-*acquis communautaire*'.[21] The Committee on Legal Affairs of the European Parliament points out, in its Report on the Implementation of the InfoSoc Directive from May 2015, 'that the existence of copyright and related rights inherently implies territoriality'.[22] It continues to emphasise, however, 'that there is no contradiction between that principle and measures to ensure the portability of content'.[23] In other words, in the EU, copyright consists of a bundle of twenty-eight nationally awarded exclusive rights, which are conferred and exploited at the national level.[24]

---

[18] A. Peukert, 'Territoriality and Extraterritoriality in Intellectual Property Law' in G. Handl, J. Zekoll and P. Zumbansen (eds.), *Beyond Territoriality: Transnational Legal Authority in an Age of Globalization* (Brill Academic Publishing, 2012), p. 4: http://ssrn.com/abstract=1592263. Although this is the prevailing view, it is not completely uncontested, as Ohly notes. See A. Ohly, 'Geoblocking zwischen Wirtschafts-, Kultur-, Verbraucher- und Europapolitik', *Zeitschrift für Urheber-und Medienrecht* [2015], 942, 943.

[19] See, e.g., Case 78/70, *Deutsche Grammophon Gesellschaft mbH* v. *Metro-SB-Großmärkte GmbH & Co. KG* [1971] ECR 487, ECLI:EU:C:1971:59; Case 62//79, *Coditel* v. *Ciné Vog Films* [1980] ECR 882–905, ECLI:EU:C:1980:84, paras. 15–17.

[20] Case C-192/04, *Lagardère Active Broadcast* v. *Société pour la perception de la rémunération équitable (SPRE), Gesellschaft zur Verwertung von Leistungsschutzrechten mbH (GVL), and, as third party, Compagnie européenne de radiodiffusion et de télévision Europe 1 SA (CERT)* [2005] ECR I-7218, ECLI:EU:C:2005:475, para. 46 (emphasis added).

[21] J. Gaster, 'Das urheberrechtliche Territorialitätsprinzip aus Sicht des Europäischen Gemeinschaftsrechts', *Zeitschrift für Urheber- und Medienrecht* [2016], 8, 9, cited in KEA European Affairs and Mines ParisTech, 140.

[22] European Parliament, 'Report on the implementation of Directive 2001/29/EC of the European Parliament and of the Council of 22 May 2001 on the harmonisation of certain aspects of copyright and related rights in the information society (2014/2256(INI))', Recital 6.

[23] Ibid., Recital 6.

[24] See L. Guibault, 'Individual Licensing Models and Consumer Protection', Amsterdam Law School Legal Studies Research Paper No. 2016–01 (2016), 12: http://ssrn.com/abstract=2713765; and Mazziotti, 'Is Geo-blocking a Real Cause for Concern?', 367.

At the same time, the territoriality principle does not, as Trimble points out, 'mandate the partitioning of markets for IPR-protected works'.[25] In combination with contractual freedom and the exclusivity principle, it follows that rights holders are, in principle, free to grant licences restricted to certain territories. For example, the Court of Justice recognised the audiovisual industry's dependence on territorial licences in its *Coditel II* judgment of 1982:

> The characteristics of the cinematographic industry and of its markets in the Community, especially those relating to dubbing and subtitling for the benefit of different language groups, to the possibilities of television broadcasts, and to the system of financing cinematographic production in Europe serve to show that an exclusive exhibition licence is not, in itself, such as to prevent, restrict or distort competition.[26]

All three concepts – exclusivity, contractual freedom and territoriality – are at the very heart of licensing of and access to copyright-protected works on the Internet, as the following sections will show.

2.2   An Intertwined Relationship: Multi-Territorial Licensing and Cross-Border Access

In order better to understand the topics of this book, it is useful to examine the relation between the phenomena at stake: multi-territorial licensing and cross-border access. The following conceptual model attempts to shed some light on this intertwined relationship. For the sake of clarity and abstraction, the model is based on a couple of simplifying assumptions: first, I abstain from differentiating between different forms of copyright-protected goods (in this case, between music and audiovisual works).[27] Secondly, for the sake of this section, I focus exclusively on the theoretical prospect of consumers accessing copyright-protected works in certain cross-border situations. This presupposes the existence of a (commercial) demand for multi-territorial licences. Thirdly, this overview disregards the different underlying institutional arrangements.

When taking *cross-border licensing* as a starting point, two scenarios need to be differentiated: first, licensing foreign content in the domestic territory, and, secondly, licensing domestic content abroad. For this section,

---

[25] M. Trimble, 'The Territoriality Referendum', *World Intellectual Property Organization Journal* [2014], 89, 96.

[26] Case 262/81, *Coditel and Others* [1982] ECR 3382–3403, ECLI:EU:C:1982:334 para 16.

[27] This differentiation will become relevant again in the following sections of the book. In reality, 'musical works' and 'audiovisual content' refer to rather different market contexts, as will be explored below.

multi-territorial licensing is understood simply as the licensing of content for more than one territory.[28]

The concept of *access* can again be looked at from at least two different viewpoints, which are arguably two sides of the same coin: consumers who have access to works and rights holders who make the content accessible, either directly or via intermediaries. *Cross-border access* is understood as embracing both situations covered by portability (i.e. a consumer from Member State A accessing its online content services from Member State A while physically present in Member State B) and geo-blocking (i.e. a consumer from Member State A being restricted from accessing online content services in another Member State). Another way of thinking about the different shades of the cross-border access concept finds its link in the four freedoms of the internal market. Portability is somewhat linked to the free movement of persons, in that the individual consumer is translocating to another Member State. An example of this scenario is a Danish consumer who is temporarily in Germany trying to access the content of an online content service from its home country, Denmark. Situations captured by geo-blocking (or 'true' cross-border access), on the other hand, are linked to the free movement of services, in that online content services are accessed from another Member State. An example of this scenario is a Danish customer trying to access the content of an online content service from Germany while being in Denmark or another third country. This is illustrated by Figure 2.

In a first scenario, let us assume that an online content provider can acquire multi-territorial licences for the relevant content through the different institutional arrangements.[29] In principle, this implies two things regarding the availability of content and territorial restrictions: first, that online content providers are hypothetically able to provide their services to consumers from different Member States, and, secondly, that they are able to offer portability to their consumers. In the absence of a legal obligation, though, this does not entail that online content providers are actually doing so: commercial considerations such as competition, price discrimination or premium payments for portability, as well as legal considerations such as applicable local laws, could provide

---

[28] The European legislator defines a 'multi-territorial licence' in Art. 3(m) Directive 2014/26/EU tautologically, as a licence that covers the territory of more than one Member State (and correspondingly in Art. 1(d) of the Online Music Recommendation (2005/737/EC), with the same wording).

[29] In Chapters 3 and 4, I will reintroduce the differentiation among the different cross-border elements as regards multi-territorial licensing: cross-border provision for users (to users from another Member State; or for use in another Member State) and cross-border provision to rights holders (representing rights of rights holders from other Member States).

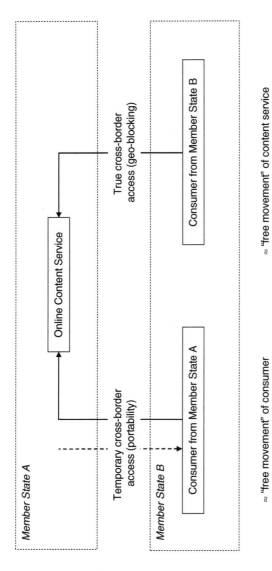

Figure 2: Visualisation of geo-blocking and portability

incentives for the online content provider to refrain from offering portability or to respond to consumer requests from other Member States.

Now, let us turn to the flip side: in this second scenario, let us assume that cross-border access, in the forms of both portability and geoblocking, is ensured, e.g. by a legal obligation on online service providers. This implies that consumers are hypothetically able to access online content from their resident and different Member States – irrespective of their location within the EU. In this scenario, though, the online content provider would still need to clear the relevant rights for the respective territories. Yet another question, however, is whether rights holders (licensors) are interested in entering into licensing agreements with service providers (licensees) for several Member States or all of the EU territory, and vice versa. Considering contractual freedom, rights holders without any obligations or restrictions would be free to license their content (or not) as they pleased, i.e. for the territories of their choice. Additionally, rights holders could oblige commercial users to put in place, for example, technological protection measures in order to enforce territorial delineations,[30] which, again, would cancel out the effect of cross-border access.

Licensing and Access: Interdependence or Just Some Overlap?

These two scenarios are naturally restricted in their insights. They do not account for considerations other than access from the consumer's perspective. Yet, this top-level view might inform the subsequent analysis and discussion. One first reflection is that, in order to make online content accessible to consumers in the EU, both multi-territorial licences and cross-border access are limited in what they can facilitate – at least without changing the current rights landscape or the modus operandi of the different arrangements. In the chapters that follow, this book will elaborate on the overlap and interplay between the different strains of action. Another insight is that licensing, on the one hand, seems to be primarily guided by the relationship between rights holders and online service providers, whereas the access dimension, on the other hand, includes both the relationship between consumers and online service providers and, to a certain degree, in an indirect fashion, rights holders. While the differentiation between the different relationships (licensor–licensee;

---

[30] Given the significant leverage that rights holders enjoy with exclusive rights, in situations in which the licensee does not have sufficient bargaining power, licensing terms are more likely to be dictated by rights holders.

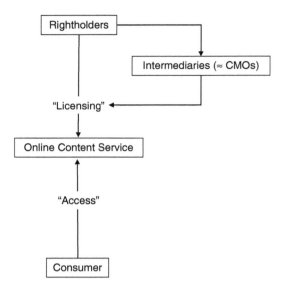

Figure 3: Simplified licensing and access scheme

licensor–licensor; and licensor/online content service consumer) is not always clear cut, this is illustrated in a simplified form in Figure 3.

It is self-evident that multi-territorial licensing has an inherent reflection on cross-border access, simply in that it enables it.[31] For the following analysis, it is important to note two major cross-border dimensions in the downstream relationship – namely, licensing foreign content in the domestic territory and licensing domestic content abroad. In the case of intermediaries, such as CMOs, yet another cross-border dimension is the provision of administration services to foreign rights holders.

In this context, it seems useful briefly to consider why multi-territorial licensing situations have received such a high level of attention, and whether the topic deserves this much emphasis. In Chapter 1, we have

---

[31] See, e.g., C. Castets-Renard, '"Digital Single Market": the European Commission presents its first measures in Copyright Law', *French Review: Recueil Dalloz*, n° 7, 2016, 388 (forthcoming), 6: http://ssrn.com/abstract=2802729. Kautio et al., for example, suggest that the 'lack of access to copyrighted works could also be explained by malfunctioning market for copyrighted products and services': T. Kautio, N. Lefever and M. Määttä, *Assessing the Operation of Copyright and Related Rights Systems, Methodology Framework* (Foundation for Cultural Policy Research (Cupore), Cupore publication 26 2016), p. 119. The project represents an interesting attempt to provide a methodology framework (primarily directed towards lawmakers) for the empirical examination of different aspects of the operation of copyright.

already visited the policy goal of the completion of the Digital Single Market. In a single market, cross-border and multi-territorial situations are inherent. The Internet has led to an unprecedented rise in cross-border access to content in all facets. While many aspects of copyright have been harmonised, the principle of territoriality is deeply rooted in copyright law and its exercise. This creates the (traditional) stress field of territoriality and the completion of a common Digital Single Market, in which national regulatory solutions are not feasible. Multi-territorial licensing can also be inextricably intertwined with mono-territorial licensing (i.e. licensing for a single territory), as the following subject matter-specific example illustrates. For this purpose, let us briefly re-introduce the differentiation between audiovisual and music content: as will be explored further below, developments in music licensing have led to a situation in which it can be necessary for a licensee to clear rights for a single territory, both with national CMOs and multi-territorial licensing entities. Furthermore, more than one right holder is often involved in the same category of work, such as when musical works have several authors.[32] In such cases of split copyright, the rights holders involved might have assigned their rights to different CMOs or intermediaries. Finally, the aggregation of a broad, or even the global, (music) repertoire constitutes a main commercial concern for online service providers,[33] in which, to a large extent, repertoires constitute complementary products rather than substitutes.

2.3   The Age of Access and Its Business Models

Digitalisation and the Internet have profoundly impacted the way in which we exploit and consume copyright-protected works.[34] Much has been written about the transformative effects, and this is not the place in which to provide a full-blown analysis of all aspects. Instead, let me rely

---

[32] See Recital 37 of Directive 2014/26/EU. See also P. Gyertyánfy, 'Collective Management of Music Rights in Europe after the CISAC Decision', *International Review of Intellectual Property and Competition Law* [2010], 59, 65; E. Anthonis, 'Will the CRM-directive succeed re-aggregating the mechanical reproduction rights in the Anglo-American music repertoire?', *International Journal of Intellectual Property Management*, 7 (2014), 151, 152.

[33] L. Guibault, 'The Draft Collective Management Directive' in I. A. Stamatoudi and P. Torremans (eds.), *EU Copyright Law: A Commentary* (Edward Elgar, 2014), p. 770.

[34] See, in the United States context, e.g., J. C. Ginsburg, 'From Having Copies to Experiencing Works: the Development of an Access Right in U.S. Copyright Law', *Journal of the Copyright Society of the USA*, 50 (2003), 113. More broadly on the impact of digitalisation on the music industry, see, e.g., M. Peitz and P. Waelbroeck, 'An Economist's Guide to Digital Music' (2004) CESifo Working Paper No. 1333: cesifo.oxfordjournals.org/content/51/2–3/359.full.pdf

on some of the sketched overall tendencies of the shift towards access-based business models for content distribution. Hilty and Köklu divide the digital age into three main periods. First, there is the transition of works from analogue to digital 'disembodied' formats, which has legally been dealt with by the first-sale doctrine.[35] Secondly, there is the digital age, in which the distribution of tangible copies has been replaced by the consumer's own devices, which means that the consumer 'produces' a physical copy of the work itself, e.g. on hard disks and other storage media (such as by downloading a work), and in which the first-sale doctrine is no longer directly applicable 'without over-stretching its interpretation'.[36] The third period that they identify is characterised by a total absence of tangible copies of the relevant work, in which the 'ability to have access to digital works is more important than acquiring "owner-ship" in the respective digital work by purchasing a digital copy'.[37] Again, they argue, '[a]s there are no more tangible copies involved, the first-sale doctrine in particular is now unsuitable for application – again at least not without over-stretching its interpretation'.[38] The business models of downloads and streaming have in common the fact that they are normally governed by direct contractual relationships between rights holders and end users, which are 'often unilaterally declared by rightholders as licen-sing or access terms'.[39] As they point out, this might lead to major insufficiencies in the existing legal framework, undermining the 'envi-saged balance of involved interests in copyright law'.[40]

Ricolfi remarks that the Internet has also enabled creators to rely on a 'short route', 'which puts in direct contact creators and the public'.[41] This, he argues, might lead to a gradual replacement of the 'long route',

[35] R. M. Hilty and K. Köklu, 'Limitations and Exceptions to Copyright in the Digital Age' in I. A. Stamatoudi (ed.), *New Developments in EU and International Copyright Law* (Kluwer Law International, 2016), p. 287.
[36] Ibid., p. 288. Notably, the authors, in 2016, find this phase to be still ongoing and currently predominant. As regards the background of the developments in recent years in streaming both audiovisual works and music, this seems unconvincing. In Norway and Denmark, for example, streaming accounted for 81 per cent and 72 per cent of music revenues respec-tively. See S. F. Schwemer, 'Kollektiv forvaltning i informationssamfundet og det nye regime under direktivet 2014/26/EU i Danmark', *Nordiskt Immateriellt Rättsskydd* [2015], 697, with further evidence.
[37] Hilty and Köklü, 'Limitations and Exceptions to Copyright in the Digital Age', p. 289. In a similar vein, Guibault refers to streaming as 'one step further in the "dematerializa-tion" of content': see Guibault, 'Individual Licensing Models and Consumer Protection', 8.
[38] Hilty and Köklü, 'Limitations and Exceptions to Copyright in the Digital Age', p. 289.
[39] Ibid, p. 290.   [40] Ibid.
[41] M. Ricolfi, 'Consume and Share: Making Copyright Fit for the Digital Agenda' in C. Geiger (ed.), *Constructing European Intellectual Property, Achievements and New Perspectives* (Edward Elgar, 2013), p. 315.

where works are handled by different intermediaries before they reach the consumer.[42] Therefore, he argues, creators are enabled to access markets 'without engaging in the trilateral relationship, which used to be characteristic of dealings in copyright'.[43] This anticipated development, however, still has to materialise.

The Case of Interactive On-Demand Streaming Service Providers

As clarified in the introductory chapter, several forms of streaming and business models can be differentiated. In the European legal framework, the lawmaker provides definitions of different services, which primarily take their starting point in the different kinds of content. A legal definition of an 'online music service', for example, was originally provided for in Article 3(m) of the Commission's proposal for the Collective Rights Management Directive (CRM Directive) as 'information society service within the meaning of Article 1(2) of Directive 98/34/EC which requires the licensing of musical works'. In Article 1(b) of the redrafted Technical Standards Directive such 'service' is defined as 'any service normally provided for remuneration, at a distance, by electronic means and at the individual request of a recipient of services'.[44] Notably, this definition has been dropped but not replaced in the final directive. Neither does Directive 2014/26/EU differentiate between on-demand and linear services.

In its Proposal for a Regulation on cross-border portability, the European Commission introduced the definition of an 'online content service', which, according to Article 2(e) of Regulation (EU) 2017/1128

means a service as defined by Articles 56 and 57 of the Treaty on the Functioning of the European Union that a service provider is lawfully providing online in the Member State of residence on a portable basis and which is an audiovisual media

---

[42] Ibid. If this was entirely manifested, though, this research endeavour would not have to look at the role of intermediaries such as CMOs. Ricolfi's point, however, seems to be confirmed, at least as regards music, where artists can self-publish their works on streaming services such as Spotify or YouTube. See, e.g., on YouTube's Content ID model, M. W. Caroll, 'A Realist Approach to Copyright Law's Formalities', *Berkeley Technology Law Journal*, 28 (2013), 1511, 1527.

[43] Ricolfi, 'Consume and Share: Making Copyright Fit for the Digital Agenda', p. 317.

[44] Directive (EU) 2015/1535 of the European Parliament and of the Council of 9 September 2015 laying down a procedure for the provision of information in the field of technical regulations and of rules on Information Society services (codification) [2015] OJ L241. The Online Music Recommendation (2005/737/EC) contains a reference to the 'commercial user', which is defined as 'any person involved in the provision of online music services who needs a licence from right-holders in order to provide legitimate online music services', – without, however, defining 'online music services'.

service within the meaning of Directive 2010/13/EU or a service the main feature of which is the provision of access to and use of works, other protected subject matter or transmissions of broadcasting organisations, whether in a linear or an on-demand manner.

Thus, the distinction between linear and on-demand services is also of minor importance in the Portability Regulation. A definition of an 'on-demand audiovisual media service', for example, is provided for in Article 1(1)(g) of the Audiovisual Media Services Directive as

an audiovisual media service provided by a media service provider for the viewing of programmes at the moment chosen by the user and at his individual request on the basis of a catalogue of programmes selected by the media service provider.

Thus, the legislator provides different notions in the context of the specific legislation, sometimes tied to the subject matter or the linear or on-demand characteristics regarding its distribution form. The European Commission differentiates between transactional services, where films or music are offered for purchase or rent on a one-off basis, and subscription services, in which service providers establish a longer-term contractual relationship with consumers.[45]

Another common differentiation between interactive on-demand streaming service providers is along the line of their business model, falling into two main categories:[46] free advertising-based models and subscription-based models. A third category combines both features in a 'freemium' model. In this context, recently a substantial amount of economic research has been devoted to the questions of how streaming affects traditional exploitation forms and' more broadly' sampling effects, i.e. the impact of free content on sales.[47]

---

[45] See Commission, 'Impact Assessment accompanying the document Proposal for a Regulation of the European Parliament and of the Council to ensure the cross-border portability of online content services in the internal market' (Commission Staff Working Document) SWD(2015) 270/final, Brussels, 9 December 2015, 7.

[46] See also G. Langus, D. Neven and S. Pouken, *Economic Analysis of the Territoriality of the Making Available Right in the EU* (Report prepared for the European Commission, DG MARKT 2014), 13.

[47] Kretschmer and Peukert piggyback on two 'quasi-experiments in the German market for online music videos to identify the effect of free sampling on physical on digital sales of recorded music'. They 'find strong evidence that online videos are complementary to digital record sales', whereas 'sales of physical records do not respond strongly to changes in the supply of online videos, which could imply lower substitutability between online video and physical sales (compared to digital)'. See T. Kretschmer and C. Peukert, 'Video Killed the Radio Star? Online Music Videos and Digital Music Sales' (2015), 20–21: http://ssrn.com/abstract=2425386. Aguiar and Waldfogel analyse the relation of streaming and music sales and conclude that 'interactive streaming appears to be revenue-neutral for the recorded music industry' (L. Aguiar and J. Waldfogel, 'Streaming Reaches Flood Stage: Does Spotify Stimulate or Depress Music Sales?'

Relatively little empirical evidence is available as to the distribution of revenues, which is outside the scope of this book. According to industry sources, interactive on-demand music streaming services pay out approximately 70 per cent of their revenue to rights holders.[48] The pay-out is usually calculated on a pro rata basis (personal streams divided by the total amount of streams) corresponding the percentage of the respective repertoire of total plays in the period.[49] According to information available to the European Commission, approximately 12 per cent of revenues of online music service providers go to CMOs (and option 3 publishers), whereas approximately 60 per cent of revenues go to record companies.[50] This seems especially noteworthy when considering that the regulatory focus (both competition proceedings and legislative measures) is almost exclusively directed towards the situation of collective management.[51] A specific market dynamic in online music streaming services is observed, in that major record labels sometimes have a (minority) equity ownership in service providers. It has been commented that such equity positions have been acquired by licensing their content catalogues at sub-market rates.[52]

(2015) NBER Working Paper Series, Working Paper 21653: www.nber.org/papers/w2 1653). In a similar vein, DangNgyuen et al. empirically analyse whether streaming and other music consumption modes are substitutes or complements (G. Dang Nguyen, S. Dejean and F. Moreau, 'Are Streaming and Other Music Consumption Modes Substitutes or Complements?': http://ssrn.com/abstract=2025071). Based on a survey of 2,000 French individuals, they find that streaming has no significant effect on CD purchase but is a complement to buying music online. Another interesting study performed by George and Peukert focuses on the cultural convergence between video (YouTube) and recorded music (see L. M. George and C. Peukert, 'YouTube Decade: Cultural Convergence in Recorded Music' (2014) NET Institute, Working Paper # 14–11: http://ssrn.com/abstract=2506357).

[48] Rethink Music, 'Fair Music: Transparency and Payment Flows in the Music Industry, Recommendations to Increase Transparency, Reduce Friction, and Promote Fairness in the Music Industry' (2015) Rethink Music, Berklee ICE, Boston, 14: www.rethink-music.com/research/fair-music-transparency-and-payment-flows-in-the-music-industry. This represents the same share as on iTunes download sales.

[49] This pay-out model is not uncontested. The issue of whether to go over to a user-centric model, where the pay-out would depend on actual plays of an individual subscriber, has been raised. This is argued to alleviate the imbalance in the current system, in which major artists benefit the most: see, e.g., A. Maasø, *User-centric settlement for music streaming; A report on the distribution of income from music streaming in Norway, based on streaming data from WiMP Music* (Clouds & Concerts research group, University of Oslo, 2014).

[50] See *PRSfM/STIM/GEMA/JV* (Case M.6800), Commission Decision of 16 June 2015 declaring a concentration to be compatible with the internal market and the EEA agreement, C(2015) 4061 final, Brussels, 16 June 2015, Public Version, Recital 296.

[51] The criticism has been that only little information is available on the proceedings within record labels as regards deductions and recouping of costs: see, e.g., Rethink Music, 'Fair Music', 14.

[52] Ibid., 17. This is argued to be problematic because ownership shares are not paid out to artists.

2.4   Online Licensing of Copyright-Protected Works

Let us now turn towards the specific market developments and current practices regarding (multi-territorial) licensing to set the scene for the forthcoming analysis of the legal framework. In Section 2.4.1, the focus is on the institutional arrangements and the licensing relationship between collective management organisations (CMOs) as intermediaries and commercial users. The use of these intermediaries is predominant in music licensing practice, whereas the online licensing arrangements for audiovisual content have evolved in a different fashion. The latter licensing practices will be addressed in Section 2.4.2.

2.4.1   Licensing by Collective Management Organisations

2.4.1.1   Intermediaries as a Solution to Market Failure

The market for collective administration of copyright has developed for well over 250 years.[53] Whereas this is not the place to present a comprehensive overview of the various aspects of collective management, some basic features are essential. 'Collective management comes in many shapes and sizes', as Gervais notes, and there is an ongoing debate about what constitutes collective management, notably referring to the level of solidarity and ideological differences between the United States–American and the continental European traditions.[54] In the

---

[53] The idea of institutionalised collective management is often said to date back to the eighteenth century, when French playwright Pierre-Augustin Caron de Beaumarchain kickstarted the debate that laid the foundation for the French Society of Drama Authors. More well known is the fact that French authors Honoré de Balzac and Victor Hugo established the Society of French Writers in 1838 (see, e.g., D. Gervais and A. Maurushat, 'Fragmented Copyright, Fragmented Management: Proposals to Defrag Copyright Management', *Canadian Journal of Law and Technology*, 2 (2003), 15, 16; or D. Gervais, 'Collective Management: Theory and Practice in the Digital Age' in D. Gervais (ed.), *Collective Management of Copyright and Related Rights*, 2nd edn. (Wolters Kluwer, 2010), pp. 3ff). Also popular is the anecdote of French composer Ernest Bourget in 1847, which led to the creation of the predecessor of French author CMO SACEM, as retold in, e.g., M. Kretschmer, 'The Failure of Property Rules in Collective Administration: Rethinking Copyright Societies as Regulatory Instruments', *European Intellectual Property Review* [2002], 126, 127. For developments in the United States–American context, see, e.g., S. M. Besen, S. N. Kirby and S. C. Salop, 'An Economic Analysis of Copyright Collectives', *Virginia Law Review*, 78 (1992), 383, 385–390.

[54] D. Gervais, 'Keynote: The Landscape of Collective Management Schemes', *Columbia Journal of Law & the Arts*, 34 (2011), 423 for an overview of the discussion on specifically the difference in the United States–American and European traditions, mainly regarding the level of solidarity. See also C. Handke, 'Collective Administration' in R. Watt (ed.), *Handbook on the Economics of Copyright* (Edward Elgar, 2014), pp. 192 ff. For an exploratory study on European CMOs' operation in the digital environment (pre-

European tradition, solidarity aspects of CMOs have been underlined time after time. Artists whose works are performing well economically support those whose works are less successful. At a more conceptual or functional level, the legal and the economic literature commonly identify three basic economic features of all CMOs:[55] after having entrusted rights from rights holders for representation, a CMO: (1) negotiates and grants licences for the use of works in its repertoire; (2) monitors usage, enforces and collects royalties; and (3) distributes revenues to its members.

CMOs hold not their own copyright, but what Schovsbo calls a 'derived administration right of copyright-character'.[56] In other words, CMOs act as intermediaries in a two-sided market by providing services to both rights holders and licensees (commercial users).[57] Towards commercial users, CMOs usually operate by issuing blanket licences, which means the whole catalogue of the represented repertoire is made available for a specific use in a single transaction.[58] This practice again bears aspects of the solidarity aspects mentioned above. Systematically, thus, CMOs, as 'private transactional mechanisms',[59] facilitate what Merges coined 'contracting into

---

streaming), see P. Gilliéron, 'Collecting Societies and the Digital Environment', *International Review of Intellectual Property and Competition Law* [2006], 939.

[55] See, e.g., Gervais, 'Keynote: The Landscape of Collective Management Schemes' 427; Gervais, 'Collective Management: Theory and Practice in the Digital Age', 6–9; R. Towse, 'Economics of collective management organisations in the creative industries' (WINIR conference, 4–6 April 2016), 3; M. Hviid, S. Schroff and J. Street, 'Regulating CMOs by competition: an incomplete answer to the licensing problem?' (2016) CREATe Working Paper 2016/03 (March 2016), 2. Hollander defines CMOs' functions as: '(1) they grant licenses for the use of works in their repertory, (2) they negotiate and collect royalties, and distribute them to their members, (3) they take legal action against those who infringe the copyrights to which they hold title.' (A. Hollander, 'Market Structure and Performance in Intellectual Property', *International Journal of Industrial Organization*, 2 (1984), 199, 200.)

[56] J. Schovsbo, *Grænsefladespørgsmål mellem immaterialretten og konkurrenceretten* (Jurist- og Økonomforbundets Forlag, 1996), p. 27.

[57] See, e.g., J. Drexl, 'Collective Management of Copyrights and the EU Principle of Free Movement of Services after the OSA Judgment – In Favour of a More Balanced Approach' in K. Purnhagen and P. Rott (eds.), *Varieties of European Economic Law and Regulation, Liber Amicorum for Hans Micklitz*, vol. 3 (Springer, 2014), p. 463.

[58] See Hollander, 'Market structure and performance', 203, who notes that blanket licensing 'offers considerable advantages from the point of view of transaction costs'. See also, more recently, Gervais, 'Keynote: The Landscape of Collective Management Schemes', 431; Towse, 'Economics of Collective Management Organisations', 5. The interface of blanket licensing with competition law is not unproblematic: see, e.g., Hollander, 'Market Structure and Performance', 203; and A. Katz, 'The Potential Demise of Another Natural Monopoly: Rethinking the Collective Administration of Performing Rights', *Journal of Competition Law and Economics*, 1 (2005), 541, 544.

[59] R. P. Merges, 'Contracting into Liability Rules: Intellectual Property Rights and Collective Rights Organizations', *California Law Review*, 84 (1996), 1293, 1295.

a liability rule'[60] or, as Hilty and Nérisson articulate, it 'facilitates the fundamental shift in copyright from a half-functioning system based on proprietary rules to an efficient system based on liability rules'.[61] The contractual freedom of the participating right holder and commercial users is limited, individual rights are pooled and the exclusive right is reduced to an entitlement of remuneration in form of a pro rata share.[62]

CMOs usually operate on a non-profit basis. However, this is not conditional on their not operating on a profit-maximising basis. Quite the opposite: a central objective of such organisations is maximising profits for their 'shareholders', i.e. rights holders who enshrined their exclusive rights in them. In a similar vein, Schovsbo notes that it is 'important to bear in mind that authors' organisations like all other institutions have a vested interest in maintaining a system which is dependent on their services'.[63]

CMOs as Natural Monopolies: a Tale of Economies of Scale and Scope   According to economic theory, a natural monopoly arises from economies of scale and scope.[64] Conventionally it is argued that CMOs are able to produce economies of scale both on the supply side and on the demand side, through bundling of various activities.[65] That is to say, the average cost per unit falls as output, for example transactions, increases.

[60] Merges bases this on the Calabresi-Melamed framework (1972) in entitlement theory, who 'describe all legal entitlements as protected by either "property rules" or "liability rules"' (ibid., 1302). This figurative notion has been used by many scholars with more or less clear attribution to Merges.

[61] R. Hilty and S. Nérisson, 'Collective Copyright Management and Digitization: The European Experience', Max Planck Institute for Intellectual Property and Competition Law Research Paper No. 13–09 (Max Planck Institute for Intellectual Property and Competition Law, 2013), 7: http://ssrn.com/abstract=2247870

[62] See ibid., 2; Ricolfi, 'Consume and Share: Making Copyright Fit for the Digital Agenda', p. 325.

[63] Schovsbo, 'The Necessity to Collectivize Copyright – and Dangers Thereof', 9.

[64] See K. E. Train, *Optimal Regulation: The Economic Theory of Natural Monopoly*, 3rd edn. (MIT Press, 1994), p. 5. See also R. Ghafele, 'Europe's Lost Royalty Opportunity: a Comparison of Potential and Existing Digital Music Royalty Markets in Ten Different E.U. Member States', *Review of Economic Research on Copyright Issues*, 11 (2014), 60, 62–63; A. M. Peréz Gómez and M. A. Echavarría Arcila, 'Collective Administration of Online Rights in Musical Works: Analysing the Economic Efficiency of Directive 2014/26/EU', *International Journal of Intellectual Property Management*, 7 (2014), 103, 109. It is important to differentiate between the legal monopoly conferred by copyright on the right holder and the concept of an economic monopoly, as remarked by Posner, 'Transaction Costs and Antitrust Concerns in the Licensing of Intellectual Property', 329.

[65] See, e.g., R. Towse, 'Economics of Copyright Collecting Societies and Digital Rights: is there a Case for a Centralised Digital Copyright Exchange?', *Review of Economic Research on Copyright Issues*, 9 (2012), 3, 12; Watt, *Copyright and economic theory: friends or foes?*, p. 163.

Katz describes that 'a natural monopoly exists whenever the costs of production are such that it is less expensive for market demand to be met by one firm than by more than one'.[66] In other words, it is optimal to have only one firm providing the activity.[67] In the context of CMOs, Towse explains:

It costs very little to offer these services to additional members and works once the initial investment in the structure of licensing, fee setting and monitoring is in place – hence the natural monopoly.[68]

The traditional economic concern with monopoly power relates to deadweight losses, 'which are irrecoverable losses in social welfare when compared to the utopian state of perfect competition'.[69] Deadweight losses are argued to arise, for example, when a monopolistic CMO exploits its dominant position by setting prices above the competition level.[70] Kretschmer analyses that CMOs hold such a market position in at least two respects – namely the demand and the supply sides:

(1) towards the users of protected works who may have just one legitimate supplier of licenses, and (2) towards the individual owners of protected works who may have no alternative provider of a rights administration infrastructure.[71]

Despite these potential negative effects for social welfare, CMOs are often set up as *de jure* or *de facto* monopolies.[72] In the absence of a legal

---

[66] Katz, 'The potential demise of another natural monopoly: rethinking the collective administration of performing rights', 552 points towards the fact that natural monopolies are usually associated with utilities.

[67] See Train, *Optimal Regulation*.

[68] Towse, 'Economics of copyright collecting societies and digital rights: is there a case for a centralised digital copyright exchange?', 12.

[69] Watt, 'Copyright Collectives: Some Basic Economic theory', p. 167.

[70] Katz, 'The potential demise of another natural monopoly: rethinking the collective administration of performing rights', 548.

[71] Kretschmer, 'The Failure of Property Rules in Collective Administration: Rethinking Copyright Societies as Regulatory Instruments', 126.

[72] In 2014, the CJEU confirmed the compatibility of a national monopoly with EU law in Case C-351/12 *OSA – Ochranný svaz autorský pro práva k dílům hudebním o.s.* v. *Léčebné lázně Mariánské Lázně a.s.* [2014] ECLI:EU:C:2014:110. On Italy, see more specifically the case study by G. M. Riccio and G. Codiglione, 'Copyright Collecting Societies, Monopolistic Positions and Competition in the EU Single Market', *Masaryk Journal of Law and Technology*, 7 (2013), 287. Generally, there are '(m)yriad ways to set up and operate CMOs': see Gervais, 'Keynote: The Landscape of Collective Management Schemes', 427. In a similar vein, see W. Liu, 'Models for Collective Management of Copyright from an International Perspective: Potential Changes for Enhancing Performance', *Journal of Intellectual Property Rights*, 17 (2012), 46, who provides an overview of different regulatory models in and outside the EU. The monopoly of CMOs derives from the law and market sources (C. Handke and R. Towse, 'Economics of Copyright Collecting Societies' (2007): http://ssrn.com/abstract=1159085).

monopoly, legislators still 'may react to the development of natural monopolies with specific regulation' such as the authorisation system in German law.[73] In other words, CMOs

[i]n addition to being natural monopolies in the economic sense (...) also acquire monopoly control of the rights they manage since they require the exclusive assignment of a specific bundle of rights as a condition of membership, thereby enabling them to offer a blanket licence.[74]

Competition constrains the market power of CMOs.[75] Handke and Towse point to three mitigating factors regarding the monopoly problem of CMOs: regulation, bilateral monopoly and price discrimination.[76] CMOs are often restricted in tariff setting, subject to an obligation to contract to a certain degree, as well as to non-discrimination principles.[77] Until the recent entry into force of Directive 2016/24/EU, however, the degree of governance and regulation of CMOs varied widely across European countries.[78]

---

[73] See J. Drexl, 'Competition in the Field of Collective Management: Preferring "Creative Competition" to Allocative Efficiency in European Copyright Law' in P. Torremans (ed.), *Copyright Law, A Handbook of Contemporary Research* (Edward Elgar, 2007), p. 263. A similar system seems to have been in place in parts of central and Eastern Europe. For a comprehensive overview, see R. Matanovac Vuckovic, 'Implementation of Directive 2014/26 on Collective Management and Multi-territorial Licensing of Musical Rights in Regulating the Tariff-setting Systems in Central and Eastern Europe', *International Review of Intellectual Property and Competition Law*, 47 (2016), 28, 30.

[74] Towse, 'Economics of copyright collecting societies and digital rights: is there a case for a centralised digital copyright exchange?', 13.

[75] Besen, Kirby and Salop, 'An Economic Analysis of Copyright Collectives', 397.

[76] Handke and Towse, 'Economics of Copyright Collecting Societies', 4, also Handke, 'Collective administration', p. 194.

[77] Schovsbo, *Grænsefladespørgsmål mellem immaterialretten og konkurrenceretten*, p. 75. In Germany, for example, CMOs were, by sector-specific regulation, obliged to contract in two ways, namely in the licensor–right holder relationship to represent rights holders at their request and in the licensor–licensee relationship to grant licences on request to everyone on reasonable terms, which corresponds to the general EU competition law principles.

[78] In Schwemer, 'Emerging models for cross-border online licensing', I relate the degree of regulation to the autonomy space in the user generated law methodology. Already, Besen and Kirby provide an overview of how CMOs in several countries have been regulated (S. Besen and S. N. Kirby, *Compensating Creators of Intellectual Property* (The RAND Corporation, 1989)). A comprehensive overview of the former German regulatory framework is provided by J. Reinbothe, 'Collective Rights Management in Germany' in D. Gervais (ed.), *Collective Management of Copyright and Related Rights*, 2nd edn. (Kluwer Law International, 2010). Rochelandet found that higher regulation in Germany yielded better results, inter alia in terms) of administration costs (F. Rochelandet, 'Are copyright collecting societies efficient? An evaluation of collective administration of copyright in Europe' (The Society for Economic Research on Copyright Issues, Inaugural Annual Congress, Madrid, 2002)).

Traditional Justifications for Collective Administration   From the 1980s, collective management has attracted increasing attention among economists and led the way to the seminal literature for the first analytical study by Hollander in 1984 and further work by Besen and Kirby in 1989 and Besen et al. in 1992. Today, there exists a small but growing literature on the economics of 'copyright collectives'.[79]

The collective administration of rights is argued to be a 'spontaneous market response'[80] to the difficulty of licensing and enforcing multiple rights to many licensees (on secondary markets) and thereby alleviates inefficiencies of individual rights management;[81] thus, it can be seen 'as a response to market failure in the individual contracting over property rights'.[82] Watt argues that

> the exploitation of copyrights collectively may actually be better for society than the alternative of individual suppliers all competing for the attention of the users of creative works.[83]

Besen et al. identify two rationales for the formation of CMOs: first, cost savings from the collective administration, and secondly the acquisition of market power through cooperative price setting.[84] As regards the latter, it is argued that the elimination of price competition between rights holders ensures fair remuneration and 'act[s] as necessary counterbalance to the superior market power of industrial right users'.[85] By equalising prices of works irrespective of their popularity, a solidarity consideration becomes apparent. In a similar vein, CMOs have been argued to resemble trade unions for authors.[86] Others refer to an argument in addition to the transaction costs rationale, namely the establishment of effective control systems.[87] In his case studies, Merges detects expert tailoring

---

[79] See, e.g., Towse, 'Economics of copyright collecting societies and digital rights: is there a case for a centralised digital copyright exchange?', 12; R. Aoki and A. Schiff, 'Intellectual Property Clearinghouses: The Effects of Reduced Transaction Costs in Licensing', *Information Economics and Policy*, 22 (2010), 218, 219.

[80] Towse, 'Economics of collective management organisations in the creative industries', 3 and 9.

[81] See, e.g., Gervais and Maurushat, 'Fragmented Copyright, Fragmented Management: Proposals to Defrag Copyright Management', 15.

[82] Kretschmer, 'The Failure of Property Rules in Collective Administration: Rethinking Copyright Societies as Regulatory Instruments'. See also M. Ricolfi, 'Collective Rights Management in a Digital Environment' in G. Ghidini and L. Mariano Genovesi (eds.), *Intellectual Property and Market Power, ATRIP Papers 2006–2007* (Eudeba, 2008), p. 385.

[83] Watt, 'Copyright collectives: some basic economic theory', p. 167.

[84] Besen, Kirby and Salop, 'An Economic Analysis of Copyright Collectives', 384.

[85] I. Brinker and T. Holzmuller, 'Competition Law and Copyright – Observations from the World of Collecting Societies', *European Intellectual Property Review*, 32(11) (2010), 553, 554.

[86] Ibid.

[87] Drexl, 'Competition in the field of collective management: preferring "creative competition" to allocative efficiency in European copyright law', p. 260.

and reduced political economy problems as distinct advantages.[88] Finally, especially in the European context, non-economic rationales such as socio-cultural functions and cultural policy,[89] play an important role, too.

The standard economic theory rationale explains the formation of CMOs with the existence of transaction (or licensing) costs, which outweigh the disadvantages from the monopolistic structure.[90] This traditional transaction cost rationale has been well explored in the organisational economics literature.[91] Williamson coined the analogy of transaction costs as the economic equivalent of friction in physical systems.[92] As regards collective management, this argument takes its starting point in the observation that:

Many individual uses of copyrighted works have relatively small value to users, and it is often not economically feasible for copyright holders to monitor and obtain payment for each such use.[93]

Thus, due to prohibitive transaction costs, Besen and Kirby argue that 'unless there is collective administration, there may be no market for these rights because administration costs exceed the revenues from licensing'.[94] In a two-sided market, collective administration saves transaction costs for rights holders and commercial users.[95] For example, Posner argues, in

[88] Merges, 'Contracting into Liability Rules', 1295.
[89] Drexl, 'Competition in the field of collective management: preferring "creative competition" to allocative efficiency in European copyright law', p. 262.
[90] Hollander, Besen, Kirby and Salop, 'An Economic Analysis of Copyright Collectives'. In fact, to a wide extent, legal research relies on this rationale too: see Posner, 'Transaction Costs and Antitrust Concerns in the Licensing of Intellectual Property', 328; Drexl, 'Competition in the field of collective management: preferring "creative competition" to allocative efficiency in European copyright law', p. 260; Ghafele, 'Europe's Lost Royalty Opportunity', 61–62; Gómez and Arcila, 'Collective administration of online rights in musical works', 107; Handke, 'Collective administration', p. 183.
[91] Transaction Cost Economics (TCE) goes back to R. H. Coase, 'The Nature of the Firm', Economica (1937), 386–405, but did not really take off until some decades later (R. H. Coase, 'The Problem of Social Cost', Journal of Law and Economics, 3 (1960), 1–44). It was further developed under Williamson (from 1971) as a branch of the New Institutional Economics research tradition. See O. E. Williamson, The Economic Institutions of Capitalism (The Free Press, 1985), p. 16.
[92] See Williamson, The Economic Institutions of Capitalism, p. 19. Williamson continues: 'the absence of friction in physical systems is cited to illustrate the analytic power associated with "unrealistic" assumptions'.
[93] Besen, Kirby and Salop, 'An Economic Analysis of Copyright Collectives', 383. See also, in a similar fashion, Besen and Kirby, Compensating Creators of Intellectual Property, pp. 1 and 3, in which they refer to them as 'small rights'. See, more broadly, in a similar fashion: Posner, 'Transaction Costs and Antitrust Concerns in the Licensing of Intellectual Property'.
[94] Besen and Kirby, Compensating Creators of Intellectual Property, pp. 1 and 3.
[95] Drexl, 'Competition in the field of collective management: preferring "creative competition" to allocative efficiency in European copyright law', p. 260.

the United States–American context, that the existence of private intellectual property rights organisations 'testifies to the significance of licensing costs in the IP field, most dramatically in the case of the musical performing-rights organizations'.[96] The same can be argued for their emergence in the continental-European context.

Transaction costs exist in two stages: first, *ex ante* transaction costs regarding search and information cost of identifying and locating rights holders as well as costs related to bargaining, negotiation and decision of the contract terms;[97] and, secondly, *ex post* transaction costs in relation to monitoring and enforcement as well as adjustment.[98] CMOs have been argued to reduce all those costs. The pooling of rights minimises *ex ante* transaction costs.[99] Blanket licensing creates economies of scope in addition to functioning as a risk management tool.[100] Standardised contracts and procedures further foster economies of scale.[101] The crucial question in this setting, for regulators and academics alike, has been whether transaction cost savings are larger than the deadweight loss incurred by the monopoly of the CMOs.

Justifications for Collective Management in the Digital Age   In the digital landscape, this traditional (economic) rationale for the collectivisation of rights management is challenged. A stream of research questions whether the collective exercise of rights is necessary after all.[102] Others predict the exact opposite.[103] But the curiosity as to what 'improvements in the technology of transacting'[104] signify for the institutional arrangements of collective administration is not novel. More than 20 years ago, Merges commented:

[96] Posner, 'Transaction Costs and Antitrust Concerns in the Licensing of Intellectual Property', 329.
[97] See G. Hansen and A. Schmidt-Bischoffshausen, *Economic Functions of Collecting Societies – Collective Rights Management in the Light of Transaction Cost- and Information Economics* (2007). See also Williamson, *The Economic Institutions of Capitalism*, p. 20; Langus, Neven and Pouken, *Economic Analysis*, p. 88; and Kautio, Lefever and Määttä, *Assessing the Operation of Copyright and Related Rights Systems, Methodology Framework*, p. 126.
[98] See Hansen and Schmidt-Bischoffshausen, *Economic Functions of Collecting Societies – Collective Rights Management in the Light of Transaction Cost- and Information Economics*; Williamson, *The Economic Institutions of Capitalism*, p. 21.
[99] See, e.g., Ghafele, 'Europe's Lost Royalty Opportunity', 63.
[100] Ibid. and Katz, 'The potential demise of another natural monopoly: rethinking the collective administration of performing rights', 576 (with critical remarks).
[101] Schovsbo, 'The Necessity to collectivize copyright – and dangers thereof', 5.
[102] Already, Merges, 'Contracting into Liability Rules', 1381 remarks: 'Some even argue that exchange technologies could be "a replacement for, rather than an adjunct to, private exchange institutions."'
[103] S. Nérisson, 'Has Collective Management of Copyright Run Its Course? Not so Fast', *International Review of Intellectual Property and Competition Law* [2015], 505.
[104] Merges, 'Contracting into Liability Rules', 1381.

The possibility of technological exchange systems suggests an interesting issue for transaction cost analysis: under what circumstances will firms adopt a comprehensive transactional technology to replace a cooperative governance structure? In other words, when will technical means for facilitating direct, bilateral exchange be superior to an institution?[105]

It is obvious that the transition from an analogue to a digital environment comes with such improvements. Drexl argues that the Internet 'considerably facilitates direct transactions between right-holders and users'.[106] In fact, in his opinion, '[l]arge internet music platforms may replace the functions of collecting societies'.[107] Also, Towse acknowledges, more cautiously, that

[t]he advent of digitization has offered the possibility of individual transactional licensing and this forms the basis of the belief that competition can improve the administrative and economic efficiency of collecting societies, replacing [collective rights management].[108]

Also, the second traditional rationale, monitoring and enforcement, is under pressure in the online world. More than 25 years ago, Besen and Kirby argued that collective management 'should be limited to instances in which infringements cannot be dealt with individually'.[109] In their opinion, 'the sole rationalization for the use of collective administration should be that it lowers costs'.[110] Nowadays, technical protection measures seem to make the individual control for rights holders over their works possible, at least to some degree.[111] In the *Simulcasting* decision of 2002, the European Commission considered regarding the monitoring and enforcement rationale from the earlier case law in *Tournier* and *Lucazeau*:

The licensing of copyrights and related rights in the online environment is significantly different from the traditional offline licensing, in that no physical monitoring of licensed premises is required. The monitoring task must necessarily

---

[105] Ibid., 1382.

[106] Drexl, 'Competition in the field of collective management: preferring "creative competition" to allocative efficiency in European copyright law', p. 261. See also A. Katz, 'The Potential Demise of Another Natural Monopoly: New Technologies and the Administration of Performing Rights', *Journal of Competition Law and Economics*, 2 (2006), 245, 247; Hviid, Schroff and Street, 'Regulating CMOs by competition', 5.

[107] Drexl, 'Competition in the field of collective management: preferring "creative competition" to allocative efficiency in European copyright law', p. 261.

[108] Towse, 'Economics of collective management organisations in the creative industries', 5.

[109] Besen and Kirby, *Compensating Creators of Intellectual Property*, p. 79.

[110] Ibid., pp. 79–80.

[111] Nérisson, 'Has Collective Management of Copyright Run Its Course?', 505.

be carried out directly on the Internet. The crucial requirements in order to be able to monitor the use of copyrights and related rights are therefore a computer and an Internet connection. This means that monitoring can take place from a distance. In this context, the traditional economic justification for collecting societies not to compete in cross-border provision of services does not seem to apply.[112]

Katz notes that regulation is deemed to be the optimal response rather than fostering competition, as a result of the assumption of a natural monopoly.[113] This assumption, however, is contested. As regards economies of scale and scope on the supply side, Katz argues that the argument only implies that individual authors are inefficient, which is 'sufficient to explain the existence of intermediaries' but 'insufficient to support a conclusion that it is inefficient to have more than one intermediary'.[114] That is to say, it does not follow that these economies of scope and scale 'can be realized fully only when a single firm administers the entire worldwide copyright repertoire'.[115] He concludes that '[e]ven if *monitoring* and *enforcement* tend to exhibit characteristics of a natural monopoly, the case for collective *licensing* of music is much weaker'.[116] Katz also criticises the rationales regarding the reduction of search and negotiation costs on the demand side. For example, the high number of licensees does not imply 'that most users need to negotiate with such a large number of them'.[117] In view of the high concentration in the music industry, in which major publishing companies control the majority of the market, Katz additionally makes the point that many of the benefits that are associated with collective management of performing rights may be overstated.[118] In essence, his main point is not that benefits do not exist, but rather whether they can be achieved only under a monopoly.[119] In a similar vein, Kretschmer has already argued that the transaction cost rationale

---

[112] *IFPI – 'Simulcasting'* (Case COMP/C2/38014) Commission Decision 2003/300/EC of 8 October 2002 [2003] OJ L107/58 Recital 61.

[113] Katz, too, applies a notion of regulation, which includes 'not only regulation by a specific regulatory body but also intervention (...) under antitrust law': see Katz, 'The potential demise of another natural monopoly: rethinking the collective administration of performing rights', 543. For a different assessment, see Gómez and Arcila, 'Collective administration of online rights in musical works', 109; E.-J. Mestmäcker, 'Collecting Societies' in C.-D. Ehlermann (ed.), *The Interaction between Competition Law and Intellectual Property Law* (European Competition Law Annual, Hart Publishing, 2005), p. 344.

[114] Katz, 'The potential demise of another natural monopoly: rethinking the collective administration of performing rights', 556.

[115] Ibid., 554.   [116] Ibid., 558.   [117] Ibid., 573.   [118] Ibid., 590–91.   [119] Ibid., 590.

may support not a universal rights administration system (to which all right-holders have access on similar terms), but a system where the major rightholders selectively decide, supported by sophisticated information technology, whether collecting license fees is worthwhile.[120]

In his opinion, the transaction cost rationale thus only supports some form of collective administration, 'but not remotely in the shape of a traditional, membership based collecting society, even if we strip out all the socio-cultural functions'.[121] On the other hand, Merges has argued that direct licensing mechanisms could be inferior despite their technical feasibility, and has pointed towards the cost associated with the fact that 'few copyright owners will have the time and resources to deal directly with each individual licensee'.[122] Such risks, he argues, underline comparative advantages of semi-internalised exchange through institutions.[123] According to Merges, such institutions, how-ever, would come close to the way in which CMOs and some patent pools operate, due to the different institutional arrangements necessary, such as internal governance or arbitration.[124] Katz suggests that existing collective licensing bodies 'could change their functions and reposition themselves in the new market as new digital merchants' and function as 'mere agents for individual rights-holders' or as 'distributors who obtain the right to license from the copyright holders and then resell it'.[125] Another important role of existing arrangements would be to assist 'in creating standards that will be necessary for the efficient operation of these markets'.[126]

Yet another rationale that is especially popular among European legal scholars is the 'cultural dimension' of collectivisation.[127] This string of

---

[120] Kretschmer, 'The Failure of Property Rules in Collective Administration: Rethinking Copyright Societies as Regulatory Instruments', 133.
[121] Ibid., 127.
[122] Merges, 'Contracting into Liability Rules', 1382 also points towards the risk of infringe-ment and royalty waste when 'content posted to the system is not owned by the party who posted it', and also towards the risk of piracy.
[123] Ibid.   [124] Ibid.
[125] Katz, 'The potential demise of another natural monopoly: New technologies and the administration of performing rights', 274.
[126] Ibid., 276. See also Schovsbo, 'The Necessity to collectivize copyright – and dangers thereof', 5, with a similar reference to scale benefits due to standardised contracts and procedures.
[127] See, e.g., Schovsbo, who differentiates between two basic arguments for collectivisation, namely an economic referring to transaction costs and a cultural (Schovsbo, 'The Necessity to collectivize copyright – and dangers thereof', 4). See also C. B. Graber, 'Collective Rights Management, Competition Policy and Cultural Diversity: EU Lawmaking at a Crossroads', *World Intellectual Property Organization Journal*, 4 (2012), 35, 36, pointing to cultural and social funds that are operated by

justification builds around an analogy to unionisation.[128] Collective negotiation increases bargaining power and enables rights holders to achieve better results compared with individual contracting.[129] As opposed to the economic argument based on transaction costs, which 'only sees collective licensing as "second best" solution' Schovsbo notes that '[t]he cultural argument (...) sees collective rights administration as having an inherent value of its own such as the "protection of authors" or even "culture"'.[130] In addition to increased bargaining power, CMOs regularly also come with a redistribution among all rights holders, which benefits less popular repertoires and thereby cultural diversity.

Katz notes that it is likely that other explanations regarding the efficiency have not been discovered yet.[131] Watt finds a rationale for the mere 'existence of collective management and blanket licensing that is not dependent upon the existence of transaction costs'[132] in that 'economies of aggregation are only partially dependent upon the sharing of transaction costs'. Instead, he points to risk-sharing functions. In another paper, Handke notes that private for-profit online platforms are taking on core functions of joint copyright management and finds that its efficient scale and scope 'will increase as copyright works are increasingly traded via digital ICT networks' and that a change from collective rights management to commercial exchange platforms would weaken the position of rights holders.[133]

A final aspect, which has received relatively little attention in the existing literature on CMOs, relates to the political economy and specifically to aspects of path dependency in these institutional licensing

most CMOs; and Street et al., who 'explore the role of intermediary institutions in promoting creativity and cultural diversity in the music industry, and the impact of cultural policy on the performance of those intermediaries' and suggest that CMOs are 'important but neglected intermediaries' (J. Street, D. Laing and S. Schroff, 'Regulating for creativity and cultural diversity', 2).

[128] Kretschmer, 'The Failure of Property Rules in Collective Administration: Rethinking Copyright Societies as Regulatory Instruments', 134; also Schovsbo, 'The Necessity to collectivize copyright – and dangers thereof', 5.

[129] Kretschmer, 'The Failure of Property Rules in Collective Administration: Rethinking Copyright Societies as Regulatory Instruments', 134; Graber, 'Collective rights management, competition policy and cultural diversity', 36.

[130] Schovsbo, 'The Necessity to collectivize copyright – and dangers thereof', 6.

[131] Katz, 'The potential demise of another natural monopoly: New technologies and the administration of performing rights', 280.

[132] R. Watt, 'The Efficiencies of Aggregation: An Economic Theory Perspective on Collective Management of Copyright', *Review of Economic Research on Copyright Issues*, 12 (2015), 26, 43.

[133] C. Handke, 'Joint Copyright Management by Collecting Societies and Online Platforms: An Economic Analysis': http://ssrn.com/abstract=2616442

arrangements.[134] Katz notes the historical dimension of the prevalence and persistence of such collective arrangements around the world.[135] Schovsbo, too, points towards the observation that 'collective administration has long been part of the very fabric of international copyright'.[136] Ricolfi also remarks that some of the features of CMOs 'cannot be explained only in terms of overcoming market failures' but 'regulation has been at work there and indeed it has been regulation in view of non-economic externalities'.[137]

The Traditional Cross-Border Dimension of CMOs: Reciprocal Representation Agreements   Let us now get to one of the most relevant aspects of collective rights management for this book: its cross-border dimensions. The inherent international dimension of the collective management system was recognised early on, and led, for instance, to the foundation of the authors' societies' umbrella organisation, International Confederation of Societies of Authors (CISAC), in 1926. In order to enable and simplify the correct clearance of foreign rights, CMOs have traditionally bilaterally entered into reciprocal representation agreements (RRAs) with each other. In 1989, the Court of Justice offered a definition of such agreements:

(. . .) to mean a contract between two national copyright-management societies concerned with musical works whereby the societies give each other the right to grant, within the territory for which they are responsible, the requisite authorizations for any public performance of copyrighted musical works of members of the other society and to subject those authorizations to certain conditions, in conformity with the laws applicable in the territory in question.[138]

Also, the Online Music Recommendation 2005/737/EC offers a slightly more concise definition, in Article 1(i), as 'any bilateral agreement between collective rights managers whereby one collective rights manager grants to the other the right to represent its repertoire in the territory of

---

[134] On path dependence and new institutional economics (NIE), see, e.g., P. A. David, 'Why are Institutions the "Carriers of History"?: Path Dependence and the Evolution of Conventions, Organizations and Institutions', *Structural Change and Economic Dynamics*, 5 (1994), 205; and A. Kay, 'A Critique of the Use of Path Dependency in Policy Studies', *Public Administration*, 83 (2005), 553.

[135] Katz, 'The potential demise of another natural monopoly: New technologies and the administration of performing rights', 280. Katz points towards the historical dimension, in that these collective arrangements emerged at a time when competition law was not established. See ibid., 282.

[136] Schovsbo, 'The Necessity to collectivize copyright – and dangers thereof', 7.

[137] Ricolfi, 'Collective Rights Management in a Digital Environment', p. 387.

[138] Case 395/87, *Ministère Public* v. *Jean-Louis Tournier* [1989] ECR 2565–2581, ECLI:EU: C:1989:319, para. 17.

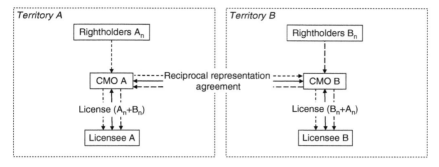

Figure 4: Functioning of reciprocal representation agreements

the other'. In *Tournier* and *Lucazeau*, the Court continues to identify two main purposes of the RRAs:

first, they are intended to make all protected musical works (...) subject to the same conditions for all users in the same Member State, in accordance with the principle laid down in the international provisions; secondly, they enable copyright-management societies to rely, for the protection of their repertoires in another State, on the organization established by the copyright-management society operating there, without being obliged to add to that organization their own network of contracts with users and their own local monitoring arrangements.[139]

More recently, in *OSA*, in reference to the *Tournier* and *Lucazeau* cases, the Court recalled that RRAs are intended

(...) inter alia, to enable those societies to rely, for the protection of their repertoires in another State, on the organisation established by the collecting society operating there, without being obliged to add to that organisation their own network of contracts with users and their own local monitoring arrangements.[140]

The functioning of RRAs is illustrated in Figure 4.

CMOs A and B contractually grant each other the right to represent their respective repertoire in the territory of the other, on a bilateral basis.[141] The effect of this arrangement is that CMO A obtains the right to license the repertoire (rights holders B_n) of CMO B by virtue of the

---

[139] Case 395/87, *Tournier*, para. 19. See also A. Capobianco, 'Licensing of Music Rights: Media Convergence and EC Competition Law', *European Intellectual Property Review*, 26 [2004] 113, 115.

[140] Case C-351/12, *OSA*, para. 75.

[141] Cf. definitions in Commission, 'Impact Assessment accompanying the document Proposal for a Directive of the European Parliament and of the Council on collective management of copyright and related rights and multi-territorial licensing of rights in musical works for online uses in the internal market' (Commission Staff Working Document) SWD(2012) 204/2, 195.

RRA, and vice versa. In other words, RRAs enable CMOs to license, in their respective territory, the widest possible repertoire, depending on the total of bilateral arrangements with a number (*n*) of other CMOs. In this traditional set-up, the cross-border dimension is on the supply side, or more specifically the inter-licensor relationship, with the goal of cross-border repertoire aggregation, ultimately to aggregate the 'worldwide repertoire'.

2.4.1.2 *Multi-Territorial Mono-Repertoire Licensing and the Disaggregation of Repertoire*

The traditional arrangement consisted of licensing on a national basis constructed via RRAs. In early 2006, this licensing landscape was transformed significantly when a first major music publisher withdrew its mechanical rights for the online use of its Anglo-American repertoire from the respective national CMOs.[142] Instead, the music publisher let a 'customized licensing entity' license this single repertoire on a multi-territorial basis.[143] This example was followed by other major as well as independent publishers. Notably, these newly formed entities and arrangements were often structured as subsidiaries of existing CMOs.[144] The main attribute of these arrangements is that they license a single repertoire on a multi-territorial basis somewhat akin to a direct licence in the sense that it resembles individual management. Primarily Anglo-American rights holders have effectively withdrawn their 'online rights from the conventional collective administration system based on interacting national monopolies, opting for bilateral contracts and joint

---

[142] For a more detailed overview, see S. F. Schwemer, 'The Licensing of Online Music Streaming Services in Europe' in R. Watt (ed.), *Handbook on the Economics of Copyright* (Edward Elgar, 2014), pp. 153–155.

[143] S. F. Schwemer, 'Emerging Models for Cross-border Online Licensing' in T. Riis (ed.), *User Generated Law, Re-Constructing Intellectual Property Law in a Knowledge Society* (Edward Elgar, 2016), p. 83. The notions used for this organisational set-up differ: Mazziotti, 'New Licensing Models for Online Music Services in the European Union: From Collective to Customized Management', Public Law & Legal Theory Working Paper Group Paper Number 11–269, Columbia Law School: http://ssrn.com/abstract =1814264 uses the term 'customized' collective rights management; V. Dehin, 'The Future of Legal Online Music Services in the European Union: A Review of the EU Commission's Recent Initiatives in Cross-Border Copyright Management', *European Intellectual Property Review*, 32 (2010), 220, 228 refers to it as 'new rights managers model'; and Hilty and Nérisson, 'Collective Copyright Management and Digitization: The European Experience', 8–9 as 'hybrid entities'.

[144] See, e.g., A. Wolf (GEMA), 'Collecting societies as enablers for multiterritorial licensing of music', EP Hearing on Collective Rights Management in the Digital Era, 1 October 2012.

ventures with a single CMO to administer their rights'[145] on a multi-territorial basis.

The impact of these developments is better understood when looking at the market share of major music labels and publishers: in 2015, the three major music labels (Sony Music Entertainment, Universal Music Group and Warner Music Group) dominated more than 70 per cent of the record label market, whereas three major music publishers (Sony/ATV Music Publishing, Universal Music Publishing and Warner/Chappell Music) dominated more than 60 per cent of the music publishing market. On the one hand, this high concentration implies that, for a majority of the (used) repertoire, multi-territorial licences are available. While larger CMOs have gained the exclusive or non-exclusive administration in subsidiaries, it also entails that small CMOs, as Hilty and Nérisson note, lost economies of scale because the most successful part of their repertoire was taken away.[146] Towards the background of the importance of the global repertoire, on the other hand, this development effectively meant additional licensors and an increase in transaction costs given the further fragmentation of repertoire:[147] effectively, a licensee needs to obtain licences both from the respective national CMOs and from the mono-repertoire licensing entities.

I have argued earlier that '[t]he development of these novel direct licensing arrangements is to be seen in the context of the two actions taken by the EU Commission which sought to foster multi-territorial licensing of music rights for the Internet: the CISAC proceedings and Recommendation 2005/737/EC'.[148] Some commentators see a causal relationship between these regulatory interventions and the disaggregation of the Anglo-American repertoire.[149] Because of the Online Music Recommendation from 2005, the respective rights holders are also referred to as 'option 3 publishers'.[150] However, in the stakeholder consultation in connection with the Online Music Recommendation, some music publishers had already indicated 'that they, regardless of any Commission action, will withdraw their repertoire from the existing

---

[145] C. Handke, J. P. Quintais and B. Balazs, 'The Economics of Copyright Compensation Systems for Digital Use' (SERCI Annual Congress 2013, Paris, July 2013), 5.

[146] Hilty and Nérisson, 'Collective Copyright Management and Digitization: The European Experience', 9; also L. Guibault and S. van Gompel, 'Collective Management in the European Union', p. 161.

[147] See, e.g., T. Riis, 'Collecting Societies, Competition, and the Services Directive', *Journal of Intellectual Property Law & Practice*, 6 (2011), 482; Schwemer, 'Emerging models for cross-border online licensing', p. 83.

[148] Schwemer, 'Emerging models for cross-border online licensing', p. 84.

[149] See Anthonis, 'Will the CRM-directive succeed re-aggregating the mechanical reproduction rights in the Anglo-American music repertoire?'.

[150] See, e.g., *Commission Decision PRSfM/STIM/GEMA/JV*, Recital 28.

reciprocal agreements and tender it for a single EU wide license'.[151] This is probably to be seen in the advantages of individual licensing on a pan-European basis for option 3 publishers, such as the freedom to set prices and 'extract more value from their rights than under collective management'.[152] In a similar vein, another explanation could lie in varying administration fees for collective management across Europe as well as the differences in the United States–American system, in which the acceptance of deductions for cultural purposes or management fees might be lower.[153] This aspect will again become relevant in Chapter 3.

2.4.1.3 Re-Aggregation and (Some) Direct Licensing?

Following the disaggregation of repertoires, several CMOs have joined forces in forming 'licensing hubs' in order to offer a (multi-repertoire, multi-territorial) licensing one-stop shop for the online use of their joint repertoires.[154] In recent merger proceedings, the DG Competition noted that these initiatives appear in various forms and can be categorised according to their scope, i.e. whether they concern one or more of the 'copyright service administration services layers':[155] front-, back-, or middle-office functions. As of 2015, the EU Commission observed several cooperation initiatives between CMOs 'which are aimed at the provision of multi-territory copyright administration services to other CMOs'.[156] Again, it is difficult to obtain a complete picture of these arrangements due to limited public insights available,[157] especially as to

---

[151] Commission, 'Impact Assessment reforming cross-border collective management of copyright and related rights for legitimate online music services', 35–36.

[152] Anthonis, 'Will the CRM-directive succeed re-aggregating the mechanical reproduction rights in the Anglo-American music repertoire?', 160. See also Kretschmer, 'The Failure of Property Rules in Collective Administration: Rethinking Copyright Societies as Regulatory Instruments', 132–134, with further evidence from as early as 1996, reports that 'the four major media companies (...) have discovered a commercial logic for withdrawing from the current regime of collective administration altogether'. Notably, Anglo-American rights holders were 'enraged by (...) deductions': GEMA, however, on its website, states for one of the novel licensing initiatives, PAECOL, that it was founded because of the Recommendation. See www.gema.de/die-gema/organisation/tochtergesellschaften/

[153] Subsequent to the European developments, publishers in the United States have also withdrawn their repertoires from the respective performance rights organisations ASCAP and BMI. See, e.g., B. Farrand, *Networks of Power in Digital Copyright Law and Policy* (Routledge, 2014), p. 147.

[154] Schwemer, 'Emerging models for cross-border online licensing', p. 85.

[155] *Commission Decision PRS/M/STIM/GEMA/JV*, para. 166.   [156] Ibid.

[157] The recent merger proceedings provide some valuable insights, which are restricted due to the redacted public version. Whereas some of the initiatives have communicated in form of websites or press releases, others appear to operate largely without public information.

whether the specific arrangements perform just specific functions in the administration layer or as to the assignment of rights for licensing purposes.

Already announced in 2007 by the Spanish, French and Italian CMOs, the joint licensing platform Armonia licensed its first deal in 2012.[158] It refers to itself as the 'first pan-European hub licensing musical works for digital music services worldwide'.[159] According to information by the DG Competition, however, Armonia provides a joint negotiating platform limited to front-office services.[160] Another cooperation model has existed between Nordic and Baltic CMOs since 2009, and provides a joint entry point for mechanical reproduction and performance rights for online exploitation.[161] The Amsterdam Initiative explored a common licensing arrangement between sixteen small and medium sized CMOs that 'would be set up on a non-exclusive basis, that is to say, its members could also decide to join another licensing and/or copyright administration hub',[162] which, however, seems not to have produced any tangible results. In November 2014, the British, Swedish and German CMOs PRS for Music, STIM and GEMA notified the EU Commission of their joint venture regarding 'multi-territorial multi-repertoire licensing activities for mechanical and performing rights of authors in musical works for online and mobile exploitation; copyright database management and online licenses processing'.[163] This constitutes the first case in which the Commission had to assess a concentration involving copyright administration services, and, in June 2015, following observations by interested third parties, the

---

[158] Apparently, another hub initiative, SOLEM, was developed in 2007 by Belgian CMO SABAM, but put on hold in 2008. Later, other CMOs joined the Armonia collaboration, which covers repertoires of SACEM (France and Luxembourg), SGAE (Spain), SIAE (Italy), SPA (Portugal), SABAM (Belgium), Artisjus (Hungary), SUISA (Switzerland), AKM (Austria) and the bulk of Anglo-American and Latin-American works. See also Schwemer, 'The licensing of online music streaming services in Europe', p. 159 and 'Emerging models for cross-border online licensing', p. 85.

[159] See www.armoniaonline.com

[160] *Commission Decision PRSfM/STIM/GEMA/JV*, para. 167.

[161] Schwemer, 'The licensing of online music streaming services in Europe', p. 159 and 'Emerging models for cross-border online licensing', p. 85. Back- and middle-office services (management, administration, operation and processing of recorded media data) are offered by NMP, a joint venture owned by PRS for Music and NCB, which, however in the context of multi-territorial licensing, according to the DG Competition, is less relevant. See *Commission Decision PRSfM/STIM/GEMA/JV*, paras. 168–173.

[162] According to DG COMP, the initiative was led by KODA and BUMA/STEMRA. According to industry information, this is not accurate, but see merger procedure: European Commission, *Commission Decision PRSfM/STIM/GEMA/JV*, para. 172.

[163] *PrSfM/STIM/GEMA/JV* (Case M.6800) Prior notification of a concentration (2014/C 438/13) OJ 438/13.

joint venture was approved under the EU Merger Regulation, after the concerned parties offered commitments.[164]

Related to the licensing hub models are emerging horizontal collaborations on several functions of the services layer, which will be discussed below. This trend towards licensing hubs (or the horizontal collaboration on front-, back-, or middle-office functions) of CMOs, as I have argued earlier, can partially be seen in the context of the multi-territorial licensing regime that Directive 2014/26/EU proposes with the aim of facilitating the re-aggregation of rights for online use, where the European Commission expects that, by encouraging the voluntary aggregation of music repertoire, the number of licences that a user needs to obtain in order operate a multi-territorial service shall be reduced.[165]

In addition to these multiple transformations in the market for online licensing, given controversies related to, inter alia, the operations of intermediaries and against the background of the critiques of collective management in the digital age, there might also be an increase in direct licensing activities and other novel arrangements and players.[166] Suffice it here to note that the CRM Directive opens up for direct licensing of rights currently enshrined in CMOs with respect to multi-territorial licensing under certain conditions in order to prevent a national repertoire lock-in.[167] Additionally, it also foresees new forms of entities ('independent management entities'), which would be in competition with traditional CMOs. Yet, it seems we are still to witness a move towards direct licensing or new entities. New forms of arrangements and organisations may emerge in the market for collective rights management, both on a traditional territorial and on a larger transnational level. In Germany, for example, a new CMO, Cultural Commons Collecting Society (C3S SCE), was founded in September 2013 as a 'fair alternative' to incumbent author CMO GEMA.[168] Organisations on a transnational level are also

---

[164] See, e.g., E. Rotondo, 'Three in One–Online: Collecting Society Joint Venture Cleared by the Commission', *Journal of Intellectual Property Law & Practice*, 11 (2016), 16, 17.

[165] See Commission, 'Impact Assessment accompanying the document Proposal for a Directive of the European Parliament and of the Council on collective management of copyright and related rights and multi-territorial licensing of rights in musical works for online uses in the internal market', 163; Schwemer, 'The licensing of online music streaming services in Europe', p. 157, and 'Emerging models for cross-border online licensing', pp. 85–86.

[166] For the example of an American player, Global Music Rights (GMR), see Schwemer, 'Emerging models for cross-border online licensing', p. 87.

[167] See Chapter 4.

[168] In 2016, the organisation was still awaiting its authorisation from the relevant German authority.

emerging.[169] Existing organisations may also expand further into the provision of multi-territorial services. In fact, some traditional CMOs also operate on a supranational level outside their territory and even license directly on a pan-European basis.[170]

In conclusion, the status quo of arrangements is complex and a mixed bag of licensing by mono-territorial and multi-territorial licensing from traditional CMOs and novel direct licensing entities, which represent different repertoires. Option 3 publishers have exacerbated the problem of repertoire disaggregation.[171] It has been noted that the changes 'are symptomatic of a radical rearrangement and gradual dissolution of established functionalities of collective rights management which is beginning to take shape' where specialisation among the different functions (i.e. front-, back- and middle-office) takes place.[172] The licensing of music for online purposes has an inherit cross-border dimension both at licensor–licensor level and at licensor–licensee level. The regulatory interventions will be discussed in the following chapters.

2.4.2   *Licensing Arrangements of Audiovisual Works*

The licensing environment is, as illustrated, highly complex and has evolved specific to the copyright-protected subject matter. It has been noted by others before that debates about content licensing often do not distinguish between the different content forms – in the context of this book, notably audiovisual content and music.[173] Compared with the collective management of rights (predominantly within music), much less scrutiny from economic and legal scholars has been devoted to the licensing relationship within the audiovisual vertical.[174] Apart from leaks, the content of licensing agreements in the audiovisual sector is a well-kept

---

[169] For example, Kobalt positions itself as 'the first global, direct, digital mechanical and performing rights society' (see www.kobaltmusic.com). It has acquired AMRA, which positions itself as 'global digital music collection society' (www.amermechrights.com).

[170] For example, the French CMO SACEM is also active in Luxembourg.

[171] According to Hoeren, 40 per cent of CELAS works are split copyright: see T. Hoeren, *Collecting Societies and Cultural Diversity in the Music Sector* (2009); p. 6. See also Hviid, Schroff and Street, 'Regulating CMOs by competition', 16 and 18; Langus, Neven and Pouken, *Economic Analysis*, p. 92.

[172] M. Kivistö, 'Multi-territorial online licensing in the light of Title III of the Directive on collective rights management', *Nordiskt Immateriellt Rättsskydd* [2015], 706, 709.

[173] KEA European Affairs and Mines ParisTech, 61. In their methodology, Kautio, Lefever and Määttä, *Assessing the Operation of Copyright and Related Rights Systems, Methodology Framework*, p. 126 suggest analysing 'the different types of activities and industries (. . .) separately' because licensing channels as well as architecture of value creation differ between industries.

[174] Samuelson notes that '[e]conomic research on intellectual property issues has tended to focus on subjects for which funding from government or foundation grants is available':

secret. Thus, relatively little is known about the evolving arrangements and practices in the licensing of audiovisual works for streaming, which is why this section relies on anecdotal evidence in order to highlight some of the more remarkable differences and tendencies. It will be for future research to provide a detailed exploratory study of the arrangements and their legal framework.

2.4.2.1 A Minor Role for Intermediaries

Traditionally, the licensing of audiovisual works has been described as less complex, because licensees (commercial users) regularly 'have to negotiate with only one party, which concentrates all the commercial exploitation rights of a film'.[175] Individual direct licensing is prevalent,[176] which is to say that collective management of rights has played a much smaller and different role than for musical works. This has been explained, for example, by there being relatively fewer transactions as compared with music rights.[177] This resonates with the rationales for why CMOs emerge in the first place. Merges notes that only repeated transactions among rights holders give rise to private exchange institutions, which are intended to reduce transaction costs and to increase the value of the assets.[178] In 2005, in its Study on a community initiative on the cross-border collective management of copyright, the European Commission argued that:

A successful transition to the emerging market for the distribution of films over digital networks will continue to be based on direct licensing with collective management playing a role in certain cases to secure remuneration for the use of their works for some right holders.[179]

Nonetheless, content aggregation appears to be topical for video on demand (VOD) service providers, too. A 2010 report for the European

P. Samuelson, 'Should Economics Play a Role in Copyright Law and Policy?', *University of Ottawa Law & Technology Journal*, 1 (2004), 1, 8.

[175] KEA European Affairs and Mines ParisTech, 61; see also Mazziotti, 'Is Geo-blocking a Real Cause for Concern?', 366; Langus, Neven and Pouken, *Economic Analysis*, p. 25.

[176] See, e.g., Commission, 'Impact Assessment accompanying the document Proposal for a Directive of the European Parliament and of the Council on collective management of copyright and related rights and multi-territorial licensing of rights in musical works for online uses in the internal market', 9; L. Guibault and J. P. Quintais, 'Copyright, Technology and the Exploitation of Audiovisual Works in the EU', Iris plus, 7, 12.

[177] KEA European Affairs and Mines ParisTech, 61.

[178] Merges, 'Contracting into Liability Rules', 1318–1319.

[179] Commission, 'Study on a Community Initiative on the Cross-Border Collective Management of Copyright' (Commission Staff working Document), Brussels, 7 July 2005, 22–23.

Commission argues that 'voluntary collective licensing may play a more important role in future digital audiovisual markets'[180] and finds evidence for different voluntary market-driven collective initiatives.[181] These arrangements are described as providing a high flexibility to encompass opt-outs in cases in which individual licensing is preferred.[182] The emergence of these arrangements finds its cause in the demand of VOD service providers (licensees), who require different licensing models. Contemplating high *ex ante* transaction costs related to the identification and acquisition of rights,[183] there exists a demand for increased transparency in content catalogues. The evidence suggests a shift in the importance of repertoire: VOD platforms compete among customers with a broad offering of content and therefore have an increased interest in acquiring content catalogues as opposed to individual titles. Empirical evidence shows that online service providers 'stress the need to make rights licensing more efficient by streamlining licensing processes, and by establishing more "one-stop shops" particularly because they are often interested in buying catalogues of rights rather than individual titles'.[184] An incentive to collectivise is also present for smaller rights holders, 'who lack the bargaining power to negotiate favourable deals in such large transactions'.[185]

2.4.2.2 Territorial Dimensions in the Licensing of Audiovisual Works

Another aspect regards the exclusivity of licences in the licensor–licensee relationship. In the licensing of musical works for online exploitation, rights are regularly not licensed exclusively to one licensee. According to reports for the European Commission, audiovisual content for VOD exploitation has been licensed on a non-exclusive and short-term basis.[186] This shows a similarity with the licensing of musical works but contrasts with licensing based on exclusive rights of more traditional forms in the exploitation chain,[187] such as theatrical, broadcasting or

---

[180] KEA European Affairs and Mines ParisTech, 61.   [181] Ibid., 63.
[182] Ibid., bringing large owners of content catalogues as examples, which already possess the structures to facilitate licensing processes.
[183] Ibid., 62.   [184] Ibid., 4.   [185] Ibid., 62.
[186] Ibid., 4. See also Langus, Neven and Pouken, *Economic Analysis*, p. 26, who identify different licensing patterns for online on-demand television, such as in the form of catch-up services.
[187] Another important practical difference is the practice of exploitation windows, in which an audiovisual work goes through different defined stages (e.g. cinema, downloads, rental, on-demand services, free TV). Curiously, some similar developments can be observed as regards music: first, launching downloads and only later being available on streaming platforms. See more broadly on the value chain, Langus, Neven and Pouken, *Economic Analysis*, pp. 18–20.

DVD exploitation, which returns higher revenues.[188] Reasons given for the non-exclusivity in VOD agreements are the limited financial means of VOD services, as well as uncertainty about market developments, which makes it favourable to spread rights over a larger sample of services.[189] Some large European VOD service providers have obtained exclusive licences from major Hollywood studios 'against paying minimum guarantees'.[190] As regards this forms of premium content, such as films of particular interest for the audience, an Impact Assessment from 2015 notes that the general practice is territorial exclusivity licensing.[191]

In addition, VOD rights seem to be licensed primarily on a territorial basis.[192] Also, sports content is usually licensed on an exclusive (territorial) basis. This again appears to be based on the traditional model, in which rights are licensed in exchange for up-front investments in the production of the audiovisual work in form of pre-sales, usually to distributors and broadcasters (who primarily serve linguistic, i.e. territorial markets).[193] This practice might change once VOD exploitation increases in value. Also the production of original content by service providers, such as Netflix or HBO, might alter this practice.

Multi-territorial licensing has also been briefly discussed in the context of VOD platforms. The European Commission has put forward the idea of a second multi-territorial licence,[194] which would supplement the primary territorial licence. As reported by the tender specifications for a study

[r]ights holders would be encouraged to grant, next to main distribution licence(s) which would be reserved for the country(ies) of the producer(s) where cinema and other forms of distribution are generally pre-organised (primary licence), a second multi-territory licence for online distribution, bundling all the other EU countries for which, in general, no distribution agreements exist.[195]

---

[188] KEA European Affairs and Mines ParisTech, 60.   [189] Ibid.
[190] Ibid., 61, pointing towards the danger of marginalization for European rights holders in this context.
[191] See Commission, 'Impact Assessment accompanying the document Proposal for a Regulation of the European Parliament and of the Council to ensure the cross-border portability of online content services in the internal market', 13.
[192] KEA European Affairs and Mines ParisTech, 4 and 60. Also P. I. Colomo, 'Copyright Licensing and the EU Digital Single Market Strategy' (2015) LSE Law, Society and Economy Working Papers 19/2015, 2: http://ssrn.com/abstract=2697178; Langus, Neven and Pouken, *Economic Analysis*, p. 53; Commission, 'Impact Assessment accompanying the document Proposal for a Regulation of the European Parliament and of the Council to ensure the cross-border portability of online content services in the internal market', 13.
[193] KEA European Affairs and Mines ParisTech, 59.   [194] See ibid., 159.
[195] See ibid. The objective of such a solution would be 'to ensure some exposure of European films on VOD platforms in countries where the film did not land a distribution deal' and rights holders would have to consent to the exploitation.

The study concludes that the value of the idea remains unclear and that an earlier proposal in public consultation was not welcomed by rights holders and users.[196] Commercial demand might drive the market towards multi-territorial licensing solutions, too. For example, in 2015, streaming service provider Netflix announced its goal to acquire rights on a global, i.e. pan-territorial, basis.[197] In its Digital Single Market Strategy, the European Commission in the context of territorial restrictions, relies on the facilitation of licensing as one of the aims of the copyright modernisation.[198]

The territorial delineation can be seen in direct relationship to the current practices regarding cross-border access and portability. As is sketched in Section 2.2, the access dimension is primarily guided by the relation between consumers and service providers. As introduced before, geo-blocking refers to the practice of restricting access to content to consumers, which access the site from a specific territory only. A related concept is geo-filtering, where end users are redirected to the website, which offers content at their location.[199] In essence, geo-blocking and geo-filtering are simply the technical means by which territoriality is enforced towards consumers. The European Commission identified concerns related to accessibility of digital media in cross-border situations, 'both when it comes to the portability of content available in the home country and as regards cross-border access to content from another Member State'.[200] These correlate to the two access dimensions presented in Section 2.2. A plausible hypothesis is that this relationship is guided by the underlying vertical licensing relationship between rights holders and service providers. Hence, in this context, two relationships are of interest: first, the licensing relationship between rights holders and online service providers and, secondly, the contractual relationship between online service providers and end users.

Geo-blocking measures 'are designed to make territorial agreements effective by limiting access to copyright works to a national public or

---

[196] See ibid., 160.
[197] See, e.g., S. Ramachandran, 'Netflix Says Push for Global Rights "Has Not Been an Easy Road"', *The Wall Street Journal* (7 December 2015): www.wsj.com/articles/netflix -says-push-for-global-rights-has-not-been-an-easy-road-1449508613
[198] See Commission, 'Questions and answers – Digital Single Market Strategy' (Press release) MEMO15/4920, Brussels, 6 May 2015.
[199] See Commission, 'A Digital Single Market Strategy for Europe – Analysis and Evidence Accompanying the document Communication from the Commission to the European Parliament, the Council, the European Economic and Social Committee and the Committee of the Regions', 21.
[200] Ibid., 26.

a linguistically homogenous audience located in a given territory'.[201] In practice, this is often enforced by identifying the IP address of the consumer, which reveals the country of origin. From an economic perspective, geo-blocking gives the opportunity for profit maximisation through price differentiation between national markets.[202] Accordingly, a monopolist 'can charge more to consumers who value the product highly and less to consumers who value it less'.[203] A UK citizen might, for example, have a higher willingness than an Italian citizen has to pay for watching Premier League games. Geo-blocking also allows online service providers to adjust the catalogue of available content to the location of the consumer.[204] Other frequent practices for price discrimination in the audiovisual sector are versioning (or quality pricing) and bundling.[205]

The basis for territorial limitations can be found in copyright itself, the licensing agreements between rights holders and online service providers as well as in technical protection mechanisms (TPMs), which are reinforced by the protection of TPMs in the national and international copyright legislation. It is important to note that there also exist reasons for geo-blocking other than copyright; both of commercial and legal nature. Also, language and cultural aspects can play into geo-blocking. It has been commented that geo-blocking 'reflects the economic reality, rather than a legal problem',[206] or in other words that geo-blocking is responding to a problem in the business model.

In its e-commerce sector inquiry launched in May 2015, the EU Commission asked respondents whether their licensing agreements with rights holders contain the requirement to apply geo-blocking

---

[201] Mazziotti, 'Is geo-blocking a real cause for concern?', 365, and, similarly, Trimble, 'The Territoriality Referendum', 90.

[202] Some interesting observations can be drawn from an economic analysis by Katz, who analysed territorial exclusivity in the soft drink industry. She found that the exclusive territorial franchise agreements benefit 'both by increasing bottlers' profits and by facilitating the recovery of these larger profits by the syrup manufacturers'. See B. G. Katz, 'Territorial Exclusivity in the Soft Drink Industry', *Journal of Industrial Economics*, 27 (1978), 85, 89. See also Langus, Neven and Pouken, *Economic Analysis*, p. 7.

[203] Katz, 'The potential demise of another natural monopoly: rethinking the collective administration of performing rights', 548.

[204] P. B. Hugenholtz, 'Extending the SatCab Model to the Internet' Study commissioned by BEUC (Brussels, 2015), 4.

[205] KEA European Affairs and Mines ParisTech, 26. Versioning 'consists of offering different qualities of the product at different prices, encouraging consumers themselves to select from among these versions according to their differing degrees of willingness to pay'. Other aspects of versioning could be 'means of access, the bundle of products gathered in the offer, and the level of liberalities (of use) granted to the consumer'. See also Langus, Neven and Pouken, *Economic Analysis*, pp. 78 ff.

[206] C. Barbière, 'Geo-blocking attacked from all sides' (*EurActiv*, 2015): www .euractiv.com/section/digital/news/geo-blocking-attacked-from-all-sides/

practices.[207] The Commission received information on more than 6,000 agreements between online digital content providers and rights holders and differentiated the agreements among seven categories – namely films, sports, music, fiction TV, news, children's TV and non-fiction TV.[208] According to the Commission's data, an EU average of 74 per cent of agreements regarding fiction TV, 77 per cent of agreements regarding films, and 63 per cent of agreements regarding sports require providers to geo-block content.[209] Also, 44 per cent of agreements concerning music require geo-blocking. It can be concluded from the dataset that geo-blocking is required in the majority of licensing agreements as regards audiovisual content and a large amount as regards music.[210]

Related to this aspect is the question of why digital content services are not available on a cross-border basis. More than 50 per cent of the respondents referred to the fact that content is not available for purchase in territories in which their service currently does not operate.[211] In some cases, licences are limited to specific language versions.[212] Also, costs unrelated to the licensing of rights, such as the adaptation of the business model to obtain revenue from users or insufficient consumer demand appear to play an important role in a service provider's decision to not make digital content available on a cross-border basis.[213] Whereas no conclusions can be drawn as to the correlation of the two datasets, it seems self-evident to hypothesise about the interrelation of the geo-blocking clauses and the non-availability of rights. According to the European Commission, respondents have stated that some licensing agreements are conditional 'upon the fact that the service provider undertakes to apply geo-blocking, or that the cost of making some content available without geo-blocking would be higher'.[214]

Roughly 40 per cent of respondents of online content service providers that offer their services in at least two Member States indicate that the offered content catalogue differs between the territories.[215] For the

---

[207] Commission, 'Geo-Blocking practices in e-commerce; Issues paper presenting initial findings of the e-commerce sector inquiry conducted by the Directorate-General for Competition', 54, para. 141.

[208] Ibid., paras. 142–143. [209] Ibid., 55.

[210] The Commission notes a high degree of variation among Member States, commenting that, in some, less than 50 per cent of agreements require geo-blocking of films, sports and TV series. See ibid., 55, paras. 148–149 and 58, para. 150.

[211] Ibid., 62. [212] Ibid. [213] Ibid.

[214] Ibid. Some rights holders do not allow for portability. See also KEA European Affairs and Mines ParisTech 4, who indicate a similar relationship.

[215] Commission, 'Geo-Blocking practices in e-commerce; Issues paper presenting initial findings of the e-commerce sector inquiry conducted by the Directorate-General for Competition', 65.

audiovisual sector, however, it has been indicated that such differences are caused by consumer preferences and whether consumer demand meets costs for acquisition and localisation of the content.[216] Even more than with music, there is an inherent territorial dimension in audiovisual content caused by film financing. The European Parliament recognises the importance of territorial licences in the audiovisual sector, 'which is primarily based on broadcasters' pre-purchase or pre-financing systems'.[217] In this

fragile ecosystem which produces and finances creative work, exclusive rights and freedom of contract are key components because they make for improved risk sharing, enable a range of players to get involved in joint projects for a culturally diverse audience and underpin the incentive to invest in professional content production.[218]

In Recital 13, the Parliament furthermore points out that:

the financing, production and co-production of films and television content depend to a great extent on exclusive territorial licences granted to local distributers on a range of platforms reflecting the cultural specificities of the various markets in Europe; that being so, emphasises that the ability, under the principle of freedom of contract, to select the extent of territorial coverage and the type of distribution platform encourages investment in films and television content and promotes cultural diversity; calls on the Commission to ensure that any initiative to modernise copyright is preceded by a wide-ranging study of its likely impact on the production, financing and distribution of films and television content, and also on cultural diversity.[219]

Thus, the licensing and access arrangements differ dependent on the respective subject matter. These differences are also important to acknowledge for forthcoming the analysis of the legal framework.

2.4.3   Industry-Led Arrangements, Operational Aspects and Standards

Besides regulation through secondary legislation and EU competition law, which are subject to chapters 3 to 5, different initiatives related to

[216] Ibid.
[217] European Parliament, 'Report on the implementation of Directive 2001/29/EC of the European Parliament and of the Council of 22 May 2001 on the harmonisation of certain aspects of copyright and related rights in the information society (2014/2256 (INI))', Recital 17. See also Langus, Neven and Pouken, *Economic Analysis*, p. 21.
[218] European Parliament, 'Report on the implementation of Directive 2001/29/EC of the European Parliament and of the Council of 22 May 2001 on the harmonisation of certain aspects of copyright and related rights in the information society (2014/2256 (INI))', Recital 29.
[219] Ibid., Recital 13.

the licensing and more broadly the establishment of a Digital Single Market have been put in place; either with the support or on the initiative of the European institutions or on private initiative. An exhaustive account of the initiatives in the field of cross-border access and multi-territorial licensing of musical and audiovisual works is beyond the objective of this chapter. Rather, this section focuses on a few specific initiatives, which become relevant as perspectives in the forthcoming discussion. From a regulatory perspective, these arrangements can be understood in the broader context of new governance and the Better Regulation framework, as explored in Chapter 1.[220]

Initiatives Addressing Operational Efficiency

A first strain of initiatives regards the operations of CMOs: one key issue in relation to the licensing of music rights has been the identification of repertoire and rights holders, i.e. *ex ante* transaction costs.[221] The demand for a centralised transnational works database has also been addressed in economic research.[222] Several industry initiatives have been put in place to simplify the access to information about ownership and control of the different rights. Dating back to 2008, the Global Repertoire Database (GRD) was an industry initiative started with the goal of creating a joint database covering ownership and control of musical works.[223] The working group was initiated by former Commissioner Neelie Kroes and initially attracted broad support from different stakeholders but eventually, in 2014, the initiative fell apart.[224] Earlier or parallel unsuccessful attempts include the International Music Joint Venture in 2000, which was formed by several CMOs in Europe and North-America, and a project initiated by the World Intellectual Property Organization (WIPO) aimed at the establishment of a common rights

---

[220] These arrangements are also relevant insofar as they provide evidence as to the need for legislative intervention. Additionally, industry standards become relevant in the context of legislation. The CRM Directive, for example, refers to industry standards as a yardstick.

[221] At the same time, the identification of repertoire is also relevant in *ex post* transaction costs. Some have underlined similar difficulties in the audiovisual sector.

[222] See, e.g., Ghafele, 'Europe's Lost Royalty Opportunity', 84, who argues: 'If any collective rights management system is to work for digital music, it requires a centralized transnational database of musical works that overcomes some of the problems associated with fragmented repertoires.'

[223] Schwemer, 'Emerging models for cross-border online licensing', p. 88.

[224] It is being reported that United States–American PRO ASCAP was the first to pull out, which eventually led to the failure of the initiative. See K. Milosic, 'The Failure of the Global Repertoire Database' (*Hypebot*, 31 August 2015): www.hypebot.com/hypebot/2015/08/the-failure-of-the-global-repertoire-database-effort-draft.html

database in 2011. Other initiatives address the identification of repertoire.[225]

A second concern regards *ex post* transaction costs, which arise in relation to the operation of licensing agreements.[226] Many challenges in relation to online music are not directly related to licensing but reside in operational processes such as documentation and reporting from online service providers about played tracks and the payment of royalties from the respective organisations to their rights holders. For example, it has been reported that a significant amount of royalties is paid to the wrong party due to identification issues.[227] There have been several initiatives put in place to mitigate some of these operational challenges, mostly in form of industry standard setting.[228] In this context, several CMOs have started to develop IT systems or created affiliated service providers that cover different layers of these administration services. Towse comments on the de-bundling of front and back office structures, in which large players establish

their own arrangements for cross-border licensing (front office) using various national CMO's back office facilities for processing revenues and their distribution, for which the CMO charges and administration fee (thereby assisting with economies of scale and the sunk costs of investment in IT).[229]

Already in 2007, the Swedish CMO STIM started a supplier for business process outsourcing services, International Copyright Enterprise (ICE), in a joint venture with the British CMO PRS for Music, which was joined by German GEMA in 2015. At the core of ICE is the 'integration of front and back office functions with the particular benefit of multi-territorial licensing across the EU',[230] which 'will both meet the needs of the new landscape by supporting the European Commission's Option 3

---

[225] For example, IFPI developed a unique identifier system, GRiD (Global Release Identifier); CISAC developed, in collaboration with ISO, an Internal Standard Musical Work Code (ISWC), 'a unique, permanent, and internally recognized reference number for the identification of musical works'. For further references, see Katz, 'The potential demise of another natural monopoly: New technologies and the administration of performing rights', 276.

[226] Directive 2014/26/EU regulates not only the initial licensing but also operations.

[227] See, e.g., Rethink Music, 'Fair Music', 14.

[228] For example, standards such as DDEX, CCID or ISNI have been developed for tasks like reporting and invoicing, which have been adopted by several CMOs.

[229] Towse, 'Economics of collective management organisations in the creative industries', 8 also points towards the opportunities opened up in the CRM Directive. See also, more broadly, Hviid, Schroff and Street, 'Regulating CMOs by competition', 8.

[230] Towse, 'Economics of collective management organisations in the creative industries', 8–9.

recommendation, and provide the services that writers, publishers and societies will require in the future'.[231] Another service provider, Network of Music Partners (NMP), which is jointly owned by NCB and PRS for Music, was founded in 2012 and offers services around on the administrative processes of invoicing for use of music and distributing royalties.[232] The services by NMP and ICE are already used by other European CMOs.[233] Yet another initiative from 2014, Polaris Nordic, by Nordic collective rights management organisations Koda, Teosto and Tono, aims to improve cross-border cooperation by developing and running 'joint back-end systems for music reporting and distribution of the revenues collected by the organizations'.[234] These different providers seem to be intertwined; Polaris Nordic, for example, will source its back- and middle-office services from ICE, 'as ICE will manage all of Polaris Nordic's copyright documentation for both domestic and international repertoire'.[235] By the investment in new IT systems, according to Towse, economies of scale, scope and networks can be achieved.[236] She comments that '[g]iven the increasing returns inherent in natural monopoly, there are clear winner-takes-all advantages' in these arrangements, which puts smaller CMOs at a considerable disadvantage.[237]

Initiatives Aimed at the Facilitation of Licensing

A second, different, line of intervention regards the facilitation of industry-led solutions for (multi-territorial) licensing, put in place by the European Commission and other stakeholders. In its *Communication on content in the Digital Single Market* of 2012, the European Commission envisioned that a stakeholder dialogue 'can work as an incubator for

---

[231] International Copyright Enterprise (ICE), 'Response, Global Repertoire Database Request for Information' (2010), 3.

[232] NMP handles the administrative back office, inter alia for the Nordic-Baltic online markets and the pan-European central licensing of the EMI catalogues. Front-office activities, such as licensing and member services, remain with the parent companies (NCB and PRS for Music). See Schwemer, 'Emerging models for cross-border online licensing', p. 88.

[233] See, e.g., NCB, 'Buma/Stemra teams up with ICE and NMP for online administration services' *Press release* (Copenhagen, 3 December 2014).

[234] Thereby the CMOs aim 'to further reduce costs and create higher efficiency, resulting in greater value for composers, song-writers, lyricists and music publishers'; see POLARIS Nordic, 'Ground breaking initiative: Cross-border alliance lead the way for future rights management', Press release (3 February 2014).

[235] *Commission Decision PRS/M/STIM/GEMA/JV*, para. 169.

[236] Towse, 'Economics of collective management organisations in the creative industries', 9.

[237] Ibid. At the time of writing, the predominance of Northern European CMOs at the time of writing is also striking.

innovative win-win solutions for all stakeholders', which are vital for the establishment and complement the other initiatives.[238] In the stakeholder dialogue, four working groups were established on cross-border access and portability of services; user generated content and micro-licensing; audiovisual heritage and text and data mining. The goal of the working group regarding cross-border access had been to

identify the main categories of restrictions on cross-border access and portability (...) and the main reasons behind these restrictions. On this basis it should take stock of current industry initiatives and deliver practical solutions to promote multi-territory access.[239]

The outcome of the ten months' stakeholder dialogue 'Licenses for Europe' has been subject to widespread criticism, given its limited results in the form of ten pledges to bring more content online. In relation to this book, pledges 1 and 3 are especially noteworthy. Regarding cross-border portability of subscription services (pledge 1), the audiovisual industry issued a joint statement:[240]

affirming their willingness to continue to work towards the further development of cross-border portability. Consumers will increasingly be able to watch films, TV programmes and other audio-visual content for which they have subscribed to at home, when travelling in the EU on business or holidays. This is already largely the case with music, e-books, magazines and newspapers.[241]

Regarding easier licensing for music (pledge 3), the music sector[242] promised inter alia:

For authors and publishers, their collective rights management societies have committed to spreading best practice on existing licensing schemes. This will make small-scale licences available in all EU countries, e.g. for background music on websites and small-scale web/podcasting.[243]

---

[238] Initially, the stakeholder dialogue was referred to as 'Licensing Europe': Commission, 'Content in the Digital Single Market', 5.

[239] Ibid., 3.

[240] The signatories include: Association of Commercial Television (ACT), European Coordination of Independent producers (CEPI), Europa Distribution, EUROVOD, Federation of European Film Directors (FERA), International Federation of Film Distributors Associations (FIAD), International Federation of Film Producers Associations (FIAPF), Independent Film & Television Alliance (IFTA), International Video Federation (IVF), Motion Picture Association (MPA), Sports Rights Owners Coalition (SROC), Society of Audiovisual Authors (SAA).

[241] See Licenses for Europe, 'Ten pledges to bring more content online' (13 November 2011) 4: http://ec.europa.eu/internal_market/copyright/docs/licences -for-europe/131113_ten-pledges_en.pdf

[242] International Federation of the Phonographic Industry (IFPI) and the European Grouping of Societies of Authors and Composers (GESAC).

[243] See Licenses for Europe, 5.

A rather different line of action is funding programmes to support the audiovisual sector. In this context, the Creative Europe initiative, launched in 2014, has as one of its main objectives 'to strengthen the demand for films, to improve their distribution across borders'.[244] The framework has a budget of 1.46 billion euros until 2020, which it spreads across different initiatives. As regards online distribution, 'Creative Europe provides support for transnational marketing, branding and distribution of European audiovisual and video-on-demand service' in the form of funding for support to video-on-demand services, support to the development of 'On Line Ready' packages and support to innovative, multi-platform releases.[245] One of its predecessors, the MEDIA Programme, ran from 2007 until 2013, with similar aims.[246]

2.5   Summary

This chapter has put forward some of the essential aspects of the underlying economic rationales as well as the market context as a primer for the following analysis of the regulatory framework.

Multi-territorial licensing and cross-border access are intertwined. However, the issues have to be seen in their specific context, which is, to a great extent, subject matter specific. The fragmentation of rights, rights holders and repertoires across countries is at the core of high transaction costs,[247] which collectivisation of rights management originally aimed to reduce. Yet, more recently, the traditional rationale has been questioned and the emergence of novel arrangements in the marketplace could be witnessed, which have at first glance aggravated the disaggregation of repertoire. Historically, this has been much less a concern as regards audiovisual content, where the territorial delineation seems to follow a price discrimination rationale. Given the multiple differences regarding rights holders and exercise of rights between musical and audiovisual works, the licensing of audiovisual content is much less defined by collective management. In the online music rights landscape, exclusivity has been a concern primarily as to territorial

---

[244] See, e.g., Commission, 'Lack of choice driving demand for film downloads'.

[245] See Commission, 'Creative Europe, Supporting Europe's cultural and creative sectors' (*European Commission*, 2016): https://ec.europa.eu/programmes/creative-europe/media/online-distribution_en

[246] Namely, inter alia to '[i]ncrease the circulation of European audiovisual works inside and outside the European Union': see ibid. The media programs ran for more than 20 years.

[247] KEA European Affairs, *Licensing Music Works and Transaction Costs in Europe* (2012), 51.

licensing exclusivity by the respective CMOs for a given territory. In the audiovisual rights licensing landscape territorial exclusivity appears to be prevalent in the market delineation for licensees. The chapters that follow turn to consider the governance and regulation of licensing and access in the EU.

3   Licensing and Access from a Competition Law Perspective

Let us briefly remind ourselves of the concept of regulation, which is applied in this book: regulation is to be understood broadly, as embracing competition proceedings as well as codifications and industry solutions. The objective of this chapter is to examine how content access and licensing in cross-border situations is being dealt with from a competition law angle, i.e. the application of the standard EU competition rules in Articles 101 and 102 of the Treaty on the Functioning of the European Union (TFEU) through the European Commission in its function as competition authority as well as in the courts.

For this purpose, let us briefly recall the scope of EU competition law: as a starting point, Article 101(1) TFEU prohibits vertical and horizontal agreements, decisions and concerted practices that have as their object or effect the prevention, restriction or distortion of competition within the internal market. Guidance on the application of Article 101(1) TFEU, as well as the cumulative conditions for an exemption under Article 101(3) TFEU, is found in the Commission's guidelines on vertical restraints,[1] horizontal cooperation agreements[2] and technology transfer agreements[3] as well as on the application of Article 101(3) TFEU.[4] Article 102 TFEU does not ban a dominant position as such but prohibits the abuse by one or more undertakings of a such position within the internal market or in a substantial part of it.[5]

The nature of collective management of copyright, i.e. the pooling of monopoly rights in intermediaries, as such, has been cause for particular difficulties from a competition law perspective, under the competition

---

[1] Commission, 'Guidelines on Vertical Restraints' (Information) [2010] OJ C130/1.
[2] Commission, 'Guidelines on the applicability of Article 101 of the Treaty on the Functioning of the European Union to horizontal co-operation agreements' (Communication – 2011/C11/01) [2011] OJ C11/1.
[3] Commission, 'Guidelines on the application of Article 101 of the Treaty on the Functioning of the European Union to technology transfer agreements' (Communication) [2014] OJ C89/3.
[4] Commission, 'Guidelines on the application of Article 81(3) of the Treaty' (Communication – Notice 2004/C101/08) [2004] OJ C101/97.
[5] Whether the undertakings hold a dominant position is not relevant for Art. 101 TFEU.

rules, and appears prima facie 'extremely problematic'.[6] Collective management organisations (CMOs), as Schovsbo notes, commit some of competition law's 'deadliest sins' in the form of horizontal price-fixing agreements and blanket licensing.[7] European case law, from the Court of Justice of the European Union (CJEU) as well as the Commission, has consistently held that CMOs are subject to the competition rules in Articles 101 and 102 TFEU.[8] First, CMOs are 'undertakings' within the meaning of Article 101(1) TFEU 'because they participate in the commercial exchange of services and are therefore engaged in the exercise of economic activities',[9] 'irrespective of whether they make profit or not'.[10] Secondly, CMOs are deemed to hold a dominant position within the meaning of Article 102 TFEU, because of their *de facto* monopoly in the market.[11] On an EU level, until 2005, collective management of copyright was almost exclusively addressed and controlled through competition law, in which the European competition authority has traditionally put much emphasis on the music vertical.[12] Over time, 'an impressive

---

[6] M. Kretschmer, 'Access and Reward in the Information Society: Regulating the Collective Management of Copyright' (2007) CIPPM Working Paper 2007, 3: http://dx.doi.org/10.2139/ssrn.2739837. See, from 20 years ago, J. Schovsbo, *Grænsefladespørgsmål mellem immaterialretten og konkurrenceretten* (Jurist- og Økonomforbundets Forlag 1996), p. 19 or A. Hollander, 'Market structure and performance in intellectual property', *International Journal of Industrial Organization*, 199(2) (1984), 201.

[7] J. Schovsbo, 'The Necessity to collectivize copyright – and dangers thereof' (2010), 15: http://ssrn.com/abstract=1632753

[8] E. J. Mestmäcker, 'Collecting Societies' in C.-D. Ehlermann (ed.), *The Interaction between Competition Law and Intellectual Property Law* (European Competition Law Annual 2005 edn. Hart Publishing, 2005), p. 344; L. Guibault and S. van Gompel, 'Collective Management in the European Union' in D. Gervais (ed.), *Collective Management of Copyright and Related Rights*, 2nd edn. (Kluwer Law International, 2010), p. 138; also C. B. Graber, 'Collective Rights Management, Competition Policy and Cultural Diversity: EU Lawmaking at a Crossroads', *World Intellectual Property Organization Journal*, 4 [2012], 35, 37; M. Hviid, S. Schroff and J. Street, 'Regulating CMOs by competition: An incomplete answer to the licensing problem?' (2016) CREATe Working Paper 2016/03 (March 2016), 4.

[9] See, e.g., *Commission Decision IFPI – "Simulcasting"*, para. 59 citing, e.g., Joined Cases 55/80 and 57/80, *Musik-Vertrieb membran GmbH and K-tel International* v. *GEMA – Gesellschaft für musikalische Aufführungs- und mechanische Vervielfältigungsrechte* [1981] ECR 147, ECLI:EU:C:1981:10; Case 7/82, *Gesellschaft zur Verwertung von Leistungsschutzrechten mbH (GVL)* v. *Commission* [1983], ECR 483, ECLI:EU:C:1983:52, para. 32; Joined Cases C-92/92 and C-326/92, *Phil Collins* v. *Imtrat Handelsgesellschaft mbH and Patricia Im- und Export Verwaltungsgesellschaft mbH and Leif Emanuel Kraul* v. *EMI Electrola GmbH* [1993] ECR I-5145, ECLI:EU:C:1993:847.

[10] Guibault and van Gompel, 'Collective Management in the European Union', pp. 138–139.

[11] In addition to potential legal monopolies. Case 7/82, *GVL* v. *Commission*, para. 44. See also Schovsbo, 'The Necessity to collectivize copyright – and dangers thereof', 15.

[12] With a few exemptions, such as, for example, in Council Directive 93/83/EEC of 27 September 1993 on the coordination of certain rules concerning copyright and rights

body of jurisprudence'[13] has been assembled in a multitude of competition cases testing CMOs' alleged anti-competitive behaviour regarding, among other factors, e.g., national discrimination,[14] mandate relationship between rights holders and CMOs,[15] or the relationship between CMOs and their members.[16] These decisions by the European Commission and the CJEU can be roughly categorised according to the respective relationships that they are addressing: the relationship of CMOs with their members (rights holders); the relationship of CMOs with commercial users (licensees);[17] and the relationship between CMOs in form of reciprocal representation agreements (RRAs). In the context of multi-territorial access and licensing, the latter are of special interest regarding their territorial limitations. But also the relationship of CMOs to their users or commercial users, respectively, becomes relevant. This is the focus of Section 3.1 on the licensor–licensor relationship.

Outside the collective management arena, licensing agreements (i.e. the licensor–licensee relationship) and territorial restrictions regarding copyright-protected content have triggered scrutiny under the EU competition rules. Given the sectoral differences regarding audiovisual content, such as the prevalence of direct licensing, the exclusivity of licensing agreements and the lower number of parties involved, EU competition law has had a different emphasis there. Traditionally, competition law looks much stricter on horizontal than vertical agreements, and, as Rognstad notes, '[t]o what extent vertical restraints represent a competition issue is a long-disputed issue'.[18] On a broader scale, '[i]ntellectual property contracts are dealt with by the EU Commission by way of a block exemption',[19] in which '[t]raditionally though copyright

related to copyright applicable to satellite broadcasting and cable retransmission [1993] OJ L248/15.

[13] Guibault and van Gompel, 'Collective Management in the European Union', p. 137.

[14] E.g., *Commission Decision GVL* (IV/29.839 – GVL) [1981] OJ L370/49.

[15] E.g., *Banghalter & de Homem Christo/SACEM ('Daft Punk Decision')* (COMP/37.219) [2002] SG(2002)231176.

[16] E.g., GEMA decisions. See Schovsbo, 'The Necessity to collectivize copyright – and dangers thereof', 18, who observes that competition law, on the one hand, 'looks upon authors in their capacity as "members" and "commercial entities"', whereas the copyright perspective focuses on the creative artist and personal and individual rights.

[17] Here, primarily the calculation of royalties has been in the focus: see Schovsbo, 'The Necessity to collectivize copyright – and dangers thereof', 16 for more.

[18] See O.-A. Rognstad, 'The Multiplicity of Territorial IP Rights and its Impact on Competition' in J. Rosén (ed.), *Individualism and Collectiveness in Intellectual Property Law* (Edward Elgar, 2012), p. 61. For economic arguments, see G. Langus, D. Neven and S. Pouken, *Economic Analysis of the Territoriality of the Making Available Right in the EU* (Report prepared for the European Commission, DG MARKT 2014) 2014), pp. 48 ff.

[19] P. Torremans, 'Questioning the Principles of Territoriality: The Determination of Territorial Mechanisms of Commercialisation' in P. Torremans (ed.), *Copyright Law, A Handbook of Contemporary Research* (Edward Elgar, 2007), p. 469.

contracts have been excluded, mainly because they are seen to have an additional cultural element'.[20] The very first major decision by the Court of Justice involving Article 101 TFEU, in 1966, related to absolute territorial restrictions in a case involving an exclusive distribution agreement of electronic products. In Joined Cases, 56/64 and 58/64, *Consten Grundig*, the Court established that such agreements are restrictive of competition by object and held that 'an agreement between producer and distributor which might tend to restore the national divisions in trade between Member States might be such as to frustrate the most fundamental objections of the Community'.[21]

According to the Guidelines on the application of Article 81(3) of the Treaty, absolute territorial protection can fall outside Article 101(1) TFEU, 'when the restraint is objectively necessary for the existence of an agreement of that type or that nature'.[22] For more than three decades, since the CJEU's judgments in *Coditel I*, *Lucazeau* and *Tournier*, it seemed, as Brinker and Holzmuller note, more or less established that a limitation of 'a copyright licence to the territory of a single Member State is no restriction to competition in the sense of [Article 101(1) TFEU]'.[23] The refusal to license and compulsory licensing have been topical, too.[24]

Chapter 3 first looks at model contracts, which are frequently used by CMOs in the sphere of music licensing. These model contracts have been subject to several competition proceedings regarding territorial delineations. Secondly, I look at licensing contracts in the audiovisual sector and territorial delineation, which has an intrinsic relationship with EU competition rules. This corresponds roughly with the differentiation between horizontal agreements and vertical agreements.

3.1   Licensor–Licensor Relationship: Model Contracts and Territorial Restrictions

The first strand of conduct regards the contractual relationship between licensors and, to a certain degree, also involves the underlying relation

---

[20] Ibid.

[21] Joined Cases 56 and 58/64, *Établissements Consten S.à.R.L. and Grundig-Verkaufs-GmbH* v. *Commission* [1966] ECR 301–351, ECLI:EU:C:1966:41, ECR 340.

[22] See Commission, 'Guidelines on the application of Article 81(3) of the Treaty', para. 18.

[23] I. Brinker and T. Holzmuller, 'Competition Law and Copyright – Observations from the World of Collecting Societies', *European Intellectual Property Review* 32(11) (2010), 553, 555 with further references.

[24] Regarding the 'exceptional circumstances' test, see, e.g., C. Ahlborn, D. S. Evens and A. J. Padila, 'The Logic & Limits of the "Exceptional Circumstances Test" in Magill and IMS Health', *Fordham International Law Journal*, 28 (2004), 1109.

between licensors and rights holders.[25] The inter-licensors relationship finds its roots in the objective of repertoire aggregation for a specific territory and is (therefore) specifically relevant in the context of CMOs and musical rights.

Let us briefly recall the conventional set-up, as described above in Chapter 2: traditionally, mass uses of copyright protected works have been confined to the territory of specific countries. Rights holders (i.e. authors, composers, publishers, performers, and record labels for secondary uses) regularly assign the administration of their rights to the respective national CMO.[26] In order to be able to offer broad licences for the domestic market covering non-domestic repertoire, authors' organisations have entered into a network of RRAs with each other.[27] These RRAs were based on non-mandatory model contracts between members of the CMOs' umbrella organisation, the International Confederation of Societies of Authors and Composers (CISAC).[28] The model contract dates back to as early 1936 and in fact 'one of the major objectives of CISAC is to promote reciprocal representation among collecting societies by means of model contracts'.[29] Based on this contractual web, CMOs obtain the right to license the repertoire of the CMOs with which it has a bilateral agreement. In effect, the traditional licensing arrangement in the sector has developed around national 'one-stop shops' that licensed the entire world music repertoire for use in their respective domestic territories.[30]

RRAs raise concerns in relation to possible market partitioning, as illustrated by the European Commission, for example, in its *Simulcasting* decision, in which it points to the exclusion of reciprocal vertical agreements from the scope of the Commission Block Exemption

---

[25] See also S. F. Schwemer, 'Emerging Models for Cross-border Online Licensing' in T. Riis (ed.), *User Generated Law, Re-Constructing Intellectual Property Law in a Knowledge Society* (Edward Elgar, 2016) and 'The licensing of online music streaming services in Europe' in R. Watt (ed.), *Handbook on the Economics of Copyright* (Edward Elgar, 2014).

[26] See Schwemer, 'Emerging models for cross-border online licensing', p. 79, with additional sources.

[27] This remains the norm. See Recital 40 of Directive 2014/26/EU. See also V. Dehin, 'The Future of Legal Online Music Services in the European Union: A Review of the EU Commission's Recent Initiatives in Cross-Border Copyright Management', *European Intellectual Property Review*, 32 (2010), 220, 223; and Guibault and van Gompel, p. 135.

[28] Especially for the licensing of public performance rights: *CISAC* (Case COMP/C-2/38.698) Commission Decision C(2008) 3435 final of 16 July 2008 [2008] OJ C323/12 Recital 13. See also more broadly on industry model contracts the methodology model by T. Kautio, N. Lefever and M. Määttä, *Assessing the Operation of Copyright and Related Rights Systems, Methodology Framework* (Foundation for Cultural Policy Research (Cupore), Cupore publication 26 2016), p. 90.

[29] *Commission Decision CISAC*, Recital 6.

[30] See Schwemer, 'Emerging models for cross-border online licensing', p. 79, with additional sources.

Regulation (EU) 330/2010 in Article 2(4)[31] and the reference made in the Guidelines on the applicability of Article 101 of the Treaty on the Functioning of the European Union to horizontal co-operation agreements.[32] Back in the 1970s, however, the Commission did not have concerns regarding CMOs' territorial practices.[33]

On 13 July 1989, the Court of Justice had already addressed the reciprocal relationship between CMOs in two seminal cases: C-395/87, *Tournier*[34] and Joined Cases C-110/88, C-241/88 and C-242/88, *Lucazeau*.[35] In the *Tournier* case, among other things, the Court had to assess whether the organisation of a '*de facto* monopoly in most countries of the European Community' via '[a] group of agreements' constitutes a concerted practice and thus facilitates the abuse of a dominant position.[36] The Court concluded that the RRAs were not, as such, restrictive of competition under Article 101(1) TFEU, provided that no concerted practice was demonstrated.[37] The Court continued to find that

[c]oncerted action by national copyright-management societies with the effect of systematically refusing to grant direct access to their repertoires to foreign users must be regarded as amounting to a concerted practice restrictive of competition and capable of affecting trade between the Member States.[38]

However, the Court reflects that (prohibited) concerted action cannot be presumed where the mere (permitted) parallel behaviour can be accounted for by other reasons. In the specifics of the case, the Court found that

[s]uch a reason might be that copyright-management societies of other Member States would be obliged, in the event of direct access to their repertoires, to organize their own management and monitoring system in another country.[39]

---

[31] Commission Regulation (EU) No 330/2010 of 20 April 2010 on the application of Article 101(3) of the Treaty on the Functioning of the European Union to categories of vertical agreements and concerted practices [2010] OJ L102/1.

[32] See, e.g., Commission, 'Guidelines on the applicability of Article 101 of the Treaty on the Functioning of the European Union to horizontal co-operation agreements', para. 226. See also *Commission Decision IFPI – "Simulcasting"*, Recital 116.

[33] P. Gyertyánfy, 'Collective Management of Music Rights in Europe after the CISAC Decision', *International Review of Intellectual Property and Competition Law*, 59 [2010], 69, pointing towards *GEMA* (Case IV.26.760) Commission Decision 71/224/EEC [1971] OJ L134/15.

[34] See Case 395/87, *Tournier*.

[35] See Joined Cases 110/88, 241/88 and 242/88, *Lucazeau and Others* v. *Sacem and Others* [1989] ECR 283-2835, ECLI:EU:C:1989:326.

[36] See referred question 2 para. 7 of Case 395/87 *Tournier* and referred question 2 para. 7 of Joined Cases 110/88, 241/88 and 242/88, *Lucazeau*.

[37] Case 395/87, *Tournier*, para. 20. See also Guibault and van Gompel, p. 144.

[38] See Case 395/87, *Tournier*, para. 23 and Joined Cases 110/88, 241/88 and 242/88, *Lucazeau*, para. 18.

[39] See Case 395/87, *Tournier*, para. 24 and Joined Cases 110/88, 241/88 and 242/88, *Lucazeau*, para. 18.

In conclusion, the Court of Justice held that:

Article 85 of the EEC Treaty [Article 101 TFEU] must be interpreted as prohibiting any concerted practice by national copyright-management societies of the Member States having as its object or effect the refusal by each society to grant direct access to its repertoire to users established in another Member State.[40]

As was highlighted by Guibault and van Gompel, RRAs 'appeared in those days to be economically justified in a context in which physical monitoring of copyright usage was required'.[41] The competition authority's interest resurrected with the emergence of Internet-related uses, such as for on-demand streaming.

3.1.1   Barcelona and Santiago Agreements

In the early 2000s, the CMOs' umbrella organisations, Bureau international des sociétés gérant les droits d'enregistrement et de reproduction mécanique (BIEM) and CISAC, developed two standard contracts for RRAs, which amended their respective pre-existing models for bilateral agreements for their members:[42] the so-called 'Santiago Agreement', covering online public performance (e.g., regarding webcasting and on-demand services, as well as music included in video transmitted online)[43] by the author CMOs' umbrella organisation CISAC;[44] and the so-called 'Barcelona Agreement', covering digital reproduction (e.g., webcasting and on-demand services) issued by the mechanical CMOs' umbrella organisation BIEM.[45]

---

[40] Case 395/87, *Tournier* 2 and 3, and Joined Cases 110/88, 241/88 and 242/88, *Lucazeau* 1 and 2. The Court continues: 'The refusal by a national society for the management of copyright in musical works to grant the users of recorded music access only to the foreign repertoire represented by it does not have the object or effect of restricting competition in the common market unless access to a part of the protected repertoire could entirely safeguard the interests of the authors, composers and publishers of music without thereby increasing the costs of managing contracts and monitoring the use of protected musical works'. It was then for the national courts to determine whether a concerted action has taken place.

[41] Guibault and van Gompel, p. 144.

[42] Schwemer, 'The licensing of online music streaming services in Europe', p. 151.

[43] Named after the CISAC World Congress 2000, which took place in Santiago de Chile. See *BUMA, GEMA PRS, SACEM – 'Santiago'* (Case COMP/C2/38.126) Notification of cooperation agreements [2001] OJ C145/2, Recital 2.

[44] In 1987, i.e. before the SatCab Directive, CISAC had already addressed cross-border activities of direct broadcasting satellites in its amendment in the 'Sydney Agreement'. See P. Gilliéron, 'Collecting Societies and the Digital Environment', *International Review of Intellectual Property and Competition Law* [2006], 939, 943, with further evidence.

[45] See *BIEM – "Barcelona Agreements"* (Case COMP/C-2/38.377) Notification of cooperation agreements [2002] OJ C132/18, Recital 2.

The respective pre-existing RRAs were modified so that that each CMO could license non-exclusively its own repertoire as well as those of organisations with which it had an agreement on an EU and world-wide basis (i.e. multi-repertoire, multi-territorial). Thus, the model represented an attempt to overcome territoriality and to construct a licensing scheme that facilitates multi-territorial online music licensing, while at the same time safeguarding the monopolistic position of CMOs in the respective territory.[46] These 'second-generation'[47] RRA agreements secured that each CMO acts as a 'one-stop shop' regarding both users and rights holders.[48] Both standard agreements included an identical rule that determined which CMO had the authority to license:[49]

(a) by the society operating in the country corresponding to the URL (uniform resource locator) used by the content provider, where the primary language used at the site of the content provider is the primary language of that country; or

(b) otherwise by the society operating in the country where the content provider is incorporated.

If the content provider has its economic residence in a different country from the countries set forth above, the licence will be granted by the society operating in that country.

In other words, licensees (i.e. online content providers) were 'routed towards the CMO of the country of their "economic residence"'.[50] As I have noted earlier, tariffs were applied according to the destination principle, which ensured that price differences between the local tariffs would not lead to 'tariff shopping'.[51] In effect, the monopolistic position of each CMO in its respective territory as licensor for the worldwide repertoire was ensured.

The European Commission's Directorate-General for Competition received notifications regarding the Santiago Agreement in May 2001

---

[46] See, e.g., G. Poll, 'CELAS, PEDL & Co.: Metamorphose oder Anfang vom Ende der kollektiven Wahrnehmung von Musik-Online-Rechten in Europa?', *Zeitschrift für Urheber- und Medienrecht* [2008], 500, 501; and G. Petteri, 'Harmonising Collective Rights Management and Multi-Territorial Licensing of Music for Online Use in the European Union: A Review of the Collective Rights Management Directive 2014/26/EU', *Nordiskt Immateriellt Rättskydd* [2015], 150, 155; Capobianco, 115.

[47] E. Bonadio, 'Collective management of music copyright in the Internet age and the EU initiatives: from reciprocal representation agreements to open platforms' World Library and Information Congress, Helsinki, 2012, 3: www.ifla.org/past-wlic/2012/148-bonadio-en.pdf

[48] R. M. Vuckovic, 'Implementation of Directive 2014/26 on collective management and multi-territorial licensing of musical rights in regulating the tariff-setting systems in Central and Eastern Europe', *International Review of Intellectual Property and Competition Law*, 47 (2016), 28, 42–43.

[49] See *Santiago Agreement* Recital 2 and *Barcelona Agreement*, Recital 3.

[50] Vuckovic, 'Implementation of Directive 2014/26', 42–43.

[51] See Schwemer, 'The licensing of online music streaming services in Europe', p. 151.

and regarding the Barcelona Agreement in February 2002, respectively, and published a notice inviting third parties to submit their observations.[52] In May 2004, the Commission officially opened proceedings on the Santiago Agreement and in August 2005 published its market test notice.

Despite 'strong support' for the 'one-stop shop' principle,[53] the Commission expressed concerns regarding the 'economic residence clause'/customer allocation clause that granted each CMO 'absolute exclusivity for its territory as regards the possibility of granting multi-territorial/multi-repertoire licences for online music rights'.[54] As result of the Commission's opinion, the agreements were not renewed and concluded respectively, and escaped further action such as a decision.[55] Effectively, the CMOs returned to the *'status quo ante'*.[56] Without being able to rely on a national 'one-stop shop', commercial users had to license territorially limited online rights from the different national CMOs.[57]

3.1.2   Simulcasting Agreement

In relation to the aforementioned standard contracts for bilateral reciprocal representation agreements, the Simulcasting Agreement also becomes relevant: the proceedings regard the licensing of neighbouring rights for simulcasting or webcasting, i.e. the non-interactive broadcasting of musical works via the Internet. Thus, it falls outside the narrower scope of this book, which focuses on interactive on-demand streaming. Nonetheless, the *Simulcasting* model offers some important reflections on the licensing for interactive on-demand streaming purposes and the models that the Commission deemed permissible under the competition rules. In addition, the CISAC decision of 2002, constitutes the first decision by the Commission concerning the licensing of musical works on the Internet by CMOs.

---

[52] See also ibid.

[53] See, e.g., Commission, 'Commission opens proceedings into collective licensing of music copyrights for online use' (Press release) IP/04/586, Brussels, 3 May 2004.

[54] *Santiago Agreement*, Recital 6. See also Schwemer, 'The licensing of online music streaming services in Europe', p. 152, with further sources.

[55] Case T-442/08, *CISAC* v. *European Commission* [2013] ECLI:EU:T2013:188, para. 109. See also Schwemer, 'The licensing of online music streaming services in Europe', p. 152; J. Drexl, 'Competition in the field of collective management: preferring "creative competition" to allocative efficiency in European copyright law', in P. Torremans (ed.), *Copyright Law, A Handbook of Contemporary Research* (Edward Elgar, 2007), p. 258.

[56] See Case T-442/08, *CISAC* v. *Commission*, paras. 110–111.

[57] See Drexl, 'Competition in the field of collective management', p. 258; and M. Ricolfi, 'Individual and Collective Management of Copyright in a Digital Environment' in P. Torremans (ed.), *Copyright Law, A Handbook of Contemporary Research* (Edward Elgar, 2007), p. 294.

The proceedings date back to November 2000, when the record producers' umbrella organisation, International Federation of the Phonographic Industry (IFPI), applied for negative clearance or an antitrust exemption for an experimental amendment of its reciprocal representation model agreement.[58] The goal of the amendment was to replace the mono-territorial licensing practice and enable commercial users (broadcasters) to 'obtain a multi-territorial licence from any one of the rights administration societies (...) established in the EEA which are party to the Reciprocal Agreement to simulcast into the signatories' territories'[59] – thus, effectively establishing a 'one-stop shop'.[60] Originally, the agreement contained a clause that required commercial users to approach the CMO in their own Member State. This was later amended so that commercial users could approach any CMO that takes part of the contractual web based on RRAs within the EEA.[61]

In its decision of 8 October 2002, the Commission granted an exemption for the trial period of the agreement because it assessed that the Simulcasting Agreement included a number of factors that would create competition between CMOs and thus 'dissipate the concern regarding possible market or customer sharing'.[62] The freedom of commercial users to seek multi-territorial licensing from a CMO of their choice within the European Economic Area (EEA) was especially welcomed by the Commission as 'major evolution' from the traditional system of national *de facto* monopolies, which enables CMOs 'to actually compete and to differentiate themselves in terms of efficiency, quality of service and commercial terms'.[63] The DG Competition deemed that

---

[58] In the course of the proceedings, a second amendment regarding tariffs was included: see *Commission Decision IFPI – "Simulcasting"* Recital 4. Notably, the Simulcasting Agreement was modelled after the Sydney Agreement, See Gilliéron, 'Collecting Societies and the Digital Environment', 943, with more details.

[59] *Commission Decision IFPI – "Simulcasting"* Recital 3.

[60] Or, as R. Hilty and S. Nérisson, 'Collective Copyright Management and Digitization: The European Experience' (2013) Max Planck Institute for Intellectual Property and Competition Law Research Paper No. 13–09 (Max Planck Institute for Intellectual Property and Competition Law), 7: http://ssrn.com/abstract=2247870 put it: the system 'aimed to safeguard the traditional system of a one-stop-shop for multi-repertoire licenses while adding the crucial feature that online use can be multi-territorial'.

[61] *Commission Decision IFPI – "Simulcasting"* Recital 28. The amendment was required by the Commission: see, e.g., Hilty and Nérisson, 'Collective Copyright Management and Digitization', 7.

[62] *Commission Decision IFPI – "Simulcasting"* Recital 116. More specifically, an exemption according to Art. 101(3) TFEU; in the decision both the promotion of technical and economic progress (Recitals 84–88) and improvements in the distribution of goods (Recitals 89–92) as well as the benefits for consumers have been considered; indispensability (Art. 101(3)(a) TFEU) and no elimination of competition (Art. 101(3)(b) TFEU).

[63] Ibid., Recital 119.

competition between CMOs would be safeguarded by clearly separating royalties from administrative fees.[64] Another concern, namely the calculation of a global tariff for the multi-territorial licence based on 'the aggregate of the royalties of the participating CMOs would charge individually for their respective territory', however, was accepted despite its potentially limiting effects on competition between CMOs.[65] Thus, the Commission's exemption was based on the hypothesis that commercial users would be able to choose between several CMOs, which compete on cost and efficiency for the granting of multi-territorial licences.

A couple of interesting insights can be drawn from comparing the *Simulcasting* model with the *Barcelona* and *Santiago* models: compared with the latter agreements, the main difference is that rights holders, or rather their intermediaries, were steadfast on an economic residence clause, whereas the former allows competition to a limited extent and therefore was exempted from Article 101 TFEU.[66] It appears that one crucial rationale behind the economic residence clause in the agreements concerning author and mechanical rights related to competition worries about price dumping: even ten years after the *Simulcasting* decision, the Impact Assessment accompanying the proposal Commission's proposal for the CRM Directive notes that some consulted organisations insist that 'customer allocation would be essential as competition between [CMOs] could lead to "a race to the bottom"'.[67] This concern, it seems, has not been shared by owners of neighbouring rights.[68] The Commission's underlying rationale, on the other hand, appears to be that CMOs 'are unlikely to improve efficiency according to economic theory' in the absence of competition based on the quality of their services and management costs.[69] The *Simulcasting* model is not without its drawbacks either, though, as Drexl points out. The reliance on RRAs 'necessarily create[s] additional costs of administration and may incite individual societies to

---

[64] Graber, 'Collective rights management', 38. See also J. Axhamn and L. Guibault, *Cross-border extended collective licensing: A solution to online dissemination of Europe's cultural heritage?* (Final report prepared for EuropeanaConnect, 2011), 22.

[65] Graber, 'Collective rights management', 38.

[66] Drexl, 'Competition in the field of collective management: Preferring "creative competition" to allocative efficiency in European copyright law', p. 257.

[67] Commission, 'Impact Assessment accompanying the document Proposal for a Directive of the European Parliament and of the Council on collective management of copyright and related rights and multi-territorial licensing of rights in musical works for online uses in the internal market', 47.

[68] See also, as regards the Santiago Agreement, Hilty and Nérisson, 'Collective Copyright Management and Digitization', 8.

[69] Petteri, 'Harmonising Collective Rights Management', 155.

discriminate against right-holders of other societies when it comes to the distribution of royalties'.[70]

3.1.3   CISAC Saga (2000–2013)

The CISAC proceedings again dealt with the (non-binding) CISAC model contract and, inter alia, the territorial delineation of licensing activities and its compatibility with Article 101(1) TFEU. The CISAC saga spans a staggering thirteen years and its factual background dates back to two separate complaints from commercial users: in 2000 by RTL Group and in 2003 by Music Choice Europe, respectively.[71]

In the case, the Directorate-General Competition assessed the RRAs, which were based on the CISAC model contract, between twenty-four European author CMOs. The relevant clauses in the competition case were:

(a) membership restrictions contained in the reciprocal representation agreements which prevent competition between EEA CISAC members for the provision of their services to authors; and

(b) territorial restrictions which prevent competition between EEA CISAC members for the licensing of performing rights to commercial users; the territorial restrictions take the form of express exclusivities in the reciprocal representation agreements and a concerted practice on the territorial delineation of the scope of the licence.[72]

In 2006, the Commission issued a Statement of Objections (SO) and, after an oral hearing and further requests for information, CISAC and eighteen of the concerned CMOs offered several commitments, such as discontinuing their recommendation of the membership and territoriality clauses in 2007.[73] However, based on a market test conducted by the Commission, it was concluded 'that the proposed commitments would not give an appropriate answer to the competition concerns'.[74] On 16 July 2008, the Commission issued its Decision addressed to the respective twenty-four European CMOs, containing as many as 265 recitals.

---

[70] Drexl, 'Competition in the field of collective management: Preferring 'creative competition' to allocative efficiency in European copyright law', p. 273.

[71] In 2000, RTL filed a complaint against German CMO GEMA after being denied a pan-European multi-repertoire licence, which had been rejected because GEMA only held multi-repertoire rights for Germany. In 2003, Music Choice Europe (MCE) filed a complaint against the umbrella organisation CISAC, claiming that the model standard contract was a concerted practice to avoid competition between CMOs. The cases were merged. See *Commission Decision CISAC*, Recital 3.

[72] Ibid., Recital 74. See also Case T-442/08 *CISAC* v. *Commission*, para. 11.

[73] See Case T-442/08, *CISAC* v. *Commission*, paras. 7–10.

[74] *Commission Decision CISAC*, Recital 72.

As regards membership clauses (based on Article 11(II) of the model contract),[75] the Commission relates to the previous case law and restates 'clear indications concerning the limitations which competition law imposes on the relationship' between CMOs and their members.[76] It finds that the membership restrictions affect both competition between CMOs as regards the provision of their services to rights holders and, indirectly, competition between the CMOs as regards the licensing of rights to commercial users[77] and therefore constitute infringements of Article 101 TFEU.[78]

The second aspect regarded exclusive representation, which safeguards that CISAC members abstain from operating in the territory of another CMO (based on Articles 1 and 6(II) of the model contract).[79] The Commission in this context reminds us of the CJEU case law in *Tournier* and *Lucazeau* from 1989 regarding territorial restrictions and the licensing for physical premises such as discotheques, hotels and bars, in which it was made clear that there exist competition concerns, if CMOs undertake not to allow access to their own repertoire for uses outside their domestic territory[80] and applies the established test to the 'new forms of exploitation such as the Internet'.[81] Regarding the former Article 1 of the model contract, the Commission found that this exclusivity in the form of a non-intervention clause[82] was restrictive of competition and had a foreclosure effect in the domestic market of CMOs (closing of direct access to one's repertoire in the other CMO's

---

[75] See ibid., Recitals 19–21. Notably, Art. 11(II) was deleted in June 2004. The relevant clause read: 'While this contract is in force neither of the contracting Societies may, without the consent of the other, accept as a member any member of the other society or any natural person, firm or company having the nationality of one of the countries in which the other Society operates'. However, it was held that 'it cannot be excluded that a number of RRAs still contain such a clause': see ibid., Recitals 35, 125.

[76] Namely the 1971 GEMA decision and the Court's findings in *GVL* from 1983: see ibid., Recitals 75–76.

[77] Ibid., Recital 126.   [78] See ibid., Recitals 123–137.

[79] See ibid., Recitals 145–152. Art. 6(II) of the model contract is at the core of the considerations. Whereas Art. 1 of the model contract no longer contains the exclusivity clauses, Art. 6 continued to have the territorial clauses (see, to that extent, Recitals 28 and 29). Art. 6(I) concerns the territory of the licence and Art. 6(II) provides that: 'For the duration of the present contract, each of the contracting Societies shall refrain from any intervention within the territory of the other Society in the latter's exercise of the mandate conferred by the present contract'. For the relationship between Arts. 1 and 6, see ibid., Recital 26.

[80] See *Commission Decision CISAC* Recital 145 and Recitals 77–80, with specific reference to Case 395/87, *Tournier*, para. 20, and Joined Cases 110/88, 241/88 and 242/88 *Lucazeau*, para. 14.

[81] *Commission Decision CISAC*, para. 80.

[82] Case T-442/08, *CISAC* v. *Commission*, paras. 13–14.

market).[83] As regards the exclusivity clause in Article 6(II), the concerned parties argued that the Commission 'completely misinterpreted' it, as it 'as imposing any form of exclusivity'.[84] Recognising that some CMOs started to remove Article 6(II) from their agreements, the Commission refrained from intervention:

insofar as CISAC and its EEA members understand it simply to mean that a collecting society will not interfere with the other society's ability to grant licences and that the clause is not interpreted as in any way limiting the possibility for the former to grant direct licences covering its own repertoire.[85]

A third aspect related to whether the territorial delineation of the authority to license constitutes a concerted practice.[86] The Commission considered, inter alia, that neither were the territorial restrictions explained by the territorial nature of copyright[87] or the need for a local presence[88] nor was the practice the outcome of individual market reaction;[89] thus, it concluded that a concerted practice would be the only possible explanation for the market outcome.[90]

Based on this assessment, the Commission held that several CMOs had infringed Article 101(1) TFEU by using the membership restrictions based on Article 11(II) of the model contract[91] (or by *de facto* applying those membership restrictions), (2) 'by conferring, in their reciprocal representation agreements, exclusive rights as provided for in Article 1 (I) and (II) of the CISAC model contract'[92] and (3) finally 'by coordinating the territorial delineations in a way which limits a licence to the domestic territory of each collecting society'.[93] Notably, the Commission found that

[c]ultural diversity (...) is not called into question by the Decision, which neither prohibits the reciprocal representation system as such, nor the possibility for collecting societies to introduce a certain territorial delineation together with certain commercial conditions in their representation contracts.[94]

Instead of creating an incentive for CMOs to abandon the system of reciprocal representation, it was deemed to

[offer] collecting societies the possibility to adapt the system of reciprocal representation to the needs of the online environment and to thereby make it more attractive for both right holders and users.[95]

---

[83] See *Commission Decision CISAC*, Recitals 140–144.
[84] See ibid., Recitals 146 and 152.   [85] Ibid., Recital 152.   [86] See ibid., Recital 153.
[87] Ibid., Recitals 159–160.   [88] Ibid., Recitals 171ff.   [89] See ibid., Recitals 166–170.
[90] See ibid., Recital 222.   [91] Ibid., Art. 1.   [92] Ibid., Art. 2.   [93] Ibid., Art. 3.
[94] Ibid., para. 95.   [95] Ibid.

The defendant CMOs satisfied their obligation to cease the alleged concerted action, and were obliged bilaterally to renegotiate their representation agreements.[96] Given the confidentiality of the agreements, the exact content or extent of potentially re-negotiated RRAs is not publicly available.[97] It has been commented that the Commission's findings were 'no surprise' in light of the authority's and the CJEU's case law.[98] Quite the opposite: Drexl expresses surprise that, more than thirty years after the *GEMA I* decision and the *GVL* judgment, the Commission still found restrictions in the RRAs.[99] The decision, nonetheless, was subject to widespread criticism.[100] Some argued that the proposed new system was in 'stark contrast' to the existing licensing regime.[101] Others found it 'an admirable attempt to remedy the previous system that was a product of its time'.[102] The European Parliament, in its resolution regarding the Online Music Recommendation of 2005, also criticises the DG Competition's intervention and:

(...) points out that the effect of the decision taken in this regard will be to preclude all attempts by the parties concerned to act together in order to find appropriate solutions – such as, for instance, a system for the clearing of rights at the European level – and to leave the way open to an oligopoly of a number of large collecting societies linked by exclusive agreements to publishers belonging to the worldwide repertoire; believes that the result will be a restriction of choice and the extinction of small collecting societies to the detriment of minority cultures.[103]

---

[96] See Gyertyánfy, 'Collective Management of Music Rights', 73. See also Art. 4(1) and (2) of the CISAC decision (immediately as regards membership restrictions and the conferral of exclusive rights in Art. 1(I) and (II) and within 120 days as regards the concerted practice of territorial delineation).

[97] See, e.g., G. Mazziotti, 'New Licensing Models for Online Music Services in the European Union: From Collective to Customized Management', Public Law & Legal Theory Working Paper Group Paper Number 11–269, Columbia Law School, 10: http://ssrn.com/abstract=1814264; Commission, 'Impact Assessment accompanying the document Proposal for a Directive of the European Parliament and of the Council on collective management of copyright and related rights and multi-territorial licensing of rights in musical works for online uses in the internal market', 149.

[98] Guibault and van Gompel, p. 147, specifically referring to *GEMA I decision* and Case 7/82 *GVL* v. *Commission* regarding membership discrimination clauses, and the *Tournier* decision regarding territorial licensing restrictions.

[99] Drexl, 'Collective Management of Copyrights and the EU Principle of Free Movement of Services after the OSA Judgment—In Favour of a More Balance Approach', p. 466.

[100] See, e.g., J. Wern Loong Yow, '"Creative Competition" with a Pan-European Licensing Body: Reconsidering the European Commission's Approach to Collecting Societies', *World Competition* 34 (2011), 287 and 308.

[101] C. Langenius, 'The ramifications of pan-European licensing for Nordic collective rights management', *Nordiskt Immateriellt Rättskydd* [2008], 29.

[102] Yow, 'Creative Competition', 292.

[103] European Parliament, 'Resolution of 25 September 2008 on collective cross-border management of copyright and related rights for legitimate online music services' P6_TA (2008)0462 (2010/C 8 E/19) OJ 8 E/105, 3.

In October 2008, CISAC and most (twenty-one out of twenty-four) CMOs appealed the decision and brought an action for the partial annulment of the Commission's decision because it allegedly failed to prove the existence of a concerted practice with regard to the national territorial limitations.[104] On 12 April 2013, after a hearing lasting almost five years, the General Court[105] in *CISAC* v. *Commission* partially annulled the DG COMP's decision in its comprehensive 184-paragraph judgment, yet only in respect of the question of whether the CMOs had engaged in concerted action, not in respect of membership and exclusivity clauses.[106] CISAC welcomed the decision. The implication of the annulment of Article 3 of the Commission's decision seems somewhat unclear, though. It is also important to note that the decision in each case had been annulled only in so far as it concerned the respective applicant.[107] Neither the membership nor the exclusivity clauses were any longer part of the CISAC model contract, which explains CISAC's focus on Article 3 of the decision. Nonetheless, the Court in *CISAC* v. *Commission* remarked, as regards the model contract, that 'it does not expressly provide for national territorial limitations, but merely invites the

---

[104] Some CMOs applied for interim suspension of the decision at the General Court, which was rejected because the CMOs could not convince it of urgency and evidence for the suspension.

[105] Formerly the Court of First Instance, which it was called at the date of filing. The following section takes the proceedings in Case T-442/, *CISAC* v. *Commission* as a starting point. The relevant parallel proceedings by the other CMOs are: T-451/08, *Stim* v. *Commission*; T-434/08, *Tono* v. *Commission*; T-433/08, *SIAE* v. *Commission*; T-432/08, *AKM* v. *Commission*; T-428/08, *STEF* v. *Commission*; T-425/08, *Koda* v. *Commission*; T-422/08, *SACEM* v. *Commission*; T-421/08, *Performing Right Society* v. *Commission*; T-420/08, *SAZAS* v. *Commission*; T-419/08, *LATGA-A* v. *Commission*; T-418/08, *OSA* v. *Commission*; T-417/08, *Sociedade Portuguesa de Autores* v. *Commission*; T-416/08, *Eesti Autorite Ühing* v. *Commission*; T-415/08, *Irish Music Rights Organisation* v. *Commission*; T-414/08, *Autortiesību un komunicēšanās konsultāciju aģentūra/Latvijas Autoru apvienība* v. *Commission*; T-413/08, *SOZA* v. *Commission*; T-411/08, *Artisjus* v. *Commission*; T-410/08, *GEMA* v. *Commission*; T-401/08, *Säveltäjäin Tekijänoikeustoimisto Teosto* v. *Commission*; T-398/08, *Stowarzyszenie Autorów ZAiKS* v. *Commission*; T-392/08, *AEPI* v. *Commission*.

[106] The Court held that it '[a]nnuls Article 3 of Commission Decision (...) in so far as it concerns (...) CISAC' in accordance with CISAC's claim (see ibid., para. 61). In the case involving the Danish CMO, Case T-425/08, *KODA* v. *Commission* [2013] ECLI: EU:T:2013:183, the applicant claimed that the decision as a whole should be annulled and subsidiarily that the decision as far as it regards KODA should be annulled or Art. 3 and Art. 4(2) and (3) should be annulled, or Art. 3 and Art. 4(2) and (3) should be annulled as far as they regard KODA, and even more subsidiarily that Art. (3) and Art. 4(2) and (3) should be annulled as regards administration and licensing of rights for cable retransmission: see para. 58 of the case (in Danish).

[107] In Case T-425/08, *KODA* v. *Commission* and in Case T-434/08, *TONO* v. *Commission* [2013] ECLI:EU:T:2013:187, the applicants were seeking annulment of Art. 3 also in respect of the other addressed CMOs. The Court, based on previous case law, deemed these claims as 'clearly inadmissible': see ibid., para. 159.

collecting societies to define the territorial scope of the mandates they grant each other in the RRAs'.[108]

The cases regarding the twenty-one CMOs have been considered in parallel proceedings (not reported), which seem to deviate from each other and the CISAC case to some extent, mainly as to the applicants' claims. In several cases, for example the Danish proceedings in Case T-442/08 and the German proceedings in Case T-410/08, third parties intervened on behalf of the European Commission.[109] Notably, the plea in law in the proceedings regarding the Swedish CMO, *STIM* v. *Commission*, diverged substantially from the other cases.[110] There, the applicant relied on an alleged breach of the cultural diversity consideration in Article 167(4) TFEU.[111] The case as a whole – one out of two of the total twenty-two proceedings[112] – was dismissed, inter alia due to the inadmissibility of the claim relating to the lack of evidence of the concerted practice.[113] The Swedish proceedings nonetheless offer some important – and, it seems from the literature, sometimes overlooked – insights into the General Court's reasoning.[114]

Regarding the actual scope of the restriction on competition arising from the concerted practice relating to the national territorial limitations, STIM argued that such clauses in the RRAs were objectively necessary, because in the 'absence of RRAs it would not be possible to grant licences covering several repertoires'.[115] The General Court started with stating that the necessity to cooperate between CMOs in order to be able to grant licences comprising several repertoires does not imply that every form of cooperation is in accordance with Article 101(1) TFEU, and recalled that such limitations must be objectively necessary and not only correspond to

---

[108] See Case T-442/08, *CISAC* v. *Commission*, para. 108.

[109] In the Danish (Case T-425/08, *KODA* v. *Commission*) and German (Case T-401/08, *GEMA* v. *Commission* [2013] ECLI:EU:T:2013:171) proceedings, for example IFPI and several media companies.

[110] Similar to the other proceedings, STIM (Case T-451/08, *STIM* v. *Commission* [2013] ECLI:EU:T:2013:189) sought annulment of Art. 3, Art. 4(2) and Art. 4(3) of the Commission's decision, the latter only insofar they regard Art. 3.

[111] Ex-Art. 151(4) TEC.

[112] The other action that was dismissed on procedural grounds was that regarding SGAE: see J. P. Quintais, 'The Empire Strikes Back: CISAC beats Commission in General Court', *Journal of Intellectual Property Law & Practice*, 8 (2013), 680, 682.

[113] See Case T-451/08, *STIM* v. *Commission*, paras. 63–72. The General Court held that the related arguments were introduced as a new plea which only was broad forward in the hearings and thus inadmissible.

[114] The General Court held that the single plea is composed of three parts 'relating to, first, the consequences which the prohibition of the concerted practice relating to national territorial limitations has on cultural diversity in the European Union, secondly, the actual scope of the restriction on competition arising from that concerted practice and, thirdly, the application of Article 81(3) EC.': see ibid., para. 61.

[115] See ibid., para. 89.

the rational behaviour of the CMO.[116] Based on the consideration 'that the system of territorial limitations is not the sole possible method allowing the grant of multi-repertoire licences and that other initiatives are possible', the Court concluded that such national territorial limitations in all RRAs cannot be considered as being objectively necessary.[117] Rather, the Court considers that the system

conceived of and used for decades for traditional forms of copyright exploitation, was also applied to new forms of exploitation, pending the discovery of other solutions which could meet the new challenges posed by those new forms of exploitation while ensuring an adequate level of protection of the rights in question.[118]

Thus, the Court in *STIM* presents a nuanced view to its finding in the CISAC case, in which it held that

[t]he arrival of new information technologies allowing the exploitation of works online does not mean that those structures are suddenly obsolete or that the economic operators concerned should immediately demonstrate their intent to compete.[119]

A second line of argumentation by STIM was built around the claim that 'national territorial limitations do not restrain competition because they do not prevent the grant of direct licences'.[120] Recalling that partial restrictions on competition are sufficient for a breach of Article 101 TFEU,[121] the Court goes on to consider national territorial limitations:

the removal of the national territorial limitations is intended to enable competition other than that made possible by the grant of direct licences. The national territorial limitations prevent two collecting societies, which grant direct licences, from competing to obtain the rights to the repertoire of another collecting society which does not grant direct licences, in order to add it to the direct licences they grant.

Finding that STIM's behaviour restricted at least one form of competition, the Court confirmed the Commission in its conclusion 'that the conduct censured by Article 3 of the contested decision was anti-competitive'.[122] In *STIM*, as opposed to the other proceedings, the Court also considered the exemption of Article 101(1) TFEU according

---

[116] See ibid., para. 90.   [117] See ibid., para. 92.   [118] Ibid., para. 92.
[119] Case T-442/08, *CISAC* v. *Commission*, para. 130. The Court continues: 'Thus, the mere fact that, after the deletion of the exclusivity clause, the collecting societies did not quickly modify the national territorial limitations could show that those limitations are explained by reasons other than the continuation, in another form, of the exclusivity'.
[120] See Case T-451/08, *STIM* v. *Commission*, para. 93.   [121] See ibid., para. 94.
[122] See ibid., para. 96.

to the four conditions laid out in Article 101(3) TFEU, but rejected it in line with the Commission's reasoning.[123]

Despite the judgments having been delivered several years ago and having been widely anticipated, relatively little academic scrutiny is devoted to the CISAC judgment (and the other cases regarding national CMOs). Most scholarly comments focus on the findings in the main case regarding CISAC. It has been noted, for example, that 'the decision of the (...) [General Court] could not turn back the clock'[124] because 'the change in the business models for online licensing of music had already started'. Others argue that the CISAC case 'undermines the Commission's justification for the proposed MTL system, even if it is mostly the result of a failure by the Commission to produce evidentiary support for its claims'.[125]

The importance of the cases in front of the General Court for the licensing system as such – at least as regards the CISAC proceedings – might be overestimated. As described above, the application as such is limited to the specific appellant. In the proceedings relating to the Swedish CMO, STIM, the Court restates that even if Article 3 is annulled, the removal of the exclusivity clause in Article 2 of the decision allows the grant of direct licences, which has inevitably an effect on the competition between less commercially attractive music and more popular music, which have traditionally been bundled in the same licence.[126]

In assessing the consequences that the prohibition of the concerted practice relating to the national territorial limitations has on cultural diversity, the Court, in paragraph 79 of its *STIM* judgment, points out that

the enforcement of the contested decision could give rise to new possibilities for a collecting society to grant another collecting society the management of its repertoire. Those new possibilities would complement the existing possibilities, without replacing them. In that respect, the probability that the system of RRAs would be maintained is all the higher since, as regards the traditional forms of exploitation of copyright, the contested decision does not affect the possibility for collecting societies to continue to grant their repertoire solely to a local collecting society.[127]

Based on the findings in the *STIM* proceedings, I find it doubtful whether the Court even wanted to turn back the clock. The central aspects of the CISAC case of 2013 related to the procedural fact that

---

[123] The General Court refers specifically to section 8.3 of the CISAC Decision: see ibid., paras. 44 and 108.

[124] Vuckovic, Implementation of Directive 2014/26', 44.

[125] Quintais, 'The Empire Strikes Back', 682.

[126] See Case T-451/08, *STIM* v. *Commission*, para. 80. [127] Ibid., para. 79.

CISAC was not an addressee of the Commission decision, as well as the legal standard for the evidence for proving the existence of a concerted practice.[128] Thus, it appears, the Court has not really altered the Commission's reasoning as regards the system as such. On a broader note regarding model contracts, in its decision of 2008 the Commission questioned neither the existence of the CISAC model contract, or the system of RRAs as such, nor the necessity of cooperation between CMOs 'provided that such cooperation does not infringe the competition rules'.[129] In fact, as the Court notes, the decision does not prevent the CMOs from using some national limitations either, 'but rather it is intended to emphasise the anti-competitive nature of the coordinated approach adopted for that purpose by all of the collecting societies'.[130] As Mazziotti notes, it 'challenged the de facto exclusivity for the licensing of the aggregated repertoire'.[131]

3.2   Licensor–Licensee Relationship: Licensing Contracts and Territorial Restrictions

In the previous section, we saw how reciprocal representation agreements between CMOs based on model contracts played a vital role in multi-territorial and cross-border arrangements and how territorial exclusivity has been high on the agenda in competition proceedings. Let us now look towards the second strand of conduct: territorial restrictions and partitions in licensing agreements with commercial users, which are prevalent in the audiovisual sector. Whereas the previous section looked at (horizontal) territorial restrictions between rights holders, or rather their intermediaries, this section is devoted to (vertical) territorial restrictions applied in licensing contracts between rights holders (or their intermediaries) and commercial users (licensees). First, I look at the combined cases *Premier League and Murphy*, in which the Court of Justice had to consider the territorial delineations in content licensing agreements and their compatibility with Article 101 TFEU.[132] Whereas the case in hand does not relate to exploitation of

---

[128] See Case T-442/08, *CISAC* v. *Commission*, para. 182; and Quintais, 'The Empire Strikes Back', 680.

[129] Case T-442/08, *CISAC* v. *Commission*, paras. 83 and 106; Case T-451/08, *STIM* v. *Commission* para. 78.

[130] Case T-451/08, *STIM* v. *Commission*, para. 78.

[131] Mazziotti, 'New Licensing Models for Online Music Services in the European Union: From Collective to Customized Management', 9.

[132] Joined Cases C–403/08 and C–429/08, *Football Association Premier League Ltd and Others* v. *QC Leisure and Others* [2011] ECR I-9159, ECLI:EU:C:2011:631.

content in the form of online streaming, it is nevertheless relevant given its potential significance for other forms of access. Then, I look at the competition investigation into pay-TV services, which find their basis in the Court's case law.

Yet another, earlier and somewhat related, competition investigation concerned downloads from Apple's iTunes store, in which the European Commission assessed whether the practice that the iTunes store was accessible only in specific Member States constituted an unjustifiable partition of the market. The investigation dates back to a complaint by a major UK consumer protection organisation about the territorial segmentation of iTunes.[133] In April 2007, DG Competition sent a Statement of Objections against alleged territorial restrictions to major record companies and Apple, regarding their respective licensing agreements for online music sales.[134] The main concern was that consumers could purchase music in the form of downloads from the iTunes store only in their country of residence, which restricted their choice, the availability of music and its price, and thus allegedly constituted a violation of Article 101(1) TFEU.[135] In January 2008, the Commission announced that Apple equalised prices among the stores.[136] The respective press release reads that the proceedings also clarified that the territorial organisation of the iTunes store is not due to the agreements between Apple and the record companies, but rather the structure was chosen 'to take into account the country-specific aspects of copyright laws'.[137] As a result, the Commission closed the investigation without making a formal decision.[138]

---

[133] Commission, 'Antitrust: European Commission welcomes Apple's announcement to equalise prices for music downloads from iTunes in Europe' (Press release) IP/08/22, Brussels, 9 January 2008. The example used referred to the UK iTunes Store, where music downloads were nearly 10 per cent more expensive than in the euro-zone. Which? is the largest consumer organisation in Europe. The case was relocated from the national competition authority to the Commission: see R. Whish and D. Bailey, *Competition Law*, 8th edn (Oxford University Press, 2015), p. 305.

[134] See Commission, 'Competition: European Commission confirms sending a Statement of Objections against alleged territorial restrictions in on-line music sales to major record companies and Apple' (Press release) MEMO/07/126, Brussels, 3 April 2007.

[135] See ibid.

[136] See Commission, 'Antitrust: European Commission welcomes Apple's announcement to equalise prices for music downloads from iTunes in Europe'.

[137] See ibid.

[138] See Commission, 'COM/C-2/39154 (PO/iTunes) and COMP/C-39174 (Which/itTunes)'. Note available at: http://ec.europa.eu/competition/antitrust/cases/dec_docs/39154/39154_629_10.pdf

3.2.1   Football Association Premier League and Murphy

3.2.2.1 Factual Background and Issues at Stake

Football Association Premier League Ltd (FAPL) organises and commercially exploits the leading professional football league competition in England.[139] In this context, FAPL grants exclusive packages of broadcasting rights for live transmission for three-year periods on a territorial basis, which usually corresponds to a Member State in the EU, in order to maximise the commercial value of its rights.[140] The territorial scope of the licences is caused by the demand in the tender process; whereas bids on a global, regional or territorial basis are possible, 'as a rule', demand corresponds to national markets or neighbouring territories with a common language.[141] This territorial exclusivity is protected by contractual obligations that require licensees 'to prevent the public from receiving their broadcasts outside the area for which they hold the licence',[142] which is achieved by encryption and prohibition of supply of decoders 'for the purpose of being used outside the territory for which they hold the licence'.[143] This is what resembles the geo-blocking practice regarding online streaming.

Due to substantial local price differences in subscriptions, some subscribers purchased decoder cards and decoder devices from providers in other Member States – in the present case, Greece.[144] In *Murphy*, pub owners acquired 'Greek private viewing licences, satellite decoders and decoding cards allowing them to access and display (. . .) matches (. . .) at a fraction of the cost, i.e. approximately £70 per month',[145] notably by providing false names and addresses.

Whereas these decoder cards have been manufactured and marketed with the authorisation of the rightholder, 'they are subsequently used

---

[139] Joined Cases C-403/08 and C-429/08, *Premier League and Murphy*, paras. 30–31.
[140] Ibid., paras. 32 and 34. See also Football Association Premier League Ltd and Others v. QC Leisure and Others (Joined Cases C-403/08 and C-429/08) [2011] ECLI:EU: C:2011:43, Opinion of AG Kokott (3 February 2011), paras. 32–36.
[141] Joined Cases C-403/08 and C-429/08, *Premier League and Murphy*, para. 33.
[142] Ibid., para. 35.   [143] Ibid., para. 35.
[144] Ibid., para. 42. According to J. Lindholm and A. Kaburakis, 'Cases C-403/08 and C-429/08 FA Premier League Ltd and Others v. QC Leisure and Others; and Karen Murphy v. Media Protection Services Ltd, 4 Oct 2011' in J. Andersen (ed.), *Leading Cases in Sports Law* (Springer, 2013), p. 273, these price differences amount to between £500 and £1,500 per month. However, the licences have only covered personal viewing and not public viewing. According to Adrian Wood, 'The CJEU's ruling in the Premier League pub TV cases – the final whistle beckons: joined cases Football Association Premier League Ltd v. QC Leisure (C-403/08) and Murphy v. Media Protection Services Ltd (C-429/08)', *European Intellectual Property Review*, 34 (2012), 203, prices amount to £700 per month with Sky, or £800 per year with the Greek supplier.
[145] Lindholm and Kaburakis, 'Cases C-403/08 and C-429/08', 273.

in an unauthorised manner' because they breach the respective licensing agreements.[146] The licensor, FAPL, argues that these activities 'are harmful to its interests because they undermine the exclusivity of rights granted by the licence in a given territory and hence the value of those rights'.[147] FAPL was concerned that the cheapest decoder cards seller would potentially become a broadcaster at the European level,

which would result in broadcast rights in the European Union having to be granted at European level. This would lead to a significant loss in revenue for both FAPL and the broadcasters, and would thus undermine the viability of the services that they provide.[148]

Against this background, the licensor proposed bringing three test cases against suppliers of decoder cards and the Greek broadcaster, as well as licensees and operators of pubs, before the High Court of Justice of England and Wales (C-403/08).[149] In a separate proceeding, criminal actions against a local pub manager, Karen Murphy, were pursued (C-429/08).[150]

In essence, the references for preliminary ruling by the national court relate to the compatibility of 'the practice of territorially restricting access to encrypted sports broadcasts which are transmitted via satellite to various Member States' with the internal market.[151] The courts consider this issue from a 'multitude of varying perspectives, which have generated a large number of different questions'.[152] In its comprehensive 211-paragraph judgment, the Court of Justice considers its preliminary ruling in C-403/08 regarding ten questions and more than twenty sub questions regarding rules relating to the reception of encrypted broadcasts from other Member States[153] and rules relating to the use of the broadcasts once they are received[154] – dealing with fundamental freedoms, competition and intellectual property law.

Advocate General Kokott took the view that, as regards use of Greek decoder cards, the case essentially dependended on 'the application of freedom to provide services and, moreover, the question of communication to the public (Article 3 of Directive 2001/29) is of great interest and

---

[146] Joined Cases C-403/08 and C-429/08, *Premier League and Murphy*, para. 42.
[147] Ibid., para. 43.   [148] Ibid.   [149] Ibid., para. 44.   [150] Ibid., para. 50.
[151] See *AG Kokott Opinion*, para. 45.   [152] See ibid.
[153] Hereunder Directive 98/84/EC of the European Parliament and of the Council of 20 November 1998 on the legal protection of services based on, or consisting of, conditional access [1998] OJ L 320/54 and the Treaty provisions of free movement of goods and services and competition. One of the main focuses of the question that was referred, was linked to the Conditional Access Directive.
[154] Hereunder reproduction right provided for in Art. 2(a) of the Copyright Directive, exception in Art. 5(1) of the Copyright Directive to the reproduction right, 'communication to the public' within the meaning of Art. 3(1) of the Copyright Directive, and effect of the Satellite Broadcasting Directive (Question 7 in Case C-403/08).

foremost'.[155] In its judgment the Court also seems to follow this reasoning.

3.2.1.2 Free Movement and Competition Law Aspects

Under UK legislation, the use of decoder cards to receive unauthorised broadcasts can constitute an offence under the Copyright, Designs and Patents Act 1988.[156] In the national proceedings, there arose the question whether the respective UK legislation was compatible with the Treaty provisions on free movement, and the following was referred to the Court

whether, on a proper construction of Articles 34 TFEU, 36 TFEU and 56 TFEU, those articles preclude legislation of a Member State which makes it unlawful to import into and sell and use in that State foreign decoding devices which give access to an encrypted satellite broadcasting service from another Member State that includes subject-matter protected by the legislation of that first State.[157]

The CJEU observed that the free movement of services is applicable, because the decoding devices are only an instrument to receive broadcasting services.[158] It is important to recall that Article 56 TFEU does not have direct horizontal effect, i.e. confers only an obligation on the Member States. In conclusion, the Court held that Article 56 TFEU precludes national legislation that prohibits the import, sale or use of foreign decoding devices that give access to an encrypted satellite broadcast from another Member State that includes protected subject matter.[159]

Whereas the Court primarily assessed the issue at stake from a free movement perspective, the competition aspects of the case appear especially relevant in the context of this book. The Court had to consider whether

The clauses of an exclusive licence agreement concluded between a holder of intellectual property rights and a broadcaster constitute a restriction on competition prohibited by Article 101 TFEU where they oblige the broadcaster not to supply decoding devices giving access to that right holder's protected subject-matter outside the territory covered by the licence agreement concerned.[160]

The section of the judgment dealing with territorial restrictions and competition is the shortest section of the 211 paragraph-long judgment.[161] In its competition assessment, the Court mainly refers to

---

[155] *AG Kokott Opinion*, para. 47.
[156] Joined Cases C-403/08 and C-429/08, *Premier League and Murphy*, para. 52.
[157] Ibid., para. 76.   [158] Ibid., para. 84.   [159] Ibid., 3.   [160] Ibid., para. 134.
[161] S. de Vries, 'Sport, TV and IP Rights: Premier League and Karen Murphy', *Common Market Law Review*, 50 (2013), 591, 616, notes that the CJEU 'could, considering the

its analysis regarding the freedom to provide services. More specifically, regarding restrictions of this freedom, the Court assessed whether the protection of industrial and commercial property can justify the restrictions.

Two licensing relations can be differentiated in the case: first, between FAPL and the licensee for a certain territory and, secondly, between the licensee and its customers (subscribers).[162] Lindholm and Kaburakis observe that the CJEU has paid only limited attention to the terms of the consumer licence and instead focused on the underlying licensing agreement between rights holders and service providers.[163]

Notably, in paragraph 107 of its judgment, the Court recalls that intellectual property is intended to ensure protection of the right commercially to exploit the protected subject matter by the grant of licences[164] and then in the following paragraph notes that the 'specific subject matter' of intellectual property does not guarantee the opportunity to demand the highest possible remuneration.[165] Instead, such remuneration must be 'reasonable' in relation to the economic value concerned and in particular in relation to the actual or potential numbers of persons who enjoy or wish to enjoy the service.[166] In this respect, the difference from the earlier case law seems to be that it became technically feasible for rights holders to track the use of their services.[167] In the case, the Court

importance of the license agreements, have focused on Article 101 TFEU alone in this case'. On the other hand, many of the paragraphs regarding free movement are relevant in the context of the competition analysis as well.

[162] Joined Cases C-403/08 and C-429/08, *Premier League and Murphy*, paras. 32–41.

[163] See Lindholm and Kaburakis, 'Cases C-403/08 and C-429/08', 277. In the footnote they note that 'it would not have been out of character for the CJEU to take the liberty of addressing the validity and interpretation of the consumer contract, notwithstanding that is had not being asked to do so by the referring national court'.

[164] Referring to the settled case law in Joined Cases 55/80 and 57/80, *Musik-Vetrieb and K-tel* v. *GEMA*, para. 12 and Joined Cases C-92/92 and C-326/92, *Phil Collins and Others* para. 20. AG Kokott, in her opinion, underlines the importance of intellectual property protection starting her opinion by stating: 'Protecting the economic interests of authors is becoming increasingly important. Creative works must be properly remunerated'. See *AG Kokott Opinion*, para. 1.

[165] See Joined Cases C-403/08 and C-429/08, *Premier League and Murphy*, para. 108. See also R. Clark, 'Exhaustion, geographical licensing restrictions and transfer prohibitions: two surprising decisions', *Journal of Intellectual Property Law & Practice*, 8 (2013), 460, 462.

[166] See Joined Cases C-403/08 and C-429/08, *Premier League and Murphy*, para. 109. See also Case 62/79, *Coditel I*, para. 13; and Case 395/87, *Tournier*, para. 12. In the following paragraph the Court specifies remuneration for television broadcasting. D. Doukas, 'The Sky is Not the (only) Limit: Sports Broadcasting without Frontiers and the Court of Justice: Comment on Murphy', *European Law Review*, 37 (2012), 605, 612 suggests that this narrows down the core of copyright.

[167] See Joined Cases C-403/08 and C-429/08, *Premier League and Murphy*, para. 133. See also B. Batchelor and L. Montani, 'Exhaustion, essential subject matter and other CJEU

concludes that the premium paid by broadcasters to rights holders in order to be granted absolute territorial exclusivity results in partitioning and that such an artificial price difference between the partitioned national markets is irreconcilable with the completion of the internal market.[168]

In their action, the plaintiffs relied on the earlier case law of the Court of Justice in *Coditel I*, in which it was held that:

> the rules of the Treaty cannot in principle constitute an obstacle to the geographical limits which the parties to a contract of assignment have agreed upon in order to protect the author and his assigns in this regard. The mere fact that those geographical limits may coincide with national frontiers does not point to a different solution in a situation where television is organized in the Member States largely on the basis of legal broadcasting monopolies, which indicates that a limitation other than the geographical field of application of an assignment is often impracticable.[169]

In *Premier League and Murphy*, the Court disregarded this objection in line with the Opinion of AG Kokott because of the different context of the case in hand[170] and the development of EU legal instruments aimed at the transition from a national to a 'single programme production and distribution market'[171] that has been going on in the meantime. The Court deemed that the context of *Premier League and Murphy* was not comparable to the context in *Coditel I*.[172] The latter related to the unauthorised cross-border cable retransmission, where the relevant communication took place in the country of origin and no remuneration was paid.[173] In the present case, on the other hand, the communication to the public

---

judicial tools to update copyright for an online economy', *Journal of Intellectual Property Law & Practice*, 10 (2005), 591, 597. However, for a more critical stance, see Doukas, 'The Sky is not the (only) limit',611.

[168] See Joined Cases C-403/08 and C-429/08, *Premier League and Murphy*, para. 115.

[169] Case 62/79, *Coditel I*, para. 16.

[170] See Joined Cases C-403/08 and C-429/08, *Premier League and Murphy*, para. 119.

[171] Ibid., para. 121. The Court makes specific reference to the Council Directive 89/552/EEC of 3 October 1989 on the coordination of certain provisions laid down by Law, Regulation or Administrative Action in Member States concerning the pursuit of television broadcasting activities [1989] OJ L298/23, the predecessor of the Audiovisual Media Services Directive (2010/13/EU), and the SatCab Directive (93/83/EEC).

[172] In line with AG Kokott: see *AG Kokott Opinion*, paras. 193–199. Notably AG Kokott refers to Case 62/79, *Coditel I*, underlining 'at the time', 'From the perspective of the 1970s' and 'At that time' – implying that *Coditel I* has to be seen in its distinct historical context, which supposedly is different from the one in the present case. See also Doukas, 'The Sky is not the (only) limit', 625, who argues that *Coditel I* is reaffirmed in the case, but see Batchelor and Jenkins, 'FA Premier League: the broader implications for copyright licensing', 158, who argue that *Coditel I* was 'heavily distinguished' from the present proceedings.

[173] Joined Cases C-403/08 and C-429/08, *Premier League and Murphy*, para. 119.

took place in the country of origin, while having an authorisation and paying remuneration.[174] No piracy or unauthorised decoding of the signals took place. Thus, the Court notes differences when it comes to both remuneration and technology. In her Opinion AG Kokott comments that '[r]ather, the direct aim of partitioning the markets is to optimise exploitation of the same work within the different market segments'.[175]

As regards the licensing agreements, the Court recalls that exclusive agreements are not *per se* contrary to Article 101(1) TFEU.[176] However, it is also points out that

(. . .) in accordance with the Court's case-law, an agreement which might tend to restore the divisions between national markets is liable to frustrate the Treaty's objective of achieving the integration of those markets through the establishment of a single market. Thus, agreements which are aimed at partitioning national markets according to national borders or make the interpenetration of national markets more difficult must be regarded, in principle, as agreements whose object is to restrict competition within the meaning of Article 101(1) TFEU (...).[177]

In the present case, the contractual obligations on the licensees, namely to ensure compliance with territorial limitations, were deemed to grant the licensees (broadcasters) absolute territorial exclusivity in their respective territories, thus eliminating all competition between them.[178] After a brief reference and the negation of the exemption in Article 101(3) TFEU, the Court held that

clauses of an exclusive licence agreement concluded between a holder of intellectual property rights and a broadcaster constitute a restriction on competition prohibited by Article 101 TFEU where they oblige the broadcaster not to supply decoding devices enabling access to that right holder's protected subject-matter with a view to their use outside the territory covered by that licence agreement.[179]

In other words, rights holders may delineate the market geographically but not prohibit licensees from supplying decoders outside the territory of the licence agreement.[180]

---

[174] See ibid., para. 120.   [175] *AG Kokott Opinion*, para. 197.

[176] Joined Cases C-403/08 and C-429/08, *Premier League and Murphy*, para. 137 citing Case 262/81, *Coditel II*, para. 15.

[177] Ibid., para. 139.

[178] See Joined Cases C-403/08 and C-429/08, *Premier League and Murphy*, paras. 141–142.

[179] See ibid., para. 146 and at 4.

[180] See also de Vries, 'Sport, TV and IP rights', 617; P. I. Colomo, 'The Commission Investigation into Pay TV Services: Open Questions', *Journal of European Competition Law & Practice*, 5 (2014), 531, 534; and T. Riis and J. Schovsbo, 'Den grænseløse onlinebruger – geografisk opdeling af markedet for online- og streamingtjenester' in *Liber Amicorum Jan Rosén* (eddy.se, 2016), p. 668.

3.2.1.3 (Absolute) Territorial Exclusivity after Premier League and Murphy

Generally, it has been noted that the Court's findings in *Premier League and Murphy* have proved difficult to interpret. Initially, the Court's considerations regarding free movement and copyright have mainly grasped the attention of legal scholars, whereas the judgment has later been considered especially in relation to its competition aspects.[181] According to some scholars, the Court could have just focused on the competition aspects instead of a full approach also taking into account free movement . De Vries hypothesises that the Court might be sending a message about how competition law is concerned with market integration, as well as the growing importance of consumer welfare because of the role that competition rules play in the creation of the internal market.[182] We should, however, not forget that the application of EU competition law arguably generally leads to a similar result as the free movement route.[183] Also, AG Kokott confirms that 'the examination of freedom to provide services confirms this conclusion since conflicting assessments of the fundamental freedoms and competition law are to be avoided in principle'.[184] It is also noteworthy that the Court, while basing its reasoning on freedom of movement of services, rather handles it as it would do freedom of movement of goods.[185] The approach by AG Kokott has been described as 'being extremely pro-consumer, and must be viewed in the light of criticism from consumer groups who argue that the copyright *acquis* does not satisfactorily address consumer rights'.[186]

---

[181] See, e.g., E. Szyszczak, 'Current Intelligence Karen Murphy: Decoding Licences and Territorial Exclusivity', *Journal of European Competition Law & Practice* [2011] 1, 2, who comments that '[the] focus on the Internal Market provisions is remarkable given that the crux of disputees is essentially a horizontal issue of EU law between non-State (private) parties'.

[182] de Vries, 'Sport, TV and IP rights', 617.

[183] See, e.g., earlier case law on exhaustion, which at times is decided under competition law and at times under freedom of movement.

[184] *AG Kokott Opinion*, para. 249.

[185] To this extent, see Dreier's interesting editorial, in which he looks at the Court's case law in *Premier League and Murphy* and *UsedSoft*. In the latter, the Court relied on the free movement of goods, despite no physical copies were involved. He argues that in *UsedSoft* the result of exhaustion could only be achieved on the basis of freedom of movement of goods. For the present case he supposes that 'a similar outcome-oriented line of argumentation can be observed in Murphy, where the CJEU tried to overcome all potentially opposing legal hurdles – rules on conditional access, opposing copyrights – in order to enforce the freedom of movement of services as regards encrypted satellite signals within the EU.' see: T. Dreier, 'Online and Its Effect on the "Goods" Versus "Services" Distinction', *International Review of Intellectual Property and Competition Law* 44 (2013), 137, 138. See also Clark, 'Exhaustion, geographical licensing restrictions and transfer prohibitions', 463f.

[186] Clark, 'Exhaustion, geographical licensing restrictions and transfer prohibitions', 463, referring to *AG Kokott Opinion*, paras. 183–187.

Many commentators in the immediate aftermath agreed that the decision is likely to 'reshape broadcast licensing practices in Europe within and beyond sports',[187] because the territorial practice is fundamental to the current licensing arrangements. De Vries, on the other hand, concludes that 'FAPL may still license to just one licensee per member state, but it may not prohibit licensee from supplying decoder devices outside its own territory'.[188] On a broader scale for audiovisual services, he deems 'it is clear that these services can no longer be provided through a system of absolute territorial protection.'[189] Wood comments that the judgment:

offer[s] a potential skeletal framework within which a less rigid territorially based system of copyright licensing could evolve across the European Union, without undermining drastically the potential for right holders to achieve an appropriate level of remuneration.[190]

Lindholm and Kaburakis assess its potential impact and responses, in differentiating between larger and smaller sport leagues.[191] As a potential response, they point towards circumvention of the restrictive effects of the case by self-broadcasting.[192] A second alternative would be that 'major media conglomerates would bid for EU-wide rights',[193] which, however, could be met by competition concerns. Another alternative, according to them, is the business model proposed by the Court of Justice, in which rights holders 'should conduct auctions where broadcasters bid for the right to broadcast and remuneration is based on actual and potential viewers'.[194] In this regard they note the potential difficulty to find competitive buyers for an exclusive pan-European broadcasting licence.[195] Lindholm and Kaburakis suggest that the only permitted division of broadcasting rights given by the Court in *Premier League and Murphy* is by language version.[196] They conclude that most feasible future business models would be to consumers' detriment in the long term, because the judgment incentivises rightholders to 'adapt more restrictive business practices'.[197]

---

[187] Lindholm and Kaburakis, 'Cases C-403/08 and C-429/08', 281. See also Doukas, 'The Sky is not the (only) limit', 605 and 623; Clark, 'Exhaustion, geographical licensing restrictions and transfer prohibitions', 460.

[188] de Vries, 'Sport, TV and IP rights', 621 with further sources in Dutch.   [189] Ibid.

[190] Wood, 'The CJEU's ruling in the Premier League pub TV cases', 203.

[191] Lindholm and Kaburakis, 'Cases C-403/08 and C-429/08', 281.

[192] Ibid., 281; also Wood, 'The CJEU's ruling in the Premier League pub TV cases', 207.

[193] Lindholm and Kaburakis, 'Cases C-403/08 and C-429/08', 282.

[194] Ibid., 283; also Wood, 'The CJEU's ruling in the Premier League pub TV cases', 207.

[195] Lindholm and Kaburakis, 'Cases C-403/08 and C-429/08', 283.

[196] Ibid. See, similarly, Doukas, 'The Sky is not the (only) limit' 623.

[197] Lindholm and Kaburakis, 'Cases C-403/08 and C-429/08', 284. See also, to some extent, Doukas. 'The Sky is not the (only) limit', 623.

Several commentators have criticised the judgment for not taking sufficient consideration of the specifics of the subject matter: Riis and Schovsbo note that, to their surprise, the CJEU did not put more emphasis on the protection of copyright's 'specific character' ('specific subject-matter'), which, in the earlier case law of the CJEU, has given copyright rights holders broader room for operation.[198] On the other hand, as Batchelor and Montani note, the Court applied the 'essential subject-matter doctrine' and assessed whether the restriction was permissible.[199] Indeed, the Court in *Premier League and Murphy* uses the same notion of 'specific subject matter' as in earlier case law.[200] Lindholm and Kaburakis, on the other hand, note that while the CJEU did not consider 'whether the characteristics of sports could warrant the measures falling outside of Article 101 TFEU', it did 'address sport's specificity with regards to the application of free movement of services'.[201] More broadly, both the Opinion of the Advocate General and the judgment of the CJEU are criticised for their brevity on whether Article 101(3) TFEU can justify the agreements.[202] At the same time, it is also apparent from AG Kokott's

---

[198] See Riis and Schovsbo, 'Den grænseløse onlinebruger', 669, commenting in the accompanying footnote that the Commission still refers to Case 262/81, *Coditel II* in its Commission, 'Guidelines on the application of Article 101 of the Treaty on the Functioning of the European Union to technology transfer agreements' point 50, as well as to the 'specificities of the work and the way in which it is exploited' and the particular issues in the licensing of rental rights and public performance rights protected by copyright, in particular for films or music. As regards the concept of the 'specific character of copyright', Schovsbo, 'The Necessity to collectivize copyright – and dangers thereof', p. 18 remarks that it is '[n]ot only (. . .) a somewhat unclear concept (to say the very least) but even if such "characters" could be identified one would still have to make a separate assessment of the business of the collecting society'. On the notion of 'specific subject-matter', see also Case 78/70, *Deutsche Grammophon*, para. 11; M. van Eechoud and others, *Harmonizing European Copyright Law, The Challenges of Better Lawmaking*, vol. 19 Information Law Series (P. Bernt Hugenholtz (ed.), Wolters Kluwer, 2009), p. 310.

[199] See Batchelor and Montani, 'Exhaustion, essential subject matter and other CJEU judicial tools to update copyright for an online economy', 597 with reference to the judgment in paras. 137–138 and 104–105. See also Doukas, 'The Sky is not the (only) limit', 610 ff, who remarks that '[t]he ruling signifies a revival of the "specific subject-matter" test, which has been used to limit the circumstances in which the exercise of intellectual property rights can justify restrictions on free movement' and, similarly, Wood, 'The CJEU's ruling in the Premier League pub TV cases', 205.

[200] See Joined Cases, C-403/08 and C-429/08 *Premier League and Murphy*, paras. 106–108. Cf. Case 78/70, *Deutsche Grammophon*, para. 11: 'specific subject-matter of such property'.

[201] Lindholm and Kaburakis, 'Cases C-403/08 and C-429/08', 279. Notably, this has apparently only been the second reference to the specifics since its introduction in Art. 165(1) TFEU, which is, however, deemed by the authors to be largely symbolic. This is also noted by de Vries, 'Sport, TV and IP rights', 592. See also *AG Kokott Opinion*, para. 46.

[202] de Vries, 'Sport, TV and IP rights', 618.

Opinion that 'similar considerations should apply [regarding Article 101(3) TFEU] as in the examination of whether a restriction of freedom to provide services is justified'.[203]

The relationship of the CJEU's decision in *Premier League and Murphy* to the Court's previous decisions is rather intriguing and has attracted the interest of several scholars. Colomo comments that it is not easy to interpret, specifically in relation to the *Coditel II* decision from 1982.[204] In contrast to its findings in the present case, in *Coditel II* the CJEU held that an exclusive territorial licence does not, as such, restrict competition. Thus, in essence, this means that, for almost thirty years, despite the effect of portioning the internal market, exclusive territorial licences did not infringe Article 101 TFEU. Hugenholtz in this context underlines that the 'Court expressly rejected the argument of price discrimination – i.e. the possibility of differentiating consumer prices – as a valid justification for segmenting markets inside the EU'.[205] *Premier League and Murphy* thus 'suggests that the court is not afraid to re-cast legislation and discard long held orthodoxies to achieve a digital single market'.[206] Martin-Prat calls it an intervention 'with the clear objective of removing obstacles to the internal market, even when required to bend some copyright principles', in which '[t]he CJEU occasionally comes very close to establishing new rules'.[207] In trying to find a balance between territorial exploitation 'and the freedom to provide and receive services across borders', the Court of Justice is, according to Martin-Prat, 'actively shaping EU copyright rules to inject a degree of internal market friendliness where the legislator – or the market – may have failed to do so'.[208] De Vries, on the other hand, points towards 'the consistency in the Court's approach since *Consten and Grundig* to territorial restrictions and market integration'.[209]

---

[203] *AG Kokott Opinion*, para. 250.

[204] P. I. Colomo, 'Copyright reform through competition law? The Commission's statement of objections in the pay TV investigation' (*Chillin'Competition*, 24 July 2015): https://chillincompetition.com/2015/07/24/copyright-reform-through-competition-law-the-commissions-statement-of-objections-in-the-pay-tv-investigation/

[205] P. Bernt Hugenholtz, 'Harmonisation or Unification of European Union Copyright Law', *Monash University Law Review*, 38 (2012), 4, 12, referring to Joined Cases C-403/08 and C-429/08, *Premier League and Murphy*, para. 115.

[206] Batchelor and Montani, 'Exhaustion, essential subject matter and other CJEU judicial tools to update copyright for an online economy', 592, also referring to Case C-128/11, *UsedSoft GmbH* v. *Oracle International Corp.* [2012] ECLI:EU:C:2012:407.

[207] M. Martin-Prat, 'The Future of Copyright in Europe', *Columbia Journal of Law & the Arts*, 38 (2014), 29, 35, also referring to Case C-128/11, *UsedSoft*.

[208] Martin-Prat, 'The Future of Copyright in Europe', 36.

[209] de Vries, 'Sport, TV and IP rights', 622.

Riis and Schovsbo note, as do several others, that the findings in the case correlate to the general principle of competition law in which agreements containing territorial delineations may contain restrictions on 'active sales' but not on 'passive sales'.[210] The Commission's Guidelines on Vertical Restraints define 'active sales' as

actively approaching individual customers by for instance direct mail, including the sending of unsolicited e-mails, or visits; or actively approaching a specific customer group or customers in a specific territory through advertisement in media, on the internet or other promotions specifically targeted at that customer group or targeted at customers in that territory. Advertisement or promotion that is only attractive for the buyer if it (also) reaches a specific group of customers or customers in a specific territory, is considered active selling to that customer group or customers in that territory.[211]

'Passive sales', on the other hand, relates to

responding to *unsolicited requests from individual customers* including delivery of goods or services to such customers. General advertising or promotion that reaches customers in other distributors' (exclusive) territories or customer groups but which is a reasonable way to reach customers outside those territories or customer groups, for instance to reach customers in one's own territory, are considered passive selling. General advertising or promotion is considered a reasonable way to reach such customers if it would be attractive for the buyer to undertake these investments also if they would not reach customers in other distributors' (exclusive) territories or customer groups.[212]

Another relevant question is how broadly or narrowly the Court's findings apply: do the findings apply to other forms of dissemination, especially in an online context? Do the findings apply to other subject matters, especially copyright-protected works? In an online exploitation of works, the 'country of origin' principle would not apply.[213] In other

---

[210] See Riis and Schovsbo, 'Den grænseløse onlinebruger', 668. See also: M. von Albrecht, A. Mutschler-Siebert and T. Bosch, 'Die Murphy-Entscheidung und ihre Auswirkungen auf Sport- und Filmlizenzen im Online-Bereich, Die exklusive territoriale Rechtevergabe ist kein Modell der Vergangenheit!', *Zeitschrift für Urheber- und Medienrecht* [2012] 93, 99; Doukas, 'The Sky is not the (only) limit', 616.

[211] Commission, 'Guidelines on Vertical Restraints', Recital 51.

[212] Ibid., Recital 51 (emphasis added).

[213] See, e.g., Batchelor and Montani, 'Exhaustion, essential subject matter and other CJEU judicial tools to update copyright for an online economy', 598. See also von Albrecht, Mutschler-Siebert and Bosch, 'Die Murphy-Entscheidung', 92 regarding Bogsch theory. See Colomo, 'Copyright Licensing and the EU Digital Single Market Strategy', 7, however noting 'the reality that emerged in the years that followed the adoption of the [SatCab] Directive', where rights holders rely on encryption technologies and license content to a local broadcaster in each Member State. See also P. Torremans, 'The Future Implications of the UsedSoft Decision' CREATe Working Paper 2014/2

words, a licensee (the online service provider) would need to clear rights for all territories, despite the ban of the contractual provision in the licensing agreement. As Batchelor and Montani note, this seems also to be confirmed in the more recent case law of the Court in *OSA*, in which it noted that:

As regards the question whether such legislation goes beyond what is necessary in order to attain the objective of protecting intellectual property rights, it must be pointed out that (...) legislation such as that at issue in the main proceedings forms part of a context of territory-based copyright protection.[214]

Batchelor and Montani conclude: '[w]hether the Premier League rule can be read beyond satellite to internet or other forms of dissemination remains, therefore, an open question'.[215] Let us come back to that assessment in the section that follows.

The second aspect that seems worth considering is the following: in the case, the Court deemed the underlying football matches not worthy of copyright protection. Thus, the case does not relate to copyright law but merely related subject matter. The question at hand is whether the outcome of the case would be different if it concerned a copyright-protected subject matter. This view is supported by Doukas as regards the full copyright protection argument, and in his eyes is supported by the fact that the Court leaves *Coditel I* intact.[216] Wood, on the other hand, argues that the

core principles in the judgment should be transferable to many other forms of exclusive licence agreements in which absolute territorial restrictions feature, such as licences to receive satellite pay-TV services and film distribution agreements.[217]

Batchelor and Montani again comment that it remains open as to what extent the findings also apply to other copyright-protected subject

---

(February 2014), 2: www.create.ac.uk/publications/wp000012 who remarks: '[a]dmittedly, the decoder cases were potentially only about hard copies'.

[214] Case C-351/12, *OSA*, para. 73; See also Batchelor and Montani, 'Exhaustion, essential subject matter and other CJEU judicial tools to update copyright for an online economy', 598.

[215] Batchelor and Montani, 'Exhaustion, essential subject matter and other CJEU judicial tools to update copyright for an online economy', 598. On the other hand, Doukas, 'The Sky is not the (only) limit', 612 argues that 'the Court's reasoning seems to be heavily informed by the central role of the country of origin (...) principle (...)'. See also Colomo, 'Copyright Licensing and the EU Digital Single Market Strategy', 8, who notes: '[SatCab] seems to have proved determinant in its outcome'.

[216] See Doukas, 'The Sky is not the (only) limit', 625. See also Szyszczak, 'Current Intelligence Karen Murphy'.

[217] Wood, 'The CJEU's ruling in the Premier League pub TV cases', 207.

matter.[218] However, one should not forget that in *Premier League and Murphy*, too, some copyright-protected subject matter was contained in the broadcasts (e.g., the opening sequence and other graphics).[219] As I will also discuss below in connection with the pay-TV investigation, it appears that the Court's findings are indeed relevant beyond broadcasts and football matches.

Yet another aspect is that the Court in *Premier League and Murphy* relates to additional obligations in the licensing agreements, namely those regarding the sale of (physical) decoder devices. The question is whether this could be translated into the context of exploitation on the Internet and obligations in the licensing agreements, in which service providers are obliged to geo-block access.[220] Doukas argues that the geo-blocking is different from the territorial exclusivity in *Premier League and Murphy*, in that the geo-blocking practice

> does not constitute an additional obligation but an inherent component of the award of territorially exclusive online licences and the determination of remuneration, which would otherwise be impossible owing to worldwide internet access.[221]

Lindholm and Kaburakis, on the other hand, argue that 'contractual obligations forcing broadcasters to employ geo-blocking (...) are rendered unlawful according to Murphy since they serve to setup the artificial trade barriers and national borders the EU abolished'.[222] On the background that geo-blocking effectively serves the same purpose as the use of physical decoders and that both are governed by the contractual arrangements between rights holders and service providers, a differentiation seems unconvincing.[223] This, it seems, is also the rationale around which the Commission builds its pay-TV proceedings. In conclusion, the key question seems to be how far reaching *Premier League and Murphy* is to be interpreted, where the Court has left us with open questions.[224] The following section will shed some light on the European Commission's view.

---

[218] Batchelor and Montani, 'Exhaustion, essential subject matter and other CJEU judicial tools to update copyright for an online economy', 598.

[219] See Joined Cases C-403/08 and C-429/08, *Premier League and Murphy*, para. 149.

[220] See also Szyszczak, 'Current Intelligence Karen Murphy', 5.

[221] Doukas, 'The Sky is not the (only) limit', 625.

[222] See Lindholm and Kaburakis, 'Cases C-403/08 and C-429/08', 284.

[223] See also Wood, 'The CJEU's ruling in the Premier League pub TV cases', 207.

[224] Or as Doukas, 'The Sky is not the (only) limit', 623, puts it: 'The Court of Justice avoided drawing any parallels with other audiovisual media services that are characterised by a similar partitioning of the internal market into distinct national markets, and especially the distribution of audiovisual works, such as computer software, musical works, e-books or films, over the internet'.

3.2.2   Application of Premier League and Murphy

3.2.2.1 Background of the Pay-TV Investigation

The territorial delineation of the European content market (and geo-blocking as an enforcement mechanism), can be traced back to clauses in the bilateral contractual arrangements between rights holders and service providers. These licensing contracts and territorial restrictions regarding audiovisual content have come under scrutiny by the European competition authority. Following a fact-finding investigation in 2012,[225] in January 2014, the DG Competition announced the opening of formal antitrust proceedings 'to examine certain provisions in licensing agreements between several major US film studios[226] (...) and the largest European pay-TV broadcasters'.[227] In particular, the Commission is interested in investigating whether provisions in the licensing agreements between rights holders and broadcasters

prevent broadcasters from providing their services across borders, for example by refusing potential subscribers from other Member States or blocking cross-border access to their services.[228]

The proceedings stand in direct relationship to the previous case law of the Court of Justice in *Premier League and Murphy*. In the background to the investigation, the Commission points explicitly to the Court's case law. Thus, Colomo argues that the sector inquiry 'can be seen as an attempt by the Commission to explore the outer boundaries of Murphy'.[229] The Commission says that the proceedings

will examine whether provisions of licensing arrangements for broadcasting by satellite or through online streaming between US film studios and the major European broadcasters, which grant to the latter "absolute territorial protection", constitute an infringement of EU antitrust rules that prohibit anticompetitive agreements.[230]

---

[225] See Commission, 'Antitrust: Commission investigates restrictions affecting cross border provision of pay TV services' (Press release) IP/14/15, Brussels, 13 January 2014.

[226] Namely Twentieth Century Fox, Warner Bros., Sony Pictures, NBC Universal and Paramount Pictures. On 23 July 2015, the Commission extended the ongoing proceedings to The Walt Disney Company.

[227] See Commission, 'Antitrust: Commission investigates restrictions affecting cross border provision of pay TV services'.

[228] Ibid.

[229] Colomo, 'The Commission Investigation into Pay TV Services: Open Questions', 532 and 'Copyright Licensing and the EU Digital Single Market Strategy', 10.

[230] See Commission, 'Antitrust: Commission investigates restrictions affecting cross border provision of pay TV services'.

In July 2015, the Commission adopted a Statement of Objections (SO) on the cross-border provision of pay-TV services available in the UK and Ireland. Regarding the licensing agreement between Paramount and Sky UK, the Commission noted two types of clauses:[231] the first set of contractual obligations prohibits or limits the licensee, Sky UK, 'from making its retail pay-TV services available in response to unsolicited requests from consumers residing or located' outside the licensed territory[232] – that is to say, a clause in the licensing agreement that requires the licensee to block passive sales from consumers abroad, i.e. consumers located in a Member State in which the licensee is not actively promoting its services. The second set of contractual obligations requires the licensor, Paramount, to prohibit or limit broadcasters located outside the licensed territory of the licensee, Sky, from 'making their retail pay-TV services available in response to unsolicited requests from consumers residing' in the licensed territory.[233]

The Commission preliminarily concluded that the conduct of the licensor in the specific case of Paramount constituted an infringement of Article 101(1) TFEU because the objective of the clauses was the restriction of competition and there existed 'no circumstances falling within the economic and legal context of the clauses that would justify the finding that they are not liable to impair competition'.[234] Effectively, according to the Commission, the relevant provisions in the bilateral agreements grant absolute territorial exclusivity to the respective broadcasters. Finally, the clauses, according to the preliminary conclusion, do not satisfy the four conditions laid out in Article 101(3) TFEU and therefore cannot benefit from an exemption from Article 101(1) TFEU.[235]

The concerned parties were invited to present justifications for their agreements and a hearing behind closed doors took place in January 2016. While Paramount disagreed with the Commission's concerns, on 14 April 2016 it nonetheless offered several commitments to meet the concerns. On 22 April 2016, the European Commission published the proposed commitments together with a market test notice and an accompanying press release. The key elements of the commitment are summarised as follows:[236]

---

[231] The proceedings regarding the other parties are ongoing: see *Cross-border access to pay-TV* (Case AT.40023) Communication from the Commission published pursuant to Article 27(4) of Council Regulation (EC) No 1/2003 (2016/C 141/07) [2016] OJ C141/13, para. 6.
[232] See ibid., para. 4.   [233] See ibid.   [234] See ibid., para. 5.   [235] See ibid.
[236] See ibid., para. 7(a).

Paramount should not enter into, renew or extend a Pay-TV Output Licence Agreement (1) that, with respect to any territory in the EEA, (re)introduces any Additional Obligations. These are defined as:

– contractual obligations of the type identified in the SO preventing or limiting a Broadcaster from responding to unsolicited requests from consumers residing and located in the European Economic Area but outside of such Broadcaster's licensed territory ('Broadcaster Obligation'),
– contractual obligations of the type identified in the SO requiring Paramount to prohibit or limit Broadcasters located within the European Economic Area but outside a Broadcaster's licensed territory from responding to unsolicited requests from consumers residing and located inside such Broadcaster's licensed territory ('Paramount Obligation').

The Commission invited third parties to submit their comments on the proposed commitments within a month of the Communication. On 26 July 2016, the Commission accepted the offered commitments, which will be in force for five years and apply to both linear pay-TV services and subscription video-on-demand services.[237] Notably, the commitments do not imply an admission of the alleged infringements of Article 101(1) TFEU. In January 2018, the Commission closed the antitrust proceedings against Paramount concerning cross-border access to pay-TV in France, Spain, Germany and Italy, while simultaneously extending the open proceedings against NBC Universal to its subsidiary, given changes in its corporate structure.

3.2.2.2 Implications of the Investigation

Before the specific proceedings regarding UK broadcaster Sky, the European Commission had already devoted scrutiny to the licensing agreements between the major US film studios and major European broadcasters in France, Italy, Germany and Spain, in which it continued to examine cross-border access to the respective pay-TV services.[238] Several proceedings are ongoing and, at the time of writing, it is unclear how the cases will develop. Thus, the following careful discussion can provide only some limited insights based on general observations.

It has been noted that Paramount in its commitments has effectively offered to the Commission that it will cease its geo-blocking practice

---

[237] See ibid., paras. 8 and 9. Commission, 'Antitrust: Commission accepts commitments by Paramount on cross-border pay-TV services' (Press release) IP/16/2645, Brussels, 26 July 2016; *Commission Decision Paramount* (Case AT.40023) Commission Decision of 26 July 2016 notified under C(2016) 4740 final.
[238] See Commission, 'Antitrust: Commission investigates restrictions affecting cross border provision of pay TV services'.

through licensing agreements.[239] In this context, two aspects seem relevant to discuss: first, provided that the practice in the licensing agreements is ceased, what this implies for cross-border access to content. Secondly, it is interesting to ask whether or how the Commitments might influence other ongoing proceedings.

Before assessing these two aspects, clarification of the proceedings by current Commissioner for Competition, Margrethe Vestager, might come handy: she clarifies that the Commission is not questioning territorial exclusivity, i.e. 'the studios' ability to grant broadcasters the exclusive rights to broadcast content in a certain territory only',[240] as such. Instead, the focus is on the absolute territorial protection granted by contractual restrictions in the licensing agreements preventing licensees from supplying passive sales.[241] On the one hand, this seems reasonable against the background of territoriality in copyright (as well as contractual freedom and exclusive rights as such) and seems in line with the Court's considerations in *Premier League and Murphy*. On the other hand, the distinction offered is not very precise.

Now let me turn towards the first question: what could the cessation of the alleged anti-competitive clauses result in? The Commission argues that without contractual restrictions in the licensing agreements, the broadcasters would be 'free to decide on commercial grounds whether to sell pay-TV services to such consumers, taking into account the regulatory framework'.[242] In other words, the broadcasters would not 'be contractually prevented from responding to unsolicited requests coming from consumers from other countries'.[243] Mazziotti notes that if passive sales requests were to be excluded from the scope of territorial exclusivity, 'online content deliveries based on national exploitation, especially in the audio-visual and sports sectors, might easily end up being eroded, with a subsequent re-definition and re-structuring of such markets'.[244] The Commission, however, also acknowledges that contractual terms are not the only restriction for licensees in providing their services to consumers from other Member States. Regarding the relevant national

---

[239] See E. Rosati, 'Geoblocking: is the end in sight through ... competition law? Possibly not' (*IPKat*, 23 April 2016): http://ipkitten.blogspot.dk/2016/04/geoblocking-is-end-in-sight-through.html

[240] EU Commissioner for Competition Margrethe Vestager, 'Intellectual property and competition' (19th IBA Competition Conference, Florence, 11 September 2015): http://ec.europa.eu/commission/2014-2019/vestager/announcements/intellectual-property-and-competition_en.

[241] See ibid.   [242] Ibid.

[243] Ibid., pointing towards this aspect twice in a similar wording.

[244] G. Mazziotti, 'Is Geo-blocking a Real Cause for Concern?', *European Intellectual Property Review*, 38 (2016), 365, 371.

copyright laws, Commissioner Vestager continues that '[t]hese aspects may need to be tackled by changes to copyright rules, for example as part of the copyright initiatives included in the Commission's Digital Single Market Strategy'.[245] Thus, as Lamadrid points out:

even if all geo-blocking clauses were suppressed, the 'passive sales' that the Commission would like to see would not exist, because they would still be precluded by the regulatory framework (which in the online world grants copyright holders the right to authorize or prohibit communications to the public in every territory of broadcast.[246]

Cole also puts the investigation into the context of the recently approved merger proceedings regarding a Title III licensing hub joint venture between the British, German and Swedish CMOs. With the approval in the merger proceedings, she argues

[the decision] implicitly accepts that exclusive territorial licences are not by object anticompetitive, and that joint licensing is an appropriate mechanism to secure the multijurisdictional licences necessary for pan-European streaming (at least for music).[247]

This, she argues, constitutes a different route than the Commission's import of the '"passive" supply concept for the Vertical Block Exemption Regulation and Technology Transfer Block Exemption Regulation'.[248] There are also several differences in the scope of the CJEU's case law and the pay-TV competition proceedings: in *Premier League and Murphy*, the Court of Justice did not question the grant of exclusive (territorial) licences as such but rather the additional obligation on the broadcasters not to supply decoding devices.[249] The proceedings by DG Competition, on the other hand, while again not questioning the grant of exclusive licences as such, relate to direct access by consumers and not additional restrictions such as a ban on sales of decoders in certain countries.[250] Colomo remarks that this view of the Commission in the proceedings 'comes dangerously close to saying that the exhaustion doctrine applies to broadcasts'.[251] According to him, the Commission's view is incompatible

---

[245] See M. Vestager, 'Intellectual property and competition'.
[246] A. Lamadrid, 'Breaking news: Pay-TV investigation- Paramount offers commitments' (*Chillin'Competition*, 22 April 2016): https://chillingcompetition.com/2016/04/22/break ing-news-pay-tv-investigation-paramount-offers-commitments/
[247] M. Cole, 'PRSfM/STIM/GEMA/JV: Multijurisdictional Licencing for Music Streaming', *Journal of European Competition Law & Practice*, 7 (2016), 257, 258.
[248] Ibid.
[249] Joined Cases C-403/08 and C-429/08, *Premier League and Murphy*, para. 141.
[250] See Mazziotti, 'Is geo-blocking a real cause for concern?', 372.
[251] P. I. Colomo, 'Copyright reform through competition law? The Commission's statement of objections in the pay TV investigation' (*Chillin'Competition*, 24 July 2015):

with Article 3 of the InfoSoc Directive.[252] Given the delimitation of this book, this is not the place to go into depth regarding the application of the exhaustion doctrine to copyright in a digital setting. *UsedSoft*, decided by the Court just a little more than half a year after *Premier League and Murphy*, applied the exhaustion doctrine to downloaded computer software.[253] The Court of Justice has yet to clarify, whether, against the indication in Recital 29 of Directive 2001/29/EU, exhaustion applies to the harmonised rights in the digital context, too.[254] In *Premier League and Murphy*, the Court of Justice refrained from providing clarification on this issue despite German AG Kokott's call to

examine carefully whether the principle of exhaustion applies *mutatis mutandis* in the present context, that is to say, whether the specific subject matter of the rights in question requires that the internal market be partitioned.[255]

In her opinion of 3 February 2011, she held that:

in the case of products offered which, as in the main proceedings, are based on conditional access or which are downloaded only from the internet, a market delimitation can be achieved much more effectively than in the case of physical goods such as books or CDs. The latter can be traded as a result of exhaustion in the internal market. For consumers, such barriers create unnecessary incentives to procure the corresponding goods illegally, that is to say, in particular without any remuneration for the rights-holder.[256]

Batchelor and Jenkins argue nonetheless that the Court in *Premier League and Murphy* 'appears to be seeking to develop a doctrine

---

https://chillingcompetition.com/2015/07/24/copyright-reform-through-competi
tion-law-the-commissions- statement-of-objections-in-the-pay-tv-investigation/

[252] Directive 2001/29/EC of the European Parliament and of the Council of 22 May 2001 on the harmonisation of certain aspects of copyright and related rights in the information society [2001] OJ L167/10–19.

[253] Joined Cases C-403/08 and C-429/08, *Premier League and Murphy* were decided on 4 October 2011; Case C-128/11, *UsedSoft* on 3 July 2012. See, e.g., Torremans, 'The Future Implications of the Usedsoft Decision'; O.-A. Rognstad, 'Legally Flawed but Politically Sound? Digital Exhaustion of Copyright in Europe after UsedSoft', *Oslo Law Review*, 3 (2014), 1; O.-A. Rognstad, 'The CJEU's Recent Findings on Digital Exhaustion and Linking and their Impact on Nordic Copyright Law', *Nordiskt Immateriellt Rättskydd* [2015], 624.

[254] Recital 29 of the InfoSoc Directive makes clear that '[t]he question of exhaustion does not arise in the case of services and on-line services in particular'.

[255] *AG Kokott Opinion*, para. 188. Batchelor and Jenkins, 'FA Premier League', 159–60 note that '[t]he Court did not need to reach a view on the issue of copyright because, on the facts, no infringement arose in the broadcast from Greece to the UK pub. This is in contrast to the Court's Advocate General (who reached a different conclusion on copyright). Thus, it was necessary for her (but not for the Court) to consider further whether the doctrine of exhaustion of rights applied to the copyright in question'. See also Doukas, 'The Sky is not the (only) limit', 611.

[256] *AG Kokott Opinion*, para. 187.

equivalent to 'exhaustion' applicable to cross-border service provision'.[257] Doukas also notes that in light of the Court's findings in *UsedSoft*, 'the application of the "country of origin" principle to this field by analogy with satellite broadcasting remains open'.[258] A recent judgment in yet another case involving the analogue setting, *AllPosters*, has been interpreted by some as indicating that exhaustion does not apply in the digital setting.[259]

Also, the interpretation by the Commission seems to follow a narrow route, not establishing 'something akin to the exhaustion doctrine'.[260] In the present investigation, however, it seems in any event that the DG Competition quite explicitly follows the distinction of active and passive sales, rather than a broader exhaustion consideration. According to Article 4 of the Commission's Vertical Block Exemption Regulation,[261] contractual limitations on passive sales constitute hard-core restrictions that are exempt from the general exemption. Generally, the Commission considers such restrictions more harmful and imposes '*de facto* a regime very close to a *per se* prohibition for such hardcore restrictions'.[262] The Commission seems to assume that geo-blocking provisions are additional obligations within the meaning of *Premier League and Murphy*.[263] In the present proceedings, it seems, the Commission is applying this rationale to the audiovisual sector – in line with the Court's findings in *Premier League and Murphy* rather than by stretching it.

---

[257] Batchelor and Jenkins, 'FA Premier League', 160: 'namely that there can be no IP infringement where: the service provider is duly licensed in the originating state (even if the licence is a national one only); the service provider has agreed to remunerate the rightsholder for use of the rights; and the number of actual or potential viewers/users can be reliably tracked (e.g., number of decoder cards), so as to properly calculate royalties. Where tracking is impossible (e.g., number of customers in a pub), the defence does not apply'. See also Rognstad, 'Legally Flawed but Politically Sound? Digital Exhaustion of Copyright in Europe after UsedSoft', 630, who states that the Court's reasoning in Case C-128/11, *UsedSoft* 'resembles that of its development of an exhaustion rule under the free movement of goods, and also its rationale for banning national prohibition on the sale of TV decoder cards from other Member States under the free movement of services rules in the *Premier League* case'.

[258] See Doukas, 'The Sky is not the (only) limit', 624, however see the more critical Mazziotti, 'Is geo-blocking a real cause for concern?', 368.

[259] See, e.g., E. Rosati, 'Online copyright exhaustion in a post-Allposters world' forthcoming in *Journal of Intellectual Property Law & Practice*: http://ssrn.com/abstract =2613608; M. Savič, 'The CJEU AllPosters Case: Beginning of the End of Digital Exhaustion?', *European Intellectual Property Review*, 37 (2015), 389.

[260] See Colomo, 'Copyright Licensing and the EU Digital Single Market Strategy', 9.

[261] Commission Regulation (EU) No 330/2010 of 20 April 2010 on the application of Article 101(3) of the Treaty on the Functioning of the European Union to categories of vertical agreements and concerted practices [2010] OJ L102/1.

[262] Nor does the *de minimis* notice apply to hardcore restrictions. See M. Motta, P. Rey and N. Vettas, *Hardcore Restrictions under the Block Exemption Regulation on Vertical Agreements: An Economic View* (2009), 1.

[263] Colomo, 'Copyright Licensing and the EU Digital Single Market Strategy', 13.

However, in looking at both satellite and online transmissions, the Commission's investigation, as Colomo notes, 'seems to be based on the idea that [*Premier League and Murphy*] is relevant beyond the scope of the Cable and Satellite Directive'.[264]

The second question is whether, or how, the commitments might influence the other ongoing proceedings and what the commitments would imply for cross-border access to content. As some proceedings are ongoing it is difficult to say anything with certainty. Lamadrid hypothesises that 'once the Commission has accepted commitments [in Paramount] with regard to one undertaking, it could now not impose fines on others for exactly the same practices'[265] because 'commitments are only appropriate in cases where the Commission does not intend to impose fines'.[266] Thus, at least to some degree, the outcome of the Paramount case could impact on the other cases. Yet, the industry has reacted to the commitments and in December 2016 a French pay-TV provider, Canal+, with whom Paramount has a contractual relationship, brought actions to annul the Commission's acceptance.[267]

With the Commission's acceptance of the offered commitments, the restriction of passive sales in the specific licensing agreements was effectively abolished. However, it does not necessarily impact on the territorial licensing practice as such. In other words, whereas rights holders (in the present case, Paramount) are obliged to not restrict cross-border access in the form of passive sales in their licensing agreements, the service providers still have to clear rights for the respective territories. Thus, effectively, service providers could still have an incentive not to provide access in the form of passive sales in order not to infringe copyright. In its proceedings, the Commission is also quite clear that the removal of the restrictive licensing provisions alone is not sufficient to enable cross-border access (whether on an unsolicited passive sale basis or an active promotion of the services). In this context clause 2.2(a) of the offered commitments become crucial. It regulates that, from the effective date, Paramount

---

[264] Case AT.40023 *Cross-border access to pay-TV*, para. 7(a) reference to 'Additional Obligations'. See also Colomo, 'Copyright Licensing and the EU Digital Single Market Strategy', 13.

[265] A. Lamadrid, 'Breaking news: Pay-TV investigation- Paramount offers commitments' (*Chillin'Competition*, 22 April 2016): https://chillingcompetition.com/2016/04/22/break ing-news-pay-tv-investigation-paramount-offers-commitments/

[266] Colomo, 'Copyright Licensing and the EU Digital Single Market Strategy', 13.

[267] Case T-873/16, *Groupe Canal + v. European Commission* [2017] Action brought on 8 December 2016 – OJ C38, 6.2.2017, 50–52.

shall not seek to enforce or initiate proceedings before a court or tribunal for the violation of a Broadcaster Obligation in an existing Pay-TV Output License Agreement.

Such broadcaster obligation is defined in the commitments under clause 1 to mean

[r]elevant Clauses or equivalent clauses to the extent they prevent or limit a Broadcaster from responding to unsolicited requests from consumers residing and located in the European Economic Area but outside of such Broadcaster's licensed territory.

That is to say that, effectively, Paramount offers not to enforce its copyright as regards passive sales. Commitments come with the hypothetical constraint that they are binding just in the respective case, which might hamper broader influence on the industry. At the same time, given the other ongoing proceedings and the experiences from, e.g., the proceedings regarding CISAC, it can at least not be excluded that the commitments in the Paramount case would also produce tangible results outside the specific case. Yet another constraint, however, lies in the licensor–licensee relationship: considering freedom of contract, a broad interpretation of 'unsolicited requests' by service providers could, for example, impede re-negotiation of licensing agreements.

3.3   Summary

This chapter has looked at how cross-border provision and access to content – or, rather, the territorial delineation in licensing arrangements – have been dealt with from a competition law stance. A thorough discussion of the findings follows in Chapter 6, where we will contrast the competition route with the proposed or established legal framework. But let us briefly reflect on some of the immediate findings of the competition decisions and judgments in the licensor–licensor relationship (regarding model contracts for RRAs in the *Barcelona, Simulcasting, Santiago* and *CISAC* proceedings) and the licensor–licensee relationship (regarding licensing agreements in the *Premier League and Murphy* case and the investigation into pay-TV services).

First, it appears that, regarding Internet-, and more specifically on-demand streaming-, related issues, the horizontal relationship among licensors (i.e. between CMOs) has, until recently, received more scrutiny from the European Commission than the vertical contractual licensing relationship between rights holders and licensees. A continuous aspect of these proceedings regarding RRAs between CMOs seems to be the difficulty in proving concerted action. Ghafele notes that the 'position of the

European Commission seems somewhat torn between the need to establish a single market and the recognition of the principle of subsidiarity' since the Santiago Agreement and the CISAC proceedings.[268] Above all, the Commission's decision in 2008 introduced competition in the market of collective rights management.[269]

As regards RRAs, the Commission 'never stated that [they] were in themselves a distortion of competition, but it warned that the conditions included in those agreements could be anti-competitive'.[270] Something similar can be said of territorial delineation by rights holders in relation to commercial users (licensor–licensee relationship): while rights holders' behaviour represents almost an archetypical case of price discrimination based on territoriality, the Court of Justice's decision in *Premier League and Murphy* does not prohibit rights holders from delineating markets geographically 'as such',[271] but prohibits licensees from supplying decoders outside the territory of the licence agreement.[272] At least in this very general respect, *Coditel II* is not reversed, it seems,[273] however, only to the extent that exclusive licences 'as such' are not sufficient to justify the finding that it has an anti-competitive object.[274] Where a licence agreement is designed to prohibit or limit the cross-border provision, however,

it must be held that (...) it is deemed to have as its object the restriction of competition, unless other circumstances falling within its economic and legal context justify the finding that such an agreement is not liable to impair competition.[275]

In practice, the two judgments led to quite different results. Whereas the licensing practice was deemed compatible in *Coditel II*, it was held

---

[268] R. Ghafele, 'Europe's Lost Royalty Opportunity: A Comparison of Potential and Existing Digital Music Royalty Markets in Ten Different E.U. Member States' *Review of Economic Research on Copyright Issues*, 11 (2014), 60, 65.

[269] See, e.g., Yow, 'Creative Competition', 287.

[270] Vuckovic, 'Implementation of Directive 2014/26', 41, also referring to the Court in Case T-442/08, *CISAC* v. *Commission*.

[271] See Joined Cases C-403/08 and C-429/08, *Premier League and Murphy*, para. 137. More specifically, the Court refers to 'the mere fact that the right holder has granted to a sole licensee the exclusive right to broadcast protected subject-matter from a Member State, and consequently to prohibit its transmission by others, during a specified period'.

[272] See above. Also de Vries, 'Sport, TV and IP rights', 617; Colomo, 'The Commission Investigation into Pay TV Services: Open Questions', 534; Riis and Schovsbo, 'Den grænseløse onlinebruger', 668.

[273] The Court recalled: 'it is apparent from the Court's case-law', Joined Cases C-403/08 and C-429/08, *Premier League and Murphy*, para. 137. See Colomo, 'Copyright Licensing and the EU Digital Single Market Strategy', 6, 8 and 10; Doukas, 'The Sky is not the (only) limit', 622. See, however, Batchelor and Jenkins, 'FA Premier League', 158, who argue that *Premier League and Murphy* was distinguishable from *Coditel II*.

[274] See Joined Cases C-403/08 and C-429/08, *Premier League and Murphy*, para. 137.

[275] Ibid., para. 140.

incompatible in *Premier League and Murphy*. The Court in the latter confirmed, in line with previous case law from the 1960s, as Colomo notes, that 'agreements giving absolute (. . .) territorial protection to distributors within the EU are in principle restrictive of competition by object under Article 101(1) TFEU',[276] that 'this line of case law is also "fully applicable" to the cross-border provision of television services'.[277]

This also appears to be the rationale behind the ongoing proceedings in the pay-TV sector. In contrast with *Premier League and Murphy*, however, the Commission departs from this position and suggests that the contractual restriction of broadcasters in providing content outside their licensed territory (geo-blocking of passive sales) is contrary to Article 101(1) TFEU. Similar to the *Premier League and Murphy* case, the Commission in the pay-TV proceedings considers ensuring 'cross-border access to content by importing the "passive" supply concept for the Vertical Block Exemption Regulation and Technology Transfer Block Exemption Regulation'.[278] Effectively, it applies the Court of Justice's additional obligations rationale to direct access via the Internet. Notably, the factual background of the pay-TV investigation correlates much more to the background in the *Coditel II* case than *Premier League and Murphy* did. Thus, the once established and accepted commercial practice of licensing copyright-protected content on an exclusive territorial basis seems not to hold any more.

In this context, it also seems worthwhile considering the relationship of the *CISAC* and the *Premier League and Murphy* cases. The *CISAC* case was decided by the General Court in 2013, i.e. roughly two years after *Premier League and Murphy*. Farrand argues that the *CISAC* case 'has demonstrated that the EU's courts will still uphold certain types of territorial exclusion agreement, and as CISAC is a[n] organization representing collecting societies acting in the area of music rights, a decision relating to digital music services may be decided similarly'.[279] This points towards yet another aspect which is worthwhile considering: the specificity of the subject matter, first as regards rights (i.e. authors' rights and neighbouring rights) and secondly as regards works (i.e. film, music, etc.).[280]

---

[276] Colomo, 'Copyright Licensing and the EU Digital Single Market Strategy', 2–3.
[277] Ibid., 3.   [278] Cole, 'PRSfM/STIM/GEMA/JV', 258.
[279] B. Farrand, *Networks of power in digital copyright law and policy* (Routledge, 2014), p. 77.
[280] Riis and Schovsbo argue that it cannot be excluded that the fact that the subject matter in *Premier League and Murphy* regarded rights in football matches and not film, music or other copyright-protected works. They conclude, however, that it is safe to assume that the judgment has a wider impact also on online services of other copyright-protected subject matter: Riis and Schovsbo, 'Den grænseløse onlinebruger', 673.

The analysis in this chapter shows that the focus in the proceedings differs, but also that territorial delineation is a traditional and fairly complex stress field of copyright and competition law. As regards the licensor–licensor relationship, Hilty and Nérisson argue that '[t]he decisions of the European Commission design the legal frame in which [CMOs] develop their services to adapt to the emergence of a demand for uses of copyrighted works across national borders'.[281] But it is also clear, that the competition route is only one side of the coin. The legislative route will be the subject of the chapters that follow.

[281] Hilty and Nérisson, 'Collective Copyright Management and Digitization', 7.

4   Multi-Territorial Licensing from a Legislative Perspective

In the previous chapter, we saw how access to and licensing of music and audiovisual online content on the Internet are being addressed and dealt with from a competition stance. Beyond the assessments under EU competition law via the competition authorities and the courts, the European lawmaker has also scrutinised multi-territorial licensing. This is the focus of this chapter.

Both content verticals, i.e. music and audiovisual content, have been in the cross-hairs of the European lawmaker under the Digital Single Market agendas, but to a very varying degree: as the reader will notice, Chapter 4 deals primarily with multi-territorial licensing of online music rights. It analyses the development from voluntary to binding measures in the distinct European setting of harmonisation and market integration in the online music vertical. Multi-territorial licensing for online uses of audiovisual works, on the other hand, has played a much smaller role in legislative activity to date. The survey of the community *acquis* concludes with the most recent developments, which also become relevant in the context of licensing of audiovisual content. This sectoral division of this chapter follows roughly the approach by the lawmaker and is introduced for the sake of greater clarity.

First, it seems worthwhile briefly to revisit legislative competence. According to the principle of conferral in Article 5(2) of the Treaty on European Union (TEU), the European lawmaker is dependent on the legislative competence that is conferred upon it by the Member States in the Treaties in order to legislate and approximate national laws. With Article 118 of the Treaty on the Formation of the European Union (TFEU), the European legislator received a special competence to pass legislation related to intellectual property rights, which was introduced by the Treaty of Lisbon only as recently as 2009.[1] Geiger predicts that '[t]he

---

[1] See C. Geiger, 'Moving out of the economic crisis: what role and shape for intellectual property rights in the European Union?' in H. Kalimo and M. S. Jansson (eds.), *EU Economic Law in a Time of Crisis* (Edward Elgar Publishing, 2016), p. 141. Art. 118(2) contains an important restriction: 'The Council, acting in accordance with a special

Treaty of Lisbon may stimulate further changes in European union IP policy, as it mandates the establishment of a truly European IP law and creates tools towards this objective'.[2] Prior to the inclusion of Article 118 TFEU as a legal basis, the European legislator had to rely on other competences to harmonise copyright law, which constituted what has been described as a 'fragmented legal basis'.[3]

Article 114(1) TFEU provides a legal basis for acts that have as their object the establishment and functioning of the internal market. It 'remains the most commonly used legal basis to harmonize laws in order to further the internal market'[4] and has been widely used to harmonise copyright legislation of the Member States. In Case C-376/98, *Germany* v. *Parliament and Council*, the Court of Justice clarified, however, that Article 114 TFEU does not provide 'general power to regulate the internal market'.[5] Rather, it established that measures adopted on the legal basis of Article 114 TFEU 'must genuinely have as its object the improvement of the conditions for the establishment and functioning of the internal market'.[6] Notably, the Commission's proposals for a Directive on copyright in the Digital Single Market, for a Regulation on ensuring the cross-border portability of online content services and for a Regulation on addressing geo-blocking and other forms of discrimination based on customers' nationality, place of residence or place of establishment within the internal market are all based on Article 114 TFEU.[7] Other legal bases have been applied by the lawmaker, too.

---

legislative procedure, shall by means of regulations establish language arrangements for the European intellectual property rights. The Council shall act unanimously after consulting the European Parliament.'

[2] Ibid.

[3] C. Geiger (ed.), *The Construction of Intellectual Property in the European Union: Searching for Coherence* (Edward Elgar Publishing, 2013), p. 6.

[4] E. Fahey, 'Does the Emperor Have Financial Crisis Clothes? Reflections on the Legal Basis of the European Banking Authority', *Modern Law Review* (2011), 2 and 6: http://ssrn.com/abstract=1715524

[5] Case C-376/98, *Germany* v. *Parliament and Council (Tobacco Advertising)* [2000] ECR I-8419, para. 83. In the case, the Court was examining Art. 100a of the EC Treaty, which was then, after amendment Art. 95 of the Treaty Establishing the European Community (TEC), which is the predecessor to Art. 114 of the Treaty on the Functioning of the European Union (TFEU).

[6] Case C-376/98, para. 84: 'Moreover, a measure adopted on the basis of Article 100a of the Treaty must genuinely have as its object the improvement of the conditions for the establishment and functioning of the internal market'.

[7] See Commission, 'Proposal for a Regulation on ensuring the cross-border portability of online content services' COM(2015) 627 final, 2015/0284 (COD), Brussels, 9 December 2015, Explanatory Memorandum, 3; and Commission, 'Proposal for a Regulation on addressing geo-blocking and other forms of discrimination based on customers' nationality, place of residence or place of establishment within the internal market and amending Regulation (EC) No 2006/2004 and Directive 2009/22/EC' COM

Directive 2014/26/EU, for example, has its legal basis in Articles 50(1), 53(1) and Article 62 TFEU.[8]

4.1   Regulating via Soft Law

4.1.1   Background of the Online Music Recommendation

As noted above, the European Commission had collective management under its scrutiny at least early as 1995: in its *Green Paper on Copyright and Related Rights in the Information Society*, the Commission commented on the regulation of collective rights management.[9] Based on a hearing conducted in 1994, the Commission concludes that '[i]n general it does not seem that intervention on the part of the Community authorities is regarded as desirable at this stage'[10] but 'feels that the regulatory framework should be examined'.[11] Also, some years later, in the InfoSoc Directive of 2001,[12] the lawmaker singled out the need

especially in the light of the requirements arising out of the digital environment, to ensure that collecting societies achieve a higher level of rationalisation and transparency with regard to compliance with competition rules.[13]

In January 2003, shortly after or in parallel to the DG Competition's activities surrounding reciprocal representation agreements, the European Parliament authorised its Committee on Legal Affairs and the Internal Market to draw up a report on a 'Community framework for collecting societies for authors' rights',[14] which resulted in the Parliament's Resolution of 2004, in which it reflected that 'a Community approach (...) must be pursued'.[15] In April 2004, having

---

(2016) 289 final, 2016/0152 (COD), Brussels, 25 May 2016, Explanatory Memorandum, 4.

[8] See Directive 2014/26/EU, Recitals 7–8. The Explanatory Memorandum declares that the Proposal is based on Arts. 50(2)(g), 53 and 62 TFEU as facilitating the free provision of services.

[9] Commission, 'Green Paper on Copyright and Related Rights in the Information Society' COM(95) 382 final, Brussels, 19 July 1995, 69–78.

[10] Ibid., 75.   [11] Ibid., 78.

[12] Directive 2001/29/EC of the European Parliament and of the Council of 22 May 2001 on the harmonisation of certain aspects of copyright and related rights in the information society [2001] OJ L167/10–19.

[13] Recital 17 of InfoSoc Directive.

[14] See European Parliament, 'Report on a Community framework for collecting societies for authors' rights (2002/2274(INI))' Committee on Legal Affairs and the Internal Market, Rapporteur: Raina A. Mercedes Echerer, A5-0478/2003 FINAL, 11 December 2003, 4.

[15] European Parliament, 'Resolution on a Community framework for collective management societies in the field of copyright and neighbouring rights (2002/2274(INI))'

observed the market for collective management of copyright for several years, the Commission also reflected that 'more common ground on several features of collective management is required' in order to achieve the Single Market.[16] In its Communication on *The Management of Copyright and Related Rights in the Internal Market*, the Commission held that abstaining from legislative measures was no longer feasible.[17] The Commission went on to reflect that '[t]o rely on soft law, such as codes of conduct agreed upon by the market place, appears to be no appropriate option'[18] regarding the establishment and status of collective management organisations (CMOs), and the relationship of CMOs to users and rights holders as well as external control of CMOs. In addition, the Commission deemed that EU-wide licences were necessary for new Internet-based services and blamed the absence of those 'as one factor that has made it difficult for new internet-based music services to develop their full potential'.[19] Nonetheless, the Commission opted for a soft-law instrument and, in May 2005, published its Recommendation 2005/737/EC on collective cross-border management of copyright and related rights for legitimate online music services ('Online Music Recommendation').

Before we turn towards this regulatory approach taken by the Commission, let us briefly recall the situation before the Online Music Recommendation: on the basis of a contractual network of reciprocal representation agreements (RRAs) between CMOs, a CMO licensed the world repertoire for exploitation in the domestic market as a monopolistic provider. Based on the country of destination principle, one licence per country was necessary in order to operate. At the time of the Recommendation, DG COMP had received complaints that led to the CISAC case, but did not issue its statement of objections before 2006. Regarding the Santiago Agreement, an investigation had officially been opened since May 2004, and a market test notice followed shortly after the Recommendation in August 2005.

P5_TA(2004)0036 OJ C 92 E/425, Recital 12. For a thorough walk-through of the Parliament's and Commission's activities at the time, see L. Guibault and S. van Gompel, 'Collective Management in the European Union' in D. Gervais (ed.), *Collective Management of Copyright and Related Rights*, 2nd edn. (Kluwer Law International, 2010), pp. 150–155.

[16] See Commission, 'The Management of Copyright and Related Rights in the Internal Market' (Communication from the Commission to the Council, the European Parliament and the European Economic and Social Committee) COM(2004) 261 final, Brussels, 16 April 2004, 19.

[17] Ibid.   [18] Ibid.

[19] E. Anthonis, 'Will the CRM-directive Succeed Re-aggregating the Mechanical Reproduction Rights in the Anglo-American Music Repertoire?', *International Journal of Intellectual Property Management* (2014) 7, 151,152.

In its Impact Assessment accompanying the Recommendation, the Commission took as a starting point that

online content providers require a licence for more than one territory which gives legal certainty and insurance against infringement suits for all territories (multi-territorial licence).[20]

In order to reach this goal, the European Commission considered three policy options: to refrain from intervention as baseline scenario (option 1); to eliminate territorial restrictions and customer allocation provisions in existing RRAs (option 2); or to give rights holders the additional choice to appoint a collective rights manager for the online use of their musical works across the entire EU (option 3).[21]

In addition to the Parliament's call for a 'Community approach', the stakeholder consultation demonstrated broad consensus that keeping the *status quo* was not an option. Under option 2, ultimately, all CMOs would offer the same repertoire based on RRAs.[22] Under option 3, on the other hand, CMOs 'would have to compete among themselves to attract right-holders'.[23] Thus, the Commission effectively had the choice between introducing competition at the level of commercial users, i.e. the licensees, (option 2) and introducing competition in the relationship between rights holders and CMOs (option 3).[24] Option 2 is also to be seen in the context of the concluded and ongoing competition proceedings at the time. Notably, author CMOs, major record producers and commercial users (online music providers), as well as consumer organisations, favoured this option.[25] The Commission, however, expressed concerns that under this model all competing CMOs would offer an identical product.[26] Option 3, on the other hand, was deemed to

---

[20] Commission, 'Impact Assessment reforming cross-border collective management of copyright and related rights for legitimate online music services' 5. See also Online Music Recommendation (2005/737/EC). Empirical evidence does not entirely support this hypothesis, though.
[21] See Commission, 'Impact Assessment reforming cross-border collective management of copyright and related rights for legitimate online music services', 5, 17–18.
[22] See ibid., 26.   [23] See ibid.
[24] See ibid. See also Max Planck Institute for Intellectual Property, Competition and Tax Law, 'Stellungnahme des Max-Planck-Instituts für Geistiges Eigentum, Wettbewerbs- und Steuerrecht zuhanden des Bundesministeriums der Justiz betreffend die Empfehlung der Europäischen Kommission über die Lizenzierung von Musik für das Internet vom 18. Oktober 2005 (2005/737/EG)' (2006), 1: www.ip.mpg.de/fileadmin/ipmpg/content/stellungnahmen/stellungnahme-lizenzierung musik1_01.pdf
[25] See Commission, 'Impact Assessment reforming cross-border collective management of copyright and related rights for legitimate online music services', 35–36.
[26] See ibid., 27.

create the competitive discipline that forces rights managers to compete among themselves for right-holders and offer optimal EU-wide management services, e.g. by competing on the technological solutions they are offering to protect and monitor copyright. If their services were either inefficient or too expensive, right-holders would move to another rights manager. This level of competitive threat would counteract any tendency toward monopoly at the Community level.[27]

This model found mainly the support of music publishers, who were likely seeing a chance to maximise returns of their repertoire, and independent record producers, because it would allow them to establish their own licensing entity.[28] The Commission opted for the latter option 3.

4.1.2   Competition for Rights Holders

The Recommendation was addressed to Member States and to 'all economic operators which are involved in the management of copyright and related rights within the Community'.[29] Aiming to introduce competition both up- and downstream,[30] the Recommendation advocated the introduction of multi-territorial licences and stipulated that rights holders should have the right to assign the management of their online rights necessary to operate online music services to a CMO of their choice, irrespective of the residence or the nationality of either the CMO or the right holder. The key recommendation aims to introduce competition between CMOs over rights holders and is enshrined in Article 3 in the section on the relationship between rights holders, collective rights managers and commercial users:

Right-holders should have the right to entrust the management of any of the online rights necessary to operate legitimate online music services, on a territorial scope of their choice, to a collective rights manager of their choice, irrespective of the Member State of residence or the nationality of either the collective rights manager or the right-holder.[31]

The Commission expected that the chosen policy option 3 'would attempt to create a multi-territorial license for legitimate online music

---

[27] Ibid.
[28] See ibid., 35–36. Publishers, however, would be able to withdraw their rights anyway.
[29] See Art. 19 of Online Music Recommendation (2005/737/EC).
[30] T. Lüder, 'First experience with EU wide online music licensing', GRUR *International* (2007) 649, 656.
[31] As the Max Planck Institute points out, the Commission refrains from specifying further how rights holders' right to choose a CMO for exploitation of online rights, is to be understood in legal terms. They conclude that such right can neither economically nor legally be justified. See: Max Planck Institute for Intellectual Property, Competition and Tax Law, 'Stellungnahme', 2.

services by giving right-holders across the EU the additional possibility to appoint any rights manager of their choice for the EU-wide exploitation of their online music rights'.[32] Consequently, a CMO can license repertoire for several territories, but not containing the world repertoire as before but merely the represented rights holders,[33] unless RRAs are additionally concluded. As Drexl notes, the Commission expected that CMOs would specialise in specific categories of music, 'which would much better target the needs of commercial uses (. . .) that likewise concentrate their programs on specific types of music'.[34] In other words, competition would exist on the basis of not only price but also repertoire.[35] As can be seen more than a decade later, that expectation did not materialise. Drexl remarks that, in utilising this model, the Recommendation opted for a 'totally new system of direct licensing without relying on reciprocal representation agreements'[36] instead of recommending a system similar to the International Federation of the Phonographic Industry (IFPI)/*Simulcasting* model for RRAs. Others shared the observation that the chosen approach entails a complete rearrangement of the European market for online rights.[37]

Besides this central provision, the Recommendation sets out a number of principles, such as the equal treatment of categories of rights holders and the equitable distribution of royalties. It also calls on CMOs to provide commercial users with sufficient information on tariffs and repertoire in advance of the negotiations. Finally, it regulates accountability, rights holders' representation in the decision-making bodies of CMOs, and dispute resolution, which are not directly relevant in the context of multi-territorial licensing. In Article 16 of the Recommendation, the Commission invited Member States to report on a yearly basis on the measures adopted.

---

[32] Commission, 'Impact Assessment reforming cross-border collective management of copyright and related rights for legitimate online music services', 18.

[33] Similarly, see G. Poll, 'CELAS, PEDL & Co: Metamorphose oder Anfang vom Ende der kollektiven Wahrnehmung von Musik-Online-Rechten in Europa?', *Zeitschrift für Urheber- und Medienrecht* [2008], 500, 502.

[34] J. Drexl, 'Competition in the Field of Collective Management: Preferring 'Creative Competition' to Allocative Efficiency in European Copyright Law' in P. Torremans (ed.), *Copyright Law, A Handbook of Contemporary Research* (Edward Elgar, 2007), p. 269, with more evidence.

[35] R. Matulionyté, 'Cross-Border Collective Management and Principle of Territoriality: Problems and Possible Solutions in the EU', *Journal of World Intellectual Property* (11) (2009), 467, 467.

[36] Drexl, 'Competition in the field of collective management', p. 280.

[37] See, e.g., Poll, 'CELAS, PEDL & Co', 503.

4.1.3   *Criticism and Reactions in the Marketplace*

The Recommendation constitutes the first (soft) law-making activity of the European Commission aimed at regulating the collective management of online rights, and more broadly the online music licensing landscape. Its main mechanism aims at a model whereby competition between CMOs is introduced via rights holders and not commercial users. Thus, as the Max Planck Institute points out, the Commission's reasoning stands and falls with the creation of permanent competition between CMOs over rights holders.[38]

However, soon after the Recommendation was adopted, it was faced with heavy criticism from next to all stakeholders. The Max Planck Institute even went as far as recommending that the German lawmaker not act on the Recommendation due to numerous flaws.[39] Academics and various stakeholders point towards consequences that it had for licensing practice. Other main concerns have been that the solution was not deemed user friendly and to disregard the territoriality principle. Guibault assesses that the

majority of scholarly commentators, policy makers and stakeholders agree that the intention behind the Recommendation of fostering competition between individual collective management organisations has created chaos rather than anything else.[40]

The Recommendation has been described as 'riding on the wind generated by an oversized ambition of the European Commission'[41] and as 'poorly informed and badly succeed intervention'[42] that was 'rushed'.[43] Another criticism points towards the exclusive focus on online licensing in the music sector, whereas the system should not differ for online licensing regarding audiovisual works.[44] Others note that it does not differentiate between those who create and perform the work and those who just

---

[38] See Max Planck Institute for Intellectual Property, Competition and Tax Law, 'Stellungnahme', 1.

[39] See ibid., 4.

[40] L. Guibault, 'The Draft Collective Management Directive' in I. A. Stamatoudi and P. Torremans (eds.), *EU Copyright Law: A Commentary* (Edward Elgar, 2014), p. 763.

[41] R. M. Vuckovic, 'Implementation of Directive 2014/26 on Collective Management and Multi-territorial Licensing of Musical Rights in Regulating the Tariff-setting Systems in Central and Eastern Europe', 47 (2016) *International Review of Intellectual Property and Competition Law*, 28, 29.

[42] M. Ficsor, 'Collective Management and Multi-territorial Licensing: Key Issues of the Transposition of Directive 2014/26/EU' in I. A. Stamatoudi (ed.), *New Developments in EU and International Copyright Law* (Kluwer Law International, 2016), p. 239.

[43] Guibault and van Gompel, 'Collective Management in the European Union', p. 156.

[44] Drexl, 'Competition in the field of collective management', p. 258. See also Guibault and van Gompel, 'Collective Management in the European Union', p. 156.

exploit it.[45] The Max Planck Institute makes the criticism that the Recommendation refrains from touching upon individual rights management.[46]

Furthermore, the Recommendation has been criticised for its potential negative effects on cultural diversity. Drexl, for example, points out that the proposed model 'promotes the interest of music publishing companies holding large repertoires in mainstream popular music'.[47] Ricolfi also argues that, in the long term, the chosen route would lead to an advantage for commercially successful, English language music, 'to the detriment of minor music communities, which will have to fall back on the series of smaller shrinking national CMOs'.[48] Drexl continues that the model fails to take the creativity-enhancing rationale of copyright itself into consideration, and is based on a 'purely static competition policy (...) that focuses exclusively on output and price'.[49] In a purely economic efficiency perspective, others argue, 'CMOs would have difficulties to fulfil their public interest functions', i.e. cultural and social functions, thereby harming cultural diversity.[50] In a similar vein, Poll comments on the general agitation, and claims that it is caused is by the fact that the Recommendation is oriented towards the internal market and uses copyright-protected goods just as any others without realising their culture-political dimension.[51]

Yet another concern related to the prediction that the implementation of the Recommendation would lead to the emergence of monopolies or regional oligopolies,[52] because larger music publishers would take their repertoire to a few large licensing entities. Others argued that the system would lead to a gradual break-up of the system of RRAs and ultimately to

---

[45] C. B. Graber, 'Collective Rights Management, Competition Policy and Cultural Diversity: EU Lawmaking at a Crossroads', *World Intellectual Property Organization Journal*, 4 [2012] 35, 39.

[46] See Max Planck Institute for Intellectual Property, Competition and Tax Law, 'Stellungnahme', 2.

[47] Drexl, 'Competition in the field of collective management: preferring "creative competition" to allocative efficiency in European copyright law', p. 251. Drexl further criticises that the policy serves 'the average taste of consumers across Europe and tries to maximise the income of the undertakings in control of the rights in such mainstream music'.

[48] M. Ricolfi, 'Individual and Collective Management of Copyright in a Digital Environment' in P. Torremans (ed.), *Copyright Law, A Handbook of Contemporary Research* (Edward Elgar, 2007), p. 297.

[49] Drexl, 'Competition in the field of collective management: preferring 'creative competition' to allocative efficiency in European copyright law', p. 281.

[50] Graber, 'Collective rights management, competition policy and cultural diversity: EU lawmaking at a crossroads', 39.

[51] Poll, 'CELAS, PEDL & Co', 503.

[52] E.g. Guibault and van Gompel, 'Collective Management in the European Union', p. 160; Ricolfi, 'Individual and collective management of copyright in a digital environment', p. 297.

a market with just a few CMOs,[53] which, however, has not materialised in the aftermath of the Recommendation. On the other hand, it is noted that, against the background of the situation without the RRAs, 'we may also understand why the EU Commission decided with uncharacteristic speed to do something about this unfortunate situation'.[54] It is important to recall, though, that European CMOs ceased their practice of their old RRAs first in 2008, i.e. in the aftermath of the CISAC decision.

Legal practitioners made the criticism that the Recommendation appears incongruous, because it opens up for competition while CMOs are generally non-profit organisations and have as their primary purpose the protection of the rights of its members.[55] Dutch CMO Buma/Stemra argued that option 3 would only benefit American repertoire and industry umbrella organisations. GESAC made the criticism that it would weaken local author CMOs and thereby undermine cultural diversity.[56] IFPI, too, argued that the one-stop multi-territorial multi-repertoire regime based on RRAs 'is quite simply a superior product to the multi-territory, mono-repertoire licence that would be the result of the Option 3'[57] – a concern that the Commission disregarded as 'premature'.[58] A report prepared for the European Commission in 2010 notes that whereas licensees welcome competition CMOs, they regret the withdrawal of RRAs, which led to fragmentation and increased transaction costs.[59] Thus, the Recommendation 'disappoint[s] both rights holders and users alike',[60] because licensees (commercial users) 'seem to be asking for blanket licenses covering all the necessary rights required to operate a distribution service'.[61]

One of the harshest criticisms of the Commission's approach was formulated by the European Parliament in 2007, in the form of a resolution.[62] In its Impact Assessment accompanying Directive 2014/26/EU, the Commission acknowledges that the Recommendation was 'coldly received by the European Parliament'.[63] First, the European

---

[53] Poll, 'CELAS, PEDL & Co', 502.

[54] Ricolfi, 'Individual and collective management of copyright in a digital environment', p. 294.

[55] C. Langenius, 'The ramifications of pan-European licensing for Nordic collective rights management', *Nordiskt Immateriellt Rättskydd* [2008], 29.

[56] See Commission, 'Impact Assessment reforming cross-border collective management of copyright and related rights for legitimate online music services', 22.

[57] Ibid., 25.   [58] See ibid.   [59] KEA European Affairs and Mines ParisTech, 158.

[60] Ibid.   [61] Ibid.

[62] European Parliament, 'Resolution of 13 March 2007 on the Commission Recommendation of 18 October 2005 on collective cross-border management of copyright and related rights for legitimate online music services (2005/737/EC) (2006/2008(INI))'.

[63] Commission, 'Impact Assessment accompanying the document Proposal for a Directive of the European Parliament and of the Council on collective management of copyright

Parliament points towards procedural omissions of the Commission: it failed to undertake a consultation with interested parties and the Parliament.[64] Besides adverse effects on cultural diversity, it continues to criticise the lack of precision, and the abolition of the system of RRAs. The Parliament predicts:

there is a risk that right-holders complying with the recommendation in respect of their interactive online rights would deprive local collective rights managers (CRMs) of other rights (e.g. those relating to broadcasting), thus preventing users of those rights from acquiring user rights for a diversified repertoire from one and the same CRM.[65]

The Parliament continues to encourage the Commission to

avoid the over-centralisation of market powers and repertoires by ensuring that exclusive mandates may not be granted to a single or a very few CRMs by major right-holders, thereby guaranteeing that the global repertoire remains available to all CRMs for the granting of licences to users.[66]

Under point 1 of the resolution, the European Parliament 'invites' the Commission to revisit its approach and propose a framework directive 'as soon as possible'. In February 2008, the Commission followed up in the form of a Monitoring Report on Recommendation 2005/737/EC and recognised a 'nascent market for EU-wide licensing of music for online services'.[67] The report concludes that the Recommendation 'seems to have produced an impact on the licensing market place' and received endorsement by some CMOs, music publishers and users.[68] A second resolution by the European Parliament in September 2008 continues to criticise the Commission's 'refusal to legislate – despite various European Parliament resolutions'.[69]

---

and related rights and multi-territorial licensing of rights in musical works for online uses in the internal market', 106.

[64] European Parliament, 'Resolution of 13 March 2007 on the Commission Recommendation of 18 October 2005 on collective cross-border management of copyright and related rights for legitimate online music services (2005/737/EC) (2006/2008 (INI))' Lit. A and C. The Parliament notes that 'it is unacceptable that a "soft law" approach was chosen without prior consultation and without the formal involvement of Parliament and the Council, thereby circumventing the democratic process, especially as the initiative taken has already influenced decisions in the market to the potential detriment of competition and cultural diversity'.

[65] Ibid., lit. E.   [66] Ibid., point 6.

[67] Commission, 'Monitoring of the 2005 Music Online Recommendation' Brussels, 07 February 2008, 1.

[68] Ibid., 8.

[69] European Parliament, 'Resolution of 25 September 2008 on collective cross-border management of copyright and related rights for legitimate online music services' point 2.

Nine years after the Recommendation, the European legislator reflected, in Recital 39 of the CRM Directive,[70] that the soft law measure 'encouraging MS to improve their legal framework and stakeholders to develop self-regulatory approaches'[71] has not been sufficient to encourage widespread multi-territorial licensing or to address specific demands. In retrospective, it appears, the Commission sees the deficits of the Recommendation mainly in its legal nature. A recommendation is a non-binding instrument introduced under Article 288 TFEU. Thus, Recommendation 2005/737/EC was arguably limited in scope and was followed only unevenly.[72] There exist doubts, however, whether a legislative instrument would have found the support of the Council and the European Parliament at the time.[73]

Much of the criticism appears to be justified, but the European Commission reflected in its Impact Assessment, that '[i]ntroducing direct EU-wide mandates alongside existing reciprocal representation agreements requires a two-phase approach'.[74] The Commission actually recommended that Member States take all measures deemed necessary, including national legislation, to ensure the full application of the recommended practice.[75] In a second phase, the Recommendation reserves the 'Commission's right to propose legislation should the self-regulatory voluntary approach not foster the policy objective set forth'.[76] In this context the Impact Assessment also relates the Recommendation to the Better Regulation principles.[77]

In the marketplace, the Recommendation, as well as the above-mentioned competition actions by the Commission, led to direct consequences in the licensing practice: as seen above, major rights holders with Anglo-American repertoires, as well as some independents,

---

[70] Directive 2014/26/EU of the European Parliament and of the Council of 26 February 2014 on collective management of copyright and related rights and multi-territorial licensing of rights in musical works for online use in the internal market [2014] OJ L84/72–98.

[71] Commission, 'Impact Assessment accompanying the document Proposal for a Directive of the European Parliament and of the Council on collective management of copyright and related rights and multi-territorial licensing of rights in musical works for online uses in the internal market', 53.

[72] Recital 6 of Directive 2014/26/EU.

[73] Drexl, 'Competition in the field of collective management: preferring 'creative competition' to allocative efficiency in European copyright law', p. 269.

[74] See Commission, 'Impact Assessment reforming cross-border collective management of copyright and related rights for legitimate online music services', 39.

[75] See ibid., 36.

[76] See ibid., 39. Whereas a Recommendation is a soft law tool, it is taken into account by the CJEU when interpreting the acquis communitaire and likely had a signalling effect to stakeholders.

[77] See ibid.

withdrew their online rights from the traditional system based on national monopolies, thereby effectively increasing transaction costs for online service providers. The Commission's approach seems to have produced, as some note, 'the opposite effect' by shifting from country-based multi-repertoire licensing to EU-wide mono repertoire licensing.[78] On the other hand, it seems that the Recommendation intended just that.

Among academic commentators there appears to be, as noted before, broad consensus that these developments have to be seen in a causal relationship with the Online Music Recommendation.[79] But, as was seen in Chapter 2, music publishers have indicated their wish to withdraw their repertoire from the existing RRAs, regardless of any intervention by the Commission.[80] Thus, whereas the Recommendation might have contributed to or accelerated the disaggregation of rights, it can hardly be seen as the sole cause. Having said that, the Impact Assessment accompanying the Proposal for the CRM Directive in 2012 acknowledges that the soft law approach, on the one hand, has contributed to industry-driven developments, whereas, on the other, it clearly 'has not been sufficient to trigger the necessary changes in national laws and in stake-holders' practices'. Thus, the Commission itself seems to see a certain causal relationship between the soft law measure or 'self-regulatory approach'[81] and industry developments.

4.2   Legislative Intervention and Codification

4.2.1   Background of Directive 2014/26/EU

Against the background of the widespread criticism of the Online Music Recommendation, the Commission continued to have multi-territorial licensing on its legislative agenda. Despite calls to revisit its chosen route, in 2008 the Commission, however, went on to follow market

---

[78] G. Petteri, 'Harmonising Collective Rights Management and Multi-Territorial Licensing of Music for Online Use in the European Union: A Review of the Collective Rights Management Directive 2014/26/EU', *Nordiskt Immateriellt Rättskydd* [2015], 150, 156.

[79] See, e.g., Guibault and van Gompel, 'Collective Management in the European Union', p. 160; R. Hilty and S. Nérisson, 'Collective Copyright Management and Digitization: The European Experience' (2013) Max Planck Institute for Intellectual Property and Competition Law Research Paper No. 13–09 (Max Planck Institute for Intellectual Property and Competition Law), 8: http://ssrn.com/abstract=2247870

[80] Commission, 'Impact Assessment reforming cross-border collective management of copyright and related rights for legitimate online music services', 35–36.

[81] Commission, 'Impact Assessment accompanying the document Proposal for a Directive of the European Parliament and of the Council on collective management of copyright and related rights and multi-territorial licensing of rights in musical works for online uses in the internal market', 53.

developments in the expectation that the market would bring forward solutions.[82] Under the second Barroso Commission (2010–14),[83] the simplification of copyright clearance, management and cross-border licensing spearheaded the Commission's Digital Agenda of 2010 as 'Key action 1'. This simplification was envisioned to be achieved by

[e]nhancing the governance, transparency and pan European licensing for (online) rights management by proposing a framework Directive on collective rights management by 2010.[84]

Originally expected in 2010, the introduction of measures to improve multi-territorial licensing was later postponed to the end of 2011.[85] Only on 11 July 2012, the Directorate-General for Internal Market and Services (DG MARKT)[86] presented its proposal for a Directive on collective management of copyright and related rights and multi-territorial licensing of rights in musical works for online uses in the internal market. Following intensive debate, a trilogue agreement was reached on 4 November 2013 under the Lithuanian Presidency, succeeding the positions of the Legal Affairs committee of the EU Parliament and the Council in July 2013.[87] While the Commission's proposal has been subject to criticism, it has been noted by myself and others that it was approved by the European Parliament with notable unanimity.[88]

---

[82] For further evidence, see Petteri, 'Harmonising Collective Rights Management and Multi-Territorial Licensing of Music for Online Use in the European Union'.

[83] The first Barroso Commission ran from 2004 to 2009.

[84] Commission, 'A Digital Agenda for Europe' (Communication from the Commission to the European Parliament, the Council, The European Economic and Social Committee and the Committee of the Regions) COM(2010) 245 final/2, Brussels, 19 May 2010, 9.

[85] Commission, 'A Single Market for Intellectual Property Rights, Boosting creativity and innovation to provide economic growth, high quality jobs and first class products and services in Europe' (Communication from the Commission to the European Parliament, the Council, The European Economic and Social Committee and the Committee of the Regions) COM(2011) 287 final, Brussels, 24 May 2011, 10. The legislative initiative has been postponed several times in the indicative roadmap and expressed the expectation to adopt a proposal by March 2012.

[86] Within the DG MARKT, the initiative stems from Directorate D, Unit D1 under Maria Martin-Prat. Martin-Prat's appointment was controversial because of her background from the record industry organisation the International Federation of the Phonographic Industry (IFPI).

[87] See Commission, 'Commissioner Michel Barnier welcomes the trilogue agreement on collective rights management', (Press release) MEMO/13/955, Brussels, 5 November 2013.

[88] The European Parliament adopted the text by 640 votes to 18, with 22 abstentions. See E. Steyn, 'Collective Rights Management: Multi-territorial Licensing and Self-regulation', *Entertainment Law Review*, 25 (2014), 143, 144. For an earlier view, see S. F. Schwemer, 'The way forward to the Collective Rights Management Directive' (*The 1709 Blog*, 25 February 2014): http://the1709blog.blogspot.dk/2014/02/way-forward-to-collective-rights.html

In February 2014, the Council adopted the Directive, which was subsequently published in the *Official Journal* in March 2014 as Directive 2014/26/EU, which came into force on 10 April 2014.

The draft Directive contained forty-four articles and forty-four recitals, whereas the final CRM Directive grew to fifty-eight recitals and forty-five articles plus annex, making it the most comprehensive Directive within the broader copyright sphere to date. Structurally, the Directive is divided into five titles: I General provisions; II Collective management organisations; III Multi-territorial licensing of online rights in musical works by collective management organisations; IV Enforcement measures; and V Reporting and final provisions. The Commission explains that the legislative initiative deals with 'two distinct but interrelated problem areas', namely, first, problems affecting collective management of rights in general by any CMO and, secondly, the specific issues of the online market for music licences.[89] Directive 2014/26/EU partly builds on the goals set forth in Recommendation 2005/737/EC and pursues two complementary objectives as laid out in Article 1 of the CRM Directive:[90]

This Directive lays down requirements necessary to ensure the proper functioning of the management of copyright and related rights by collective management organisations. It also lays down requirements for multi-territorial licensing by collective management organisations of authors' rights in musical works for online use.

This roughly correlates to Chapter II on collective rights management organisations and Chapter III on multi-territorial licensing of online rights in musical works by collective management organisations, respectively.

Regarding the chosen policy tool, as noted above, the Commission contemplates in its Impact Assessment that the previously chosen non-binding route was insufficient 'to trigger the necessary changes in national laws and in stakeholders' practices'.[91] Thus, a legislative instrument was

---

[89] See Commission, 'Impact Assessment accompanying the document Proposal for a Directive of the European Parliament and of the Council on collective management of copyright and related rights and multi-territorial licensing of rights in musical works for online uses in the internal market', 32–33.

[90] See also Recital 40 of the Directive; and P. Quintais, 'Proposal for a Directive on Collective Rights Management and (some) Multi-territorial Licensing', *European Intellectual Property Review*, 35 (2013), 65, 67. Initially, the focus of the establishment of a regulatory framework was on establishing principles of good governance, see Guibault and van Gompel, 'Collective Management in the European Union', p. 137.

[91] Commission, 'Impact Assessment accompanying the document Proposal for a Directive of the European Parliament and of the Council on collective management of copyright and related rights and multi-territorial licensing of rights in musical works for online uses in the internal market', 53.

deemed more appropriate to address the identified issues, because '[o]nly a binding instrument can guarantee that the policy options are introduced in all MS and that improvements follow for all CS across the EU'.[92]

A Regulation as policy tool was discarded for several reasons: first, the objective of the lawmaker was not a full harmonisation, but rather to leave Member States some flexibility.[93] More profoundly, the legal basis for the action, inter alia the freedom to provide services, does not foresee Regulations.[94] A third consideration was directed towards the varying traditions of collective management in the different Member States, which would hamper cultural diversity and not be compatible with the subsidiarity and proportionality principle.[95] Thus, a Directive was deemed the most suitable legal instrument. In order to satisfy the need for quick implementation, which was evaluated as main advantage of a Regulation, the Commission considered proposing a short transposition deadline.[96] Despite this consideration in the Impact Assessment, the Commission suggested a standard two-year implementation deadline. After publication in the *Official Journal*, the Directive had to be implemented by the Member States by 10 April 2016.

There exist no rules in the international conventions or EU rules regarding the collective management of copyright and related rights.[97] The comprehensive framework introduced by the Directive was expected to result in 'substantial changes' in the laws of most Member States.[98] As to the degree of harmonisation, the EU lawmaker envisioned a minimum harmonisation.[99] This reflects with the expressed aim for a minimum implementation in the Danish[100] and Swedish[101]

---

[92] Ibid.   [93] Ibid., 54.   [94] Ibid.   [95] Ibid.   [96] Ibid.
[97] See J. Axhamn, 'Nya normer för kollektiv rättighetsförvaltning på upphovsrättens område', *Nordiskt Immateriellt Rättskydd* [2015], 675, 679, who points towards rules in the conventions that nonetheless can play a role in relation to collective management of rights in that individual administration is the starting point.
[98] Commission, 'Proposal for a Directive of the European Parliament and of the Council on collective management of copyright and related rights and multi-territorial licensing of rights in musical works for online uses in the internal market' COM(2012) 372/2, 2012/0180 (COD) Annex II, 43. See also Ficsor, who raises the point that '[t]here is hardly any EU Member State whose national law contains as detailed regulation on collective management of copyright and related rights as the [CRM] Directive does' (Ficsor, 'Collective Management and Multi-territorial Licensing: Key Issues of the Transposition of Directive 2014/26/EU', p. 212).
[99] See Commission, 'Proposal for a Directive of the European Parliament and of the Council on collective management of copyright and related rights and multi-territorial licensing of rights in musical works for online uses in the internal market', Annex II, 45.
[100] For details on the discussion around the Danish implementation, see S. F. Schwemer, 'Kollektiv forvaltning i informationssamfundet og det nye regime under direktivet 2014/26/EU i Danmark', *Nordiskt Immateriellt Rättskydd* [2015], 697.
[101] For a detailed report on the Swedish implementation process, see, e.g., Axhamn, 'Nya normer för kollektiv rättighetsförvaltning på upphovsrättens område', 678.

implementations, which is not going beyond what is necessary, because more extensive regulation could inter alia lead to competitive disadvantages.[102] In both Scandinavian countries the implementation was conducted by the introduction of a new law (*lov om kollektiv forvaltning af ophavsret* and *lag om kollektiv rättighetsförvaltning på upphovsrättsområdet* respectively) and changes to the existing copyright acts. In Germany, substantial existing legislation on collective management in the *Urheberrechtswahrnehmungsgesetz* was replaced by a new law: *Verwertungsgesellschaftengesetz*. In the United Kingdom, the government had published minimum standards at the end of 2012 and the Copyright (Regulation of Relevant Licensing Bodies) Regulations of 2014,[103] which have been revoked in favour of a new legislative instrument in the form of the Collective Management of Copyright (EU Directive) Regulation.

4.2.2   Scope of Directive 2014/26/EU

Collective Management Organisations

Whereas the Commission's Proposal referred to 'collecting societies', the notion was later adjusted to CMOs. In earlier legislative acts, 'collecting society' had been defined by the European legislator for the purpose of the SatCab Directive in Article 1(4), as 'any organisation which manages or administers copyright or rights related to copyright as its sole purpose or as one of its main purposes'.[104] The somewhat more general term in the CRM Directive was preferred to ensure a level playing field and accommodate different national approaches.[105] In Article 3(a) of Directive 2014/26/EU such a CMO is defined as:

---

[102] Ibid.

[103] See UK Intellectual Property Office, 'Collective rights management in the digital single market, Consultation on the implementation of the EU Directive on the collective management of copyright and multi-territorial licensing of online music rights in the internal market' (2015), 5; also A. Ross, 'The new regulatory regime for collective rights management – the Government consults on how to implement', *Entertainment Law Review*, 26 (2015), 130.

[104] Council Directive 93/83/EEC of 27 September 1993 on the coordination of certain rules concerning copyright and rights related to copyright applicable to satellite broadcasting and cable retransmission [1993] OJ L248/15–21.

[105] See Quintais, 'Proposal for a Directive on collective rights management and (some) multi-territorial licensing', 67; Schwemer, 'The way forward to the Collective Rights Management Directive'; and J. Drexl, 'Collective Management of Copyrights and the EU Principle of Free Movement of Services after the OSA Judgment – In Favour of a More Balanced Approach' in K. Purnhagen and P. Rott (eds.), *Varieties of European Economic Law and Regulation, Liber Amicorum for Hans Micklitz*, vol. 3 (Springer, 2014), p. 460 n. 6. See also J. Drexl and others, 'Comments of the Max Planck Institute for Intellectual Property and Competition Law on the Proposal for a Directive of the

any organisation which is authorised by law or by way of assignment, licence or any other contractual arrangement to manage copyright or rights related to copyright on behalf of more than one rightholder, for the collective benefit of those rightholders, as its sole or main purpose, and which fulfils one or both of the following criteria:
  (i) it is owned or controlled by its members;
  (ii) it is organised on a not-for-profit basis

A comparison with the definition of a 'collecting society' in the draft Directive reveals that only minor changes to the wording have been carried out – namely specifying that the authorisation is not only 'by more than one rightholder' but 'on behalf of more than one rightholder' and adding the alternative criteria of an organisation organised on a non-profit basis.[106] Ficsor criticises this definition verbatim as 'dysfunctional', mainly because its reference to 'on behalf of more than one rightholder', which implies that an organisation that is 'managing rights on behalf of as few as two rightholders is supposed to be recognized as CMO'.[107] The definition in Article 3(a) of the Directive is complemented by Recital 14, in which it is specified that CMOs do not have to adopt a specific legal form, however, an association seems to be the standard form that the Directive looks at.[108] Both the definition in the SatCab Directive and that in the CRM Directive respectively put special emphasis on the activity being the organisation's 'sole or main purpose'. The Commission expressed for the CRM Directive that this criterion is to be understood objectively, e.g., looking at the activities of a certain organisation.[109]

Independent Management Entities

Additionally, the legislator introduced the novel notion of so-called 'independent management entities' (IMEs) in Article 3(b) Directive

---

European Parliament and of the Council on Collective Management of Copyright and Related Rights' (2012) Max Planck Institute for Intellectual Property and Competition Law Research Paper No. 13–04, 3, n. 2: http://ssrn.com/abstract=2208971

[106] Art. 3(a) of the draft Directive defined 'collecting society' as 'any organisation which is authorised by law or by way of assignment, licence or any other contractual arrangement, by more than one rightholder, to manage copyright or rights related to copyright as its sole or main purpose and which is owned or controlled by its members'

[107] M. Ficsor, 'Collective Management and Multi-territorial Licensing: Key Issues of the Transposition of Directive 2014/26/EU', p. 234.

[108] In the Swedish implementation, the lawmaker takes that all legal forms are to be seen as being embraced by the Directive: see Axhamn, 'Nya normer för kollektiv rättighetsförvaltning på upphovsrättens område', 683. Stokkmo comments that the 'CRM Directive is agnostic with respect to the legal personality of CMOs': see O. Stokkmo, 'The EU Collective Rights Management Directive and the RRO', *International Journal of Intellectual Property Management*, 7 (2014), 120, 127.

[109] See Recitals 2 and 16 of the Directive.

2014/26/EU.[110] In Recital 15, it is reflected that rights holders should be free to entrust the management of their rights to IMEs. As I have pointed out earlier, the main difference between CMOs and IMEs lies in their ownership or control structure, in that the latter is neither owned nor controlled by rights holders and is organised on a for-profit basis.[111] In the Swedish and Danish implementations, respectively, 'entity' ('enhet', 'enhed') was replaced by 'organisation' (idem in Swedish and Danish). The Swedish implementation provides as explanation for the redraft that the Directive does not contain a definition of 'entity'.[112] IMEs are not equated with CMOs; they are subject primarily to information duties and excluded from several provisions of the Directive.[113] The rationale behind seems to be that, due to the lack of a membership structure, IMES do not run into all issues that the Directive is aiming to solve.[114] There exists, however, ambiguity and uncertainty as to what undertakings the European law-maker had in mind. The Directive offers only negative criteria, namely in Recital 16, in which it lists examples of players that should not be regarded as IMEs: first, audiovisual producers, record producers, broadcasters, book, music and newspaper publishers that license rights of authors on the basis of individually negotiated agreements because they act in their own interests; secondly, authors' and performers' managers and agents acting as intermediaries and representing rights holders in their relation with CMOs, 'since they do not manage rights in the sense of setting tariffs, granting licences or collecting money from users'.[115] The German implementation, for example, notes that

---

[110] Art. 3(b) defines 'independent management entity' as 'any organisation which is authorised by law or by way of assignment, license or any other contractual arrangement to manage copyright or rights related to copyright on behalf of more than one right-holder, for the collective benefit of those rightholders, as its sole or main purpose, and which is: (i) neither owned nor controlled, directly or indirectly, wholly or in part by rightholders; and (ii) organised on a for-profit basis'. Whereas the draft Directive made reference to independent management entities in Recital 4, a definition was first included in the final Directive.

[111] See Schwemer, 'Emerging models for cross-border online licensing', 87–88.

[112] Axhamn, 'Nya normer för kollektiv rättighetsförvaltning på upphovsrättens område', 686. Kulturministeriet, 'Forslag til Lov om kollektiv forvaltning af ophavsret' (2015) Dok nr. 2772691, Bemærkninger til lovforslaget, 96.

[113] See Art. 2(4) and Recital 15 of the CRM Directive.

[114] This can be drawn from the reverse argument in Recital 15, second sentence, of the Directive. See also Quintais, 'Proposal for a Directive on collective rights management and (some) multi-territorial licensing', 68, pointing to Recital 4 of the draft Directive, which was, however, not adopted.

[115] Recital 16 of Directive 2014/26/EU. An interesting question, which is outside the scope of this book, is whether this means that tariff setting, granting licensing and collecting royalties from users a contrario are essential aspects of the activity of CMOs that should be considered in the definition in Art. 3(a).

undertakings such as 'Rechtemakler' (rights agents), which could be understood as such entities, so far have hardly any practical relevance.[116] It remains a matter of speculation as to whether the European legislator had more direct licensing developments as pointed out above in mind.[117]

In the German implementation, the wording was left unaltered ('unabhängige Verwertungseinrichtung'), but the legislator additionally specified a third type: a so-called 'dependent management entity' ('abhängige Verwertungseinrichtung', § 3(1) VGG), which embraces controlled entities as envisioned under Article 2(3) of the Directive, which refers to an entity which is partly owned by a CMO.[118] The Danish and Swedish legislators refrained from introducing a similar definition, but instead implemented a rule closer to Article 2(3) of Directive 2014/26/EU, according to which the relevant provisions also

apply to entities directly or indirectly owned or controlled, wholly or in part, by a collective management organisation, provided that such entities carry out an activity which, if carried out by the collective management organisation, would be subject to the provisions of this Directive.

The provision serves to safeguard the freedom of CMOs in having certain aspects of their activities being carried out by, e.g., subsidies, while ensuring that this cannot serve as a loophole.[119]

---

[116] Bundesministerium der Justiz und für Verbraucherschutz, 'Referentenentwurf des Bundesministeriums der Justiz und für Verbraucherschutz Entwurf eines Gesetzes zur Umsetzung der Richtlinie 2014/26/EU über die kollektive Wahrnehmung von Urheber- und verwandten Schutzrechten und die Vergabe von Mehrgebietslizenzen für Rechte an Musikwerken für die Online-Nutzung im Binnenmarkt sowie zur Änderung des Verfahrens betreffend die Geräte- und Speichermedienvergütung (VG-Richtlinie-Umsetzungsgesetz)' (2015) 09.06.2015, 69.

[117] Given the reference to 'collective benefit' in the definition of an independent management entity, the feature that rights holders have no control makes the provision somewhat contradictory. In the Consultation on the implementation of the CRM Directive, the UK Intellectual Property Office, for example, asked whether rights holders or licensees have either managed or obtained their licences from an organisation that they think is an IME. This indicates that also national governments were unsure about this new type of organisation. One example for an IME is Soundreef, which provides administration of publishing rights and master recording rights for background music in stores and at live events. According to its website, it is competing with traditional CMOs and registered in the UK. See www .soundreef.com

[118] Verwertungsgesellschaftengesetz vom 24. Mai 2016 (BGBl. I S. 1190), das zuletzt durch Artikel 14 des Gesetzes vom 17. Juli 2017 (BGBl. I S. 2541) geändert worden ist.

[119] See Recital 17 of the CRM Directive. On umbrella structures, which are common in Scandinavia, see Schwemer, 'Kollektiv forvaltning i informationssamfundet og det nye regime under direktivet 2014/26/EU i Danmark'.

Hybrid Option 3 Licensing Entities

As seen in Chapter 2, new licensing arrangements by option 3 publishers have emerged, which license mono-repertoire on a multi-territorial basis. Surprisingly, the Directive makes no direct reference to these licensing arrangements. Thus, it is relevant to ask whether such arrangements fall within the scope of the Directive.

The details of these arrangements remain blurred, but several key features are essential in determining the applicability of Directive 2014/26/EU: the most obvious feature is that these entities represent and license only a single repertoire.[120] Thus, they might not satisfy the condition of representing more than one right holder contained in Article 3 (a) Directive 2014/26/EU, in order to qualify as CMOs or IMEs.[121] A second feature is that these entities appear to be regularly established as fully owned subsidiaries of one or several CMOs. Thus, the relevant provisions of the Directive could apply to licensing arrangements of option 3 publishers, according to Article 2(3) of the Directive. The second condition of Article 2(3) refers to the activity of the entity and whether, if carried out by the CMO, it would be subject to the provisions of this Directive. This appears to be the case as regards the licensing hub by CMOs as recently formed by STIM, GEMA, and PRS. On a macro level, option 3 publisher licensing entities, too, seem to perform activities, foremost the licensing of their rights, which constitute central activities of CMOs. Given the central role of the developments

---

[120] See also Hilty and Nérisson, 'Collective Copyright Management and Digitization: The European Experience', 8–9.

[121] See also the definition of 'rightholder' in Art. 3(c) of the Directive. Additionally, it seems questionable whether such entities or arrangements would satisfy the other criteria set out in the provision, such as the 'not-for-profit basis' or the reference to 'collective benefit'. Regarding the point that the first essential condition of 'more than one rightholder', something different could potentially be argued of ARESA, which represents the former EMI and Sony/ATV repertoire following their merger; thus, ARESA holds technically two repertoires. In Germany, the District Court of Munich in *MyVideo* v. *CELAS* (LG München I, 25.06.2009 – 7 O 4139/08) dealt with a case involving CELAS. The case was upheld at the Higher Regional Court (OLG München, 29.04.2010 – 29 U 3698/09); an appeal to the German Federal Court of Justice (BGH I ZR 116/10) was withdrawn. The Court, however, explicitly refrained from commenting on whether CELAS could qualify as a CMO under German law. Hoeren and Altemark, for example, argue that CELAS qualified as a CMO in the sense of the former Urheberrechtswahrnehmungsgesetz. See Thomas Hoeren and Christine Altemark, 'Musikverwertungsgesellschaften und das Urheberrechtswahrnehmungsgesetz am Beispiel der CELAS', GRUR [2010] 16. The Max-Planck Institute recommended clarifying the definition in Art. 3(a) with the effect that the Directive also applies to entities as CELAS. See Drexl and others, 'Comments of the Max Planck Institute for Intellectual Property and Competition Law on the Proposal for a Directive of the European Parliament and of the Council on Collective Management of Copyright and Related Rights', 21, para. 29.

around these multi-territorial mono-repertoire publishers, it is odd looking that the European legislator does not mention option 3 publishers in the Directive or its preparatory documents and has chosen not to explicitly clarify their role, despite the high level of uncertainty. The Commission clearly did not envision having every possible licensing entity fall under the Directive; instead, it supposes that licensing entities operating under the passport requirements in Title III would be in competition with other licensing agents, which fall outside the scope of Directive, 'for attracting repertoire with the licensing entities operating under passport requirements'.[122] On the other hand, Article 2(3) was first introduced in a comparable form in the report on the proposal for the CRM Directive by the Committee on Legal Affairs, which can explain the lack of reflections in the Commission's preparatory works.[123] The European umbrella consumer protection association also pointed, in its statement in relation to the Draft Directive, towards the fact that the proposed definitions let subsidiaries such as CELAS fall outside the scope of the Directive.[124] According to BITKOM, a major German digital industry association, § 3 of the German implementation (dependent management entity) comprises option 3 publishers.[125]

But if the Directive were to apply partly to the current licensing arrangements of option 3 publishers, it might create an incentive to

---

[122] Commission, 'Impact Assessment accompanying the document Proposal for a Directive of the European Parliament and of the Council on collective management of copyright and related rights and multi-territorial licensing of rights in musical works for online uses in the internal market' 162. See also discussion of the passport model below.

[123] See European Parliament, 'Report on the proposal for a directive of the European Parliament and of the Council on collective management of copyright and related rights and multi-territorial licensing of rights in musical works for online uses in the internal market (COM(2012)0372 – C7-0183/2012 – 2012/0180(COD))' Committee on Legal Affairs, Rapporteur: Marielle Gallo, 2012/0180(COD), 4 October 2013 Amendment 38.

[124] Bureau Européen des Unions de Consommateurs (BEUC), 'Collective Management of Copyright and Related Rights and Multi-territorial Licensing of Rights in Musical Works for Online, Proposal for a Directive' *Ref.: X/2013/001* (Brussels, 08 January 2013): https://ameliaandersdotter.eu/sites/default/files/beuc_-_crm.pdf

[125] In the context that also option 3 publishers need to be authorised by the German Patent and Trademark Office (DMPA), see Bundesverband Informationswirtschaft Telekommunikation und Neue Medien e.V. (bitkom), 'Stellungnahme zum Regierungsentwurf eines Verwertungsgesellschaftengesetzes (VGG)' (Berlin, 14 January 2016). The explanatory statement of the draft by the federal government, however, does not refer to these licensing entities: Bundesregierung, 'Entwurf eines Gesetzes zur Umsetzung der Richtlinie 2014/26/EU über die kollektive Wahrnehmung von Urheber- und verwandten Schutzrechten und die Vergabe von Mehrgebietslizenzen für Rechte an Musikwerken für die Online-Nutzung im Binnenmarkt sowie zur Änderung des Verfahrens betreffend die Geräte- und Speichermedienvergütung (VG-Richtlinie-Umsetzungsgesetz)' (2015) RegE Gesetzentwurf der Bundesregierung, 11. November 2015, 88.

remodel the respective systems to escape compliance. By forming their own licensing entities, which are not subsidiaries of CMOs, they would effectively enter the Directive's 'no man's land'. This could have adverse effects on a level playing field and it seems questionable whether the legislator intended this scenario.[126] In a similar vein, Anthonis argues, on the other hand, that option 3 publishers operating under a lower regulatory burden might create an incentive for CMOs to create work-arounds to escape the scope of the Directive.[127]

Teleologically, it seems that Article 2(3) could also be primarily directed towards the outsourcing of certain 'own' functions of CMOs,[128] such as front-, middle- or back-office activities. This interpretation is supported by Recital 17 of Directive 2014/26/EU, which specifies that

> Collective management organisations should be free to choose to have certain of their activities, such as the invoicing of users or the distribution of amounts due to rightholders, carried out by subsidiaries or by other entities that they control. In such cases, those provisions of this Directive that would be applicable if the relevant activity were carried out directly by a collective management organisation should be applicable to the activities of the subsidiaries or other entities.

In addition, it is worth recalling that licensing activities of option 3 publishers would notably not be carried out by CMOs in the first place, as rights holders withdrew their repertoire from the system of CMOs as such. Another consequence, however, would be that, e.g., rules on licensing such as non-discriminatory terms of the Directive would not apply. Yet, the general principles, as refined by the courts, might do. Against this background, it seems unclear at best, and unconvincing at worst, that Article 2(3) is the norm that expands the scope of the Directive to the licensing arrangements of option 3 publishers. This view also implies that subsidiaries by CMOs, which have their function outside the activities specified in Recital 17, would only be comprised by the Directive in a teleological reading.[129]

---

[126] Also considering the detailed refinement of an IME; as noted, the IME is a form of organisation that has yet to emerge on a broader scale. The argument might not convince, if CMOs could 'simply', by starting subsidiaries for each individual right holder, escape the application of the Directive.

[127] See Anthonis, 'Will the CRM-directive succeed re-aggregating the mechanical reproduction rights in the Anglo-American music repertoire?', 159, noting that CELAS (nowadays SOLAR), for example, 'could change that relationship to an agency contract'. More generally, see also Schwemer, 'Kollektiv forvaltning i informationssamfundet og det nye regime under direktivet 2014/26/EU i Danmark' 702.

[128] See also Recital 43 of Directive 2014/26/EU.

[129] Similarly, see K.-N. Peifer, 'Umsetzung der EU-Richtlinie für Verwertungsgesellschaften in deutsches Recht, Umsetzungsbedarf aus wissenschaftlicher Sicht', *Zeitschrift für Urheber- und Medienrecht* [2014], 453, 455.

Finally, further legal uncertainty comes with the reference to '[t]he relevant provisions of this Directive' in Article 2(3): the Directive does not specify what is to be understood as relevant. In an extensive interpretation, it seems reasonable that Title III is to be understood as such a set of rules. Some have argued that if Title III applied to subsidiaries of CMOs,[130] it 'would guarantee that option 3 platforms, that are owned in whole or in part, by a CMO (. . .) fall under the scope of Title [III] of the Directive'.[131] However, this view overlooks the fact that, according to Article 2(2), Title III only to CMOs managing authors' rights in musical works and not related-rights owners.[132]

In conclusion, it appears that licensing entities of option 3 publishers are left in the Directive's 'no man's land', where it is up to the discretion of the national legislator to clarify the scope, as for example in the German implementation, and ultimately the interpretation by the Courts.

CMOs from Outside the European Economic Area (EEA)

Recital 10 of the CRM Directive opens up the opportunity for Member States to apply the rules based on the Directive also to CMOs, which are established outside the Union, but which operate in the respective Member State.[133] When considering the goal of creating a level playing field, the application of the rules to non-EEA CMOs seems appropriate. Otherwise, CMOs operating outside the scope of the Directive could, for example, face lower compliance costs. At the same time, however, there are a couple of unknown factors, such as whether it is possible to cherry-pick which rules to apply and how those rules could effectively be enforced. At least the rules regarding multi-territorial licensing (Title III of the Directive) apply pursuant to Article 2(3) only to CMOs established in the Union. Otherwise, the Directive is silent on this matter. In Denmark, for example, the legislator has chosen to apply the implementing law only to CMOs that are established in Denmark.[134]

---

[130] See Art. 2(3) of Directive 2014/26/EU or Art. 31 of the draft Directive.

[131] See also Anthonis, 'Will the CRM-directive succeed re-aggregating the mechanical reproduction rights in the Anglo-American music repertoire?', 159.

[132] See also Drexl and others, 'Comments of the Max Planck Institute for Intellectual Property and Competition Law on the Proposal for a Directive of the European Parliament and of the Council on Collective Management of Copyright and Related Rights' 19, para. 26.

[133] Notably, according to Art. 2(3) of the Directive, Title III applies only to CMOs established in the Union.

[134] Schwemer, 'Kollektiv forvaltning i informationssamfundet og det nye regime under direktivet 2014/26/EU i Danmark', 703.

4.2.3   Administrative Part: Governance and Transparency Framework (Title II)

The first objective of the Directive, namely to increase transparency and efficiency in the functioning of CMOs, is addressed in the provisions on Collective Management Organisations in Title II of Directive 2014/26/EU. In contrast with the provisions on multi-territorial licensing, which apply to author CMOs only, the governance and transparency framework applies to all CMOs, irrespective of their sector of operation or rights concerned.

The Commission considered four policy options in order to achieve its goals: retaining the status quo as baseline scenario (A1), in which the legislator would rely on the market pressure and self-regulation. The Commission contented that the cross-border issues would not be solved in this scenario.[135] Policy option A2 aimed at the better enforcement of existing EU law, where neither operating conditions for CMOs would be harmonised nor 'issues outside the scope of the existing principles' would be resolved.[136] A third policy option (A3), the codification of existing principles from the case law of the CJEU, the EU Commission's competition decisions, and the Online Music Recommendation but was deemed to fail to address 'more recently identified problems in relation to financial transparency and control by rightholders'.[137] Thus, the Commission opted to 'codify the existing principles and provide a more elaborate framework of rules on governance and transparency, increasing the possibilities of control over collecting societies'.[138]

Title II consists of five chapters governing representation of rights holders and membership and organisation of CMOs (Chapter 1), management of rights revenue (Chapter 2), management of rights on behalf of other CMOs (Chapter 3), relations with users (Chapter 4) as well as transparency and reporting (Chapter 5).

During the implementation of the Directive especially the governance and transparency framework has been in focus.[139] As noted, Title II codifies certain principles of the CJEU's case law and the Commission's

---

[135] Commission, 'Proposal for a Directive of the European Parliament and of the Council on collective management of copyright and related rights and multi-territorial licensing of rights in musical works for online uses in the internal market', Explanatory Memorandum, 6. In more recent proposals, the baseline scenario is not sketched as policy option.

[136] Ibid., Explanatory Memorandum, 6.   [137] Ibid.

[138] Ibid. Such as Case 395/87, *Tournier*; Joined Cases 110/88, 241/88 and 242/88, *Lucazeau* and *Commission Decision CISAC*.

[139] On implementation in Denmark and some of the issues, especially in relation to Title II, see the earlier work by Schwemer, 'Kollektiv forvaltning i informationssamfundet og det nye regime under direktivet 2014/26/EU i Danmark'.

competition decisions in addition to comprehensive additional rules. Whereas this framework *prima facie* has little to do with the provision of cross-border licences, there are several aspects that are relevant for licensing.

4.2.3.1 General Licensing Provisions

In Chapter 4 of Title II, the Directive sets general principles for the relationship with the organisations' (commercial) users, i.e. licensees. Article 16 Directive 2014/26/EU harmonises, inter alia, that negotiations are to be conducted in good faith and under the provision of all necessary information.[140] It continues to govern that licensing terms are to be based on objective and non-discriminatory criteria. This is particularly important, according to Recital 31, in order to ensure that licensees can obtain licences and to ensure the appropriate remuneration of rights holders. Article 16(2) codifies the Court's case law and sets out that tariffs

shall be reasonable in relation to, inter alia, the economic value of the use of the rights in trade, taking into account the nature and scope of the use of the work and other subject-matter, as well as in relation to the economic value of the service provided by the collective management organisation.

Notably, Article 16(2), in its second sentence, allows for the setting of licensing terms for new types of online services, which have been available to the public for less than three years, without the risk for CMOs that those terms could be used as precedent for other licences. As Recital 32 clarifies, this is anticipated to give CMOs the flexibility 'required to provide, as swiftly as possible, individualised licences for innovative online services' for 'totally new forms of exploitation and business models'. In the draft Directive this provision was contained in Article 32, which meant that it only applied to author CMOs for online rights in multi-territorial situations. It has already been referred to as 'one of the most ambiguous provisions'.[141] The legislator refrained from providing further definitions of what should be understood as 'innovative' services.

---

[140] The Max Planck Institute advocated the introduction of a general obligation to contract with rights holders. See Drexl and others, 'Comments of the Max Planck Institute for Intellectual Property and Competition Law on the Proposal for a Directive of the European Parliament and of the Council on Collective Management of Copyright and Related Rights', 7, para. 10.

[141] Quintais, 'Proposal for a Directive on collective rights management and (some) multi-territorial licensing', 71. But Quintais also sees the article as a derogation from the objective criteria such as 'the economic value of the use of the rights in trade', which made sense under the structure of the draft Directive, where the derogation from the general rule in Art. 15 was contained in Art. 32. In the final Directive, however, the derogation comes before the general rule, thereby rendering this argument less valid.

Article 16(3) of Directive 2014/26/EU sets out to speed up the processing of licensing requests and obliges CMOs, without undue delay, to 'offer a licensee or provide the user with a reasoned statement explaining why it does not intend to license to a particular service'. Connected to this, Article 17, on the other hand, obliges licensees to provide relevant information on the use of the rights, whereby voluntary industry standards should be taken into account as far as possible.[142]

As regards licensing for non-commercial purposes such as, e.g., uses falling under Creative Commons licences, Article 5(3) has been added during the legislative process, stipulating:[143]

rightholders shall have the right to grant licenses for non-commercial use of any rights, categories of rights or types of works and other subject matter, provided that their management falls within the scope of its activity.

Recital 19 clarifies that this should include 'inter alia, a decision by the collective management organisation on the conditions attached to the exercise of that right as well as the provision to their members of information on those conditions'.

4.2.3.2 General Provisions of the Governance and Transparency Framework

In addition to the specific rules on licensing, the Directive's governance and transparency framework also becomes relevant in the licensing relationship. The general framework builds upon the premise that

---

[142] See also Ross, 'The new regulatory regime for collective rights management – the Government consults on how to implement', 132.

[143] The Danish author CMO KODA was one of the first to introduce a Creative Commons scheme for non-commercial purposes in 2008. See KODA, 'Creative Commons nu i Danmark' *KODA* (Copenhagen, 24 January 2008). In France, Denmark, the Netherlands and Sweden, there have been projects between CMOs and Creative Commons, allowing CMO members to apply for non-commercial licences for some of their music. 'This possibility of individual treatment of single works is a big step', as noted by Hilty and Nérisson, 'Collective Copyright Management and Digitization: The European Experience', 11. In Germany, rights holders were required to withdraw all their rights from the respective CMO, GEMA, in order to license for creative uses: see A. Metzger and T. Heinemann, 'The Right of the Author to Grant Licenses for Non-Commercial Use: Creative Commons Licenses and the Directive on Collective Management', *Journal of Intellectual Property, Information Technology and Electronic Commerce*, 6 (2015), 11, 13. The EP's Committee on International Trade suggested that not only commercial uses but also placement in the public domain should be included. See European Parliament, 'Opinion of the Committee on International Trade for the Committee on Legal Affairs on the proposal for a directive of the European Parliament and of the Council on collective management of copyright and related rights and multi-territorial licensing of rights in musical works for online uses in the internal market (COM(2012)0372 – C7-0183/2012 – 2012/0180(COD))' Committee on International Trade, Rapporteur: Helmut Scholz, 2012/0180(COD), 20 June 2013, 8.

governance rules increase competition. Additionally, the Commission expected the general framework to have a positive impact on licensees (commercial users) as 'they would obtain access to the most information and would have the right to bring disputes before the dispute resolution body'.[144]

Chapter 1 of Title II regulates the representation of rights holders and membership and organisation of CMOs with, e.g., rules on membership and general assembly. Most relevant, Article 5(2) of Directive 2014/26/EU codifies the right of rights holders to authorise CMOs of their choice as envisioned in the Online Music Recommendation. It reads:

> Rightholders shall have the right to authorise a collective management organisation of their choice to manage the rights, categories of rights or types of works and other subject-matter of their choice, for the territories of their choice, irrespective of the Member State of nationality, residence or establishment of either the collective management organisation or the right holder. Unless the collective management organisation has objectively justified reasons to refuse management, it shall be obliged to manage such rights, categories of rights or types of works and other subject-matter, provided that their management falls within the scope of its activity.

Thereby it makes it compulsory to adopt the core principle of the Recommendation. In contrast with the Recommendation, however, the right to withdraw is not limited to 'any of the online rights necessary to operate legitimate online music services' but applicable to all rights and rights holders.[145]

4.2.4 Multi-Territorial Licensing Framework (Title III)

In the context of multi-territorial licensing, the second part of the Directive, i.e. Title III on multi-territorial licensing of online rights in musical works by collective management organisations, is most relevant: it aims to

> provide a set of rules prescribing basic conditions for the provision by collective management organisations of multi-territorial collective licensing of authors' rights in musical works for online use.[146]

---

[144] Commission, 'Impact Assessment accompanying the document Proposal for a Directive of the European Parliament and of the Council on collective management of copyright and related rights and multi-territorial licensing of rights in musical works for online uses in the internal market', 39.

[145] See also E. Arezzo, 'Competition and Intellectual Property Protection in the Market for the Provision of Multi-territorial Licensing of Online Rights in Musical Works – Lights and Shadows of the New European Directive 2014/26/EU', *International Review of Intellectual Property and Competition Law*, 46 (2015), 534, 540.

[146] Recital 40 Directive 2014/26/EU; see also Art. 23 Directive 2014/26/EU.

Structurally, Title III is one of the shorter sections of the Directive, encompassing just ten articles.[147] Compared with the governance and transparency framework, the scope of the set on rules on multi-territorial licensing is narrower: the rules continue the regulatory focus on author CMOs (including lyrics) and licensing for online use on a multi-territorial basis, which stems from Recommendation 2005/737/EU. Thus, whereas the main use case is likely to evolve around streaming services (and, to a lesser degree, downloading), it also covers the use of music in games or audiovisual content.[148] Furthermore, the rules of Title III apply only to CMOs that are established in the EU.[149] It is important to recall that the rules on multi-territorial licensing also apply to subsidiaries or other entities directly or indirectly owned or controlled by a CMO under certain conditions.

4.2.4.1 *Considered Policy Options*

In its comprehensive, 197-pages-long Impact Assessment accompanying the proposal for the Directive, the Commission lays out the five policy options that it had considered on multi-territory licensing for online use of musical works: retaining the *status quo* (B1); European licensing passport (B2); parallel direct licensing (B3) ; extended collective licensing (B4); and a centralised portal (B5).

Policy option B1, retaining the *status quo* as a baseline scenario, was dismissed because the licensing of online rights would remain complex and cumbersome.[150] Policy option B2, a European licensing passport,

---

[147] The part on multi-territorial licensing of the draft Directive was slightly longer and consisted of twelve articles; inter alia Art. 27 (draft Directive on outsourcing) was dropped (contained in Recital 43 of the final Directive) and Art. 32 (draft Directive on licensing terms for services that have been available to the public for less than three years) was moved.

[148] See Recital 40 of the CRM Directive. Online services that solely provide access to musical works in the form of sheet music are not covered by Title III, according to Recital 40 of the CRM Directive. Art. 32 of the Directive contains a derogation of Title III for the multi-territorial licensing of online music rights that are required for simultaneous and delayed online transmission of radio and television programs. This derogation finds its basis in the licensing situation, where broadcasters rely on a licence from a local CMO for their own broadcasts of television and radio programs. See Recital 48 of Directive 2014/26/EU.

[149] See Art. 2(2) Directive 2014/26/EU.

[150] Commission, 'Impact Assessment accompanying the document Proposal for a Directive of the European Parliament and of the Council on collective management of copyright and related rights and multi-territorial licensing of rights in musical works for online uses in the internal market' 27; Commission, 'Proposal for a Directive of the European Parliament and of the Council on collective management of copyright and related rights and multi-territorial licensing of rights in musical works for online uses in the internal market', Explanatory Memorandum, 6.

would focus on encouraging the aggregation of repertoire 'through effective and responsive MT licensing infrastructure'.[151] The details of this model, which has been chosen, will be discussed in the designated section below.

Policy option B3, parallel direct licensing, which was advocated by some music publishers, 'would have given rightholders the ability to conclude direct licences with users, in parallel with their membership of a CMO'.[152] In this model, CMOs would be required to manage the rights of rights holders on a non-exclusive basis.[153] Thus, rights holders would be able to conclude direct licences with licensees, without having to withdraw their rights from the respective CMO.[154] The Commission presumed that direct licences could be 'more responsive, flexible and adapted to the needs of users' in the case of licensing of 'new forms of services where licensing terms and conditions have not yet been tested'.[155] This option was deemed to 'improve the ability of publishers to aggregate all the rights needed for the exploitation of musical works on line (i.e. the mechanical and the performing rights) directly across the entire EU both as regards the Anglo-American and the continental repertoire'.[156] Direct licensing by individual authors, on the other hand, was deemed unlikely to be a viable economic proposition.[157]

A fourth policy option (B4), an extended collective licensing (ECL) model paired with a 'country of origin' principle, was considered. This model, inspired by the Scandinavian ECL-regime, is based on an extension effect of the licence provided the respective organisation is representative, which the presumption that each author CMO 'has the authority to grant "blanket" licenses for online uses covering the entire repertoire'.[158] The Commission evaluated that this system would support the

---

[151] Commission, 'Impact Assessment accompanying the document Proposal for a Directive of the European Parliament and of the Council on collective management of copyright and related rights and multi-territorial licensing of rights in musical works for online uses in the internal market', 42.

[152] Anthonis, 'Will the CRM-directive succeed re-aggregating the mechanical reproduction rights in the Anglo-American music repertoire?', 157.

[153] Commission, 'Impact Assessment accompanying the document Proposal for a Directive of the European Parliament and of the Council on collective management of copyright and related rights and multi-territorial licensing of rights in musical works for online uses in the internal market', 44.

[154] Ibid.   [155] Ibid.   [156] Ibid., 165.

[157] Ibid. Parallel direct licensing was not ultimately not chosen as a policy option, inter alia because obtaining consent from the individual rights holders would be time consuming and create legal uncertainty; furthermore, the Commission deemed it unclear whether the number of licences would be reduced; finally, a negative impact on cultural diversity could not be ruled out, because smaller rights holders would be in a weaker bargaining position.

[158] Ibid., 45.

aggregation of rights within each local CMO and improve legal certainty.[159] In order to ensure that one licence is sufficient to cover the entire EU territory, it was suggested that the model be combined with a 'country of origin' principle, as used, for example, in the SatCab Directive.[160] Some public broadcasters advocated this model in stakeholder dialogue. Data processing problems such as repertoire identification, on the other hand, were deemed not to be solved but simply shifted 'to the "back office" of collective management'.[161] Thus, the Commission contemplated, there would be little incentive for CMOs to become more efficient. The main concern, however, was addressed in the prediction that publishers and some CMOs would opt out of the extended licences on a large scale – an effect that was deemed to be most likely regarding commercially valuable repertoire.[162] Repertoire would be further disaggregated and in effect be detrimental to multi-territorial licensing.[163] In order to avoid such opt-outs, local CMOs, on the other hand, would have an incentive to maintain 'a very conservative licensing policy to the detriment of innovative services'.[164] In this model 'commercial users still need to get a number of licences from rightholders and CS (as under the baseline scenario) as well as an extended licence from the society in their country of origin'.[165]

Finally, the Commission considered a centralised portal as option B5. In this scenario, CMOs would pool their repertoires for multi-territorial licensing on voluntary basis,[166] thereby effectively creating a 'one-stop shop' with a *de facto* monopoly power. The Commission reflects that this model would 'exacerbate competition restrictions, notably customer allocation (because the portal rather than a commercial user would choose the licensing society) and price fixing (as administration fees would be decided by the portal rather than different CS)'.[167] While this solution was supported by some CMOs, it was ruled out due to competition concerns and not further assessed as to its impacts.[168]

---

[159] Ibid., 44 and 170.   [160] Ibid., 46.   [161] Ibid., 171.   [162] Ibid., 170.

[163] See Commission, 'Proposal for a Directive of the European Parliament and of the Council on collective management of copyright and related rights and multi-territorial licensing of rights in musical works for online uses in the internal market', Explanatory Memorandum, 6.

[164] Commission, 'Impact Assessment accompanying the document Proposal for a Directive of the European Parliament and of the Council on collective management of copyright and related rights and multi-territorial licensing of rights in musical works for online uses in the internal market', 170.

[165] Ibid. The Commission also notes that the system lacks the flexibility of other licensing processes as regards choice of service providers.

[166] Ibid., 46.   [167] Ibid., 47.

[168] Ibid. This has been considered a premature assessment: see, e.g., Drexl and others, 'Comments of the Max Planck Institute for Intellectual Property and Competition Law

4.2.4.2 The European Licensing Passport

The Commission found that policy option B2, a model coined in the Commission's work as 'European licensing passport', would be most suitable to achieving the objectives of both facilitating repertoire aggregation for multi-territorial licensing and increasing legal certainty. The notion of the passport model was only used in the Commission's working documents and the Explanatory Memorandum accompanying the proposal for the directive; hence it does not appear in the final Directive.[169] This proposed system builds on a voluntary aggregation of repertoire, in which CMOs that do not offer multi-territorial licences can tag on their rights for multi-territorial purposes to a CMO that does. The basic idea behind the model is enshrined in Articles 24–31 of the CRM Directive. Overall, the rules on multi-territorial licensing are kept, like the rest of the Directive, fairly technical and rather detailed.

Articles 24–28 of the Directive lay out a set of minimum requirements for multi-territorial licensing. These provisions relating to capacity to process data, transparency, invoicing and payment to rights holders, aim to ensure a high standard required to provide multi-territorial licensing.[170] Article 24 of the CRM Directive, on the capacity to process multi-territorial licences, prescribes that CMOs, which grant multi-territorial licences for online rights, fulfil certain minimum requirements. These refer, inter alia, to the ability to identify the represented musical works as well as rights and corresponding rights holders. Furthermore, according to Article 24(2)(c) of Directive 2014/26/EU, passport entities need to make use of unique identifiers for rights holders and musical works, 'taking into account, as far as possible, voluntary industry standards and practices developed at international or Union level'. Article 25 of Directive 2014/26/EU governs the transparency of multi-territorial

---

on the Proposal for a Directive of the European Parliament and of the Council on Collective Management of Copyright and Related Rights', 32, para. 65; A. M. P. Gómez and M. A. E. Arcila, 'Collective Administration of Online Rights in Musical Works: Analysing the Economic Efficiency of Directive 2014/26/EU', *Journal of Intellectual Property Management*, 7 (2014), 103, 114.

[169] The European Commission has considered passport schemes as policy options in other areas, too. For instance, in the banking sector, in which a 'single passport' is used, it was established in 1989 in the Second Banking Directive (89/646/EEC). Kivistö provides anecdotal evidence from 2010 that the licensing passport model 'was the Commission's favourite long before the publication of the Impact Assessment' (M. Kivistö, 'Multi-territorial online licensing in the light of Title III of the Directive on collective rights management', *Nordiskt Immateriellt Rättskydd* [2015], 706, 707).

[170] Commission, 'Impact Assessment accompanying the document Proposal for a Directive of the European Parliament and of the Council on collective management of copyright and related rights and multi-territorial licensing of rights in musical works for online uses in the internal market', 161.

repertoire information and specifies the information that a passport entity needs to provide in response to a duly justified request. Article 26 of the CRM Directive addresses the accuracy of the multi-territorial repertoire information. Finally, Articles 27 and 28 of the CRM Directive concern financial flows: accurate and timely reporting and invoicing as well as accurate and timely payment to rights holders.

The contractual relationship between mandating and mandated CMOs is governed in Article 29 of the CRM Directive. According to Article 29(1), the representation agreement has to be concluded on a non-exclusive basis and the mandated CMO shall manage the rights of the mandating CMO on a non-discriminatory basis. In addition, Article 29(2) and (3) establishes information duties for both contracting CMOs towards their members.

A cornerstone of the passport-model consists of tag-on obligations and tag-on opportunities, which are contained in Article 30. According to Article 30(1) of Directive 2014/26/EU, a CMO that does not grant or offer to grant multi-territorial licences for the online rights in musical works in its own repertoire can request that another CMO enter into a representation agreement to represent those rights. The requested CMO is then obliged to agree to such a request if it is already granting or offering to grant multi-territorial licences for the same category of online rights in musical works in the repertoire of another CMO. It is clarified in Recital 46 of the Directive that this representation requirement does not extend to CMOs that provide multi-territorial licences only for their own repertoire. As becomes clear from this, theoretically, all CMOs could theoretically comply with the provisions of Title III, by just offering their own repertoire on a multi-territorial basis.

Article 30 of the Directive continues to lay out the conditions for the representation. Article 30(3) Directive 2014/26/EU contains a non-discrimination principle and governs that a mandated CMO has to manage the repertoire of the mandating CMO on the same conditions as its own repertoire.[171] Building on this rationale, the mandated CMO is, according to Article 30(4), also obliged to include the represented repertoire of the mandating CMO in all offers that it addresses to online service providers. The management fee for the services provided by the mandated CMO shall not exceed the costs reasonably incurred by the requested CMO, according to Article 30(5) and Recital 46 of Directive 2014/26/EU. Finally, the mandating CMO is obliged to provide repertoire information to the requested CMO, according to Article 30(6) of

---

[171] See also Recital 46 of Directive 2014/26/EU.

Directive 2014/26/EU. In cases in which the mandating CMO is not providing the information, the mandated CMO can either exclude the respective repertoire or charge for the costs reasonably incurred to meet the requirements.[172]

It is noteworthy that Article 30 of the Directive has been subject to changes from its draft version put forward by the European Commission.[173] Apart from modifications in the wording and structure, it was included in Article 30(2) that requests shall be responded to in writing and without undue delay. Furthermore, the provisions on the same conditions in Article 30(3), as well as the obligation to include the represented repertoire in all offers in Article 30(4), have been added.

The European lawmaker has also included a legal mechanism preventing the repertoire lock-in in situations in which a right holder has not offered multi-territorial licensing or allows another CMO to license the respective repertoire on a multi-territorial basis by 10 April 2017.[174] The workings and details of this mechanism will be discussed in the section below.

4.2.4.3 The Mechanism of the Passport Model

The introduced mechanism centres on the voluntary (re-)aggregation of repertoire for licensing of multi-territorial purposes.[175] This 'framework for facilitating the voluntary aggregation of music repertoire and rights' constitutes, according to the Commission, an 'absolute novelty' from a regulatory perspective.[176] In Recital 40 of the Directive, it is reflected that 'the number of licences a user needs to operate a multi-territory, multi-repertoire service' should be reduced. Besides decreased transaction costs, the option was also deemed to improve legal certainty and the quality of licensing services by, for example, better identification of rights, which should solve, besides others, the problem of double invoicing.[177] But will the model yield the desired outcome?

[172] Art. 30(6), 2nd sentence, of Directive 2014/26/EU.
[173] Art. 29 of the Draft Directive.   [174] Art. 31 of Directive 2014/26/EU.
[175] Local uses in the territory of the operating CMO would continue to be licensed by the national CMO on a mono-territorial basis. Cf. Recital 46 of Directive 2014/26/EU.
[176] Commission, 'Proposal for a Directive of the European Parliament and of the Council on collective management of copyright and related rights and multi-territorial licensing of rights in musical works for online uses in the internal market', Annex II, 43.
[177] Commission, 'Impact Assessment accompanying the document Proposal for a Directive of the European Parliament and of the Council on collective management of copyright and related rights and multi-territorial licensing of rights in musical works for online uses in the internal market', 26, 161 and 163. Data 'submitted in confidence' suggests that this concerns between 10 per cent and 30 per cent of invoices.

Incentive to Engage in Multi-Territorial Licensing   As noted above, CMOs are free to offer only their own repertoire on a multi-territorial basis; in this scenario, such CMOs would still trigger some of the requirements of Title III, such as the capacity to process multi-territorial licences according to Article 23 of the Directive. Consequently, however, neither the tag-on obligation in Article 30(1) of Directive 2014/26/EU nor the right of rights holders to withdraw their online rights and grant multi-territorial licences themselves or through any other party enshrined in Article 31 of the Directive would be triggered.

Systematically, it appears that one of the central incentives put in place to foster the aggregation of, or at least engagement in, multi-territorial licensing is the withdrawal-right in Article 31 of Directive 2014/26/EU. CMOs, which do not offer multi-territorial licences to their rights holders, would be faced with rights holders withdrawing their online rights from the administration and shop for a different organisation or entity. The lawmaker reflects that

[t]he objectives and effectiveness of the rules on multi-territorial licensing by collective management organi-sations would be *significantly jeopardised* if rightholders were not able to exercise such rights in respect of multi-territorial licences when the collective management organisation to which they have granted their rights did not grant or offer multi-territorial licences and furthermore did not want to mandate another collective management organisation to do so.[178]

In the sketched scenario, however, rights holders would nonetheless have the general right to authorise a CMO of their choice irrespective of their nationality or the residence of the CMO, in accordance with the rules and procedures laid out in Article 5 of the Directive.[179] One possible interpretation is that Article 31, as opposed to Article 5, concerns the specific situation in which a right holder is able to withdraw the relevant online rights for multi-territorial separate from online rights for mono-territorial licensing. However, it seems that Article 5(2) of the Directive, which enables rights holders to authorise a CMO 'to manage the rights, categories of rights or types of works and other subject-matter of their choice, for the territories of their choice', in connection with the general withdrawal right in Article 5(4) of the Directive, effectively creates the same possibility.[180] Thus, at first glance, Article 31 seems

---

[178] Recital 47 of Directive 2014/26/EU (emphasis added).
[179] The wording of Art. 5 of Directive 2014/26/EU could imply that this choice is restricted to CMOs; Recital 15 of the Directive clarifies that rights holders should be free to entrust the management of their rights to IMEs, see also Recital 19.
[180] See also *Banghalter & de Homem Christo/SACEM* (COMP/37.219) [2002] SG(2002) 231176 (*'Daft Punk Decision'*).

rendered redundant.[181] Arezzo argues that the distinctive feature of Article 31 is that it enables rights holders to administer their rights individually,[182] which represents an aspect that was not addressed by the Online Music Recommendation. As discussed above, Article 5 codifies the principle envisioned in the Recommendation and lacks a direct reference to individual licensing. But then Recital 19(2) complements the mechanism and makes specific reference to and opens up for individual management. Only when a Member State provides for mandatory collective management 'rightholders' choice would be limited to other collective management organisations'.[183] Article 31 has not met with the same restriction. Thus, in countries that have mandatory collective management for online music rights, this difference may be of practical importance.[184] Also, the fact that this aspect is mentioned in the recital only could indicate that Member States enjoy more freedom in implementing this rule. In addition, Article 31 contains a transitional period with a sunset date of 10 April 2017, whereas Article 5 is not met by the same constraint. On the flip side, this implies that the withdrawal mechanism (and its deterrent effect) would be present in any case in some Member States, thereby potentially rendering the effect of Article 31 less effective.

Yet another reading of Article 31 could be that it simply gives rights holders a withdrawal right irrespective of the membership contract with the respective CMO, which might have longer withdrawal notice.[185] Finally, the withdrawal is in both scenarios dependent on the initiative of the right holder. Quintais expresses criticism of the 'excessive

---

[181] See also Quintais, 'Proposal for a Directive on collective rights management and (some) multi-territorial licensing', 71; Arezzo, 'Competition and intellectual property protection in the market for the provision of multi-territorial licensing of online rights in musical works – lights and shadows of the new European Directive 2014/26/EU', 540; and Ficsor, 'Collective Management and Multi-territorial Licensing: Key Issues of the Transposition of Directive 2014/26/EU', p. 247, who share a similar observation.

[182] Arezzo, 'Competition and intellectual property protection in the market for the provision of multi-territorial licensing of online rights in musical works – lights and shadows of the new European Directive 2014/26/EU', 542–543.

[183] Recital 2, para. 2 at the end of Directive 2014/26/EU.

[184] In 2006, it was reported that eight Member States out of twenty-five had *de jure* monopoly (Austria, Belgium, Czech Republic, Denmark, Italy, Latvia and the Netherlands), see: KEA European Affairs, *The Collective Management of Rights in Europe The Quest for Efficiency* (Study commissioned by the European Commission 2006), 67.

[185] An additional problem is pointed out by the Max Planck Institute: in practice, it is often unclear whether online rights were entrusted to a CMO by the author or by the publishing company. See for more evidence Drexl and others, 'Comments of the Max Planck Institute for Intellectual Property and Competition Law on the Proposal for a Directive of the European Parliament and of the Council on Collective Management of Copyright and Related Rights', 29, para. 55.

dependence on the right holder's initiative', without, however, outlining alternative routes.[186] Guibault notes the critique expressed by the CMO umbrella organisation GESAC, which argues that the direct licensing possibility in Article 31 contradicts the principle of exclusivity in the assignments of rights in favour of the initial CMO.[187]

Continuing the line of thought, it is somehow odd that neither the European Commission nor the other institutions directly address the scenario of rights holders engaging in direct licensing, which the Directive opens up: it is clear that rights holders who directly license their repertoire on a multi-territorial basis fall outside the scope of Title III of the Directive.[188] There is no basis for reasonable assumptions as to the likelihood and the extent of this development, but it seems clear that any development in this direction would run counter to the regulatory goal of a reasonable number of licensors. As noted above, some scholars argue that large platforms could even replace CMOs. At the same time, these developments have yet to manifest themselves.

Incentives for the Creation of a Few 'Licensing Hubs' As result of the passport model, the Commission envisions, as noted, the emergence of a 'reasonable number' of passport entities, which attract a broad share of European repertoire as 'licensing hubs' – without leading to a single monopoly.[189] Such hubs would then license multi-repertoire on a multi-territorial basis. In the Annex to the Impact Assessment accompanying the draft Directive, the Commission acknowledges that '[t]he number of licensing entities which would emerge as a result (. . .) cannot be predicted with certainty' but 'should be substantially lower than today' given the standards required to engage in multi-territorial licensing and the tag-on possibilities for CMOs.[190] The hypothesis of the legislator centres on a scenario in which a CMO 'cannot or does not wish to fulfil the requirements itself'[191] or CMOs 'that are not willing or not able to grant multi-territorial licences directly in their own music repertoire'.[192] According to Recital 44, these

---

[186] Quintais, 'Proposal for a Directive on collective rights management and (some) multi-territorial licensing', 71.

[187] Guibault, 'The Draft Collective Management Directive', p. 775, with additional references.

[188] See Art. 23 of Directive 2014/26/EU. Title III does not apply to IMEs either: see Art. 2(4) of Directive 2014/26/EU.

[189] Commission, 'Impact Assessment accompanying the document Proposal for a Directive of the European Parliament and of the Council on collective management of copyright and related rights and multi-territorial licensing of rights in musical works for online uses in the internal market', 50, 160.

[190] Ibid., 160–161.   [191] Recital 40 of Directive 2014/26/EU.

[192] Recital 44 of Directive 2014/26/EU.

CMOs should be encouraged to mandate other CMOs to manage their repertoire on a voluntary basis.

The Directive itself is surprisingly silent on the more specific incentives it creates for the creation of licensing hubs and voluntary aggregation of repertoire. The Impact Assessment implies that the aggregation would be driven by market forces, which would 'build upon the current level of aggregation and market trends'.[193] As regards the creation of a few licensing hubs, one central aspect appears to be compliance costs: CMOs are required to, for example, invest in information technology (IT) infrastructure such as repertoire databases. Whereas the Commission is unable to quantify the investment required,[194] it points out that the 'added value' of the rules in Title III is that CMOs are encouraged to 'entrust their rights to passport entities instead of each investing separately'.[195] The decision not to make an investment in the capability to license on a multi-territorial basis may depend, inter alia, on the size and the position of the CMO in the market and could change over time.[196]

A second mechanism seems to centre on the hypothesis that the best-performing passport entities will attract a broad share of repertoire. The Commission assumes that '[p]ublishers (directly or through their society) and authors (through their society) would be likely, on a voluntary basis, to aggregate their rights in the best performing passport entities'[197] in order to maximise their revenues. As was seen in the section above, the corresponding legal mechanism is provided by the tag-on

---

[193] Commission, 'Impact Assessment accompanying the document Proposal for a Directive of the European Parliament and of the Council on collective management of copyright and related rights and multi-territorial licensing of rights in musical works for online uses in the internal market' 160. The Commission (162) points towards two CMOs that already aggregate repertoire for the purpose of multi-territorial licensing of online services: 'this is currently the case for the Irish society IMRO (whose rights are licensed e.g., by the UK society PRS) and for the Portuguese society PTA (whose rights are licensed e.g., by the Spanish society SGAE). These collecting societies in order to continue multi-territory licensing in aggregated repertoire would have to comply with the passport requirements. Also, as aggregators they would be subject to the tag-on obligation'.
[194] Vague information on the compliance cost of Option B2 is presented (ibid., 187): 'Investments are required in order for societies to deliver multi-territory licences. Currently, it is not possible to quantify the investments required. However, it is clear that a number of licensing entities would be expected to be able to comply with passport requirements at a reasonable cost. It is also clear that duplicating those investments would not be necessary to gain a comprehensive overview of rights ownership in the EU – there is no need for 27 databases to record the entire EU repertoire, as relatively recent databases are already in a position to reference a large share of the EU repertoire. Further, it would not be economically viable for all societies to duplicate those costs – for many, these would be unsustainable.'
[195] Ibid., 165.   [196] See ibid., 101.   [197] Ibid., 163.

opportunity for the mandating CMO in combination with the equal treatment principle. The obligation to accept the request of a mandating CMO, in the Commission's view, 'would avoid the risk of a two-tier licensing infrastructure emerging (i.e. commercially attractive repertoire being served by a better licensing infrastructure and obtaining more favourable licensing terms than small, local or niche repertoire)'.[198] The Commission assumes that thereby co-existing licensing hubs would emerge, which compete for rights holders and put pressure on them to conclude licences with, for example, innovative services.[199] This argued to be supported by the non-exclusivity rules, which are deemed useful in helping to ensure competition between a number of CMOs for the granting of pan-European licences.[200]

A third noteworthy aspect relates to the competition between CMOs that offer multi-territorial licensing and other players, which offer multi-territorial licences. This competition could emerge at two levels: first, the European Commission remarks that other licensing agents, which fall outside the scope of the Directive, 'could be in competition for attracting repertoire with the licensing entities operating under passport requirements'.[201] In other words, competition could emerge as regards rights holders. Secondly, there could also arise competition regarding (commercial) users. This, according to the Commission, would depend on the 'overlaps in the repertoire offered by passport entities and these agents'.[202] In recent merger proceedings, however, the DG Competition found it unlikely that option 3 publishers 'would have the ability and the incentive to enter the relevant market themselves'.[203]

It seems still too early to assess or predict whether the licensing hub model will be broadly used and lead to the predicted market consolidation. But the picture might not be as positive as the European lawmaker anticipated. The incentives seem to depend highly on the investment in infrastructure, which especially presents entry barriers for smaller CMOs. I will get back to this assessment in the following sections. Quite notable is also the chain of causation that the legislator suggests in Recital 44 of Directive 2014/26/EU, which does not stop at the market consolidation:

[198] Ibid., 164.   [199] Ibid., 161 and 163.
[200] Kalimo, Olkkonen and Vaario, *EU Economic Law in a Time of Crisis*, pp. 159–160.
[201] Commission, 'Impact Assessment accompanying the document Proposal for a Directive of the European Parliament and of the Council on collective management of copyright and related rights and multi-territorial licensing of rights in musical works for online uses in the internal market', 162.
[202] Ibid.
[203] M. Cole, 'PRSfM/STIM/GEMA/JV: Multijurisdictional Licencing for Music Streaming', *Journal of European Competition Law & Practice*, 7 (2016), 257, 258.

Aggregating different music repertoires for multi-terri-torial licensing facilitates the licensing process and, by making all repertoires accessible to the market for multi-territorial licensing, enhances cultural diversity and contributes to reducing the number of transactions an online service provider needs in order to offer services. This aggregation of repertoires should facilitate the development of new online services and should also result in a *reduction of transaction costs being passed on to consumers.*[204]

4.2.5 Criticism and Discussion

Overall, the Directive has been welcomed by a broad variety of stake-holders. After some initial criticism, the Directive, for example, was positively received by UK CMOs.[205] The UK Intellectual Property Office cherished the Directive as a '[g]olden opportunity for our CMOs to build on their achievements since they adopted their codes of practice in 2012'.[206] Also, the Max Planck Institute generally endorsed the initiative for a binding legal instrument.[207] Nonetheless, several aspects of the system of the CRM Directive, in either its draft or its final form, have attracted criticism from different stakeholders. Providing a thorough overview of the different aspects is outside the scope of this chapter. In the following section, therefore, I give a condensed overview of some of the main aspects relevant for the theme of this book.

The Directive is voluminous and, at places, highly detailed. In Annex II to the proposal, the Commission suggested the transmission of explanatory documents, once the transposition has taken place, 'due to the [c]omplexity of the Directive and the sector concerned'.[208] Ficsor raises doubts whether the CRM Directive, more specifically in its draft version, is compliant with the subsidiarity principle in Article 5(3) TFEU because the governance and transparency framework could have been achieved by other measures.[209] He points towards evidence from the statement of the Republic of Poland, the French senate and the Swedish Parliament, which were concerned that the draft Directive was in conflict with the principle of subsidiarity.[210] Most of

---

[204] Emphasis added.
[205] See Ross, 'The new regulatory regime for collective rights management – the Government consults on how to implement', 144.
[206] See Intellectual Property Office, Ministerial foreword, 1.
[207] See Drexl and others, 'Comments of the Max Planck Institute for Intellectual Property and Competition Law on the Proposal for a Directive of the European Parliament and of the Council on Collective Management of Copyright and Related Rights', 1.
[208] See Joint Political Declaration of Member States and the Commission on explanatory documents of 28 September 2011 (2011/C369/02) [2011] OJ C369/14.
[209] Ficsor, 'Collective Management and Multi-territorial Licensing: Key Issues of the Transposition of Directive 2014/26/EU', p. 212.
[210] Ibid., p. 214.

the tensions seem to have been alleviated in the adopted version, which is no less voluminous and detailed but has introduced certain flexibilities.

Scope of the Directive: Narrow, Yet so Broad

Systematically, the CRM Directive is rather restricted in scope: instead of providing a framework for the overall licensing process, the legislator opted for the sectoral regulation of the management of authors' rights only (and not related rights) in Title III. This may not seem surprising, given the emphasis that CMOs have received from the legislator; I find it, nonetheless, striking how little scrutiny the legislator devoted to the management of related rights.[211] On the other hand, the adopted version introduced IMEs, which have been endorsed by, for example, the European author societies' umbrella organisation, GESAC.[212] Concerning multi-territorial licensing, some also criticise the exclusive focus on musical works.[213] The EP's European Economic and Social Committee found the focus on music to be 'well chosen', underlining

the importance of music in the market for online cultural content, and that it could improve understanding of the cross-border management of rights, which could then serve as a model or, at least, as inspiration for the online sale of multimedia content and books.[214]

Another aspect that has been criticised is the geographic scope of the Directive.[215] The Committee on International Trade, for example, underlined that it

---

[211] This criticism is shared by the Max Planck Institute: see Drexl and others, 'Comments of the Max Planck Institute for Intellectual Property and Competition Law on the Proposal for a Directive of the European Parliament and of the Council on Collective Management of Copyright and Related Rights', 26, para. 48.

[212] See GESAC, 'Collective Rights Management in Europe – our thoughts on the road ahead' (Brussels, February 2013), 3. Ficsor, 'Collective Management and Multi-territorial Licensing: Key Issues of the Transposition of Directive 2014/26/EU', p. 239 notes that the 'extension of the scope of application of the Directive was supported also by real CMOs for competition reasons'.

[213] A. Strowel and B. Vanbrabant (eds.), *Copyright Licensing: A European View* (Edward Elgar 2013), p. 49; Quintais, 'Proposal for a Directive on collective rights management and (some) multi-territorial licensing', 67 and 72.

[214] European Parliament, 'Opinion of the European Economic and Social Committee on the 'Proposal for a Directive of the European Parliament and of the Council on collective management of copyright and related rights and multi-territorial licensing of rights in musical works for online uses in the internal market' COM(2012) 372 final – 2012/0180 (COD)' 2013/C 44/18 OJ C 44/104 point 1.2.

[215] GESAC, the European authors' societies' umbrella organisation, for example argued that the Directive should also apply to CMOs outside the EU to prevent off-shoring. See GESAC, 3.

wishes to make sure that the increased demands (...) do not lead to discrimination of the EU based collecting societies and commercial agents compared to their non-EU based competitors operating in the EU market, and to discourage off-shoring of collecting societies.[216]

It proposed an amendment that certain parts of the Directive also apply to CMOs established outside the EU as regards their operations within the EU and with regard to rights holders residing in or established in the EU, which, however, was not adopted in the final Directive. Instead, it has been left up to the discretion of Member States to expand the scope. As noted above, inter alia, uncertainty about enforcement and cherry-picking of rules, as well as the goal of minimum harmonisation, might have deterred Member States from expanding the scope, possibly to the detriment of a level playing field. The scope of the Directive also remains blurred as to its applicability to different entities and arrangements, such as those established by option 3 publishers.

Cultural Diversity Concerns

The Directive has been criticised for or giving up the 'traditional spirit of solidarity in collective management systems' and its general negative effect on cultural diversity.[217] A related line of criticism concerns smaller CMOs and cultural diversity concerns. The European authors' societies' umbrella organisation, GESAC, for example, remarked that the draft Directive should provide extra safeguards for smaller CMOs.[218]

The Directive, in relation to both the governance and transparency framework and the passport model, were assessed as corresponding to the goals of the Recommendation. As such, even though less vocally, some of the same concerns as with the Recommendation have been raised. In a similar vein, Hilty and Nérisson refer to the proposal for the Directive

---

[216] European Parliament, 'Opinion of the Committee on International Trade for the Committee on Legal Affairs on the proposal for a directive of the European Parliament and of the Council on collective management of copyright and related rights and multi-territorial licensing of rights in musical works for online uses in the internal market (COM(2012)0372 – C7-0183/2012 – 2012/0180(COD))', 3.

[217] Ficsor, 'Collective Management and Multi-territorial Licensing: Key Issues of the Transposition of Directive 2014/26/EU', p. 247.

[218] GESAC, 3. As regards the medium-sized Nordic CMOs, for example, Kivistö, deems that it is unlikely that it 'would alone be eligible for a "passport entity"'. See Kivistö, 'Multi-territorial online licensing in the light of Title III of the Directive on collective rights management', 710. See also Gómez and Arcila, 'Collective administration of online rights in musical works: analysing the economic efficiency of Directive 2014/26/EU', 107; and R. Towse, 'Economics of collective management organisations in the creative industries' (WINIR conference, 4–6 April 2016), 8.

figuratively as 'Band-Aid on a wooden leg', 'based on the same mistaken assumptions as the Recommendation'.[219] In particular, Article 5 of the Directive, which codifies the Recommendation's approach, has been criticised from a cultural diversity perspective, in that the Directive 'continues to treat CMOs merely as providers of services to right-holders and without distinguishing between creators and successors in title' and thereby disregards the 'important non-economic functions'.[220] Graber calls the reference to Article 167 TFEU, cultural diversity, cynical, in light of the disposal of 'reciprocal cooperation between national monopoly CMOs contribute to this end since those CMOs are obliged to represent all repertoires (and thus secure an income also to less popular creators) rather than cherry-pick popular works'.[221] At the same time, the Directive has been criticised for not going far enough, in that 'rights are still assigned on an exclusive basis and therefore cannot be assigned to several agents at the same time', which would foster further competition.[222]

Finally, in its proposal for the Directive, the Commission in Recital 3 stated that CMOs as service providers must comply with Directive 2006/213/EC.[223] This view was met with severe criticism from several stakeholders and the prevalent opinion in the literature and was eventually not implemented in the final Directive.[224] One day after adoption

---

[219] Hilty and Nérisson, 'Collective Copyright Management and Digitization: The European Experience, 9.

[220] Graber, 'Collective rights management, competition policy and cultural diversity: EU lawmaking at a crossroads', 41. See also Drexl and others, 'Comments of the Max Planck Institute for Intellectual Property and Competition Law on the Proposal for a Directive of the European Parliament and of the Council on Collective Management of Copyright and Related Rights', 13, paras. 15–18; M. Hviid, S. Schroff and J. Street, 'Regulating CMOs by competition: an incomplete answer to the licensing problem?', CREATe Working Paper 2016/03 (March 2016), 21.

[221] Graber, 'Collective rights management, competition policy and cultural diversity: EU lawmaking at a crossroads', 41.

[222] Hviid, Schroff and Street, 'Regulating CMOs by competition: an incomplete answer to the licensing problem?', 23.

[223] Also referred to as the 'Services Directive' or the 'Bolkestein Directive'. This is in line with the Commission's (non-binding) interpretation on the implementation of the Services Directive: see T. Riis, 'Collecting Societies, Competition, and the Services Directive', *Journal of Intellectual Property Law & Practice*, 6 (2011), 482, 491, with further evidence.

[224] See ibid., with further evidence. See also Drexl and others, 'Comments of the Max Planck Institute for Intellectual Property and Competition Law on the Proposal for a Directive of the European Parliament and of the Council on Collective Management of Copyright and Related Rights', 16–18, at paras. 19–24; European Parliament, 'Opinion of the European Economic and Social Committee on the 'Proposal for a Directive of the European Parliament and of the Council on collective management of copyright and related rights and multi-territorial licensing of rights in musical works for online uses in the internal market' COM(2012) 372 final – 2012/0180 (COD)' point 1.5. The Directive, now, instead makes just reference to the principle of free movements of services in Recital 4. See Drexl, 'Collective Management of Copyrights and the EU

of the CRM Directive, the CJEU delivered its judgment in Case C-351/12, *OSA* and confirmed that Article 16 of the Services Directive does not apply to the activities of CMOs.[225]

As regards the permanent critique of cultural diversity, it looks as though the position of the European lawmaker is at odds with those of most stakeholders. It recalls the importance of taking into account cultural diversity in Recital 3 of the Directive and deems, in Recital 44 of the Directive, that the multi-territorial licensing system serves to enhance cultural diversity. For the European lawmaker, it seems that cultural diversity can be achieved by other means than local CMOs protecting and promoting local rights holders and non-mainstream subcultures. This is somewhat consistent with the view of DG Competition, which, for example, in its *CISAC* 2008 decision, at paragraph 95, just points out that '[c]ultural diversity in the music sector is not called into question by this decision'. It also becomes clear from the Impact Assessment that the EU Commission has been aware of certain licensing hub developments when drafting its policy options.[226] This could indicate that the Commission wanted specifically to promote these market developments further, to the disadvantage of other models.

The Passport Model: Jack of All Trades?

Let me now turn towards the multi-territorial licensing framework and supplement on the thoughts provided above on the functioning of the system. The chosen route is built around the voluntary aggregation of repertoire. Here, it is important to distinguish between the re-aggregation of the Anglo-American repertoire and the aggregation of repertoire of different CMOs. While the Commission considered the re-aggregation of mechanical rights, the system put forward in the CRM Directive focuses on the latter.[227]

Principle of Free Movement of Services after the OSA Judgment – In Favour of a More Balanced Approach', p. 491.

[225] For a thorough discussion of the case, see Drexl, 'Collective Management of Copyrights and the EU Principle of Free Movement of Services after the OSA Judgment – In Favour of a More Balanced Approach'. However, Ficsor, 'Collective Management and Multi-territorial Licensing: Key Issues of the Transposition of Directive 2014/26/EU', p. 229 refers to a statement by former Commissioner Barnier, which could be interpreted as to 'whether or not the Services Directive is applicable to CMOs is still an open issue'.

[226] See Commission, 'Impact Assessment accompanying the document Proposal for a Directive of the European Parliament and of the Council on collective management of copyright and related rights and multi-territorial licensing of rights in musical works for online uses in the internal market', 104–105.

[227] See Anthonis, 'Will the CRM-directive succeed re-aggregating the mechanical reproduction rights in the Anglo-American music repertoire?', 157.

As to its mechanics, it appears that the proposed model is not so novel after all. In 2007, in connection with the *CISAC* proceedings, some of the concerned CMOs 'undertook to grant multi-repertoire, multi-territorial performing right licences for internet services (. . .) to each signatory society that fulfilled certain qualitative criteria'[228] in proposed commitments. But market players

generally considered that the proposed commitments would not be effective and almost none of the potential licensees would be eligible under the definitions and exceptions listed in the proposed commitments, to obtain a multi-territorial multi-repertoire licence.[229]

The Court concluded that the proposed commitments were not an appropriate answer to the raised competition concerns.

At the outset, it seems that the system in Directive 2014/26/EU follows a rationale in which the mitigation of transaction costs serves as a tool to increase access to repertoire. However, Ghafele is critical of whether the system of the CRM Directive, with its goal to increase competition between CMOs, will help to overcome the fragmentation of musical repertoires on the supply side.[230] Also, Greeley argues that the passport model 'fails to address the policy goal of repertoire aggregation and still allows for the survival of an undesirable number of inefficient CMOs'.[231] Notably, Poland was not convinced of the introduction of a system of multi-territorial licensing in Title III either, and abstained from voting in the Council.[232] Its main concern, besides potential detrimental effect on cultural diversity, relates to the hypothesis of the legislator that online service providers are 'interested in acquiring licenses for multi-repertoire and multiterritorial coverage'.[233]

Another criticism is that the Directive continues in the spirit of the Recommendation by focusing on competition in the market for rights

---

[228] *Commission Decision CISAC*, para. 71.   [229] Ibid., para. 72.

[230] R. Ghafele, 'Europe's Lost Royalty Opportunity: a Comparison of Potential and Existing Digital Music Royalty Markets in Ten Different E.U. Member States', *Review of Economic Research on Copyright Issues*, 11 (2014), 60, 66.

[231] K. Greeley, 'Recommendations, Communications, and Directives, Oh My: How the European Union Isn't Solving its Licensing Problem', *Georgetown Journal of International Law*, 44 (2013), 1523, 1536.

[232] See Council of the European Union, 'Proposal for a Directive of the European Parliament and of the Council on collective management of copyright and related rights and multi-territorial licensing of rights in musical works for online use in the internal market, Statements' ('I/A' Item Note 2014, 6434/14) Brussels, 17 February 2014, Statement by the Republic of Poland, 4.

[233] Ibid., Statement by the Republic of Poland, 4.

holders, not in relation to licensees.[234] In a two-sided market, however, a crucial question is how competition in the upstream market, i.e. the administration of rights, and in the downstream market, i.e. the streaming services, interacts.[235] Katz notes that

> it makes little sense to introduce competition in one layer, even if it were feasible, unless competition is introduced in both because any reduction in the price resulting from competition in the other layer would be captures by the monopoly in the other layer which supplies an essential complement.[236]

In a similar vein, the Max Planck Institute criticises that 'the Commission seems to fail to take account of the full legal framework and factual circumstances that have structured the current system of collective rights management'.[237] As such, it seems that the General Court's judgment in CISAC had little influence on the rules.[238] Drexl et al. stress that 'the natural monopoly of collecting societies should be accepted as an efficient market solution',[239] which is why competition should not be imposed. The envisaged competition, they continue, would be likely to lead an oligopolistic market, in which just very few – 'most likely the currently most powerful' – CMOs are able to grant such licences,[240] which is a concern that is shared by many.[241] Also, the Republic of Poland argues that

---

[234] See Drexl and others, 'Comments of the Max Planck Institute for Intellectual Property and Competition Law on the Proposal for a Directive of the European Parliament and of the Council on Collective Management of Copyright and Related Rights', 6, para. 9.

[235] See, e.g., O.-A. Rognstad, 'The Multiplicity of Territorial IP Rights and its Impact on Competition' in J. Rosén (ed.), *Individualism and Collectiveness in Intellectual Property Law* (Edward Elgar, 2012), p. 65, criticising that neither aspect has been analysed thoroughly by the European Commission in the previous proceedings.

[236] Katz, 'The Potential Demise of Another Natural Monopoly: New Technologies and the Administration of Performing Rights', *Journal of Competition Law and Economics*, 2 (2006), 245, 270.

[237] See Drexl and others, 'Comments of the Max Planck Institute for Intellectual Property and Competition Law on the Proposal for a Directive of the European Parliament and of the Council on Collective Management of Copyright and Related Rights', 6.

[238] See e.g., Hilty and Nérisson, 'Collective Copyright Management and Digitization: The European Experience', 9, who comment on the Proposal for the Directive: 'Hope remains in the legislative work of the EU parliament on the proposal and in the ruling of the ECJ regarding the CISAC case.'

[239] Drexl and others, 'Comments of the Max Planck Institute for Intellectual Property and Competition Law on the Proposal for a Directive of the European Parliament and of the Council on Collective Management of Copyright and Related Rights', 5, para. 6.

[240] Ibid., para. 7.

[241] See, e.g., Ficsor, 'Collective Management and Multi-territorial Licensing: Key Issues of the Transposition of Directive 2014/26/EU', p. 247; Gómez and Arcila, 'Collective administration of online rights in musical works: analysing the economic efficiency of Directive 2014/26/EU', 109.

it is very likely that the system will in any case lead to the reinforcement of the position of the biggest organisations representing the most popular Anglo-American repertoire.[242]

It is further stated that this would have a detrimental effect on repertoires with limited linguistic presence in the EU, and thus ultimately harm cultural diversity.[243] Also, Towse comments that 'centralising multiterritorial licensing risks the development of an even greater natural monopoly'.[244] She continues to note that the large financial investments in infrastructure preclude smaller CMOs, which 'will have to turn to the larger ones for those purposes thereby increasing their economies of scale, scope and networks'.[245] Hviid et al., too, share this concern in relation to, e.g., databases.[246]

On a broader scale, and in relation to the audiovisual sector, Hugenholtz comments on the promotion of multi-territorial licensing in contrast with, for example, a 'country of origin' approach as a 'much less ambitious' and 'more modest' solution.[247] Others ask whether a Directive in light of the General Court's judgment in the CISAC Case T-442/08 'indeed was necessary'.[248] Arezzo argues in this vein that the withdrawal right in Article 5(3) of the CRM Directive alone 'would be sufficient to open up the market for online music rights'.[249]

Finally, the European consumer organisation BEUC regards the licensing passport system as 'insufficient' because it fails 'to address the remaining obstacles and therefore it is highly unlikely that it will help boost the development of cross-border music services'.[250]

---

[242] Council of the European Union, Statement by the Republic of Poland, 4.

[243] See ibid. See also Gómez and Arcila, 'Collective administration of online rights in musical works: analysing the economic efficiency of Directive 2014/26/EU', 109.

[244] Towse, 'Economics of collective management organisations in the creative industries' (WINIR conference, 4–6 April 2016), 9.

[245] Ibid., also remarking: 'It is also the case, however, that several private rights management companies besides the ones described above have entered the market, some which simply offer to monitor the flow of royalties and others that offer an individualised rights management service with their own data systems. It is not clear whether they are able to contest the position of the CMOs.'

[246] Hviid, Schroff and Street, 'Regulating CMOs by competition: an incomplete answer to the licensing problem?', 7.

[247] P. B. Hugenholtz, 'Audiovisual Archives across Borders – Dealing with Territorially Restricted Copyright', IRIS Special, 49 [2010], 53.

[248] Petteri, 'Harmonising Collective Rights Management and Multi-Territorial Licensing of Music for Online Use in the European Union: A Review of the Collective Rights Management Directive 2014/26/EU', 170.

[249] Arezzo, 'Competition and intellectual property protection in the market for the provision of multi-territorial licensing of online rights in musical works – lights and shadows of the new European Directive 2014/26/EU', 540.

[250] Bureau Européen des Unions de Consommateurs (BEUC), 10.

Reciprocal Representation Agreements under the New Regime

Vuckovic points towards the preamble of the CRM Directive, in which Recitals 11 and 12 'unequivocally' state that nothing in the Directive precludes CMOs from concluding RRAs provided that they are not of an exclusive nature.[251] This system is especially relevant

in order to facilitate, improve and simplify the procedures for granting licences to users, including for the purposes of single invoicing, under equal, non-discriminatory and transparent conditions, and to offer multi-territorial licences also in areas other than those referred to in Title III of this Directive.[252]

The legislator continues to reflect, in Recital 44 of the Directive, that in all RRAs

[e]xclusivity in agreements on multi-territorial licences would restrict the choices available to users seeking multi-territorial licences and also restrict the choices available to collective management organisations seeking adminis-tration services for their repertoire on a multi-territorial basis.

This implies, however, *a contrario*, that the legislator does not foresee the use of RRAs for multi-territorial licensing of online music rights. In its Impact Assessment, the European Commission has already underlined that the passport model does not require RRAs.[253] Nonetheless, the model is dependent on a simple representation agreement:[254] such an agreement between the passport organisation and the mandating CMO, however, is not reciprocal, because 'it does not aim to put both societies in a position to grant licences in their combined repertoire'[255] but 'aims to set the terms under which the best placed [passport] society (. . .) can license the repertoire of another society'.[256]

---

[251] Vuckovic, 'Implementation of Directive 2014/26 on collective management and multi-territorial licensing of musical rights in regulating the tariff-setting systems in Central and Eastern Europe', at 47–48, commenting that '[t]his is not a novelty since the exclusivity clauses were already abandoned among the CISAC members. Nevertheless, the abandonment of exclusivity as such did not change the de facto situation that exclusivity is tacitly applied'.

[252] Recital 11 of Directive 2014/26/EU.

[253] Commission, 'Impact Assessment accompanying the document Proposal for a Directive of the European Parliament and of the Council on collective management of copyright and related rights and multi-territorial licensing of rights in musical works for online uses in the internal market', 49.

[254] See, e.g., Gómez and Arcila, 'Collective administration of online rights in musical works: analysing the economic efficiency of Directive 2014/26/EU', 106.

[255] Commission, 'Impact Assessment accompanying the document Proposal for a Directive of the European Parliament and of the Council on collective management of copyright and related rights and multi-territorial licensing of rights in musical works for online uses in the internal market', 49.

[256] Ibid.

Despite this, the Commission expects RRAs to continue to exist, only slightly modified and with more limited scope. First, according to the Commission, RRAs are likely to be concluded to cover the right to license small and local users.[257] This is based on the assumption that the local CMO is best placed to grant licences to local or small-scale users, 'as it knows the local market, and as a passport society will not necessarily have an interest in granting direct licences to such users'.[258] In the Explanatory Memorandum to the draft Directive, the Commission reflects that

[a] collecting society may decide not to grant multi-territorial licences for online rights in musical works, but it could continue to grant national licences for its own repertoire and/or national licences for the repertoire of other societies through reciprocal agreements.[259]

Secondly, RRAs would still cover offline use, which is not affected by the passport model.[260] Finally, mono-territorial licensing of online music rights, according to the Commission, will remain unaffected.[261] The Max Planck Institute also points towards the scenario in which a requesting CMO does not hold rights for all the EU and author and publisher have chosen different societies.[262]

In relation to the preparations for a proposal for a Directive, the accompanying Impact Assessment remarks, as noted above, that some organisations insisted that 'customer allocation would be essential as competition between CS could lead to "a race to the bottom"'.[263] The Commission reflected that the negative consequences on the internal market are well recognised by the CJEU and that, to date, no significant efficiencies for consumers outweighing the competition concerns have

---

[257] Ibid.   [258] Ibid.

[259] Commission, 'Proposal for a Directive of the European Parliament and of the Council on collective management of copyright and related rights and multi-territorial licensing of rights in musical works for online uses in the internal market', Explanatory Memorandum, 10.

[260] Commission, 'Impact Assessment accompanying the document Proposal for a Directive of the European Parliament and of the Council on collective management of copyright and related rights and multi-territorial licensing of rights in musical works for online uses in the internal market', 49.

[261] Ibid.

[262] See Drexl and others, 'Comments of the Max Planck Institute for Intellectual Property and Competition Law on the Proposal for a Directive of the European Parliament and of the Council on Collective Management of Copyright and Related Rights', 28, para. 54.

[263] Commission, 'Impact Assessment accompanying the document Proposal for a Directive of the European Parliament and of the Council on collective management of copyright and related rights and multi-territorial licensing of rights in musical works for online uses in the internal market', 49.

been demonstrated.[264] Thus, it refrained from further assessing this option.

4.3   Proposal for a Directive on Copyright in the Digital Single Market

In September 2016, the European Commission adopted its Proposal for a Directive of the European Parliament and of the Council on copyright in the Digital Single Market. The proposed Directive addresses specifically cross-border use of protected content, irrespective of content form, i.e. embracing both music and audiovisual works. Its proposed Article 1(1) reads:

This Directive lays down rules which aim at further harmonising the Union law applicable to copyright and related rights in the framework of the internal market, taking into account in particular digital and cross-border uses of protected content. It also lays down rules on exceptions and limitations, on the facilitation of licenses as well as rules aiming at ensuring a well-functioning marketplace for the exploitation of works and other subject-matter.

The Commission's proposal has been highly debated by academics and other stakeholders. Among the most controversial proposals are the introduction of a mandatory exception for text and data mining by research organisations (Article 3 on text and data mining), the introduction of a new ancillary right in press publications for publishers somewhat akin to the models introduced in Germany and Spain (Article 11 on protection of press publications concerning digital uses), and Article 13 (on use of protected content by information society service providers storing and giving access to large amounts of works and other subject matter uploaded by their users) which aims to introduce 'effective content recognition technologies' for intermediaries to identify the user-generated upload of unlicensed works. For the question of licensing of and access to protected works as such, however, these controversial provisions have little importance. Suffice it to note here that the provisions are widely debated, and recent proposals by the Presidency suggest several changes.[265]

---

[264] Ibid.
[265] On the latter, see, e.g., M. Senftleben and others, 'The Recommendation on Measures to Safeguard Fundamental Rights and the Open Internet in the Framework of the EU Copyright Reform' (2017): https://ssrn.com/abstract=3054967; S. Stalla-Bourdillon and others, 'Open Letter to the European Commission – On the Importance of Preserving the Consistency and Integrity of the EU Acquis Relating to Content Monitoring within the Information Society' (2016): https://ssrn.com/abstract=28504833

The Proposal does, however, also address licensing of copyright-protected content in Title III on measures to improve licensing practices and ensure wider access to content. First, the Commission's proposal foresees the facilitation of licences for out-of-commerce works for use by cultural heritage institutions. In the proposed Articles 7 and 8, Member States would be required 'to put in place a legal mechanism to facilitate licensing agreements of out-of-commerce works and other subject-matter' with cross-border effect.[266] Cultural heritage institutions are outside the scope of this book, but it is worth noting that institutions such as Europeana as well as national libraries in many instances offer an online catalogue of different kinds of works.[267]

As seen above, licensing for multi-territorial or cross-border purposes for musical works has been addressed by the CRM Directive (at least as regards author rights). In the short Chapter 2 on access to and availability of audiovisual works on video-on-demand platforms, the Commission's proposal suggests the introduction of a negotiation mechanisms regarding the licensing of audiovisual works. Article 10 of the proposal reads:

Member States shall ensure that where parties wishing to conclude an agreement for the purpose of making available audiovisual works on video-on-demand platforms face difficulties relating to the licensing of rights, they may rely on the assistance of an impartial body with relevant experience. The body shall provide assistance with negotiation and help reach agreements.

According to the Commission, an example for challenges in licensing relate to situations in which rights holders are either not interested in the online exploitation of their work for a certain territory or issues in relation to the industry practice of exploitation windows.[268] The envisaged solution would require Member States 'set up a negotiation mechanism allowing parties willing to conclude an agreement to rely on the assistance of an impartial body'.[269] Thus, compared with the detailed mechanism for the licensing of online music rights, the Commission envisions a weaker mechanism to facilitate the licensing of audiovisual works with large discretion for the Member States' solutions.[270]

---

[266] Commission, 'Proposal for a Directive of the European Parliament and of the Council on copyright in the Digital Single Market', Explanatory Memorandum, 10.

[267] In Denmark, for example, the streaming service offered by the public libraries (Filmstriben) offers more than 2,500 titles.

[268] See Recital 29 of Commission, 'Proposal for a Directive of the European Parliament and of the Council on copyright in the Digital Single Market'.

[269] Ibid., Recital 30.

[270] That being said, the licensing of online content by broadcasting organisations is being partly addressed in the Commission's simultaneous proposal: Commission, 'Proposal for a Regulation of the European Parliament and of the Council laying down rules on the

In October 2017, the Council of the European Union's Presidency, Estonia, sent its consolidated compromise proposal to the delegations.[271] The Presidency notably suggests the introduction of a completely new chapter on measures to facilitate collective licensing. Similar to the mechanism for out-of-commerce works and the Scandinavian model of extended collective licensing (ECL), the proposal provides a general legal basis for extended collective licensing by CMOs. According to the proposed Article 9a:

When a collective management organisation, in accordance with its mandates, enters into a collective licensing agreement for the exploitation of works or other subject- matter Member States may provide, subject to safeguards provided for in this Article, that such an agreement, as far as the use *within their national territory* is concerned, *may be extended to apply to the rights of rightholders who have not authorised the organisation to represent them* by way of assignment, licence or any other contractual arrangement, or that the organisation is presumed to represent rightholders who have not authorised the organisation accordingly.[272]

Article 9a then lays out certain restrictions and specifies safeguards. Notably, according to Article 9a(3), such mechanism

shall only be applied in certain special cases which do not conflict with a normal exploitation of the work or other subject-matter and do not unreasonably prejudice the legitimate interests of the rightholders.

Because such extended collective licensing arrangements would have no cross-border effect, the suggested mechanism would be of little relevance in these situations.

4.4   Summary

From a regulatory law-making perspective, much has happened during the last decade. In the first part on multi-territorial licensing in the online music vertical, we can witness the development from soft law to binding measures. Both regulatory measures are based, among others, on the hypothesis of the lawmaker that online service providers prefer clearing rights on a multi-territorial basis.[273] The red thread running through both

---

exercise of copyright and related rights applicable to certain online transmissions of broadcasting organisations and retransmissions of television and radio programmes'

[271] Council of the European Union, 'Note from Presidency to Delegations, Proposal for a Directive of the European Parliament and of the Council on copyright in the Digital Single Market – Consolidated Presidency compromise proposal', Brussels 30 October 2017, 13842/17, 2016/0280 (COD).

[272] Emphasis added.

[273] Anecdotal evidence paints a different picture. According to evidence from a study performed by KEA and Mines in 2010, the majority of European VOD service

measures seems to be based on a rationale whereby mitigating transaction costs is argued to increase access to repertoire. First the Recommendation of 2005 and then the CRM Directive of 2014 propose a substantially different regime than the previous system. With Recommendation 2005/737/EC, the Commission primarily had competition between CMOs (and other licensing entities) in its cross-hairs; at the expense of other, potentially more efficient (i.e. with lower transaction costs) licensing arrangements, it appears. There is little doubt that the Recommendation, while well intended, has failed on many levels. The frenzy for more competition between rights holders effectively meant a departure from the traditional system developed by the market-place, in which each CMO effectively controlled the entire world repertoire of music in its territory as a 'one-stop shop'. Instead of mono-territorial multi-repertoire licensing, an additional licensing layer in the form of multi-territorial mono-repertoire arrangements has been added, increasing the complexity in right clearance, notably.[274]

The various efforts towards the establishment of a legislative regulatory framework have culminated in the CRM Directive, which had to be transposed into national law by April 2016. The novel regime proposed in Directive 2014/26/EU is based on a voluntary aggregation, supported by the liberalisation of the market for collective management for rights holders and commercial users alike.[275] The chosen approach shows that the European lawmaker is not convinced about the natural monopoly rationale and deems that competition is both possible and desirable in the market for rights management (both between CMOs and also other licensors such as IMEs). It expands to some extent on the rationale behind the interventions of the DG Competition and continues the line of thought of Besen and Kirby, who, in a similar vein, argued more than twenty-five years earlier, '[w]here competition among rights holders is feasible, it should be promoted and should not be replaced by bilateral monopoly'.[276] Stakeholders and the literature in part heavily contest

---

providers, for example, focus on linguistic territories and thus do not demand licences covering a broader territory. See KEA European Affairs and Mines ParisTech, 65. Also the Republic of Poland underlines in the context of the CRM Directive that this hypothesis is flawed. See Council of the European Union, Statement by the Republic of Poland, 4.

[274] This is also confirmed, e.g., by the research of Hviid et al., who empirically analysed the path of a potential service provider to acquire a licence: see Hviid, Schroff and Street, 'Regulating CMOs by competition: an incomplete answer to the licensing problem?', 9–12.

[275] See Guibault and van Gompel, 'Collective Management in the European Union', p. 136, with further evidence.

[276] S. Besen and S. N. Kirby, *Compensating Creators of Intellectual Property* (The RAND Corporation, 1989), p. 79.

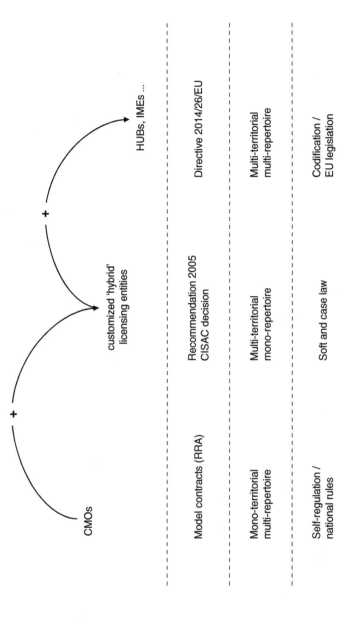

Figure 5: Evolution of licensing arrangements
Source: Thomas Riis 2016, User Generated Law: Re-Constructing Intellectual Property Law in a Knowledge Society, Edward Elgar Publishing. Re-print with permission of Edward Elgar.

whether this indeed is the optimal solution. At the same time, the law-maker, with Directive 2014/26/EU, promotes an oligopolistic system of multi-territorial licensing hubs. Figure 5 provides an overview of these distinct phases and developments.

As regards the governance and transparency framework, the Directive thereby mostly codified the CJEU competition case law and Commission decisions. For now, there seems to be relatively little consensus as to the CRM Directive's effect and its multi-territorial licensing system.[277] Some argue that the proposed system will decrease transaction costs.[278] Member States, however, have argued that 'the system does not really allow for the completion of a genuine digital single market as it does not guarantee equal access for consumers to legal online music offers in all Member States', because other barriers than licensing prevent the online services from launching a multi-territorial service.[279]

The anticipated effects of the Directive, such as a market consolidation, will only demonstrate themselves over time. For this, the Directive has put a review process in place: by 10 April 2021, the Commission is to assess, inter alia, the impact on the development of cross-border services, cultural diversity and the intra-Union operations of CMOs established outside the EU, according to Article 40 of the Directive, if appropriate, come with a new legislative proposal.[280]

As regards licensing, the Directive builds in many ways on the Recommendation of 2005 and promotes a licensing system in which hubs are expected to (re-)aggregate rights of multiple repertoires for multi-territorial licensing purposes. This voluntary regime, which is argued to not depend on the traditional contractual web of RRAs, seems to focus on the mitigation of transaction costs as a way to increase the access to repertoire. Whether this re-aggregation is likely to happen is a different question. Not much points towards this development, though. By 2009, the Danish CMO KODA, for example, was already aiming to collaborate with music publishers in order to re-establish a blanket licence that covers the world repertoire for licensing in Denmark.[281]

---

[277] In a different vertical, the text and image sector, Stokkmo evaluates, for reproduction rights organisations (RROs), that the Directive allows RROs to continue their practice with no or only minor changes: O. Stokkmo, 'The EU Collective Rights Management Directive and the RRO', International Journal of Intellectual Property Management, 7 (2014), 120.

[278] E.g. G. Langus, D. Neven and S. Pouken, *Economic Analysis of the Territoriality of the Making Available Right in the EU* (Report prepared for the European Commission, DG MARKT, 2014), 95.

[279] See Council of the European Union, Statement by the Republic of Poland, 4.

[280] This is not so uncommon: see, e.g., Art. 12(1) of Directive 2001/29/EC.

[281] See J. Hüttel (KODA), 'The CISAC Case & the 2005 Recommendation' *FEMR*, Sophienberg, 24 April 2009.

Interestingly, the Commission noted, in 2012, that some option 3 publishers are considering re-entrusting part of their rights to CMOs complying with the passport requirements.[282] Industry experts, however, find it 'unlikely that major music publishers would massively bring back their mechanical rights to collective management as a result of the CRM Directive'.[283] Also, the International Copyright Enterprise (ICE), for example, anticipates that 'the option 3 world is here to stay and will likely move in the future to traditionally licensed services'.[284]

As we have seen already in Chapter 2, up to now, a rather horizontal aggregation is taking place, instead of the expected re-aggregation of rights and repertoire. The aggregation of repertoire of CMOs is based mainly on their voluntary actions and it is too early to predict whether the licensing hub model will be more broadly used and lead to the predicted market consolidation. From the recent merger proceedings regarding the joint venture between PRS, GEMA and STIM,[285] it is evident that some first large CMOs are introducing hub models as proposed by the Directive – which can be taken as an indicator of a certain development in the direction of aggregation of repertoire from CMOs. For now, however, the picture is more complex. Only time will tell whether we are to witness more individual licensing arrangements, as described above, or IMEs, which compete with CMOs.

It is also worth noting that Recital 56 of Directive 2014/26/EU recalls that its rules are without prejudice to EU competition law.[286] In other words, multi-territorial licensing activities remain under the scrutiny of Articles 101 and 102 TFEU – given the aggregation of repertoires as well as infrastructure in the hand of a few players likely to continue to be an area of much interest of regulators and scholars alike.

Finally, with the European Commission's most recent proposal, the licensing of audiovisual content also appears on the legislative radar; for now, however, the chosen route is a reluctant facilitation approach.

---

[282] Commission, 'Impact Assessment accompanying the document Proposal for a Directive of the European Parliament and of the Council on collective management of copyright and related rights and multi-territorial licensing of rights in musical works for online uses in the internal market', 162.

[283] Anthonis, 'Will the CRM-directive succeed re-aggregating the mechanical reproduction rights in the Anglo-American music repertoire?', 160.

[284] International Copyright Enterprise (ICE), 3.

[285] *Commission Decision PRSfM/STIM/GEMA/JV* para. 34.

[286] See also L. Marchegiani, 'Le licenze multiterritoriali per l'uso online di opere musicali nella disciplina comunitaria della gestione collettiva dei diritti d'autore e dei diritti connessi', *Osservatorio del diritto civile e commerciale*, 2 (2013), 293, 306.

5   Cross-Border Access from a Legislative Perspective

In the previous chapter, we have seen the sector-specific regulatory legal framework for multi-territorial licensing – primarily within online music – that has been put in place. In this chapter, let us turn towards the second aspect: cross-border, or multi-territorial, access from a legislative perspective.

Compared with multi-territorial licensing, until recently, the question of cross-border access to online content has received less attention from lawmakers. That is not to say, though, that it has been off the regulatory radar. Historically, by 1989 the lawmaker had addressed related issues on a broader scale in secondary legislation in the form of the Television Without Frontiers Directive, which established the principle 'that Member States must ensure freedom of reception and that they may not restrict retransmission on their territory of television programmes from other Member States.'[1] It preceded the Audiovisual Media Services Directive (AVMS Directive[2]), which expanded the scope from television to audiovisual media services and governs the co-ordination of national legislation on both traditional television and on-demand audiovisual services throughout the EU. On the same day as the proposal for a Regulation on geo-blocking, the European Commission also presented its proposal for an update of the AVMS Directive,[3] following a consultation that ran from July to September 2015. The revision of the Directive is

---

[1] Art. 2(2) of Council Directive 89/552/EEC of 3 October 1989 on the coordination of certain provisions laid down by Law, Regulation or Administrative Action in Member States concerning the pursuit of television broadcasting activities [1989] OJ L298/23–30 (repealed) (Television without Frontiers Directive (TVWF)).

[2] Directive 2010/13/EU of the European Parliament and of the Council of 10 March 2010 on the coordination of certain provisions laid down by law, regulation or administrative action in Member States concerning the provision of audiovisual media services [2010] OJ L95/1–24 (Audiovisual Media Services Directive).

[3] Commission, 'Proposal for a Directive of the European Parliament and of the Council amending Directive 2010/13/EU on the coordination of certain provisions laid down by law, regulation or administrative action in Member States concerning the provision of audiovisual media services in view of changing market realities', COM(2016) 287 final, 2016/0151 (COD), Brussels, 25 May 2016, The document still contains mark-ups and seems rushed.

based on an *ex post* evaluation under the Better Regulation model (REFIT), in which it assessed, among other factors, the effectiveness, efficiency, relevance and coherence of the Directive. The overall conclusion of this evaluation was that the objectives of the Directive were still relevant and 'that the country of origin principle has enabled the development and free circulation of audiovisual media services across the EU, with legal certainty and resulted in lower compliance costs for providers and more choice for consumers'.[4] Apart from a reference to political news programmes in Recital 40, however, the Proposal does not extend the scope to the relevant subject matter of this research. Remarkably, Article 13 of the Proposal suggests a quota – namely that:[5]

Member States shall ensure that providers of on-demand audiovisual media services under their jurisdiction secure at least a 20% share of European works in their catalogue and ensure prominence of these works.[6]

The SatCab Directive of 1993[7] represents another milestone as regards rights clearance for satellite and cable broadcasters, notably with the introduction of a 'country of origin' principle. Prima facie, the Services Directive of 2006 seems relevant insofar as it prohibits geo-blocking.[8] Article 20 of the Services Directive, in the section on rights of recipients of services, stipulates that

1. Member States shall ensure that the recipient is not made subject to discriminatory requirements based on his nationality or place of residence.

2. Member States shall ensure that the general conditions of access to a service, which are made available to the public at large by the provider, do not contain discriminatory provisions relating to the nationality or place of residence of the recipient, but without precluding the possibility of providing for differences in the conditions of access where those differences are directly justified by objective criteria.

---

[4] Ibid., Explanatory Memorandum, 2.
[5] For an economic analysis, see C. Crampes and A. Hollander, 'The Regulation of Audiovisual Content: Quotas and Conflicting Objectives', *Journal of Regulatory Economics*, 34 (2008), 195.
[6] Commission, 'Proposal for a Directive of the European Parliament and of the Council amending Directive 2010/13/EU on the coordination of certain provisions laid down by law, regulation or administrative action in Member States concerning the provision of audiovisual media services in view of changing market realities', Art. 1(15).
[7] Council Directive 93/83/EEC of 27 September 1993 on the coordination of certain rules concerning copyright and rights related to copyright applicable to satellite broadcasting and cable retransmission [1993] OJ L 248/15–21 (SatCab Directive).
[8] Directive 2006/123/EC of the European Parliament and of the Council of 12 December 2006 on services in the internal market [2006] OJ L376/36. See, to this extent, P. B. Hugenholtz, 'Extending the SatCab Model to the Internet', Study commissioned by BEUC (Brussels, 2015), 6.

According to Article 2(2)(g) of Directive 2006/123/EC, audiovisual services (including cinematographic services), however, fall outside the scope of the Directive. Also, as regards other copyright-protected subject matter, Hugenholtz argues that '[a]lthough the Directive does not specify this, it is likely that the proper exercise of intellectual property rights by content providers would amount to such a justification'.[9] He concludes that 'geo-blocking for "justifiable" copyright-related reasons cannot be prohibited by direct reference to the Directive'.[10]

With the growing popularity of online content services, where the copy of the copyright-protected work is not downloaded to the consumer's device, but accessed via the Internet, the question of cross-border access to content has become more pressing. With the new Commission, discussions surrounding access to online content have been revived. In 2015, geo-blocking has become a central part of the European Commission's Digital Single Market Agenda.[11] At the same time, the European Parliament's report on the implementation of the InfoSoc Directive of June 2015,[12] however, acknowledges the multiple differences between the different issues and subject matters:

Considers that lessons may be drawn for other types of content from the approach taken in Directive 2014/26/EU on collective rights management, but that issues concerning portability and geo-blocking may not be solved by one all-encompassing solution but may require several different interventions, both regulatory and market-led;[13]

This chapter focuses on the recently introduced legal framework for multi-territorial access in favour of a discussion of the status quo until the entry into force of all discussed instruments. The chapter is structured in the following way: first, it looks at Regulation (EU) 2017/1128[14] regarding cross-border content portability and Regulation

---

[9] See Hugenholtz, 'Extending the SatCab Model to the Internet', 6.   [10] Ibid.

[11] Several non-academic sources comment on the fact that access to audiovisual content from their home country is a key concern for people working in the European institutions. See, e.g., C. Barbière, 'Geo-blocking attacked from all sides' (*EurActiv*, 2015): www.euractiv.com/section/digital/news/geo-blocking-attacked-from-all-sides/

[12] Directive 2001/29/EC of the European Parliament and of the Council of 22 May 2001 on the harmonisation of certain aspects of copyright and related rights in the information society [2001] OJ L167/10–19 (InfoSoc Directive).

[13] European Parliament, 'Report on the implementation of Directive 2001/29/EC of the European Parliament and of the Council of 22 May 2001 on the harmonisation of certain aspects of copyright and related rights in the information society (2014/2256(INI))', Recital 5.

[14] Regulation (EU) 2017/1128 of the European Parliament and of the Council of 14 June 2017 on cross-border portability of online content services in the internal market [2017] OJ L168/1–11.

(EU) 2018/302[15] regarding geo-blocking. Then, it will briefly look over the fence towards the online offerings of broadcasting organisations and touch upon the 2015 consultation on the SatCab Directive and the Commission's subsequent Proposal for a Regulation laying down rules on the exercise of copyright and related rights applicable to certain online transmissions of broadcasting organisations and retransmissions of television and radio programmes from September 2016.[16]

5.1   Status Quo and Contractual Arrangements

The question of cross-border access to digital content has only recently and only partly been addressed in the existing legal framework with Regulation (EU) 2017/1128 on cross-border content portability. Thus, there arise several issues, which can be roughly grouped into copyright-related questions, on the one hand, and contractual questions, on the other. As noted in the introduction to this book, the focus is on the exercise of copyright, not the scope of substantive rights. Also, while this chapter looks at contractual arrangements, it is outside the scope of this book to provide a thorough analysis under a contract law perspective.

As is commented on in Chapter 2, the majority of online service providers, both as regards music and to an even larger degree as regards audiovisual content, have been applying geo-blocking practices towards consumers. A first aspect, thus, relates to the contractual aspects in the relationship between service providers and rights holders – namely regarding limitations in the licensing agreements. In the absence of specific legislation, this relationship is guided by the general principles of, inter alia, contract law and competition law.

In order to provide some context, let us look at some empirical evidence from the practices of boilerplate terms in service or end-user licensing agreements of selected music and audiovisual streaming services towards their consumers from 2016.[17] The contractual relationship between end users and service providers has, relatively recently, moved into the

---

[15] Regulation (EU) 2018/302 of the European Parliament and of the Council of 28 February 2018 on addressing unjustified geo-blocking and other forms of discrimination based on customers' nationality, place of residence or place of establishment within the internal market and amending Regulations (EC) No 2006/2004 and (EU) 2017/2394 and Directive 2009/22/EC [2018] OJ L60I/1–15.

[16] Commission, 'Proposal for a Regulation of the European Parliament and of the Council laying down rules on the exercise of copyright and related rights applicable to certain online transmissions of broadcasting organisations and retransmissions of television and radio programmes'.

[17] The examined samples fall roughly into two categories: public broadcasters and private service providers. As regards private service on-demand providers, I have chosen to look at the two major video on demand (VOD) platforms Netflix and HBO Nordic, as well as

spotlight of the European lawmaker and also allows to draw conclusions regarding the licensing agreements between service providers and rights holders, as the terms provide an indication of the underlying licensing terms.

Let us first look briefly at audiovisual streaming services. According to its terms of use, Netflix grants subscribers a limited, non-exclusive, non-transferable licence to access its service and view its content, on a streaming-only basis.[18] The consumer also agrees not to use the service for public performances. With regard to content access and portability, section 4.3 notes that:

You may view the Netflix content primarily within the country in which you have established your account and only in geographic locations where we offer our service and have licensed such content. The content that may be available to watch will vary by geographic location and will change from time to time.[19]

The wording remained unchanged in April 2018, i.e. after the entry into force of the Portability Regulation. Riis and Schovsbo also look at the Danish terms of Netflix in relation to violation of contract, and point towards the indeterminacy of the rule, which restricts the geographical coverage.[20] In terms of geographical restrictions, in 2016 the terms of

major music streaming services Spotify, Apple Music and Deezer. The selection of samples does not follow a specific method and was largely guided by my knowledge of languages. Thus, the samples serve, to a large degree, as anecdotal evidence and come with the drawback that it is unsuitable to derive conclusions with broader applications. Nonetheless, the samples will provide some insights into whether and how these contractual arrangements cover the availability of content and territorial restrictions. For user-generated content sites: 'these agreements typically require users to "click through" the terms of use to indicate acceptance before accessing the website and its content. Courts have typically upheld these agreements, applying standard contract principles. Disputes over EUAs, however, have most often involved suits against user-consumers for violating the terms of use'. See J. C. Ginsburg, 'Authors' Transfer and License Contracts under U.S. Copyright Law' in J. de Werra (ed.), *Research Handbook on Intellectual Property Licensing* (Edward Elgar, 2013), p. 26.

[18] See section 4.2 of Netflix Terms of Use, available at: www.netflix.com/TermsOfUse?locale=en-GB. In comparison with the Netflix Terms of Use in 2016, a specification on the access on a streaming-only basis was dropped.
[19] See section 4.3 of Netflix Terms of Use, available at: www.netflix.com/TermsOfUse?locale=en-GB. The Danish and German versions respectively are literal translations. The section remains largely unaltered from Netflix Terms of Use from 2016, in which it was stated that: 'You may view a movie or TV show through the Netflix service primarily within the country in which you have established your account and only in geographic locations where we offer our service and have licensed such movie or TV show. The content that may be available to watch will vary by geographic location and will change from time to time'.
[20] T. Riis and J. Schovsbo, 'Den grænseløse onlinebruger – geografisk opdeling af markedet for online- og streamingtjenester' in *Liber Amicorum Jan Rosén* (eddy.se, 2016), p. 675. Notably, they find a variation in the Norwegian terms of Netflix, which specify that the service is restricted to the country of subscription.

streaming service HBO Nordic were, compared with those of Netflix, found to be more specific as well as more restrictive: section 2.1 of the terms formerly defined that the 'service may only be used in Sweden, Denmark, Norway and Finland'.[21] This formulation remained intact until at least mid-April 2018, after which the section was modified in order to accommodate the Portability Regulation.[22] According to section 15.1 on intellectual property rights, consumers are granted the non-exclusive, non-transferable and restricted right to use the content of the service. Finally, the terms also safeguard the service provider's right to cancel the agreement in case of violations.[23] The geographic availability of the VOD offering by Amazon are specified in section 3 of its terms, but only vaguely note that 'the Service is available only in certain locations' and prohibits the use of 'any technology or technique to obscure or disguise your location'.[24]

The picture looks somewhat different as regards the terms of subscription music streaming services. Spotify, one of the largest music streaming service providers, grants its users 'a limited, non-exclusive, revocable license to make use of the Spotify Service, and a limited, non-exclusive, revocable license to make personal, non-commercial, entertainment use of the Content'.[25] Notably, the terms in 2016 did not directly address content portability.[26] However, in the third condition of section 1 of the terms it was specified that an end-user needs to 'be resident in a country where the Service is available'.

In 2016, Apple Music, the on-demand streaming service of Apple provided via the iTunes platform, specified in the section on 'Requirements for use of the Apple Music Service' of its terms that the

[21] Terms available in Danish at: https://dk.hbonordic.com/account/terms

[22] Terms available in Danish at: https://dk.hbonordic.com/terms-and-conditions

[23] Section 7.2 reads: '7.2 The service may only be used in the Territory. The user may not in any way use – or encourage, promote or cause others to – use or try to use the Service outside the Territory.' (translation from Danish by the author).

[24] Amazon Prime Video Terms of Use, last updated 2 April 2018: www.primevideo.com/help?nodeId=202095490&view-type=content-only

[25] See section 4 of Spotify Terms and Conditions of Use, effective as of 3 September 2015, available at: www.spotify.com/uk/legal/end-user-agreement/

[26] The Support section under 'Travel with Spotify', however, offers some specifications: 'If you're a Premium user, you can use your Spotify account as long as you like anywhere in the world that offers unrestricted internet. You can also use offline mode to enjoy your music even if your journey takes you to corners of the earth without internet (or if you're on the plane). If you're a Free user, you can use Spotify in a different country to the one registered on your account for up to 14 days. After that, you'll need to upgrade to Premium or change the country on your account.' Thus, the portability of the service discriminates between paying and non-paying subscribers. From the wording, the clauses notably refer to the account of the user and not the content catalogue; worldwide use, not restricted to the territories in which Spotify is active. See https://support.spotify.com/is/account_payment_help/account_settings/travel-with-spotify/

service is available only in the country of the subscriber. In other words, a user of the German Apple Music service is restricted to Germany, a user of Apple Music in the United Kingdom to the United Kingdom and so on.[27] Additionally, the user agrees 'not to use or attempt to use the Apple Music Service from outside this location'.[28]

Deezer's terms of 2016 in Article 10 on 'Territory', respectively, regulate that '[t]he subscription to the Service is reserved to physical person, living in the effective country and owning a credit card produce by a bank established in this country'.[29] As regards portability, the Support page specifies that users can access the service while abroad, but safeguards that '[t]here may be some music that is not available to you because of the licensing rights in that area'.[30]

Remarkably, the commercial VOD services in the sample provided for clauses on territorial limitations in their terms. As regards commercial music streaming services, apart from Apple Music, none of the services specified the territorial scope of access in their terms; rather, they appeared in the support section. Several of the service providers specify also some kind of sales restriction ('passive sales'). Depending on the clauses in the agreements and their validity, in some cases, consumers thus might breach the subscription contract if they try to circumvent such restrictions.

This brings me to a second aspect. Here, the question is whether consumers can lawfully circumvent such geo-blocking arrangements or technological protection measures (TPMs). End users sometimes rely on tools, notably virtual private network (VPN) clients, to evade geo-blocking and to circumvent (technical) territorial restrictions.[31]

---

[27] At least, this is the case in the UK, German, Danish, Swedish, Norwegian and Italian version of the terms. See, e.g., iTunes Terms and Conditions for the UK, last updated 21 October 2015, available at: www.apple.com/legal/internet-services/itunes/uk/terms.html %23AM

[28] It continues to note that 'iTunes may use technologies to verify the compliance' of the consumer. However, no detailed information is available on whether or how the provision is enforced. These restrictions are contained in a similar wording, at least in the terms and conditions applicable in Denmark, Germany, Italy, Norway, Sweden and the United Kingdom.

[29] See, e.g., Art. 10 of Terms of Use and Sale Deezer Premium Service, available at: www.deezer.com/legal/cgu%23cgu_premium

[30] See Support section under question 'Can I use Deezer while abroad?': http://support. deezer.com/hc/en-gb/articles/201160352-What-is-Deezer-. In another Support article, it is specified that the service is available in 174 countries.

[31] A variety of other reasons for the use of VPN clients are given by consumers, such as privacy or practicality, when internet connections would not allow for direct access to certain service providers. See, e.g., M. Trimble, 'The Territoriality Referendum', *World Intellectual Property Organization Journal* [2014], 89, 92.

Netflix announced strict enforcement against VPN clients.[32] Evidence from leaked licensing contracts suggests that video streaming service providers, for example, are contractually obliged to use software to detect the use of VPN clients.[33] In this context, Riis and Schovsbo point towards three aspects: first, whether the circumvention would constitute a breach of the subscription contract.[34] Secondly, whether the circumvention infringes copyright.[35] Thirdly, whether the circumvention is contrary to the protection of TPMs. Commissioner Ansip pointed towards the use of VPNs as a legal grey area.[36] Others note that the circumvention of geo-blocking is likely to constitute an infringement of TPMs according to Article 6(3) of Directive 2001/29/EC.[37] It is outside the scope of this book to devote further scrutiny to this aspect. Suffice it to conclude here that several forms of territorial restriction are present in the contractual

[32] See, e.g., J. Greenberg, 'For Netflix, Discontent over Blocked VPNs is Boiling' (*WIRED*, 3 July 2016): www.wired.com/2016/03/netflix-discontent-blocked-vpns-boiling/. Notably, an online petition to change the policy has gained more than 36,000 signatures by subscribers.

[33] No public information is available as to how the software works, but notably the technology has been developed by rights holders. It seems likely that strict enforcement via the use of technological measures also forms part of the licensing terms by rights holders. Evidence from leaked licensing contracts in connection with the 'Sony hack' support this hypothesis. One of the licensing contracts from September 2012, a 'Subscription Video-on-demand Licence Agreement' between Netflix and rights holders, contains a section on 'Fraud detection' that reads: 'Licensee shall consistently track information indicating fraudulent viewing and distribution activity on the SVOD Service, including, without limitation, license issuances by Registered User and IP address, device registration and de-authorization, customer IDs, play data and number of current streams by Registered User and review its procedures with Licensor from time to time.' Contract available at: https://wikileaks.org/sony/docs/07/Documents/@Deals/Netflix/Sony-Netflix Nordics SVOD License Agreement D18 GPC (14–09-2012).docx

[34] This would be the case where service providers have specified this, such as, e.g., HBO Nordic. See Riis and Schovsbo, 'Den grænseløse onlinebruger – geografisk opdeling af markedet for online- og streamingtjenester', 675.

[35] This depends on the underlying licensing relationship. Thus, if a service provider has not cleared the respective rights in the territory from which the service is accessed, an infringement would occur. For more in-depth analysis, see ibid.

[36] Commissioner Andrus Ansip, 'Speech by Vice-President Ansip at the Creators Conference' (31 May 2016): https://ec.europa.eu/commission/2014–2019/ansip/annou ncements/speech-vice-president-ansip-creators-conference_en

[37] For the German context, see, e.g., M. von Albrecht, A. Mutschler-Siebert and T. Bosch, 'Die Murphy-Entscheidung und ihre Auswirkungen auf Sport- und Filmlizenzen im Online-Bereich, Die exklusive territoriale Rechtevergabe ist kein Modell der Vergangenheit!', *Zeitschrift für Urheber- und Medienrecht* [2012] 93, 97; for the Danish context, see, e.g., Riis and Schovsbo, 'Den grænseløse onlinebruger – geografisk opdeling af markedet for online- og streamingtjenester', who look at the circumvention to sub-scribe to an online service from another country, and the circumvention to enable portability, i.e. access to a subscription legally purchased in one country, but accessed from another.

arrangements between online service providers and consumers and that the legal framework did not address cross-border access until recently.

5.2   Cross-Border Portability Regulation

Just seven months after the announcement of the Digital Single Market Strategy, on 9 December 2015, the European Commission published its Proposal for a Regulation on ensuring the cross-border portability of online content services in the internal market.[38] The proposal is to be seen on the intersection with the end of roaming charges, which ended in 2017: the Commission argues that, once roaming charges fall, consumers will be able to access content while travelling.[39]

With the goal being to 'remove barriers to cross-border portability so that the needs of users can be met more effectively as well as promoting innovation for the benefit of consumers, service providers and right holders', the Commission considered the baseline scenario of no policy intervention and three policy options.[40] As a first option, the European Commission considered providing guidance and encouraging stakeholders regarding the cross-border portability of online content services.[41] Option 2 consisted of a legal mechanism to facilitate cross-border portability of such services in the EU, which entailed a legal fiction regarding the country of access to content by the consumer, but without prohibiting contractual clauses that limit or prevent the mechanism.[42] Finally, as option 3, an intervention to ensure cross-border portability of online content services in the EU was suggested, which, beyond the legal fiction of option 2, would also introduce an obligation on service providers and a prohibition on restrictions in licensing contracts.[43] The latter policy option was deemed to be the most effective in meeting the objectives of the intervention.[44]

---

[38] Commission, 'Proposal for a Regulation on ensuring the cross-border portability of online content services'.

[39] See, e.g., Commission, 'Impact Assessment accompanying the document Proposal for a Regulation of the European Parliament and of the Council to ensure the cross-border portability of online content services in the internal market', 3; Commission, 'Impact Assessment accompanying the document Proposal for a Regulation of the European Parliament and of the Council to ensure the cross-border portability of online content services in the internal market (COM(2015) 627 final) SWD(2015) 271 final}' (Commission Staff Working Document) Brussels, 9.12.2015 SWD(2015) 270 final, 3.

[40] Commission, 'Proposal for a Regulation on ensuring the cross-border portability of online content services', Explanatory Memorandum, 2.

[41] See Commission, 'Impact Assessment accompanying the document Proposal for a Regulation of the European Parliament and of the Council to ensure the cross-border portability of online content services in the internal market (COM(2015) 627 final) (SWD(2015) 271 final)', 23.

[42] See ibid., 24.   [43] See ibid., 26.   [44] See ibid., 47.

On 25 May 2016, the Council reached a general approach and envisioned that the Regulation could enter into force in 2017. Only in February 2017, however, did the Parliament and the Maltese Council presidency reach a provisional agreement on the Regulation, which exemplifies the difficulties around the proposal. On 14 June 2017, Regulation (EU) 2017/1128 on cross-border portability of online content services in the internal market was adopted. The Regulation applies from 1 April 2018.[45]

5.2.1   Scope of Regulation (EU) 2017/1128

The Commission's proposal consisted of twenty-nine recitals and eight articles, compared with thirty-six recitals and eleven articles in the final Regulation, making it a relatively concise regulatory instrument. In Article 1(1) of Regulation (EU) 2017/1128, its objective and scope are set out:

This Regulation introduces a common approach in the Union to the cross-border portability of online content services, by ensuring that subscribers to portable online content services which are lawfully provided in their Member State of residence can access and use those services when temporarily present in a Member State other than their Member State of residence.

In contrast with the Commission's proposal, apart from refining the wording, it has been clarified that the Regulation only applies to online content services that operate lawfully or, in other words, have licensed the content from rights holders. Such online content service is further defined in Article 2(5) of the Portability Regulation as:

a service as defined in Articles 56 and 57 TFEU that a provider lawfully provides to subscribers in their Member State of residence on agreed terms and online, which is portable and which is:

   (i) an audiovisual media service as defined in point (a) of Article 1 of Directive 2010/13/EU, *or*

   (ii) a service the main feature of which is the provision of access to, and the use of, works, other protected subject-matter or transmissions of broadcasting organisations, whether in a linear or an on-demand manner;[46]

---

[45] Art. 11(2) of Regulation (EU) 2017/1128; see Corrigendum to Regulation (EU) 2017/1128 of the European Parliament and of the Council of 14 June 2017 on cross-border portability of online content services in the internal market [2017] OJ L198/42.

[46] Emphasis added.

Thus, the Regulation is first directed towards audiovisual media services, according to Article 2(5)(i). According to Article 1(a)(i) of Directive 2010/13/EU, such service is

a service as defined by Articles 56 and 57 of the Treaty on the Functioning of the European Union which is under the editorial responsibility of a media service provider and the *principal purpose* of which is the provision of programmes, in order to inform, entertain or educate, to the general public by electronic communications networks within the meaning of point (a) of Article 2 of Directive 2002/21/EC. Such an audio-visual media service is either a television broadcast as defined in point (e) of this paragraph or an on-demand audiovisual media service as defined in point (g) of this paragraph;[47]

Secondly, the Geo-blocking Regulation applies to services that provide access to and use of works according to Article 2(5)(ii).[48] Regulation (EU) 2017/1128, as well as the Commission's proposal, refrain from defining the notions of 'works' or 'other protected subject matter'. As becomes apparent from the non-exclusive list in Recital 8 of the Proposal, the European Commission seems to understand as 'works or other protected subject-matter' at least books, audiovisual works, recorded music or broadcasts both in a linear or in an on-demand manner. Similarly, Recital 8 of Regulation (EU) 2017/1128 mentions books, audiovisual works, recorded music and broadcasts. Additionally, other examples can be found spread out throughout the recitals, such as music (Recitals 1 and 4), games (Recitals 1 and 4), films (Recitals 1 and 4), entertainment programmes (Recitals 1 and 4) and sports events (Recital 1; see also Recital 5). Even though these recitals stand in a different context, given the lack of other clear references it would seem incoherent for a different subject matter to apply within the meaning of the provision.[49]

In several parts of its Impact Assessment accompanying the Proposal, the European Commission commented that portability in the case of online music services seems to be a minor concern.[50] It evaluates that the licensing practice of rights holders regarding online music 'does not

---

[47] Emphasis added.

[48] And Art. 2(e) alt. 2 var. 1 of the Commission's Proposal accordingly.

[49] The recitals relate to the necessity to 'have the right to use such content for the relevant territories'. This reading is also supported by evidence from the glossary from the Impact Assessment, in which the European Commission defines 'Work' as 'creative output of authors protected by copyright. It includes: literary (books, lyrics, etc.), dramatic (plays, opera librettos, etc.), musical and artistic (photography, painting, etc.) works' and 'Other protected subject-matter' as 'output of holders of related rights i.e. performers, phonogram and film producers and broadcasting organisations'. See Commission, 'Impact Assessment accompanying the document Proposal for a Regulation of the European Parliament and of the Council to ensure the cross-border portability of online content services in the internal market (COM(2015) 627 final) (SWD(2015) 271 final)', 85.

[50] See ibid., 10 and 15.

create obstacles, beyond some legal uncertainty, to the cross-border portability of services'.[51] As one reason for this argumentation, the Commission provides 'that the vast majority of music content is not licensed on an exclusive basis (e.g. most musical works are available from multiple service providers in the same MS)'.[52] As regards the background of the identified complexities in the licensing system in the previous chapters, this assessment by the Commission seems undifferentiated. The observation that musical works are available from more than one service provider in a single Member State especially substantiates that the observation that portability is not a concern for end users of online music service providers and remains nebulous. The Proposal and the Regulation do not provide much more clarity.[53] In Recital 16, the Regulation (and in Recital 14 of the Proposal accordingly) merely refines that an online service that is not an audiovisual media service and uses the covered subject matters only in an ancillary matter should not be covered by the Regulation.[54] Thus, it seems that online music services are not precluded from its scope. This view is also supported by the draft report of the European Parliament's Committee on Legal Affairs, which suggested the amendment of Recital 4 of the Proposal by adding:

At present, the problems associated with cross-border portability of online content services differ from one sector to another: whereas the music industry *began* to resolve these problems by proposing multi-territorial or pan-European licences following the implementation of Directive 2014/26/EU of the European Parliament and of Council, the audiovisual sector, where the model of exclusive territorial licensing predominates, is having trouble in adapting to the portability approach. This Regulation should solve *all* the difficulties of adjusting to portability in *all* the sectors concerned, without affecting the high level of protection guaranteed by the copyright and related rights in the EU.[55]

The Committee's suggestion has not found its way into the final Regulation. However, Recital 12 of Regulation (EU) 2017/1128 envisions that '[t]he Regulation should ensure cross-border portability of online content services in all sectors concerned'. Read in conjunction

---

[51] Ibid., 15.   [52] Ibid.
[53] It is, however, apparent from the survey above that online music streaming services provide portability to some degree.
[54] The Regulation comes, inter alia, with the example of music used as background on a website with the main purpose of sale of goods.
[55] Emphasis added. See European Parliament, 'Draft Report on the proposal for a regulation of the European Parliament and of the Council on ensuring the cross-border portability of online content services in the internal market', Committee on Legal Affairs, Rapporteur: Jean-Marie Cavada, 2015/0284(COD), 21 June 2016, Amendment 4, 7–8.

with Recitals 4 and 8 of the Regulation (see above), it is clear that online music falls within the scope of the Regulation.

A subscriber to such online content service is defined in Article(2)(1) of Regulation (EU) 2017/1128 as

> any consumer who, on the basis of a contract for the provision of an online content service with a provider whether against payment of money or without such payment, is entitled to access and use such service in the Member State of residence.

In contrast with the Commission's draft, the legislator has chosen to move the additional criteria for free services into a separate Article 6 (Cross-border portability of online content services provided without payment of money), which will be discussed below.

The final criterion of Article 1 that is worth looking at refers to the temporary presence of the subscriber.[56] In Article 2(4), the Regulation defines 'temporarily present in a Member State' merely as 'being present in a Member State other than the Member State of residence for a limited period of time'. Article 2(d) of the Proposal defines temporary presence as 'presence of a subscriber in a Member State other than the Member State of Residence'. Thus, in contrast with the Commission's Proposal of 2015, the legislator added the criterion of a limited time period. Recital 1 of the Regulation names leisure, travel, business trips or learning mobility as examples. Notably, the Regulation does not further specify the temporality element and leaves open whether this embraces days, weeks, months or even longer periods of time.[57]

5.2.2   Legal Mechanisms for the 'Common Approach'

The Regulation contains three main mechanisms in order to facilitate its objectives, which are contained in three articles: Article 3 (on the obligation to enable cross-border portability of online content-services), Article 4 (on the localisation of the provision of, access to and use of online content services), and Article 7 (on contractual provisions). The three mechanisms roughly correlate to the respective relationships between the different parties involved, namely rights holders, online service providers (commercial users) and subscribers (end users). Figure 6 provides an overview of these relationships and serves as a reference through the following explanation.

---

[56] Notably, this criterion did not form part of the Commission's proposal for Art. 1, but was instead merely introduced in Art. 2(d) on Definitions in the proposal; Art. 2(d) thus refined Art. 1, which otherwise merely refers to the subscriber being 'temporarily present in a Member State' – thus lacking the reference to the essential translocation element.

[57] This has been subject to criticism: see below.

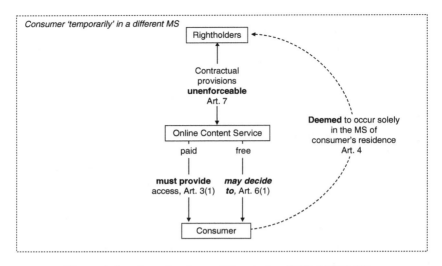

Figure 6: Legal mechanisms of Regulation (EU) 2017/1128

First, Article 3 of Regulation (EU) 2017/1128 regards the contractual arrangements between online content service providers and subscribers. Article 3(1) of the Portability Regulation sets out to install the obligation for the online content service provider, which is provided against the payment of money, to enable cross-border portability of its services to subscribers:

The provider of an online content service provided against payment of money shall enable a subscriber who is temporarily present in a Member State to access and use the online content service in the same manner as in the Member State of residence, including by providing access to the same content, on the same range and number of devices, for the same number of users and with the same range of functionalities.

It is specified in Article 3(3) and (4) that, as a basic principle, the obligation does not extend to the quality requirements of the service, unless otherwise expressly agreed by the provider, but that the provider must inform subscribers of the quality of delivery.[58] In contrast with the Commission's proposal, the legislator has also introduced an explicit prohibition on additional charges by the providers for portability in Article 3(2).

---

[58] C. Castets-Renard, '"Digital Single Market": the European Commission presents its first measures in Copyright Law', *French Review: Recueil Dalloz*, n° 7 (2016) 5: http://ssrn.com/abstract=2802729, notes on the Commission's proposal that the limitation constitutes a weakness of protection 'because the service providers could not make efforts or even voluntarily degrade the quality of their services and defeat the objective of the regulation, without engaging their liability'.

On a more abstract level, Article 4 of Regulation (EU) 2017/1128 relates to the relationship of rights holders to subscribers (and service providers). It sets out the central mechanism as regards the relevant acts relating to copyright and related rights:

The provision of an online content service under this Regulation to a subscriber who is temporarily present in a Member State, as well as the access to and the use of this service by the subscriber *shall be deemed to occur* solely in subscribers' Member State.[59]

In other words, Article 4 creates the legal fiction of the subscriber accessing the works only in its Member State of residence as regards the provision, access to and use of online content services. Thus, the mechanism constitutes the centrepiece of enabling access to copyright-protected works for which an online service provider has cleared rights in the Member State of residence (Member State A) but not necessarily in the Member State of temporary presence (Member State B). In its effect, this mechanism functions according to the 'country of origin' principle for portability.

The final mechanism relates to the relationship between online content service providers and rights holders as well as subscribers. Article 7 of Regulation (EU) 2017/1128 (Article 5(1) of the Proposal respectively) establishes that any contractual arrangements that run counter to the legal fiction in Article 4 and the obligation for online content services to provide cross-border portability in Article 3 are unenforceable. That is to say that contractual terms in the licensing agreements between rights holders and service providers, as well as terms in the contracts between service providers and subscribers, that 'limit either the consumer's possibilities as to the cross-border portability (. . .) or service provider's ability to deliver it'[60] or are 'contrary to the legal mechanism which enables service providers to comply with the cross-border portability obligation'[61] are overridden. Notably, the Regulation as a whole has retroactive effect as regards contracts concluded and rights acquired before the date of its application, i.e. 1 April 2018, according to Article 9(1).

As regards the background of industry concerns that consumers would use the mechanisms of the Portability Regulation in order permanently to access content in cross-border situations, a key concern for rights holders

---

[59] Emphasis added. Notably the Commission's proposal referenced specifically Directive 96/9/EC, Directive 2001/29/EC, Directive 2006/115/EC, Directive 2009/24 and Directive 2010/13/EU.

[60] See Commission, 'Proposal for a Regulation on ensuring the cross-border portability of online content services', Explanatory Memorandum, 8.

[61] See ibid., Explanatory Memorandum, 8–9.

centred on how to authenticate the presence of the consumer, as well as the definition of the Member State of residence. This verification of the Member State of residence has been introduced as an obligation on service providers in Article 5 (on verification of the Member State of residence).[62] The Commission's proposal foresaw that rights holders could require that

the service provider makes use of effective means in order to verify that the online content service is provided in conformity with Article 3(1), provided that the required means are reasonable and do not go beyond what is necessary in order to achieve their purpose.[63]

Under Regulation (EU) 2017/1128, the verification of the Member State depends on whether the service is provided against the payment of money, or free. Also, in its definitions the Commission's proposal differentiated among online content service provided as a subscription service (for money directly or indirectly), or free.[64] In the latter case, it was proposed that the Portability Regulation was to apply only to the extent that service providers verify the Member State of residence of their subscribers. According to Article 5(1) of Regulation (EU) 2017/1128, online service providers are obliged to verify the Member State of residence of the subscriber of a service provided against payment of money at the conclusion and upon the renewal of a contract. It further stipulates a specific verification mechanism with an exhaustive list of means of verification and obliges the online service provider to 'ensure that the means used are reasonable, proportionate and effective'.[65]

---

[62] See also Recitals 26–27 of Regulation (EU) 2017/1128.

[63] Further specified in Recital 23 of the Proposal.

[64] An example of indirect payment is a bundled package 'which combines a telecommunication service and an online content service provided by another device provider'. See Commission, 'Proposal for a Regulation on ensuring the cross-border portability of online content services', Explanatory Memorandum, 8.

[65] Namely: '(a) an identity card, electronic means of identification, in particular those falling under the electronic identification schemes notified in accordance with Regulation (EU) No 910/2014 of the European Parliament and of the Council (12), or any other valid identity document confirming the subscriber's Member State of residence; (b) payment details such as the bank account or credit or debit card number of the subscriber; (c) the place of installation of a set top box, a decoder or a similar device used for supply of services to the subscriber; (d) the payment by the subscriber of a licence fee for other services provided in the Member State, such as public service broadcasting; (e) an internet or telephone service supply contract or any similar type of contract linking the subscriber to the Member State; (f) registration on local electoral rolls, if the information concerned is publicly available; (g) payment of local taxes, if the information concerned is publicly available; (h) a utility bill of the subscriber linking the subscriber to the Member State; (i) the billing address or the postal address of the subscriber; (j) a declaration by the subscriber confirming the subscriber's address in the Member State; (k) an internet protocol (IP) address check, to identify the Member State where the subscriber accesses

In the final Regulation, the legislator has chosen to introduce a specific Article 6 (on the cross-border portability of online content services provided without payment of money). The legal mechanism for such 'free' online content services functions roughly in the same way as the mechanism for such services provided against payment: according to Article 6(1) of the Regulation, such a 'free' service 'may decide to' enable portability for its subscribers, provided that the subscribers' Member State of residence is verified. Thus, the legislator has effectively chosen an opt-in solution for those services.

Interestingly, the notion of 'subscriber' in Article 6 of the Portability Regulation still conveys a contractual relationship between the service provider and the consumer. Recital 15 clarifies that such a contract 'should be regarded as covering any agreement between a provider and a subscriber, including any arrangement by which the subscriber accepts the provider's terms and conditions for the provision of online content services'. It continues to elaborate that a 'registration to receive content alerts or a mere acceptance of HTML cookies should not be regarded as a contract'. Notably, 'the payment of a mandatory fee for public broadcasting services' is not regarded as payment of money, according to Recital 18 of the Regulation. This means that public broadcasting services are not covered by the obligation to provide portability in Article 3 (1) but fall under the opt-in regulation of Article 6. The rationale behind Article 6 becomes clearer when we look at Recital 20:

Providers of online content services which are provided without payment of money generally do not verify the Member State of residence of their subscribers. The inclusion of such online content services in the scope of this Regulation would involve a major change to the way those services are delivered and involve disproportionate costs. However, the exclusion of those services from the scope of this Regulation would mean that providers of those services would not be able to take advantage of the legal mechanism which is provided for in this Regulation and which enables providers of online content services to offer cross-border portability of such services, even when they decide to invest in means that allow them to verify their subscribers' Member State of residence. Accordingly, providers of online content services which are provided without payment of money should be able to opt to be included in the scope of this Regulation provided that they comply with the requirements on the verification of the Member State of residence of their subscribers.

the online content service'. Specifically, on IP address checks see also Recital 28 of the Regulation. Recital 17 of the Commission's draft: 'As concerns verification of the subscriber's Member State of residence, information such as a payment of a licence fee for other services provided in the Member State of residence, the existence of a contract for internet or telephone connection, IP address or other means of authentication, should be relied upon, if they enable the provider to have reasonable indicators as to the Member State of residence of its subscribers.'

If a provider of such 'free' service decides to opt in, it has to 'inform its subscribers, the relevant holders of copyright and related rights and the relevant holders of any other rights in the content of the online content service' prior to providing that service, according to Article 6(2) of the Regulation.[66]

5.2.3   *Discussion of the Portability Regulation*

Given its relatively recent adoption, the Portability Regulation has so far attracted limited academic interest. Among stakeholders, the Commission's Proposal of 2015 has partly been described as controversial.[67] Others, notably the right holder Premier League, note that '[t]he portability regulation is fine. But the European Commission should be aware that if they go beyond that we'd be very opposed'.[68] The European Broadcasting Union (EBU) welcomed the draft but argued that public service broadcasters should be free to decide whether to launch a portability service.[69] Also, the British public broadcaster's BBC iPlayer, which provides linear and on-demand access to content, supported the Commission's Proposal.[70] On a more critical note, the Communia Association welcomed the proposed regulation, which it said 'will put an end to one of the most annoying consequences of a territorial copyright system' but criticised it in that 'by making the system a little more bearable the this move can also be expected to further entrench the reality of territorial markets'.[71] It has been pointed out that some service providers are already adjusting their contracts, as in the case of the Premier League's licensing contracts, which were set to include a clause on portability in the football season following the proposal.[72] Overall, it is too early to assess the impact of the Portability

---

[66] According to Recital 20, that information on their decision to exercise that option has to be provided in a timely manner – for example, on the provider's website.

[67] For a summary of reactions, see, e.g., C. Stupp, 'Commission wants consumers to access digital content when they travel' (*EurActiv*, 9 December 2015): www.euractiv.com/sec tion/digital/news/commission-wants-consumers-to-access-digital-content-when-they-travel/

[68] Ibid.

[69] EBU, 'Satellite and Cable Licensing Solutions: The Key to Enhancing Cross-border Access to Online TV and Radio Content' *EBU* (9 December 2015): www.ebu.ch/news/2015/12/satellite-and-cable-directive-li

[70] Stupp, 'Commission wants consumers to access digital content when they travel'.

[71] P. Keller, 'Copyright Communication: the good, the bad, and the ugly' (*COMMUNIA Association*, 10 December 2015): www.communia-association.org/2 015/12/10/copyright-communication-commission-communiaction-the-good-the-ba d-and-the-ugly/

[72] Stupp, 'Commission wants consumers to access digital content when they travel'.

Regulation, but, nonetheless, some of its essential features and aspects can be pointed out.

First, the chosen legal tool, a Regulation according to Article 288 of the Treaty on the Functioning of the European Union (TFEU), presents a novelty in the copyright-related arena.[73] Farrand comments on the fact that the proposal introduces '[i]n comparison to earlier, more cautious initiatives (...) a maximum harmonisation approach'.[74] He deems that whereas the choice of legal instrument is ambitious, 'its objectives are somewhat more cautious'.[75] The decision on the necessity of adopting a Regulation vis-à-vis a Directive was not unanimous, though. In this respect, the German Federal Council (Bundesrat) requested that the Commission re-assess the necessity of the legal nature of its Proposal under the proportionality principle.[76]

There are a couple of aspects of the substantive provisions that have been refined during the legislative process. Several commentators have pointed towards the fact that 'temporary' presence was not defined specifically in the Commission's draft,[77] which was argued to hamper legal certainty of the different parties involved. In its Impact Assessment, the Commission, on the other hand, considered that a specification of the duration was not required, 'as the main defining feature is that such presence does not change the habitual residence of the subscriber' and because the concept needs to 'accommodate temporary presences of various lengths and for various purposes'.[78] Notably, the Committee on Legal Affairs agrees with the concept that the transient presence should not be limited to a specific number of days:

---

[73] See, e.g., T. Shapiro, 'The Proposed Regulation on Portability – Don't Leave Home without it', *Entertainment Law Review*, 27 (2016), 351 for a detailed walk-through. This also noted by G. Mazziotti, 'Is geo-blocking a real cause for concern?', *European Intellectual Property Review*, 38 (2016), 365, 369; and L. Guibault, 'Individual Licensing Models and Consumer Protection', Amsterdam Law School Legal Studies Research Paper No. 2016–01, 13: http://ssrn.com/abstract=2713765

[74] B. Farrand, 'The EU Portability Regulation: One Small Step for Cross-border Access, One Giant Leap for Commission Copyright Policy?'. *European Intellectual Property Review*, 38 (2016), 321, 322.

[75] Ibid.

[76] Bundesrat, 'Beschluss des Bundesrates, Vorschlag für eine Verordnung des Europäischen Parlaments und des Rates zur Gewährleistung der grenzüberschreitenden Portabilität von Online-Inhaltediensten im Binnenmarkt', *Drucksache* 167/16, 22 April 2016.

[77] E.g. ibid.

[78] See Commission, 'Impact Assessment accompanying the document Proposal for a Regulation of the European Parliament and of the Council to ensure the cross-border portability of online content services in the internal market', 24–25.

The regulation must remain simple to apply if it is to benefit the greatest possible number of people in Europe moving for shorter or longer periods within the Union, particularly for reasons of leisure, business or study.[79]

It has to be considered, however, that the interpretation in the absence of a more specific definition could be up to the discretion of rights holders and service providers, which might have a detrimental effect on the aim of the provision and harm legal certainty. As has been seen, the legislator has chosen to refrain from offering a more specific definition.

Another aspect of uncertainty, which was clarified during the legislative process, is to what extent the draft Regulation was to apply to online content services, which are accessible to the public without entering into a subscription contract but subject to terms of use, as could be the case with both public service broadcasters and (advertising-based) private service providers.[80] The Proposal did not contain a definition of what is to be understood as a contract, but, in Recital 13, merely laid out that '[a] registration to receive content alerts or a mere acceptance of HTML cookies should not be regarded as a contract for the provision of online content service for the purposes of this Regulation'.[81] In its Explanatory Memorandum, the Commission notes that

if, for example, a consumer just accepts the terms and conditions of a free of charge online content service but does not register on a website of such service (and hence the provider does not verify the Member State of residence of such a consumer), the service provider will not be obliged to provide cross-border portability for such service.[82]

This refinement, however, was not represented in the Commission's proposed text for the Portability Regulation. Furthermore, both the Impact Assessment on the chosen policy option and the Explanatory Memorandum comment that services 'that (...) do not involve the verification of the consumer's MS of residence' are outside the scope of the

---

[79] European Parliament, 'Draft Report on the proposal for a regulation of the European Parliament and of the Council on ensuring the cross-border portability of online content services in the internal market' Explanatory Statement, 34.

[80] The relevant provisions refer to the 'subscriber', who is defined in Art. 2(a) as 'any consumer who, on the basis of a contract for the provision of an online content service with a provider may access and use such services in the Member State of residence'.

[81] This is also specified in the scope of the Impact Assessment, in which the Commission notes that online content services that 'are freely accessible in the sense that they do not involve any explicit contractual relation between the service provider and the consumer or that they do not involve the verification of the consumer's MS of residence' are outside its scope. See Commission, 'Impact Assessment accompanying the document Proposal for a Regulation of the European Parliament and of the Council to ensure the cross-border portability of online content services in the internal market', 8.

[82] Commission, 'Proposal for a Regulation on ensuring the cross-border portability of online content services', Explanatory Memorandum, 8.

legislative intervention.[83] Some therefore comment that at least free-to-view services, 'which are not subject to residency verification would ostensibly not be covered'.[84] In the Regulation, the legislator has filled this and in Recital 15 defined the contract terminology.

As regards free services, the draft report by the European Parliament's Committee on Legal Affairs suggested the introduction of a new Article 3a on the cross-border portability of online content services free of charge, in which it would be up to the discretion of the online content service provider to enable portability;[85] thus effectively excluding service providers from the scope of the Regulation but holding doors open for an opt-in, provided that 'they take all necessary measures to permit verification of the Member State of residence of their users'.[86] As regards public broadcasting services, in its draft report the Committee only imprecisely added to Recital 16 that '[t]he payment of a mandatory fee for public broadcasting services must not lead to the assimilation of the latter to fee-charging online content services'.[87] Some commented therefore that public service broadcasters fell outside the scope of the

---

[83] See Commission, 'Impact Assessment accompanying the document Proposal for a Regulation of the European Parliament and of the Council to ensure the cross-border portability of online content services in the internal market', 8. It continues: 'If the service is provided free of charge, the provider would only be obliged to enable the cross-border portability if the provider can verify the subscriber's MS of residence on the basis of information or other means readily available to the provider. If a service provider offers free of charge services without such verification, they would not be obliged to ensure portability' (ibid., 37).

[84] Farrand, 'The EU Portability Regulation: one small step for cross-border access, one giant leap for Commission copyright policy?', 322.

[85] European Parliament, 'Draft Report on the proposal for a regulation of the European Parliament and of the Council on ensuring the cross-border portability of online content services in the internal market' Amendment, 34, 28. The suggested amendment reads: 'A provider of online content services provided free of charge may opt to permit his users who are temporarily present in a Member State other than their Member State of residence to access and use the online content service on condition that he complies with the technical requirements relating to verification of the Member State of residence of users under Article 3b.'

[86] Ibid., Explanatory Statement, 35.

[87] Ibid., Amendment, 12, 14. Interestingly, the UK public broadcaster the British Broadcasting Corporation (BBC), in its Terms of Use for 'BBC Online Services – Personal Use', specifies in section 3.2.1: 'You may not access, view and/or listen to certain parts of BBC Content (such as video or live television services) using BBC Online Services if you are outside the UK, although you may, in accordance with the Terms, access and view bbc.co.uk or other websites and listen to some (but not all) BBC radio content. The types of BBC Content that may be available outside the UK will usually depend on the BBC's agreements with the persons who own rights in such content.' Notably, section 3.2.2 specifies that you may not 'watch television programmes using BBC Online Services (. . .) unless you have a valid television licence'. No information is available as to whether and how the BBC enforces these restrictions. These were by far the strictest terms in a comparison across the German (ARD), Swedish (SVT), Norwegian (NRK) and Italian (RAI) broadcasters' online offering; these regularly geo-

Proposal.[88] In this vein, in its draft opinion the Committee on the Internal Market and Consumer Protection, for example, suggested adding to Recital 16 that '[t]he payment of a mandatory fee such as a broadcasting license fee should not be regarded as a payment of money to receive an online content service'.[89] The Committee on Culture and Education went even further and suggested in its opinion that Recital 13 should be specified in a way that also 'a simple log-in system such as one designed primarily for programme recommendation or personalised advertising services, a payment of a universal mandatory fee such as a broadcasting licence fee or the exchange or transfer of data' should not be regarded as a contract for the purpose of the Portability Regulation.[90] Thus, the Commission's proposal was imprecise and likely to embrace only commercial service providers. As we have seen above, the legislator has clarified these aspects in the final Regulation (EU) 2017/1128.

More broadly, the question was raised as to whether a European online content service provider would successfully be able to counter a foreign contractual partner's requirement that it accept portability without higher licensing fees, because the Portability Regulation creates a legal fiction and renders conflicting contractual provisions unenforceable.[91] Some have also pointed out that, in relation to the proposed legal fiction, the three-step test should be applied, to which neither the Commission's proposal nor the final Regulation makes reference.[92]

Surprisingly, the Commission's draft also left open the question whether service providers would be able to monetise portability by charging additional fees.[93] In its draft opinion, the Committee on the Internal Market and Consumer Protection underlines in several passages that portability of content services should be provided without additional

---

block content but in most instances provide a notice of whether the content is available or not.

[88] Shapiro, 'The proposed regulation on Portability – don't leave home without it', 354.

[89] European Parliament, 'Draft Opinion of the Committee on the Internal Market and Consumer Protection for the Committee on Legal Affairs on the proposal for a regulation of the European Parliament and of the Council on ensuring the cross-border portability of online content services in the internal market (COM(2015)0627 – C8-0392/2015 – 2015/0284(COD))'; Committee on the Internal Market and Consumer Protection, Rapporteur: Marco Zullo, PE583.879v01-00, 29 June 2016 Amendment 79, 35.

[90] See European Parliament, 'Opinion of the Committee on Culture and Education for the Committee on Legal Affairs on the proposal for a regulation of the European Parliament and of the Council on ensuring the cross-border portability of online content services in the internal market (COM(2015)0627 – C8-0392/2015 – 2015/0284(COD))'; Committee on Culture and Education, Rapporteur: Sabine Verheyen, 2015/0284 (COD) of 29 June 2016, Amendment 10, 9.

[91] Bundesrat at number 16.

[92] Shapiro, 'The proposed regulation on Portability – don't leave home without it', 355.

[93] Ibid., 358.

cost or administrative burden.[94] However, neither the opinion of the Committee on Culture and Education nor the draft report of the Committee on Legal Affairs mentions this aspect, which, again, the legislator has clarified.

As regards the application deadline of the Portability Regulation, it has been noted, mostly from the industry side, that the six–month period in Article 8 of the draft Regulation would be too short retroactively to adjust existing contracts.[95] The argument is somewhat unconvincing because the legal effect of the respective provision would simply override the relevant contractual clauses in existing contracts. In its draft opinion, the Committee on Legal Affairs has extended the period from six to twelve months.[96]

Finally, given its scope, the Regulation also has some intersections with the CRM Directive,[97] although they are limited. The Commission's Proposal does not refer to Directive 2014/26/EU but the EP's Committee on Culture and Education suggested in its opinion, for example, that Article 5 of the draft Regulation be supplemented by a new paragraph 2a that makes reference to Title III of the Directive.[98] The suggested amendment reads:

The holders of copyright and related rights or those holding any other rights in the context of an online content service may authorise service providers holding multi-territorial licenses in accordance with Title III of Directive 2014/26/EU of the European Parliament and of the Council to access and use their content under this Regulation *without verification of the Member State of residence.*[99]

---

[94] European Parliament, 'Draft Opinion of the Committee on the Internal Market and Consumer Protection for the Committee on Legal Affairs on the proposal for a regulation of the European Parliament and of the Council on ensuring the cross-border portability of online content services in the internal market (COM(2015)0627 – C8-0392/2015 – 2015/0284(COD))'.

[95] This appears to be mainly a commercial concern. See, however, Art. 7, in combination with Art. 5(1) of the Proposal as regards legal aspects.

[96] European Parliament, 'Draft Report on the proposal for a regulation of the European Parliament and of the Council on ensuring the cross-border portability of online content services in the internal market', Amendment 41, 33, based on the argument that the introduction of verification measures is likely to take more than six months. The short application deadline of six months was endorsed by, e.g., Bundesrat.

[97] Directive 2014/26/EU of the European Parliament and of the Council of 26 February 2014 on collective management of copyright and related rights and multi-territorial licensing of rights in musical works for online use in the internal market [2014] OJ L84/72–98 (CRM Directive).

[98] European Parliament, 'Opinion of the Committee on Culture and Education for the Committee on Legal Affairs on the proposal for a regulation of the European Parliament and of the Council on ensuring the cross-border portability of online content services in the internal market (COM(2015)0627 – C8-0392/2015 – 2015/0284(COD))'.

[99] See ibid., Amendment 38, 28.

The suggestion was rejected, and Recital 34 now stipulates that:

This Regulation should not affect the application of Directive 2014/26/EU of the European Parliament and of the Council (11) and in particular Title III thereof. This Regulation is consistent with the objective of facilitating the lawful access to content, which is protected by copyright or related rights, as well as services linked thereto.

Overall, the Portability Regulation is based on fairly simple and sleek legal mechanisms, which centre on a legal fiction, similar to the 'country of origin' principle in the SatCab Directive.[100] The Commission put its proposal for the Regulation from 2016 into the context of the Court of Justice of the European Union's (CJEU's) case law in *Premier League and Murphy*, in which the Court held 'that certain restrictions to the provision of services cannot be justified in light of the objective of protecting intellectual property rights' in Recital 11 of the draft preamble. This reference to the case has been removed in the Regulation's Recital 11 and replaced with a more flowery phrase, which is that:

case law of the Court of Justice of the European Union should be taken into account when balancing the objective of protecting intellectual property rights with the fundamental freedoms guaranteed by the Treaty on the Functioning of the European Union (TFEU).

It is important to recall that the Portability Regulation is rather limited in scope. It relates to the movement of the consumer but leaves untouched the second scenario, somewhat akin to a movement of the online service or content. The tangible results will therefore be restricted to the relatively small proportion of EU citizens who travel for leisure or work within the European Economic Area (EEA). Thus, it represents only one brick in the fulfilment of the Digital Single Market for copyright-protected content. As it stands, the Commission has expected that the intervention would have its biggest impact on the licensing practice of audiovisual and premium sports content sectors.[101] It has been argued that the Regulation would

provide the Commission with a quick win, either because it has realised the damaging effect of full-scale cross-border access to the European content

---

[100] Colomo refers to it as 'limited expansion of the "country of origin" principle': see P. I. Colomo, 'Copyright Licensing and the EU Digital Single Market Strategy', (2015) LSE Law, Society and Economy Working Papers 19/2015 12: http://ssrn.com/abstract=2697178

[101] Commission, 'Impact Assessment accompanying the document Proposal for a Regulation of the European Parliament and of the Council to ensure the cross-border portability of online content services in the internal market', 37.

industry, or in order to bolster its position when it tries to go further in future. It is a less controversial alternative than a blanket ban on geo-blocking.[102]

Farrand, on the other hand, comments that, the Regulation on a discursive level suggests that the small step of content portability is part of a giant leap for copyright reform regarding cross-border access'.[103] He notes that '[t]he Commission itself refers to the Portability Regulation as only constituting a "very short term" action'.[104]

5.3   Geo-Blocking Regulation (EU) 2018/302 and Its Copyright Interface

Roughly half a year after its proposal of the Cross-border Portability Regulation, on 25 May 2016 the European Commission put forward a second proposal that addressed the cross-border provision of or access to inter alia online content services as part of its e-commerce package:[105] the Proposal for a Regulation on addressing geo-blocking and other forms of discrimination based on customers' nationality, place of residence or place of establishment within the internal market and amending Regulation (EC) No 2006/2004 and Directive 2009/22/EC.[106] The broad general objective of the proposal was articulated as being

to give customers better access to goods and services in the Single Market by preventing direct and indirect discrimination by traders artificially segmenting the market based on customers' residence.[107]

This Proposal is again to be seen against the background of the Digital Single Market Agenda, in which the prohibition of 'unjust' geo-blocking

---

[102] Shapiro, 'The proposed regulation on Portability – don't leave home without it'. 359.

[103] Farrand, 'The EU Portability Regulation: one small step for cross-border access, one giant leap for Commission copyright policy?', 325.

[104] Ibid.

[105] On the same day, there were also introduced a legislative proposal on cross-border parcel delivery services to increase the transparency of prices and improve regulatory oversight and a legislative proposal to strengthen enforcement of consumers' rights and guidance to clarify, among others, what qualifies as an unfair commercial practice in the digital world, which complement the two legislative proposals from December 2015. In addition, see Proposal for a revised Directive on audiovisual media services. See also Commission, 'Commission proposes new e-commerce rules to help consumers and companies reap full benefit of Single Market' (Press release) IP/16/1887, Brussels, 25 May 2016.

[106] Commission, 'Proposal for a Regulation on addressing geo-blocking and other forms of discrimination based on customers' nationality, place of residence or place of establishment within the internal market and amending Regulation (EC) No 2006/2004 and Directive 2009/22/EC'.

[107] See ibid., Explanatory Memorandum, 2.

constitutes a key feature.[108] In 2014, the European Parliament also urged the European Commission to tackle the issues of geo-blocking. It recalls:

> that consumers are too often denied access to certain content services on geographical grounds, which runs counter to the objective of Directive 2001/29/EC of implementing the four freedoms of the internal market; urges the Commission, therefore, to propose adequate solutions for *better cross-border accessibility of services and copyright content* for consumers;[109]

The European Parliament also points out a connection to the CRM Directive, noting:

> that lessons may be drawn for other types of content from the approach taken in Directive 2014/26/EU on collective rights management, but that issues concerning portability and geoblocking may not be solved by one all-encompassing solution but may require several different interventions, both regulatory and market-led;[110]

A little under two years after the Commission's proposal, on 27 February 2018, the Council of the European Union, under its Bulgarian presidency, adopted the Geo-blocking Regulation, after it had been approved by the European Parliament earlier in February.[111]

Regulation (EU) 2018/302 applies from 3 December 2018, according to Article 11(1). Overall, it is too early to assess its impact, but some essential features and aspects of the Geo-blocking Regulation in relation to copyright-protected works can be pointed out.

5.3.1   Scope of the Geo-Blocking Regulation

The Draft Regulation comprised thirty-five recitals and eleven articles, compared with forty-three recitals and eleven articles in the final Regulation (EU) 2018/302. Systematically, the Geo-blocking Regulation was in the Commission's proposal suggested as applying to

---

[108] Under the first pillar of the DSM Strategy, which aims to tackle the existing barriers for the DSM and aims to ensure better access for consumers and businesses to online goods and services across Europe, the Commission has committed itself to 'make legislative proposals in the first half of 2016 to end unjustified geo- blocking'. The DSM Strategy proposes sixteen measures ranging from areas such as consumer contract rules and parcel delivery to audiovisual media services and telecoms rules. It seems that the notion of unjustified geo-blocking somehow mirrors or resembles the idea of lawful access.

[109] Emphasis added. Recital 4 of European Parliament, 'Report on the implementation of Directive 2001/29/EC of the European Parliament and of the Council of 22 May 2001 on the harmonisation of certain aspects of copyright and related rights in the information society (2014/2256(INI))'.

[110] Ibid., Recital 5.

[111] Council of the European Union, 'Geo-blocking: Council adopts regulation to remove barriers to e-commerce' (Press release) 95/18, 27 February 2018.

three situations, according to Article 1(2)(a)–(c) of the Proposal: first, where trader and customer are in different Member States; secondly, where trader and customer are in the same Member State, but the customer is a national of another Member State; and, thirdly, where the customer is only temporarily located in the Member State of the trader. In other words, the Commission proposal covers situations that roughly correlate to the free movement of services. In the final Regulation this distinction was dropped to the advantage of a somewhat broader definition of the purpose of Regulation (EU) 2018/302 in Article 1(1):

The purpose of this Regulation is to contribute to the proper functioning of the internal market by *preventing unjustified geo-blocking* and other forms of discrimination based, directly or indirectly, on the *customers' nationality, place of residence or place of establishment,* including by further clarifying certain situations where different treatment cannot be justified under Article 20(2) of Directive 2006/123/EC.[112]

Already the notion 'trader' conveys the focus on trade-situations and not IP-related aspects. Such a trader is defined in Article 2(18) of Regulation (EU) 2018/302 as

any natural person or any legal person, irrespective of whether privately or publicly owned, who is acting, including through any other person acting in the name or on behalf of the trader, for purposes relating to the trade, business, craft or profession of the trader.

Before the publication of the Commission's Proposal for the Geo-blocking Regulation in 2016, it had been anticipated that the legislative instrument would also apply to audiovisual services.[113] Yet, according to Article 1(3) of the Proposal in conjunction with Article 2(2) of Directive 2006/123/EC, it was proposed to exclude audiovisual services from the scope of the Regulation. The Commission reflects that

[r]egarding audiovisual services, for which the issue of territoriality of copyright is particularly relevant, a specific framework exists in the form of the Audiovisual

---

[112] Emphasis added. Purely internal situations are, besides others, excluded from the Regulation's scope according to Art. 1(2) Regulation (EU) 2018/302.

[113] The proposal was expected with great anticipation and, in May 2016, some leaks pointed towards the possible exclusion of audiovisual services from the scope of the Proposal. See, e.g., J. Plucinska, 'Leak: the Commission's latest geo-blocking plans' (*POLITICO*, 9 May 2016): www.politico.eu/pro/geoblocking-ecommerce-european-c ommission-leak-eu/. See Mazziotti, 'Is geo-blocking a real cause for concern?', 365, noting also that the exclusion is odd, given the results of the Commission's copyright consultation from 2013 to 2014. See also A. Savin, 'The Commission's New Proposals on the Digital Single Market, May 2016' (*EU Internet Law & Policy Blog*, 25 March 2016): https://euinternetpolicy.wordpress.com/2016/05/25/the-commissions-new-pro posals-on-the-digital-single-market-may-2016/

Media Services Directive and the Satellite and Cable Directive, both of which are currently under review.[114]

This restriction has not been changed. According to Article 1(3) of the final Regulation, audiovisual services are excluded in addition to other activities mentioned in Article 2(2) of the Services Directive. The provision of access to broadcasts of sports events that are provided on the basis of exclusive territorial licences is also explicitly excluded in Recital 8. Additionally, according to Article 1(5) of Regulation (EU) 2018/302, it 'shall not affect the rules applicable in the field of copyright and neighbouring rights, notably the rules provided for in Directive 2001/29/EC of the European Parliament and of the Council'.

It appears that the Commission envisioned in its proposal that the Regulation would, however, nonetheless apply to online music services. Recital 6 specifies:

As a consequence, the provisions of this Regulation should apply inter alia to non-audio-visual electronically supplied services, the main feature of which is the provision of access to and use of copyright protected works or other protected subject matter, subject however to the specific exclusion provided for in Article 4 and the subsequent evaluation of that exclusion as provided for in Article 9.

Recital 8 of Regulation (EU) 2018/302 builds upon the Commission's proposal and clarifies that consistency between the Geo-blocking Regulation and the Services Directive should be ensured:

Accordingly, this Regulation should apply, inter alia, to non-audiovisual electronically supplied services the main feature of which is the provision of access to and use of copyright protected works or other protected subject matter, subject, however, to the specific exclusion and the subsequent evaluation of that exclusion for which this Regulation provides.

5.3.2   Access to Interfaces versus Access to Goods or Services

Instead of providing a thorough analysis of the Geo-blocking Regulation, I focus on the two main mechanismsthat have been put in place on cross-border access: on access to online interfaces in Article 3 of Regulation (EU) 2018/302 and on access to goods and services according to Article 4 Regulation (EU) 2018/302.

---

[114] Commission, 'Impact Assessment accompanying the document proposal for a Regulation of the European Parliament and of the Council on adressing [sic] geo-blocking and other forms of discriminiation [sic] based on place of residence or establishment or nationality within the Single Market' (Commission Staff Working Document) SWD(2016) 173 final, Brussels, 25 May 2016, 5.

Article 3 governs access to online interfaces and has remained largely unaltered from the Commission's proposal. Such an online interface is defined in Article 2(16) of the Geo-blocking Regulation as

any software, including a website or a part thereof and applications, including mobile applications, operated by or on behalf of a trader, which serves to give customers access to the trader's goods or services with a view to engaging in a transaction with respect to those goods or services.[115]

First, Article 3(1) of Regulation (EU) 2018/302 regulates that a trader

shall not, through the use of technological measures or otherwise, block or limit a customer's access to the trader's online interface for reasons related to the customer's nationality, place of residence or place of establishment.

In Article 3(2), this obligation is extended to the redirection 'to a version of the trader's online interface that is different from the online interface to which the customer initially sought access (...) unless the customer has explicitly consented to such redirection'. However, according to Article 3(3), these prohibitions do not apply where it is 'necessary in order to ensure compliance with a legal requirement' in EU law or the national legislation.[116] Both the Commission's proposal and the final Regulation refrain from further specifying what would constitute such a legal requirement.[117]

Secondly, the key requirement to enable cross-border access is introduced in Article 4 on access to goods and services. Article 4(1) foresees three scenarios in which traders 'shall not apply different general conditions of access to goods or services, for reasons related to a customer's nationality, place of residence or place of establishment'.

The first scenario in Article 4(1)(a) relates to the sale of goods. The second scenario, Article 4(1)(b), which is most relevant in the context of this book, relates to situations in which a customer seeks to

receive electronically supplied services from the trader, other than services the main feature of which is the *provision of access to and use of copyright protected works* or other protected subject matter, including the selling of copyright protected works or protected subject matter in an intangible form.[118]

---

[115] Art. 2(f) of the Commission's proposal respectively.

[116] See Art. 3(3) and Recital 16 of Commission, 'Proposal for a Regulation on addressing geo-blocking and other forms of discrimination based on customers' nationality, place of residence or place of establishment within the internal market and amending Regulation (EC) No 2006/2004 and Directive 2009/22/EC'.

[117] Recital 16 of Commission's proposal brings as example: 'Such laws can limit customers' access to certain goods or services, for instance by prohibiting the display of specific content in certain Member States'.

[118] Emphasis added.

Finally, the third scenario, in Article 4(1)(c), relates to services other than electronically supplied services in a physical location. From Article 4(1)(b) of Regulation (EU) 2018/302 it follows that services of which the main feature 'is the provision of access to and use of copyright protected works or other protected subject matter' are excluded from the prohibition of applying different general access conditions. In other words, online platforms offering access to, e.g., e-books, music or other (non-audiovisual) copyright protected works are not prohibited from applying different general conditions. Additionally, Article 4(2) of Regulation (EU) 2018/302 stipulates that traders are still allowed to offer 'general conditions of access, including net sale prices, which differ between Member States or within a Member State and which are offered to customers on a specific territory or to specific groups of customers on a non-discriminatory basis'.

Notably, the exclusion regarding access to copyright-protected works is set to be reviewed after two years, according to Article 9(2) of the Geo-blocking Regulation, with a view to whether it should be extended to services that have copyright as their main feature, provided that the trader has the requisite right for the relevant territories.[119] As this reference is specifically made to Article 4(1)(b), the inclusion of audiovisual content under the scope seems to be not envisioned.[120] In the Impact Assessment accompanying the Commission's proposal from 2016,[121] it is further reflected that '[i]n any case, companies would not be obliged to acquire additional licences, but would potentially be subject to the provisions only if they already have the licenses for the territories in question'.[122] The Commission further explains its hesitation to apply Article 4(1)(b) right away:

---

[119] In other words, an online service could be obliged to grant access to its service to customers from a certain Member State, but only to the extent that rights are cleared for the respective territory. This resembles the 'passive sales' rationale.

[120] See also, to this extent, Commission, 'Impact Assessment accompanying the document proposal for a Regulation of the European Parliament and of the Council on adressing [sic] geo-blocking and other forms of discriminiation [sic] based on place of residence or establishment or nationality within the Single Market', 40.

[121] The Impact Assessment appears to be rushed and roughly put together (spelling mistakes in document title, different layout styles, mark-ups remaining in the Document etc.).

[122] Commission, 'Impact Assessment accompanying the document proposal for a Regulation of the European Parliament and of the Council on adressing [sic] geo-blocking and other forms of discriminiation [sic] based on place of residence or establishment or nationality within the Single Market', 40.

For the sale of electronically delivered non-audiovisual content services subject to copyright protection, such as music, e-books, software and games, if the trader has the required rights for the relevant territories, the considerations above would apply. However, given ongoing developments in the market, e.g. with respect to multi-territorial licensing, for these services the potential extension of the non-discrimination obligation requires further assessment.[123]

The European Commission specifically points to geo-blocking issues of non-audiovisual content, including e-books, music, software and games, and, while it is well aware of different treatment depending on physical or digital format, points to 'complex legal issues':[124]

For music, for example, providers will typically have obtained multi-territorial licenses which allow them to serve the European market. Nonetheless, for some of the music in their catalogues, they may only have national licenses, in which case they would not be able to give full access to their repertoire to consumers from other Member States.[125]

Article 6 of the Geo-blocking Regulation contains an important reference to 'passive sales'. The Commission proposed declaring automatically void '[a]greements imposing on traders obligations, in respect of passive sales, to act in violation of this Regulation'.[126] This legal consequence is now enshrined in Article 6(2) of Regulation (EU) 2018/302. During the law-making process, Article 6(1) was introduced, which further clarifies that the Geo-blocking Regulation

shall not affect agreements restricting *active sales* within the meaning of Regulation (EU) No 330/2010 or agreements restricting *passive sales* within the meaning of Regulation (EU) No 330/2010 that concern transactions *falling outside the scope* of the prohibitions laid down in Articles 3, 4 and 5 of this Regulation.[127]

In Recital 34, the lawmaker recalls that 'agreements imposing obligations on traders not to engage in passive sales in respect of certain customers or groups of customers in certain territories are generally considered to restrict competition' but that there is a risk that 'they could be used to circumvent the provisions of this Regulation'. As becomes clear from the Explanatory Memorandum accompanying the

---

[123] Ibid., 38.   [124] Ibid., 5.
[125] Ibid. Later on, the Impact Assessment reflects that 'these differences in access mainly seem not to be driven by objective legal reasons related to the EU copyright regime' (ibid., 10).
[126] See Art. 6 of Commission, 'Proposal for a Regulation on addressing geo-blocking and other forms of discrimination based on customers' nationality, place of residence or place of establishment within the internal market and amending Regulation (EC) No 2006/2004 and Directive 2009/22/EC'.
[127] Emphasis added.

Commission's proposal, as well as Recital 34, however, Article 6 is designed primarily to prevent the circumvention of the Geo-blocking Regulation.[128] In this respect it has been clarified that Article 6 of Regulation (EU) 2018/302 applies to both access to online interfaces and access to goods or services.

Currently, as seen above, only parts of the Geo-blocking Regulation apply to such online content services that provide copyright-protected material. Thus, the breadth of Article 6 is likely to depend on whether contractual restrictions on passive sales would distort the specific goal of the applicable rules. As noted above, however, the main provision, Article 4 on access to goods or services, does not apply to services that have as their main feature 'the provision of access to and use of copyright protected works or other protected subject matter'. Whereas it seems possible that contractual restrictions of passive sales could result in customers being frustrated in accessing an online interface, it seems to be of little use given the exclusion from the access right in Article 4 of the Geo-blocking Regulation. In the preparatory works, there is no indication of whether Article 6 would apply in the context of copyright-protected works. It is, however, noteworthy that the Impact Assessment in reference to passive sales just relies on its general competition law interface and the Vertical Block Exemption Regulation.[129] In contrast with the Commission's Proposal for the Portability Regulation, no reference to the CJEU's findings in *Premier League and Murphy* was made.

The review by 23 March 2020 of whether to include

electronically supplied services the main feature of which is the provision of access to and use of copyright protected works or other protected subject matter, including the selling of copyright protected works or protected subject matter in an intangible form, provided that the trader has the requisite rights for the relevant territories

in Article 9(2) of Regulation (EU) 2018/302 in this context is essential for the potential extension of scope. It seems to be thought that Member States are by no means aligned on this issue. Whereas Luxembourg seems supportive of the review by the Commission potentially to extent the scope of the Geo-blocking Regulation, both Germany and France, in their respective statements accompanying the Council's adoption,

---

[128] See also Commission, 'Impact Assessment accompanying the document proposal for a Regulation of the European Parliament and of the Council on adressing [*sic*] geo-blocking and other forms of discriminiation [*sic*] based on place of residence or establishment or nationality within the Single Market', 5.
[129] Regulation 330/2010.

underline the importance of a detailed impact study of a potential extension to audiovisual content.[130]

Thus, for now, it seems, the Regulation will change little regarding access to copyright-protected works, despite its initial focus on content-related restrictions. It seems that, according to Article 3 of Regulation (EU) 2018/302, mere access to the website (i.e. 'online interface') could become relevant. In other words, consumers would be able to access the website but not the content. In relation to Article 3, on access to the online interface, Recital 18 clarifies that 'the prohibition of discrimination with respect to access to online interfaces should not be understood as creating an obligation for the trader to engage in transactions with customers'.

The Commission's proposal has been criticised for its lack of ambition, besides other factors, because it does not address the main concerns 'identified by Commission in its impact assessment and its initial findings on geo-blocking – for example consumer goods (in particular clothing and electronics), airplane tickets, and copyright works (in particular digital content) – are carved out of the Proposed Regulation'.[131] This criticism is, for example, shared by Luxembourg, which, in its statement in connection with the adoption of the Geo-blocking Regulation in the Council, comments that 'Luxembourg remains sceptical as to the added value of the Regulation, which does not provide for legal certainty and which confirms, rather than removes, existing barriers'.[132]

Regulation (EU) 2018/302 will not help to overcome cross-border access to online music services in the short term, or solve the problem of customers receiving the message 'This video is not available in your country' in the long run. The Regulation is likely to have its biggest impact on online service providers that provide content other than audio-visual, or, more broadly, copyright-protected works such as online

---

[130] Council of the European Union, 'Draft Regulation of the European Parliament and of the Council on addressing unjustified geo-blocking and other forms of discrimination based on customers' nationality, place of residence or place of establishment within the internal market and amending Regulations (EC) No 2006/2004 and (EU) 2017/2394 and Directive 2009/22/EC, Statements' ('I/A' Item Note 2018, 6054/18), 2016/0152 (COD), Brussels, 19 February 2018, Statements by Germany and by France, 3–4.

[131] A. Morrison, 'European Commission's draft Geo-Blocking Regulation fails to clear the way' (*King & Wood Mallesons*, 21 June 2016): www.kwm.com/en/uk/knowledge/insigh ts/european-commissions-draft-geo-blocking-regulation-fails-to-clear-the-way-20160621

[132] Council of the European Union, 'Draft Regulation of the European Parliament and of the Council on addressing unjustified geo-blocking and other forms of discrimination based on customers' nationality, place of residence or place of establishment within the internal market and amending Regulations (EC) No 2006/2004 and (EU) 2017/2394 and Directive 2009/22/EC, Statements', Statement by Luxembourg, 2.

shopping. Thus, the geo-blocking of copyright-protected works is likely to continue to be on the legislative agenda. In November 2017, for example, the Nordic Council, a cooperation forum between Denmark, Finland, Iceland, Norway and Sweden, announced a study on how geo-blocking between Nordic countries could be abolished.[133]

5.4   Looking over the Fence: Cross-Border TV and Radio Broadcasts

5.4.1   Consultation on SatCab Directive in 2015

As laid out in its Digital Single Market Strategy, the Commission aimed to

review the Satellite and Cable Directive to assess the need to enlarge its scope to broadcasters' online transmissions and the need to tackle further measures to ensure enhanced cross-border access to broadcasters' services in Europe.[134]

In the context of the consultation on the SatCab Directive, it has been noted that it represents the only concrete measure mentioned in the European Commission's Digital Single Market Strategy of 2015.

In August 2015, the EU Commission opened a public consultation on the SatCab Directive, to review the rules that have served for little more than twenty years.[135] The SatCab Directive was adopted in 1993 with the goal of easing cross-border activity of satellite broadcasting and cable retransmission in the EU. The consultation is also significant regarding the licensing of audiovisual content beyond broadcasters. One of the central aspects of the consultation was that contained in section III on the assessment of the need for the extension of the Directive. Most prominently, the question was raised whether the 'country of origin' principle should be extended to certain Internet scenarios, namely:

- TV and radio transmissions by other means than satellite (e.g. by IPTV, webcasting)
- Online services ancillary to initial broadcasts (e.g. simulcasting, catch-up TV)

---

[133] Norden, 'Nordic Council: Digital television must be available to view throughout the Nordic Region' (*Nordic Council*, 2 November 2017): www.norden.org/en/news-and-ev ents/news/nordic-council-digital-television-must-be-available-to-view-throughout-the-nordic-region

[134] See Commission, 'A Digital Single Market Strategy for Europe'.

[135] See https://ec.europa.eu/digital-single-market/en/news/consultation-review-eu-satel lite-and-cable-directive and also S. F. Schwemer, 'Geoblocking: im Visier der EU Kommission' (*HIIG Blog*, 13. November 2015): www.hiig.de/blog/geoblocking-im-vis ier-der-eu-kommission/

- Any online services provided by broadcasters (e.g. video on demand services)

- Any online content services provided by any service provider, including broadcasters.

The differentiation goes roughly along the line of whether it should be extended only to linear or also non-linear (on demand) online services, in which content is available for the consumer on demand, e.g. via the online library of the respective service.[136] A second aspect is whether the extension should be only for broadcasters or for any service provider. In this context, the Commission was also interested in the question how the country of origin would be determined in cases of online transmission. The 2015 consultation was preceded by a consultation in 2002.[137] Already by then, the European Commission had, to an extent, laid out certain principles of the SatCab Directive, partly based on the principle of technological neutrality *mutatis mutandis* on linear cross-border situations (i.e. webcasting, but not on-demand services). Back then, it was concluded that was not 'appropriate, at this stage, to extend the mandatory collective-management regime to other categories of retransmissions'.[138]

In relation to its Cross-border Portability Proposal (Regulation (EU) 2017/1128), the Commission notes that the review of the SatCab Directive has a different scope as regards the relevant services: 'Moreover, limited or no access of consumers in a MS to online content services provided in other MS is a situation that is very different from cross-border portability'.[139]

It, is, however, not so different from cross-border access in the form of active or passive sales. It could be argued that the introduction of such a system thematically could fit better under the InfoSoc Directive, in which the delineation of the 'making available' right appears especially interesting.[140]

---

[136] The differentiation among the four scenarios has been criticised as imprecise. See, e.g., J. Enser, 'Another consultation from Brussels- anyone for SatCab?' (*IP Kat*, 27 August 2015): http://the1709blog.blogspot.dk/2015/08/another-consultation-from-brussels.html

[137] Commission, 'Report from the European Commission on the application of Council Directive 93/83/EEC on the coordination of certain rules concerning copyright and rights related to copyright applicable to satellite broadcasting and cable retransmission' COM(2002) 430 final, Brussels, 26 July 2002.

[138] Ibid., 15.

[139] Commission, 'Impact Assessment accompanying the document Proposal for a Regulation of the European Parliament and of the Council to ensure the cross-border portability of online content services in the internal market', 3.

[140] European Parliament, 'Report on the implementation of Directive 2001/29/EC of the European Parliament and of the Council of 22 May 2001 on the harmonisation of certain aspects of copyright and related rights in the information society (2014/2256 (INI))'; Schwemer, 'Geoblocking: im Visier der EU Kommission'.

On 4 May 2016, the Commission published the results of the public consultation. It had resulted in 257 responses, which was significantly fewer than in the previous copyright consultation. Unsurprisingly, the spectrum of answers varied greatly, however, although they had some common ground. End user representatives supported a broad extension of the 'country of origin' principle to cover all online services and partly argued that 'such an intervention would need to be accompanied by a rule explicitly prohibiting technical or contractual restrictions on "passive sales" across EU borders'.[141] Rights holders, on the other hand, vetoed any extension of the 'country of origin' principle, especially as regards online and VOD services, which, according to them, would lead to pan-European licences and restrict their ability to license on a territorial basis.[142] Their particular concerns regard, inter alia, negative consequences for the value chain of the production and its potential negative impact on creators' revenues, as well as the risk of forum shopping by service providers, in addition to the fact that voluntary multi-territorial licensing schemes are already in place.[143] These concerns were roughly shared by collective management organisations and commercial broadcasters.[144] Among commercial users, namely broadcasters, opinions were split along the line of public and commercial broadcasters. Whereas all broadcasters urge maintaining full contractual freedom, public broadcasters made a 'call for the application of the principle to EU broadcasters' transmissions by any technological means as well as to all broadcast-related online services'.[145] Prominently, the EBU welcomed 'a technologically-neutral application of licensing rules for online programme services' which 'would help facilitate the online and cross-border availability of broadcaster content in a way that matches consumer preferences, without undermining the contractual flexibility and territoriality options that are crucial to the development of public service media productions'.[146]

Other commercial users mostly endorsed 'a careful and measured approach'. Whereas Internet service providers comment 'that it would enable digital content providers to offer services EU-wide', other service providers argue that contractual freedom should be maintained and

---

[141] Commission, 'Synopsis Report on the Responses to the Public Consultation on the Review of the Satellite and Cable Directive', 3.
[142] Ibid.   [143] Ibid.   [144] Ibid., 4.   [145] Ibid.
[146] EBU, 'EBU Welcomes Steps to Update EU Cable and Satellite Directive for the Digital Age' (*EBU*, 26 August 2015): www.ebu.ch/news/2015/08/ebu-welcomes-steps-to-upd ate-eu

'claim that if the extension of the application of the principle were to lead to pan-European licensing, it would put European and local market players at a competitive disadvantage in relation to multinational operators as they would not have the means to acquire pan-European licences'.[147] Finally, Member States and public authorities were also reported as having called for caution, especially regarding contractual freedom, the high level of protection of IP and the exclusivity of rights.[148]

5.4.2 *Proposal for a Regulation on Online Transmissions of Broadcasting Organisations*

In proceedings regarding the Geo-blocking Regulation (EU) 2018/302, the European Commission specifically refers to the specific rights-clearance framework of the SatCab Directive and the ongoing review, and thereby explains why it is not extending the scope to audiovisual content.[149] On the background of the responses to the consultation, as well as the Commission's Communication of 2016, which refers to the facilitation of 'online distribution of TV and radio programmes across the EU',[150] however, it seemed unlikely that the Commission would extend that framework to issues outside TV and radio programmes.[151]

On 14 September 2016, the European Commission issued its Proposal for a Regulation laying down rules on the exercise of copyright and related rights applicable to certain online transmissions of broadcasting organisations and retransmissions of television and radio programmes, consisting of nineteen recitals and seven articles.[152] On 15 December 2017, the Council adopted a common stance for negotiation with the European Parliament. Interinstitutional negotiations were set to start in early 2018 but at the time

---

[147] Commission, 'Synopsis Report on the Responses to the Public Consultation on the Review of the Satellite and Cable Directive', 4.

[148] Ibid., 3.

[149] See Commission, 'Impact Assessment accompanying the document proposal for a Regulation of the European Parliament and of the Council on adressing [*sic*] geo-blocking and other forms of discriminiation [*sic*] based on place of residence or establishment or nationality within the Single Market', 5.

[150] See ibid., 3.

[151] This finds also support in Commission, 'Towards a modern, more European copyright framework', 6.

[152] Commission, 'Proposal for a Regulation of the European Parliament and of the Council laying down rules on the exercise of copyright and related rights applicable to certain online transmissions of broadcasting organisations and retransmissions of television and radio programmes'.

of writing no additional public information was available.[153] In contrast with the Commission's proposal, both the European Parliament and the Council have suggested amending the Regulation to a large extent.[154] The proposed Regulation is, given its scope on broadcasts and radio transmission, outside the scope of this book. Nonetheless, one of the central provisions is of interest. Article 2 of the proposed Regulation suggests extending the 'country of origin' principle to ancillary online services. Article 2(1) of the Proposal reads:

The acts of communication to the public and of making available occurring when providing an ancillary online service by or under the control and responsibility of a broadcasting organisation as well as the acts of reproduction which are necessary for the provision of, the access to or the use of the ancillary online service *shall*, for the purposes of exercising copyright and related rights relevant for these acts, *be deemed to occur solely in the Member State in which the broadcasting organisation has its principal establishment.*[155]

Such an ancillary online service is defined in Article 1 (a) of the Commission's Proposal as

an online service consisting in the provision to the public, by or under the control and responsibility of a broadcasting organisation, of radio or television programmes *simultaneously with or for a defined period of time after their broadcast* by the broadcasting organisation as well as of any material produced by or for the broadcasting organisation which is ancillary to such broadcast;[156]

Thus, the Regulation would effectively expand the 'country of origin' principle from linear services in the SatCab Directive to such online services of broadcasting organisations. According to Recital 2 of the proposed Regulation, such ancillary online service could consist, e.g., in the provision of simulcasting or catch-up services. Additionally, Recital 8 stipulates the subordinate character of these services vis-à-vis the broadcast. Thus, content that is offered exclusively online would not fall under the scope of the Regulation. It further envisions that this also includes services

which give access to material which enriches or otherwise expands television and radio programmes broadcast by the broadcasting organisation, including by way of previewing, extending, supplementing or reviewing the relevant programme's content.

---

[153] Council of the European Union, 'Online cross-border TV and radio broadcasts: Council agrees negotiating stance' (Press release) 808/17, 15 December 2017.
[154] See European Parliamentary Research Service, 'Regulating online TV and radio broadcasting' (Briefing, EU Legislation in Process), PE 620.217, April 2018.
[155] Emphasis added.   [156] Emphasis added.

In other words, the Proposal would lead to a situation in which broadcasting organisations need to clear the online rights for the respective ancillary online services (offered via their online portals) only in the country of origin (or, rather, country of principal establishment). The proposed Regulation, however, still foresees the rights holders' freedom 'to continue limiting the exploitation of the rights affected by the principle of country of origin laid down in this Regulation, especially as far as certain technical means of transmission or certain language versions are concerned'.[157]

The extension of the principle has attracted the criticism of various national parliaments.[158] In December 2017, the European Parliament's Committee on Legal Affairs suggested restricting the 'country of origin' principle to 'broadcasting of news and current affairs programmes'.[159] In a similar vein, in December 2017 in its general approach the Council also advocates limiting the 'country of origin' principle to programmes that are either 'related to news and current affairs' or 'fully financed and controlled by a broadcasting organisation', whereas broadcasts of sports are suggested to be generally excluded.[160] Also the choice of instrument, a Regulation instead of a Directive, has attracted criticism.

5.5   Summary

As regards on-demand streaming of music and audiovisual works, different regulatory actions based on secondary law have been taken to

---

[157] Recital 11 of the proposed Regulation.

[158] See, e.g., Folketinget, 'Political opinion on Commission proposal for reform of EU copyright rules (Erik Christensen, Orla Hav)', 11 May 2017; Bundesrat, 'Beschluss des Bundesrates, Vorschlag für eine Verordnung des Europäischen Parlaments und des Rates mit Vorschriften für die Wahrnehmung von Urheberrechten und verwandten Schutzrechten in Bezug auf bestimmte Online-Übertragungen von Rundfunkveranstaltern und die Weiterverbreitung von Fernseh- und Hörfunkprogrammen' (2016) Drucksache 566/16, 16 December 2016.

[159] European Parliament, 'Report on the proposal for a regulation of the European Parliament and of the Council laying down rules on the exercise of copyright and related rights applicable to certain online transmissions of broadcasting organisations and retransmissions of television and radio programmes (COM(2016)0594 – C8-0384/2016 – 2016/0284(COD))' Committee on Legal Affairs, Rapporteur: Tiemo Wölken, 27 November 2017, Amendment 31.

[160] Council of the European Union, 'Proposal for a Regulation of the European Parliament and of the Council laying down rules on the exercise of copyright and related rights applicable to certain online transmissions of broadcasting organisations and retransmissions of television and radio programmes – Final Presidency compromise proposal' (Note 2017, 15898/17), 2016/0284 (COD), Brussels, 19 December 2017, Art. 2(1a).

mitigate the impact of copyright territoriality (or, rather, copyright's territorial exploitation). In this chapter, I have mapped and examined the institutional legal framework based on non-binding and binding legal instruments or acts on the *ex ante* (legislative) initiative of the European Commission, which are aimed at the facilitation of cross-border access to audiovisual and musical works. The bulk of the discussion will follow in Chapter 6, but nonetheless some brief reflections are in place here.

The facilitation of cross-border access to copyright-protected works has only fairly recently (re-)joined the agenda of policymakers in the online context: both (temporary) portability and geo-blocking have recently featured prominently on the legislative agenda, however, with different scope:

'True' cross-border access to audiovisual and other copyright-protected works, i.e. situations in which citizens from one Member State (A) access the content of an online content service provider in another Member State (B), has been addressed by the European legislator only rudimentarily. The more ambitious maximum harmonisation approach in the recently adopted Geo-blocking Regulation (EU) 2018/302 is not aimed at audiovisual online services, and online music services are also hardly covered. Thus, some of the most pressing cross-border access issues remain effectively unaddressed for now. In this context, the European Commission has pointed towards the review of the SatCab and AVMS Directives. At least the latter, however, does little to mitigate territorial access restrictions. The former, based on the outcome from the stakeholder consultation, seems unlikely to expand beyond broadcasters.

The Portability Regulation (EU) 2017/1128, on the other hand, although more limited in scope insofar it addresses only transient cross-border access, addresses primarily online content services that provide access to audiovisual works. Essentially, the Portability Regulation relies on a legal fiction that creates something akin to the 'country of origin' principle of the SatCab Directive. But, as has been seen, it only solves one side of the cross-border access issue.

Thus, it appears that, for now, a patchwork of rules with carve-outs is going to address the issue of cross-border content accessibility. The European Commission as well as the European Parliament have made clear that a copyright-based solution is high on their agenda, but concrete steps have yet to materialise. The most recent copyright proposals, notably the Commission's proposals for a Directive on Copyright in the Digital Single Market[161] and for a Regulation on online transmissions of broadcasting organisations[162] only address in an ancillary manner licensing of or cross-border access to copyright protected works in the Digital Single Market.

---

[161] Commission, 'Proposal for a Directive of the European Parliament and of the Council on copyright in the Digital Single Market'.
[162] Commission, 'Proposal for a Regulation of the European Parliament and of the Council laying down rules on the exercise of copyright and related rights applicable to certain online transmissions of broadcasting organisations and retransmissions of television and radio programmes'.

6 The Regulatory System
Challenges and Solutions

In the foregoing chapters, we have seen the development of different arrangements for multi-territorial licensing and cross-border access (Chapter 2) and how they are addressed (or proposed to be addressed) by the regulatory framework – broadly understood as embracing *ex post* control under competition rules (Chapter 3) and *ex ante* sector-specific legislation (Chapters 4 and 5). In this chapter, let us focus on linking the different concepts and connecting the dots. Whereas there exists a broad variety of issues worth further scrutiny, here I prioritise the aspects most relevant for the objectives of this book as laid out in Chapter 1.

Chapter 6 is structured in the following way: First, I analyse the characteristics of the regulatory framework and its implications for multi-territorial licensing and cross-border access to content. In doing so, I further discuss some of the discovered links and some of the areas that remain open in the current regulatory framework. Then, I turn towards the EU's double approach between (copyright-related) sector regulation and competition law. I examine how the legal framework interacts with market developments and discuss how territoriality is reconciled – or suggested to be reconciled – with borderless access to audiovisual and music content. The chapter wraps up with concluding remarks.

6.1 Mapping the Regulatory Landscape

Based on the expository analysis of the different (institutional) arrangements and approaches in the foregoing chapters, the question is how to analyse these models in order to outline their characteristics, identify inconsistencies and interactions.

I have already laid out some of the apparent overlaps in Chapters 3–5. This section focuses on the macro-features in order to discover discrepancies in the regulatory framework. It is important to remind ourselves that we are looking at two different aspects of an interrelated issue: cross-

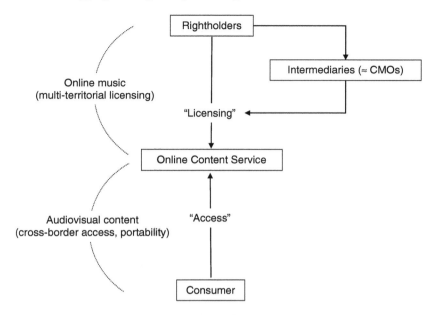

Figure 7: Simplified licensing and access scheme (adapted)

border access and multi-territorial licensing. There exist several scenarios that should be differentiated. These correlate to the conceptual model of Section 2.2: A first scenario relates to the supply side, where cross-border services (e.g. membership in a collective management organisation (CMO)) are provided by licensing entities to rights holders. This is the case when a licensor (a right holder directly or via an intermediary) located in Member State A represents rights from rights holders from another Member State B (irrespective of whether the appointment is for rights management in Member State A only or also comprises other territories). This scenario primarily relates to the aggregation of reper- toire. It is therefore of only minor importance for cross-border access and multi-territorial licensing and will be disregarded in the following discussion.

The two main scenarios regard the cross-border relationship between rights holders and licensees and that between licensees and consumers as follows. This is displayed in the adapted Figure 7 above, which takes into account that multi-territorial licensing is primarily relevant in online music, whereas the different shades of cross-border access are primarily relevant as regards audiovisual works.

Table 1: *Matrix of regulatory intervention*

Subject Matter	Cross-Border Access		Multi-Territorial Licensing		
	(licensor→ licensee→consumer)		Cross-border services to users (*licensor–licensee*)		Cross-border services to rights holders (*right holder–licensor*)
	Temporary (portability)	'True' Cross-Border access (geo-blocking)	To users from another MS	For use in another MS	Represent rights of rights holders from another MS
Music (Collective management)	*Cross-border Portability Regulation*	*(Geo-blocking Regulation)*	*(COMP) CRM Directive Recommendation*		*(COMP) CRM Directive Recommendation*
Audiovisual	*Case law ('Passive sales')*	~~*(Geo-blocking Regulation)*~~ *(COMP)*			–

1) *Cross-Border Services to Commercial Users (Licensees)*

The first scenario relates to the cross-border relationship between rights holders and licensees, namely in the provision of cross-border services to commercial users (licensees). It embraces two situations: first, a licensor located in Member State A provides licences of its own repertoire to commercial users from another Member State (Member State B). Connected to this situation is a second scenario, in which the same licensor licenses its repertoire to commercial users from any Member State (X) for several territories (i.e. multi-territorial licensing). In other words, multi-territorial licensing transforms the traditional per-territory licensing of rights to ultimately pan-European licensing, which leads to content being available in all Member States. This correlates to the right-hand column of the matrix in Table 1 above.

2) *Cross-Border Access to Content Services (Private Users/ Consumers)*

The second scenario relates to the cross-border access relationship between licensees (i.e. content services) and consumers. Again, this scenario embraces two separate situations: first, when a consumer from Member State A accesses content from a service provider in Member State A while (temporarily) present in another Member State (Member State B) (i.e. cross-border portability). In other words, portability of content covers situations in which consumers have access to content in their home country and enables (temporary) access to the content abroad. The second situation is when a consumer from Member State B accesses the content from a service provider located in Member State A in any other Member State ('true' cross-border access). These situations correlate to the left-hand column of the matrix above.

Let us now turn towards a regulatory overview. The respective rows, corresponding to the subject matter music and audiovisual content, will be discussed in the following two sections. Table 1 provides an abstract overview over the different measures:

Now a separate question is which parameters could prove useful in order better to compare the above-drafted characteristics of the different measures. There are several perspectives from which these two aspects can be compared. A first category of characteristics is looking at the policy goal of regulatory intervention (competition, Digital Single Market, harmonisation, integration or other considerations). A second category is looking at the main addressees of the intervention (rights holders, intermediaries, commercial users, consumers). A third category is looking at types of regulation (industry measures, soft law, legislative measures such as Directives or Regulations (*ex ante*), competition proceedings (*ex post*)). Yet another perspective, especially relevant in the context of competition law, is the horizontal or vertical dimension. Finally, let us recall that this book looks at two different copyright-protected subject matters: music and audiovisual content. Whereas there exists a certain regulatory overlap in some respects, others are dependent on the subject matter.

A variety of stakeholders are involved – namely rights holders, intermediaries (CMOs), licensees (online service providers) and consumers. For the sake of this section, let us focus on the consumer perspective. Thus, it seems reasonable to assume that the availability of content (both foreign and domestic) constitutes a key concern[1] in the form of a demand for as many rights or works as possible to the lowest possible price. Thus, for consumers there is likely to be a qualitative relationship between the different shades of access: EU-wide cross-border access, where consumers can access online content services from a different Member State, for example, expands the potential repertoire consumers can access. This is also facilitated for individual consumers in a similar vein in the form of 'passive sales'. Finally, portability is safeguarding access to content from a consumer's resident Member State A, when (temporarily) present in a different Member State B. As all scenarios regard slightly different situations, the qualitative relationship, i.e. which forms are most advantageous, is dependent on the specific situation.

Whereas consumers are likely to be interested in the 'last mile' only, access is also dependent on the underlying licensing arrangements (for example, efficiency aspects such as transaction costs or price and royalties).[2] Multi-territorial licensing theoretically (not addressing contractual aspects) gives the possibility of both enabling portability for customers in one Member State and setting up shop in the licensed areas in addition to increasing the offered repertoire.[3]

The Regulation of Multi-Territorial Licensing

Broadly speaking, territorial restrictions are an anomaly in the internal market. Related to the traditional rationale for collectivisation in the form

---

[1] See also, in this respect, the methodology framework by T. Kautio, N. Lefever and M. Määttä, *Assessing the Operation of Copyright and Related Rights Systems, Methodology Framework* (Foundation for Cultural Policy Research (Cupore), Cupore publication 26, 2016), p. 120.

[2] See Section 2.2.

[3] Additionally, competition and monopoly concerns are also likely to influence this picture. Yet another dimension is likely to be cultural aspects and cultural diversity.

of CMOs as intermediaries, competition aspects constitute a key concern, as seen in previous chapters. Competition can occur at two levels: in the downstream relationship (commercial users as licensees) and in the upstream relationship (exclusivity in membership relations, i.e. rights holders as members).[4]

Interestingly, it is the licensor–licensor relationship that has been in the focus of regulatory proceedings. In the discotheque cases from 1989, *Lucazeau* and *Tournier*, the Court found a territorial delineation by CMOs permissible.[5] In the absence of regulation, attributes of the licensing and access arrangements were, to a large extent, determined by industry practices.[6] For the last fifteen years, however, the European Commission made it clear that the territorial restrictions in horizontal arrangements for licensing must be reviewed. But vertical agreements, notably in the relationship between rights holders (members) and CMO, have also occupied the judiciary. The Commission's view, it appears, is primarily based on the erosion of the economic efficiency (transaction costs) argumentation in the digital landscape: on the Internet there might exist fewer objective justifications for territorial restrictions by intermediaries, if more efficient individual models become available.[7] It seems somewhat unclear to what extent the European courts share this view. In its *CISAC* judgment from 2013, the General Court held that the: '[a]rrival of new information technologies allowing the exploitation of works online does not mean that those structures are suddenly obsolete'.[8]

CMOs' answer to the digital, borderless exploitation on the Internet was envisioned in the creation of 'one-stop shops'. This system was based on their existing cross-border collaboration in the form of reciprocal representation agreements (RRAs) based on model contracts (which, however, served the purpose of repertoire aggregation within one territory), as becomes clear from the Santiago and Barcelona Agreements – and met with competition concerns due to customer allocation clauses. Earlier, the *Simulcasting* decision from 2002 showed one way that was

---

[4] G. Petteri, 'Harmonising Collective Rights Management and Multi-Territorial Licensing of Music for Online Use in the European Union: A Review of the Collective Rights Management Directive 2014/26/EU', *Nordiskt Immateriellt Rättskydd* [2015], 150, 162.

[5] See Section 3.2.

[6] In the case of reciprocal representation agreements, this might resemble a form of industry self-regulation, without going further into details here.

[7] See, e.g., J. Schovsbo, 'The Necessity to collectivize copyright – and dangers thereof' (2010), 18: http://ssrn.com/abstract=1632753; and discussion in Section 2.4.

[8] Case T-442/08, *CISAC* v. *Commission* [2013] ECLI:EU:T2013:188, para. 130, but see a more differentiated position in Case T-451/08, *STIM* v. *Commission* [2013] ECLI:EU: T:2013:189; and Section 3.1.3.

deemed permissible under EU competition law by the Directorate General for Competition (DG Competition).[9] From the Court of Justice's reasoning in the late 1980s in *Lucazeau* and *Tournier,* it appears that it encourages competition by commercial users: it held that the RRAs were not in themselves restrictive of competition, which, however, 'might be different if the contracts established exclusive rights whereby copyright-management societies undertook not to allow direct access to their repertoires by users of recorded music established abroad'.[10]

This focus has changed in the Commission's regulatory initiatives: Hviid et al. assess that '[t]he Commission shifted from viewing the CMO as necessary evil (. . .), to seeing it as unnecessary anti-competitive undertaking which harmed both right holders and users'.[11] In its Online Music Recommendation of 2005, DG MARKT envisioned enhanced competition between CMOs being driven by rights holders rather than by commercial users (licensees) – that is to say inter alia by competition over repertoire. This resonates also with previous or concurrent activity of DG Competition, as in the CISAC decision of 2008.[12] Recommendation 2005/737/EC, however, is somewhat special in that it seems to aim at the facilitation of multi-territorial licensing whereby increased competition served as a means to achieve this.[13] This again seems to constitute the premise behind the CRM Directive of 2014.[14] Multi-territorial licensing, it appears, is used in order to mitigate transaction costs as a way to increase the access to repertoire. The CRM Directive, for example, takes its starting point in the regulation of competition aspects between CMOs and creates a framework for multi-territorial licensing. Implicit in the Commission's regulatory actions (i.e. competition proceedings as well as Recommendation 2005/737/EC and Directive 2014/26/EU) appears to lie the assumption that CMOs are not natural monopolies – in that they provide for competition. Thus, *ex ante* sector regulation, as well as *ex post* control via competition law, in this respect appears fairly

---

[9] See Section 3.1.2.

[10] See Case 395/87, *Ministère Public* v. *Jean-Louis Tournier* [1989] ECR 2565–2581, ECLI: EU:C:1989:319, para. 20.

[11] M. Hviid, S. Schroff and J. Street, 'Regulating CMOs by competition: an incomplete answer to the licensing problem?', CREATe Working Paper 2016/03 (March 2016), 7.

[12] As Rognstad notes, however, the competition route 'does not necessarily do away with the one stop shop principle', see: O. A. Rognstad, 'The Multiplicity of Territorial IP Rights and its Impact on Competition' in J. Rosén (ed.), *Individualism and Collectiveness in Intellectual Property Law* (Edward Elgar, 2012), p. 64.

[13] See Petteri, 'Harmonising Collective Rights Management', 162; and Section 4.1.

[14] Directive 2014/26/EU of the European Parliament and of the Council of 26 February 2014 on collective management of copyright and related rights and multi-territorial licensing of rights in musical works for online use in the internal market [2014] OJ L84/72–98 (CRM Directive).

consistent, despite all criticism in the literature and from stakeholders as to their objectives.

Besides addressing some of the dangers associated with the collectivisation of copyright management, such as information asymmetries and greater transparency, in Title III the CRM Directive envisions a regime for multi-territorial licensing, notably (again) building on a voluntary aggregation. In this, Directive 2014/26/EU indicates supporting the creation of an oligopolistic structure, in which larger CMOs with sufficient leverage can comply with the requirements set out. This appears to be the solution to balancing the effect of repertoire fragmentation by multi-territorial licensing and the competition concerns associated with more comprehensive one-stop shop solutions. Some of the major rights holders have enshrined their rights on an exclusive basis to novel entities; thus, competition for repertoires could potentially be hampered by the concentration of rights in a few entities. Market developments indicate that, instead of or besides a re-aggregation of rights in a few licensing hubs, the horizontal aggregation of functions (i.e. front-, middle- and back-office) is one immediate advancement.[15]

Yet another observation relates to 'direct' licensing activities and other novel arrangements: the CRM Directive does not openly address new licensing entities (or, as discussed, is at least quite unclear). Thus, it seems likely that the courts will have to weigh in and determine the regulatory landscape for such entities. As noted, Directive 2014/26/EU opens up for direct licensing of rights currently enshrined in CMOs in respect of multi-territorial licensing under certain conditions in order to prevent a national repertoire lock-in, in addition to the general principles regarding direct licensing laid out in, e.g., the *Daft Punk* decision. But its effects on the market are yet to be manifested. At the same time, the latest regulatory intervention, in the form of Directive 2014/26/EU, supports the creation of new arrangements, which could take a monopolistic character such as rights databases and other horizontal operational arrangements.

As is seen throughout the book, the multi-territorial licensing of audiovisual content has been much less a concern of regulatory activities.

The Regulation of Cross-Border Access

More recently, the cross-border dimension of access to copyright-protected works has come into the crosshairs of regulatory activities.

---

[15] See, however, the discussion of merger proceedings and hub developments in Section 2.4.

Whereas competition concerns are also at the heart of the (vertical) access dimension, it has received scrutiny much later when compared with the horizontal licensing arrangements between intermediaries.

As regards cross-border portability, which, as I have noted earlier, can be linked somewhat to the free movement of consumers,[16] the Portability Regulation (EU) 2017/1128 offers an intriguing legislative solution: it establishes a legal mechanism that resembles the country of origin principle of the SatCab Directive[17] and, quite noteworthy, additionally safeguards that contractual agreements do not run counter to its objectives. In these instances, thus, multi-territorial licensing is not necessary in the first place. The Portability Regulation is, however, restricted in two dimensions, which renders it in practical terms less relevant: first, it is mandatory for paid services only, and, secondly, it is restricted to transient, temporary situations.[18]

The second, broader category of 'true' cross-border access, which finds its link to the free movement of services, concerns a slightly different situation.[19] As shown in Chapter 5, geo-blocking of services using copyright-protected works is currently exempt from the Geo-blocking Regulation (EU) 2018/302. But, as seen, in *Premier League and Murphy* the Court of Justice opened up an intriguing train of thought regarding additional obligations in licensing agreements, over content and passive sales. From different angles, both the Commission's pay-TV investigation and the Court's judgment in *Premier League and Murphy* have their point of departure in passive sales. The judgment, however, leaves us with several open questions, as seen above.[20] Its application by the DG Competition of the European Commission in the pay-TV proceedings seems to point towards a broader application of the 'passive sales' or 'additional obligations' rationale in the digital content landscape (notably regarding copyright-protected subject matter). At the same time, it is

---

[16] See Section 2.2.

[17] Council Directive 93/83/EEC of 27 September 1993 on the coordination of certain rules concerning copyright and rights related to copyright applicable to satellite broadcasting and cable retransmission OJ L248/15–21 (SatCab Directive).

[18] See Section 3.3. G. Mazziotti, 'Is Geo-blocking a Real Cause for Concern?', *European Intellectual Property Review* (2016), 365, 369 points towards the 'modest' impact, referring to EU calculations inn which, after finding that geo-blocking today affects only 0.2 per cent of EU citizens (short-term migrants, travellers and tourists), he argues that the solution is 'clearly insufficient'.

[19] See Section 2.2.

[20] See Section 3.2.2. The suggested legislative measures do not really help in interpreting the Court's line of thought either. On the one hand, it could be seen as necessity to regulate; on the other, it could be seen as implementation.

restricted in the sense that it leaves room for service providers not to respond to passive sales.[21] This application comes with an interesting twist, though: the differentiation between passive and active sales on the Internet does not seem as straightforward as in an offline context. A search engine result, for example, could hardly be qualified as active sale. Considering that search engines are a major access point to websites, the consequences, potentially in combination with the Geo-blocking Regulation (EU) 2018/302, could be quite far reaching. But, for now, legislation, on the one side, and the Court and the Commission on the other, appear to move at different speeds. With the Proposal for a Regulation on online transmissions of broadcasting organisations,[22] the European Commission again proposed a solution based on a 'country of origin' principle, at least for some content forms in the specific area of online transmissions by broadcasting organisations. It is unclear, however, what form the final Regulation will take.

Relation between EU Initiatives and Market Self-Regulation

As pointed out above, regulatory initiatives also need to be seen in the broader context of the different actors that participate and interact in the development of regulation. As noted in Chapter 1, these arrangements, for example, in the form of licensing agreements and standard contracts, can be seen both as regulatory instruments that help to shape the market and as a product of regulatory instruments (i.e. the result of regulatory intervention).

In relation to licensing of music online, the development of operational standards is prevalent.[23] But other forms, such as the 'Licences for Europe'-dialogue, have also been facilitated. These initiatives are sometimes induced by the European Commission or other governmental bodies, and sometimes by the actors or their umbrella organisations. A market-led solution to licensing based on RRAs, as seen, was refused by the European lawmaker, at least in its form safeguarding national monopolies.[24] Without detailed insight in licensing agreements, it is

---

[21] See, e.g., P. I. Colomo, 'Copyright Licensing and the EU Digital Single Market Strategy', LSE Law, Society and Economy Working Papers 19/2015 (2015), 14: http://ssrn.com/abstract=2697178

[22] Commission, 'Proposal for a Regulation of the European Parliament and of the Council laying down rules on the exercise of copyright and related rights applicable to certain online transmissions of broadcasting organisations and retransmissions of television and radio programmes'.

[23] See Section 2.4.3.   [24] See, e.g., Section 3.2.1.

likely that commercial users (online service providers) were benefiting from the traditional system based on RRAs (in terms of lower transaction costs due to fewer licensors), at least as long as they themselves did not operate on a pan-European basis.[25] The system of RRAs with mandatory dispute resolution regarding online rates was the favoured model at the time because 'their [service providers'] main interest is an EU-wide licence for the aggregate EU repertoire'.[26] The Recommendation of 2005 advocated competition between CMOs via rights holders rather than commercial users. This scheme continues under the CRM Directive of 2014, which again primarily focuses on collective management services provided to rights holders and, to a lesser degree, commercial users.

Another interesting dynamic between the regulatory intervention and market developments relates to the emergence of direct licensing of mono-repertoires on a multi-territorial basis (option 3 publishers). The traditional view in the academic literature seems to be that the Online Music Recommendation has been the driving force behind the withdrawal of the Anglo-American repertoire from the system of reciprocal representation agreements and local CMOs. But, as was discovered in Chapters 2 and 3, evidence suggests that Anglo-American publishers would have withdrawn their repertoire in any case. In that respect, it seems that the Recommendation might have accelerated the development, but only as one of several factors.

As regards cross-border access, the dynamics between market self-regulation and EU initiatives is less apparent. One indication could be how broadly the current pay-TV proceedings will transform the current

---

[25] This might also be overstated. Since the proceedings regarding the Santiago and Barcelona Agreements, no information has been available as to whether RRAs for online uses exist and what terms they have. See R. Hilty and S. Nérisson, 'Collective Copyright Management and Digitization: The European Experience' Max Planck Institute for Intellectual Property and Competition Law Research Paper No. 13–09 (Max Planck Institute for Intellectual Property and Competition Law, 2013), 8: http://ssrn.com/abstract=2247870

[26] Referred to as 'option 2' in the IA to the Recommendation, and especially the system of RRAs with mandatory dispute resolution regarding online rates. See Commission, 'Impact Assessment reforming cross-border collective management of copyright and related rights for legitimate online music services', 36. More specifically Finish CMO Teosto argued 'that users would welcome a re-launch of the Santiago/Barcelona Agreements in a revised format, to suite the DG Competition views' (Ibid., 24). See also Council of the European Union, 'Proposal for a Directive of the European Parliament and of the Council on collective management of copyright and related rights and multi-territorial licensing of rights in musical works for online use in the internal market, Statements', Statement by the Republic of Poland, 4.

licensing and access practices of audiovisual content outside the proceedings' immediate scope.

Open Issues and Missing Pieces

As becomes clear from this assessment, the regulatory framework does not address the digital reality as regards cross-border access and licensing in its entirety. Here, I supplement with some broader perspectives the multiple more detailed aspects discussed in the previous sections.

With the Geo-blocking Regulation (EU) 2018/302, the European lawmaker has (for now) chosen to not include cross-border access to audiovisual works. Given the relatively broad scope of the Regulation, which is broadly directed towards e-commerce in the EU, it might not be the most suitable legal instrument to regulate copyright-related matters in detail. Nonetheless, this seems somewhat odd given the background of the findings of the Court in *Premier League and Murphy:* at least those access restrictions stemming from contractual licensing arrangements could have been addressed.[27] This seems unsatisfactory considering the direct contractual relationship with consumers, which gives services providers as well as rights holders the possibility of unilaterally defining limitations on access.[28] The competition proceedings in the pay-TV investigation might fill this gap to some extent.

As regards licensing for online music purposes, Directive 2014/26/EU applies only to CMOs, independent management entities and, in certain cases, their subsidiaries or outsourcing services. There are, as identified, several issues that remain untouched or unclear. Also, direct licensing is touched upon only in an ancillary way.[29] On a broader scale, yet another area left open by the legislator is the licensing of online music rights by record labels (which, ultimately, again fulfil an intermediary function).[30] Thus, in both areas, further intervention might become necessary.

[27] Another boundary of the proposal is the circumvention of technological protection measures (TPMs), which it does not address.
[28] See, e.g., R. M. Hilty and K. Köklü, 'Limitations and Exceptions to Copyright in the Digital Age' in I. A. Stamatoudi (ed.), *New Developments in EU and International Copyright Law* (Kluwer Law International, 2016), p. 289; see also Section 6.3.
[29] See also KEA European Affairs, *Licensing music works and transaction costs in Europe* (2012), p. 55.
[30] See also C. B. Graber, 'Collective rights management, competition policy and cultural diversity: EU lawmaking at a crossroads', 4 *World Intellectual Property Organization Journal* [2012], 35, 42–43. The European Commission refrains from providing explanations for the regulatory focus. This seems odd in relation to the problematic nature of the record label–right holder relationship.

6.2   The EU's Double Approach

6.2.1   Ex Ante *or* Ex Post *Regulation?*

The European lawmaker seems to orbit around the central question: how to alleviate territorial borders for digital content effectively, while preserving territoriality of copyright and the specifics of the sector involved. As seen, both competition proceedings (*ex post* control under EU competition law) and legislative tools (*ex ante* sector-specific regulation) regulate the market for multi-territorial content licensing and cross-border access to various degrees.[31] But is one regulatory approach superior to the other, and do they exclude or complement each other?

Much of this discussion would lead us to the very fundamental legal and economic theories and their respective considerations regarding optimal regulation and more specifically the appropriate relationship of competition law and the (monopolistic, in economic or even legal sense) exploitation of copyright. Different rules have different rationales. Providing a contribution to these important questions is outside the scope of this book. Suffice it to note here that both competition law and rules on administration of copyright law strive to achieve common goals and that the latter is not 'completely shielded form control by competition law'.[32] Instead, let us focus on the more immediate overlaps of this book's theme.

From the outset, both forms of interventions have a distinctive playing field to navigate: on the one hand, any legislative intervention in copyright would be subject to the three-step test[33] and the subsidiarity principle, in addition to being required a legal basis in the Treaty. *Ex post* intervention based on competition law as a correcting factor, on the other hand, does

---

[31] See also, for this distinction, L. Guibault and S. van Gompel, 'Collective Management in the European Union' in D. Gervais (ed.), *Collective Management of Copyright and Related Rights*, 2nd edn. (Kluwer Law International, 2010), p. 149.

[32] T. Dreier, 'Regulating Competition by Way of Copyright Limitation and Exceptions' in P. Torremans (ed.), *Copyright Law, A Handbook of Contemporary Research* (Edward Elgar, 2007), p. 242; Schovsbo, 'The Necessity to collectivize copyright – and dangers thereof', 14. See also J. W. L. Yow, '"Creative Competition" with a Pan-European Licensing Body: Reconsidering the European Commission's Approach to Collecting Societies', 34 *World Competition* (2011), 287, 288; and on similar purposes R. M. Hilty, 'Individual, Multiple and Collective Ownership: What Impact on Competition?' in J. Rosén (ed.), *Individualism and Collectiveness in Intellectual Property Law* (Edward Elgar, 2012), p. 5 with more sources. Commission's view on Competition/IP: no inherent conflict – see, e.g., Technology Transfer Guidelines 2014/C89/03, para. 7.

[33] See, e.g., Schovsbo, 'The Necessity to collectivize copyright – and dangers thereof', 7. But see declaration by several leading academics regarding a flexible interpretation: C. Geiger and others, 'Declaration, A Balanced Interpretation of the "Three-Step Test" in Copyright Law', *Journal of Intellectual Property, Information Technology and Electronic Commerce Law*, 1 (2010), 119.

not come without constraints either. Its application is restricted to specific circumstances; unilateral business decisions or the absence of a misuse of a dominant position fall outside its effects.[34] By definition, competition law, as Dreier notes, 'only comes in late (...) and is a heavy entrustment based on a rather cumbersome enforcement mechanism'.[35]

Legislative measures can be desirable for a variety of reasons, which are not further explored here. If the existing regulatory framework, and in this case notably proceedings under competition law, however, is able to address the challenges, legislative intervention might seem much less a necessity. The DG Competition expresses – not very surprisingly, one might add, in the context of online content – that 'we should bear in mind that generally it is not more regulation that makes companies innovate and thrive'.[36] The flip side of this is that competition law (possibly in combination with fundamental freedoms as in *Premier League and Murphy*) could represent an interesting – and under certain circumstances preferable – regulatory factor to help overcome territorial delineation based on licensing agreements and arrangements.

6.2.1.1 Using Competition Law to Ensure Access to Works

Let us first revisit the situation for cross-border access. It is sensible to ask whether geo-blocking, i.e. the technical solution to enforcing territorial delineation of rights, is in fact a competition, rather than a copyright-related issue. The current Commissioner for Competition, Margrethe Vestager, underlines that the digital economy, and more specifically the 'access [to] goods, content, and other services no matter where they live and travel in Europe',[37] is a priority for competition policy.

In examining the Commission's pay-TV investigation in light of the *Premier League and Murphy* judgment, Colomo shows 'how competition law is enforced by the Commission to address concerns that are, first and foremost, the consequence of the nature and scope of national copyright regimes'.[38] As I have noted throughout the previous chapters, it is worth recalling that most of the proposed and implemented measures by the EU legislator (as well as from a competition law side) are not addressing substantial copyright as such.[39] Instead, they focus on the exercise of the rights in their respective arrangements.

---

[34] Dreier, 'Regulating competition by way of copyright limitation and exceptions', p. 242.
[35] Ibid.   [36] Margrethe Vestager.   [37] Ibid.
[38] Colomo, 'Copyright Licensing and the EU Digital Single Market Strategy', 3.
[39] This is, of course, in relation to this research. The interpretation and harmonisation of substantial copyright norms, especially in the context of the InfoSoc Directive (Directive 2001/29/EC of the European Parliament and of the Council of 22 May 2001 on the

Riis and Schovsbo argue that legal challenges of portability can indeed be solved by the existing framework, and specifically the competition rules.[40] Thus, they conclude, portability can hardly justify a modernisation of copyright rules.[41] They see this view confirmed by parts of the European Commission, namely in interpreting the DG Competition's Statement of Objections in the pay-TV proceedings.[42] More broadly, Hugenholtz finds a competition approach regarding the territorial delineation of intellectual property rights 'less structural, but sometimes effective nonetheless'.[43] Similarly, a report prepared for the EU Commission in 2010 concludes that competition proceedings are 'very effective in restricting unjustified territorial exploitation of intellectual property rights'.[44]

I argue that intervention under both competition rules and legislative intervention is necessary and, to some degree, a well-tuned or somewhat intended interplay. This leads us back to my attempt to explain the intertwined relation of multi-territorial licensing and cross-border access from Chapter 2.[45] As I have touched upon there, cross-border access, whether in the form of cross-border portability or 'true' cross-border access, is dependent, for one, on the underlying licences for the relevant repertoires. Licensing, however, is not addressed (or circumvented) by competition proceedings, but rather is dependent on the underlying substantive copyright rules. In other words, whereas absolute territorial exclusivity provided by licensing agreements might be challenged by competition law also in relation to copyright-protected subject matter, the necessity to clear the respective underlying rights is not. This is supported by evidence from the European Commission, which provides insights on its interpretation of *Premier League and Murphy*, as already noted, by its reference in the ongoing pay-TV investigation by the DG COMP. Additionally, the Commission commented on the case in its Staff Working Document accompanying the Digital Single Market Strategy of 2015:

harmonisation of certain aspects of copyright and related rights in the information society [2001] OJ L167/10–19), has been a major part of the copyright-related proceedings before the Court of Justice; see also Section 6.2.2.

[40] T. Riis and J. Schovsbo, 'Den grænseløse onlinebruger – geografisk opdeling af markedet for online- og streamingtjenester' in *Liber Amicorum Jan Rosén* (eddy.se, 2016), p. 679.

[41] Ibid., p. 666.   [42] See ibid., in footnote 2.

[43] P. B. Hugenholtz, 'Harmonization or Unification of EU Copyright Law' in J. Axhamn (ed.), *Copyright in a Borderless Online Environment* (Norsteds Juriidik, 2012), p. 198, with the same wording as had already appeared in M. van Eechoud and others, 'The Last Frontier: Territoriality' in P. B. Hugenholtz (ed.), *Harmonizing European Copyright Law: The Challenges of Better Lawmaking*, vol. 19, Information Law Series (Wolters Kluwer, 2009), p. 314.

[44] KEA European Affairs and Mines ParisTech, 155.   [45] See Section 2.2.

(. . .) right holders may nevertheless prefer to issue exclusive licences with a limited territorial scope (e.g. matching the territory of a Member State or based on linguistic criteria). In the Premier League cases (joined cases C-403/08 and C-429/08) which addressed issues related to cross-border access to satellite broadcasting services, the Court of Justice of the European Union (CJEU) concluded that right holders and service providers *may conclude licencing agreements* based on territorial exclusivity but *cannot include in such licensing agreements clauses* aiming at achieving absolute territorial exclusivity in breach of competition law and the Internal Market freedom to provide services.[46]

As for the ongoing proceedings in the pay-TV investigation, the offered commitment by one party, Paramount, to cease its geo-blocking practice, does not imply that other rights holders would do so, too.[47] In other words, there is only so much competition that proceedings can achieve. Also, Colomo looks at the two-pronged strategy and concludes that '[t]he objectives of the DSMS cannot be achieved through the reform of national copyright regimes alone. The enforcement of EU competition law is also necessary'.[48]

As to the second claim, of a well-tuned or at least intended interplay, supporting evidence can again be found with the European Commission: current Commissioner for Competition, Vestager, in a speech from September 2015, here underlined for emphasis:

Competition law can therefore complement intellectual property law in situations where the way that intellectual property law is exercised may fall short of promoting consumer welfare. Without effective competition rules, there would be higher risks that today's innovators might stifle those of tomorrow, or that consumers might not benefit from fair access to those innovations. Our task in this regard is to find the right balance between the interests of distributors, artists, inventors and creators and the interests of consumers.[49]

In what appears a fairly conscious application of both routes, i.e. competition and legislative routes, she also points towards restrictions in what competition law can and should address:

However, competition law is not the answer to everything. We cannot solve issues in today's digital world that are for the IP rules – we cannot and we should not. If those rules need to be updated, that is a task for legislators. Competition policy

---

[46] Commission, 'Impact Assessment accompanying the document Proposal for a Regulation of the European Parliament and of the Council to ensure the cross-border portability of online content services in the internal market', 28 (emphasis added).

[47] See also A. Lamadrid, 'Breaking news: Pay-TV investigation- Paramount offers commitments' (*Chillin'Competition*, 22 April 2016): https://chillingcompetition.com/2016/04/22/breaking-news-pay-tv-investigation-paramount-offers-commitments/

[48] Colomo, 'Copyright Licensing and the EU Digital Single Market Strategy', 3.

[49] Margrethe Vestager (emphasis added).

should therefore work *hand in hand* with intellectual property policy to achieve common goals.[50]

The picture for cross-border licensing by collective management obviously looks different. With the adoption of Directive 2014/26/EU, the European playing field is, to a large extent, regulated on a legislative basis.[51] But, here too, competition proceedings have played a crucial rule in paving the way to harmonisation by hard law, as will be explored in the next section. Farrand argues that 'the lack of multi-territory licenses for European digital music provision has been effectively framed as being a competition issue, rather than a harmonization one'.[52] Considering the context and content of the CRM Directive, I am inclined to agree.

6.2.1.2 Quasi-Regulatory Interventions via Competition Law

From what we have seen in Chapter 3, the use of competition proceedings in the field of cross-border access, as well as cross-border licensing, seems to be applied not purely in a traditional *ex post* but to a certain extent in a quasi-regulatory interventionist fashion: more broadly, 'the use of competition law as an alternative to, or substitute for, sector-specific regulation' is a well-recognised phenomenon, as Dunne notes.[53] Competition law as regulation, she argues, 'arises most frequently, where there has simply been a failure to enact regulation within a sector where existing regulation has gaps in coverage, rather than any decision against regulation as such'.[54] In the absence of sector-specific regulation, i.e. where competition law as regulation takes a 'gap-filling function', competition law 'may provide a second-best solution' to market failure, 'particularly those related to structural issues such as exploitation of natural or legal monopolies (...)'.[55] Even though the natural monopoly assumption is heavily contested, arguably the cross-border dimension of collective

---

[50] Ibid., (emphasis added).
[51] Obviously with some level of discretion in its implementation by Member States.
[52] B. Farrand, *Networks of Power in Digital Copyright Law and Policy* (Routledge, 2014), p. 136.
[53] N. Dunne, *Competition Law and Economic Regulation, Making and Managing Markets* (Cambridge University Press, 2015), p. 69. See also Colomo, 'Copyright Licensing and the EU Digital Single Market Strategy', 16. The 'more recent trend of competition law and competition enforcement to develop mechanisms and tools that *go beyond* mere protection of competition, but try to improve the market conditions in a *forward looking approach*, which is more typical for market regulation' has also been subject of a book edited by Di Porto and Drexl, in which various aspects are explored: see F. Di Porto and J. Drexl, 'Preface' in F. Di Porto and J. Drexl (eds.), *Competition Law as Regulation* (Edward Elgar, 2015), p. ix.
[54] N. Dunne, *Competition Law and Economic Regulation: Making and Managing Markets* (Cambridge University Press, 205), p. 70.
[55] Ibid., p. 72.

rights management is a prototype scenario of this. A somewhat similar tendency can be observed regarding audiovisual licensing agreements and cross-border access: based on the Court of Justice's case law, the DG Competition then opened proceedings into the pay-TV sector applying the Court's reasoning. Dunne further notes that 'recurrent competition law complaints or investigations may also highlight the existence of market-wide problems, which may subsequently prompt adoption of a more comprehensive regulatory solution'.[56]

Notably, the CISAC proceedings date back to two separate complaints from licensees. More generally, the proceedings centred on the CISAC and International Federation of the Phonographic Industry (IFPI) model contracts for, inter alia, reciprocal representation agreements. And indeed, with the adoption of Directive 2014/26/EU, a rather comprehensive legislative solution for the multi-territorial licensing of online music rights has been put forward.[57]

On the other hand, Dunne argues that the use of competition law to address market problems may also 'represent a deliberate policy choice to favour market-oriented solutions'.[58] This is especially relevant in the context of the European Commission's Better Regulation framework. One can hypothesise whether this, for example, is not the case with regard to option 3 publishers, and even more broadly music labels, which are not addressed by legislation. In the cross-border access relationship for audiovisual content, the competition law concerns might have highlighted the existence of market-wide issues, too. And here, too, with the recent Geoblocking and Portability Regulations, as well as the Commission's proposals, a comprehensive legislative solution has been put forward. However, as seen, again, some aspects are left unaddressed by legislation.

Whereas, for the sake of this section, I merely conclude the apparent proactive regulatory use of competition law (and not to what extent this is desirable on a conceptual level), it is necessary briefly to sketch a couple of associated drawbacks. As seen in the previous section, the Commission itself acknowledges the inadequacy of competition law in some respects. On a more conceptual level, Dunne presents several objections that point towards the danger of subverting democratic processes. A first objection relates to the constitutional separation of power: the European Commission in respect of competition proceedings holds quasi-judicial

---

[56] Ibid.

[57] Dunne points to a case that shares some common developments, it seems: relating to ground handling of airports, on which the Commission 'initially pursued a policy of competition enforcement against airport operators in order to generate political support for EU-wide regulation of such services'. See ibid., pp. 90 and 73–74.

[58] Ibid., p. 76.

powers,[59] whereas '[t]he enactment of regulation, is by contrast, a legislative task'.[60] Competition authorities therefore use 'its [enforcing competition law] (. . .) to create *de facto* regulation, given that this is a legislative task rather than an executive or judicial function'.[61]

A second objection relates to legitimacy and the rule of law; compliance 'cannot be verified (. . .) and the legitimacy of the resulting law is compromised'.[62] Similar concerns might arise in relation to other non-legislative interventions by the Commission under the Better Regulation agenda. Finally, on a more pragmatic level, Dunne articulates that 'the movement from legalistic competition law to competition law-as-regulation renders the law itself more vulnerable to political pressure and influence'.[63] If this last argument holds, it might be especially important to consider in the sphere of collective rights management. Farrand notes that '[g]iven the high complexity of collective management, combined with its very low salience, discussions concerning multi-territory licensing took place in an environment of quiet politics, which tends to benefit large business interests'.[64]

A Broad Range of Regulatory Instruments   The picture is further blurred, when looking towards a second string of thoughts, which evolves around the broader choice of regulatory instruments. As seen in the preceding chapters, the European Commission is not only proceeding from a competition and legislative side, but also operates with other instruments such as non-binding soft-law acts and by facilitating market-developments.

As regards the Online Music Recommendation 2005/737/EC, it is worth recalling that the European Parliament heavily criticised the European Commission for its instrument – on substantive and procedural grounds. It argued that the Recommendation 'clearly goes further than merely interpreting or supplementing existing rules'.[65] But, as seen, the Recommendation has also been criticised for its non-binding nature. This

---

[59] Ibid., p. 89.   [60] Ibid.   [61] Ibid.   [62] For discussion, see ibid., p. 91.
[63] Ibid., p. 95 with more evidence.
[64] Farrand, *Networks of Power in Digital Copyright Law and Policy*, p. 155. Farrand looks, anecdotally, at the media coverage in the UK accompanying the CRM Directive, which suggests that 'in the UK at least, the role and reform of collecting societies is not an issue of high political salience, meaning that businesses are able to dictate the terms of legislative developments'. He continues to track these influences – for example, in the Impact assessment in which the Commission relies on data of, e.g., the recording industry's umbrella organisation, IFPI.
[65] European Parliament, 'Resolution of 13 March 2007 on the Commission Recommendation of 18 October 2005 on collective cross-border management of copyright and related rights for legitimate online music services (2005/737/EC) (2006/2008 (INI))', lit. B.

aspect, however, has to be seen in light of the inherent threat that non-compliance would lead to regulatory intervention based on either the general competition rules or proposed legislative measures. Both these factors seem to have been at play here.[66] This also correlates well to the new modes of governance and the 'Better regulation' law-making procedure, described in Chapter 1.[67]

As regards both multi-territorial licensing and cross-border access, one can witness a wide use of the different non-legislative tools at a preparatory level, such as, for example, the discussed consultations and sector inquiries. At the same time, however, the Commission clearly seems to be of the opinion that the cross-border access dimension requires intervention with hard-binding law and a full-harmonisation approach.

6.2.2   The Interplay at an Institutional Level

The market situation of licensing and access arrangements is, as seen, characterised by scrutiny from different institutional actors. Traditionally, legal research has focused primarily on the interplay between judicial and legislative branches, rather than the fine-tuned facets within the institutions. In the field of multi-territorial licensing and cross-border access not only the interplay between the judicative and legislative actors but also intra-institutional aspects are relevant.

6.2.2.1   Intra-Institutional Interplay at the European Commission

The European Commission's most intriguing feature is its Janus face: on the one hand, it has the right of initiative in proposing legislation, and on the other it functions as a competition authority.[68] In other words, it is combining judiciary and legislative competence over several DGs. I have just explored the interplay between the former and the latter in the section above, which is why I focus on the former function in this section. In this function of proposing legislation, policy agendas are shaped by several DGs within the Commission, each of them overseeing a particular thematic area.[69] As policy areas can overlap, different DGs may be involved

---

[66] See Section 3.3 with further evidence on the 'second phase', in which the Commission reserved the right to propose legislation.
[67] The EU Commission, for example, refers to 'Better Regulation' in its Recommendation 2005/737/EC (See Commission, 'Impact Assessment reforming cross-border collective management of copyright and related rights for legitimate online music services', 39).
[68] See also above, concerns regarding the constitutional division of power problem.
[69] See, e.g., R. Ackrill and A. Kay, 'Multiple Streams in EU Policy-making: The Case of the 2005 Sugar Reform', *Journal of European Public Policy*, 18 (2011), 72, 75.

in the relevant EU action:[70] as the following examples display, the competition proceedings and decisions[71] stem from the DG Competition. The Online Music Recommendation of 2005, as well as its follow-up in the form of the Proposal for the CRM Directive of 2012, comes from DG MARKT as leading service. In this context, one explaining factor for the additional impetus for sector regulation could also be the shift of Neelie Kroes, who was Commissioner for Competition in Barroso's first Commission from 2004 to 2009, and to the Digital Agenda under Barroso's second Commission from 2010 to 2014.

The Proposals for Regulations on Geo-blocking in 2016 and on Cross-border Portability in 2015 stem from its succeeding Directorate General DG CONNECT. The former DG Information Society and Media (INFSO), which also merged into DG CONNECT, prepared the Communication on *creative content online in the Single Market* as leading DG in 2007.[72] In 2009, DG INFSO and DG MARKT published a joint reflection document on *Creative Content in a European Digital Single Market: Challenges for the Future*.[73] In other words, before the restructuring separate DGs were involved in policy making. Hoeren notes:

> The involvement of all these institutional bodies, each one with its own remit and policy agenda, creates a confusing picture and complicates follow-up. Without proper coordination and constructive inter-service and inter-institutional consultation, policy development in the field of multi-territorial rights clearance might prove a very difficult venture.[74]

As seen in Chapter 1, the two DGs involved in policy making on content on the Internal Market have merged. Thus, as shown before, the need for intra-institutional cooperation is likely to have decreased. The recent re-shuffling has thematically relocated the copyright unit from its traditional institutional proximity to other industrial property rights in DG MARKT, in a digital context surrounded by other resorts working on

---

[70] For multi-territorial licensing this is also remarked on by T. Hoeren, *Collecting Societies and Cultural Diversity in the Music Sector* (2009), pp. 13–14. R. Ackrill and A. Kay, 'Multiple Streams in EU Policy-making: The Case of the 2005 Sugar Reform', 18 *Journal of European Public Policy*, 72 (2011), 85 track the specific-agenda and decision-making structure of different DGs in the completely different field of sugar policy. Here they find 'the potential for policy (...) "endogenous" spillovers [which] mean, first, a policy issue subject to decision-making in one policy arena may affect causally decisions on that issue in other arenas. Furthermore, such spillovers affect the duration of the policy windows'.

[71] Such as the Barcelona and Santiago Agreements (2003), the Simulcasting Agreement (2002), CISAC (2008) and the pay-TV investigation (ongoing).

[72] See Hoeren, *Collecting Societies and Cultural Diversity in the Music Sector*, p. 13.

[73] Commission, 'Creative Content, in a European Digital Single Market: Challenges for the Future' (A Reflection Document of DG INFSO and DG MARKT), 22 October 2009.

[74] Hoeren, *Collecting Societies and Cultural Diversity in the Music Sector*, p. 14.

the Digital Single Market in DG CONNECT. Considering that most challenges in copyright seem to be related to its application in the digital context, this might appear to be a reasonable change. Undoubtedly, spill-over effects might occur, which, for example, could inform copyright-related proposals in their context. On the other hand, the traditional proximity to and context within the broader intellectual property sphere might diminish. Then again, it is worth recalling that copyright has a peculiar role within the intellectual property rights (IPR) landscape, as it comes with no registration requirements, around which much of the institutional setup is built. The question poses itself whether this re-shuffling can also be tracked in the legislative proposals and other initia-tives coming from the DG. Whereas it is for future research, in the legal or political sciences, to put institutional changes (and whether they for example lead to political focus on a more open than proprietary environ-ments) more closely under scrutiny, let me provide some anecdotal observations.

Starting at the most recent legislative initiative by DG CONNECT, it seems noteworthy that the Geo-blocking Regulation proposal addresses copyright-protected subject matter only at its very margin. At the same time, the Commission foresaw a review of the Geo-blocking Regulation especially as regards its applicability to copyright-protected services. The Commission's Cross-border Portability Proposal, on the other hand, came with a clear focus on online content services, i.e. services based on the provision of copyright-protected works. Here it is worth recalling the central legal mechanism, which is a legal fiction in form of a country of origin principle akin to the one we know from the SatCab Directive. Thus, it appears as if DG CONNECT, as leading Directorate-General, builds its proposals around different sectors, where copyright-protected works receive special attention.[75] Most noteworthy appears to be the choice of instrument: full-harmonisation via Regulations represents a novelty in the copyright-related field, instead of the approach up till now based on Directives.[76] Compared with Directive 2014/26/EU, the Cross-border Portability and Geo-blocking Regulations, despite their limited scope, seem more ambitious. But also under the previous institu-tional set-up, the Copyright Unit of DG MARKT, in its Public Consultation on the review of the EU copyright rules from 2013 and

---

[75] To what extent this is caused by internal agenda setting or by external stakeholders' influence is another question.

[76] In other fields of IP, regulations have been used for the introduction of unitary rights. The harmonisation of substantive copyright continues to be based on Directives: see, e.g., Commission, 'Proposal for a Directive of the European Parliament and of the Council on copyright in the Digital Single Market'.

2014, requested input on fairly far-reaching unconventional solutions, such as the adoption of a copyright registration system.[77]

Finally, the overall political discourse, which seems to have moved its agenda from protection- to access-related issues, is also likely to have influence on the agenda-setting. In conclusion, it is probably too early to track how the institutional changes impact on the proposed measures, but these recent developments might provide a first indication of the direction the relevant DG is taking.

6.2.2.2 The Role of the Court of Justice

It is also worthwhile briefly to consider the role of the Courts in this area. Hunt and Shaw point towards the 'dense network of policy actors, including referring courts, national supreme and constitutional courts, the Commission, Advocate General, member state governments and litigants'[78] in which the Court operates and where some actors are particularly privileged. In this context they recall earlier research where after 'the Court's judgments accorded with the views presented by the legal service of the Commission in 9 out of 11 cases'.[79] Conventionally, as Hunt and Shaw note, the Court has been perceived 'as a motor of integration, driving the Community ever onwards towards further and deeper integration'.[80] As regards the harmonisation of copyrights, in recent years, the Court of Justice, too, has taken a proactive stance in interpreting certain key concepts, where it tries to achieve adequate results in the respective preliminary rulings at the cost of traditional copyright principles.[81] Examples of this development can be seen regarding communication to the public and exhaustion in *UsedSoft*.[82] Others call it a 'creative interpretation of the *acquis communautaire* in the field of

---

[77] Which, in an obligatory version, would run counter to the Berne Convention.

[78] J. Hunt and J. Shaw, 'Fairy Tale of Luxembourg? Reflections on Law and Legal Scholarship in European Integration' in D. Phinnemore and A. Warleigh-Lack (eds.), *Reflections on European Integration, 50 Years of the Treaty of Rome* (Palgrave Macmillan, 2009), p. 104. This finds its expression in that some parties present the Court 'with their own perspectives on the "correct" response in particular cases and feeding into an ongoing, iterative process of policy and polity development' (ibid.).

[79] Ibid., pp. 104–105, with further evidence.   [80] Ibid., p. 100.

[81] See T. Riis, 'Ophavsrettens fleksibilitet', *Nordiskt Immateriellt Rättsskydd* [2012], 139; M. Favale, M. Kretschmer and P. C. Torremans, 'Is there an EU Copyright Jurisprudence? An Empirical Analysis of the Workings of the European Court of Justice', *Modern Law Review*, 79 (2016), 31–75: http://ssrn.com/abstract=2643699. Recently, Favale et al., for example, empirically looked at the question whether the Court of Justice had failed to develop a coherent copyright jurisprudence.

[82] See Riis, 'Ophavsrettens fleksibilitet', 139. See O. A. Rognstad, 'Legally Flawed but Politically Sound? Digital Exhaustion of Copyright in Europe after UsedSoft', *Oslo Law Review*, 3 (2014), 1; M. Martin-Prat, 'The Future of Copyright in Europe', *Columbia*

intellectual property'.[83] In looking at the approximation by the Court of Justice of the originality criteria, Bently coined the expression 'harmonisation by stealth' for this phenomenon.[84] Does this pattern repeat itself in proceedings regarding collective administration and cross-border access?

When looking at how the Court addresses the system of collective management, a more nuanced view is adequate. Several of the more recent cases relating to collective management find their basis in competition proceedings. Thus, the Court of Justice (in CISAC the General Court, i.e. former Court of First Instance) to a lesser degree needs to determine the interpretation of harmonised rights. On a broader note, Kretschmer argues that the European Courts and the European Commission have been unable clearly to articulate the aims of solving 'innovation issues in the information society where major right holders otherwise may dictate problematic terms' by ensuring that '[c]reators at the margins of commercial viability have access to a mechanism of collective bargaining against major rights exploiters, such as publishers, record labels and broadcasters'[85] as regards collective licensing. He supposes that this is 'perhaps because they cannot be easily placed within the framework of Community competencies'.[86]

As regards the territorial delineation in licensing agreements, the picture looks different, though: as seen, *Premier League and Murphy* leaves us with some open questions. The Court of Justice did not follow AG Kokott's call to 'examine carefully whether the principle of exhaustion applies *mutatis mutandis* in the present context, that is to say, whether the specific subject-matter of the rights in question requires that the internal market be partitioned'.[87] Colomo suggests a shift in the development because the courts never questioned the existence of intellectual property

Journal of Law & the Arts, 38 (2014), 29, 36; Favale, Kretschmer and Torremans, 'Is there an EU Copyright Jurisprudence?'
[83] C. Geiger (ed.), *The construction of Intellectual Property in the European Union: Searching for Coherence* (Edward Elgar, 2013), p. 13.
[84] Bently, however, points out that it was not really 'by stealth', though; L. Bently, 'Harmonization By Stealth: Copyright and the ECJ', (Fordham IP Conference, 2010): http://fordhamipconference.com/wp-content/uploads/2010/08/Bently_Harmonization.pdf
[85] M. Kretschmer, 'Access and Reward in the Information Society: Regulating the Collective Management of Copyright', CIPPM Working Paper (2007), 4: http://dx.do i.org/10.2139/ssrn.2739837
[86] Ibid.
[87] AG Kokott, *Opinion*, para. 188. See also Chapter 3. B. Batchelor and T. Jenkins, 'FA Premier League: The Broader Implications for Copyright Licensing', *European Competition Law Review*, 33 (2012), 157, 159f. note: 'The Court did not need to reach a view on the issue of copyright because, on the facts, no infringement arose in the broadcast from Greece to the UK pub. This is in contrast to the Court's Advocate General (who reached a different conclusion on copyright). Thus, it was necessary for her (but not for the Court) to consider further whether the doctrine of exhaustion of rights applied to the copyright in question.'

(IP) rights but only their exercise, which according to him is different in *Premier League and Murphy*.[88] Others have commented in this context that '[a] trans-border right of access is in fact created in an implicit manner, maybe before its explicit consecration in law'.[89] As noted in Chapter 3, however, the Court in *Premier League and Murphy* also appears to be rather activist and has begun 'to set the pace of discussion' towards enhanced integration, where services move freely over borders.[90]

6.2.3 Summary

With regard to online platforms, the European Commission refers to its approach as 'problem-driven': 'This means when we identify a particular problem, for instance in copyright, we solve it there.'[91]

The arrangements for licensing of content for online use and access in Europe are of high complexity, and so are the regulatory initiatives and interventions by the European institutions. This leads to what appears to be a piecemeal approach and comes with some inconsistencies and areas that are (sometimes deliberately) left unaddressed. But what appears to be an incoherent piecemeal approach shows some signs of a somewhat systematic arrangement of regulation or governance. In this step-by-step approach, competition law seems to be much more than an *ex post* control, potentially paving the way for legislative intervention. Additionally, it might also provide the EU lawmaker with the flexibility to avoid a legislative lock-in in over-hasty regulation. The answer to the question whether this is desirable is likely to depend on the perspective.

Towards the background of the developments that find their basis in competition proceedings, it seems that licensing of and access to copyright-protected works is moving outside the copyright-related arena and closer to competition law (and correspondingly free movement). That is

---

[88] See, e.g., P. I. Colomo, 'Copyright reform through competition law? The Commission's statement of objections in the pay TV investigation' (*Chillin'Competition*, 24 July 2015) https://chillingcompetition.com/2015/07/24/copyright-reform-through-competition-law-the-commissions-statement-of-objections-in-the-pay-tv-investigation/

[89] C. Castets-Renard, '"Digital Single Market": the European Commission Presents its First Measures in Copyright Law', *French Review: Recueil Dalloz*, 2016, n° 7, 388: http://ssrn.com/abstract=2802729

[90] Martin-Prat, 'The Future of Copyright in Europe', 124; A. Wood, 'The CJEU's ruling in the Premier League pub TV cases – the final whistle beckons: joined cases Football Association Premier League Ltd v QC Leisure (C-403/08) and Murphy v Media Protection Services Ltd (C-429/08)', *European Intellectual Property Review*, 34 (2012), 203.

[91] C. Andrus Ansip, speech by Vice-President Ansip at the Creators Conference (31 May 2016): https://ec.europa.eu/commission/2014–2019/ansip/announcements/speech-vice-president-ansip-creators-conference_en

provided, though, that it has not been primarily a competition issue in the first place. In the digital content access world, 'regular' competition law appears to take back some of the autonomy that copyright-protected subject matter has enjoyed in the offline world. At the same time, copyright, or more specifically the arrangements around its exploitation, has not lost the place in the heart of the European institutions, neither in the Courts nor the European Commission, just yet. Whereas the end goals from a cross-border access-perspective are similar, the European Commission also recognises the need to take into account subject matter-specific aspects of the different creative sectors and its market participants. In this context, the Commission's exemption of audiovisual content from the geo-blocking proposal correlates with the current scheme of things.

6.3   Reconciling the Analogue Territorial with the Digital Borderless World

So which ways are there to improve the regulatory framework beyond the aspects presented before? As noted throughout this book, its focus is on the conditions and arrangements around the exercise of copyright. This section touches upon some related suggested measures, which theoretically support the policy goal of a Digital Single Market in the sense of providing cross-border access to copyright-protected content. Providing a thorough analysis of these measures is outside the scope of this book.

Until recently, the facilitation of licences appears to have been the main regulatory response by the European lawmaker. In this context some scholars, for example, have suggested models based on centralised licensing bodies.[92] Other intriguing proposals address more substantial issues of copyright, such as alternative compensation systems[93] or the definition of a making available on the Internet right as contemplated by the European Commission. Yet another line of thought that has been put

---

[92] Yow, for example, suggests, as an alternative to the chosen model of the Commission in the *CISAC* decision of 2008, with its focus on competition between CMOs, to 'establish a centralized licensing body to grant pan-European licenses. This body should be a private collaborative effort between the collecting societies as opposed to a public licensing agency established under EU law. Additionally, the concept of "creative competition" should also be introduced within each society'. See Yow, '"Creative Competition" with a Pan-European Licensing Body', 288ff.

[93] O.-A. Rognstad, 'Restructuring the Economic Rights in Copyright – Some Reflections on an "Alternative Model"', *Journal of the Copyright Society of the USA*, 62 (2015), 503, 508 proposes an alternative model, which restructures the economic rights, 'as part about the need for more radical adjustments of the current regime'. In his model, an 'exclusive right to a *reasonable exploitation* of the work (or other protected subject matter)' would become the overriding norm.

forward – not new but often recurring both in Europe and on the other side of the Atlantic – goes along copyright formalities.[94] In relation to licensing, the (re-)introduction of formalities is most prevalent with regard to the lack of ownership information. It has been noted by many that, as regards both music and audiovisual content, rights clearance can involve major transaction costs in form of search costs. As regards orphan works, the European legislator intervened in 2012 by introducing a regulatory framework in form of a Directive.[95] In the academic literature, the introduction of formalities (on both voluntary and mandatory bases), for example, as a means to ease licensing, has been frequently suggested over time.[96] Van Gompel, for example, notes that '[t]he general idea is that more adequate and reliable information about the authors and current right owners of works would become publicly available should particular copyright formalities be reintroduced.'[97]

Also, the Copyright Consultation from 2014 asks about the value of adopting a copyright registration regime. As seen, several industry initiatives have been put in place as regards music rights.[98]

As seen in Chapter 1, the European Commission aimed to address the field in several phases. On 31 May 2016, Commission Vice-President Ansip anticipated in a speech:

Our aim is to help consumers and creators by widening access to content. This will become possible with our proposal on cross-border portability. It aims to get people to pay for content – and pull them away from piracy and legal 'grey areas' like VPNs. The second phase of the copyright reform will come later in the year. The main focus will be on widening online availability of audio-visual content: in other words, more access to culture across Europe – but without challenging the principle of territoriality.[99]

This is also underlined in another memo from 2015, in which the Commission recollects that it does not want to change the principle of territoriality but 'understands it is important for the creative sector, especially for the film industry'.[100] In other words, there can be little

---

[94] See, e.g., S. van Gompel, 'Copyright Formalities in the Internet Age: Filters of Protection or Facilitators of Licensing', *Berkeley Technology Law Journal*, 28 (2013), 1425.

[95] Directive 2012/28/EU of the European Parliament and of the Council of 25 October 2012 on certain permitted uses of orphan works [2012] OJ L299/5.

[96] See, e.g., R. P. Merges, 'Contracting into Liability Rules: Intellectual Property Rights and Collective Rights Organizations', *California Law Review*, 84 (1996), 1293.

[97] van Gompel. 'Copyright Formalities in the Internet Age', 1432.   [98] See Section 2.4.

[99] Andrus Ansip.

[100] The Memo underlines: 'Each film has its distribution strategy, its release windows system. The Commission aims to the licensing of rights and ensure a better access in the digital world. This means, for example, that if a film is available on a video-on

doubt that the territoriality principle, aptly labelled by Hugenholtz the 'Achilles heel of harmonisation',[101] in addition to its firm legal position in international treaties, is not up for discussion. Ghafele comments that

The aspiration of a Single Market and the borderless world of the Internet stand in strong contrast to a Westphalian state order as reflected in the Berne Convention. The political, economic and technological shifts present considerable challenges to the existing system. How and to what extent to adapt the system remains a challenge for European Union policy makers.[102]

Katz points towards the chilling effect that international obligations in the area of intellectual property 'might have on the ability and willingness of regulators in a single country to try to eliminate a practice widely endorsed worldwide'.[103] In the context of collective rights management and its compatibility with the Berne Convention, Schovsbo underlines the importance of making 'sure that the international copyright legal framework does not stand in the way of beneficial collectivisation'.[104]

For the remainder, I focus on two suggested measures: first, the creation of a unitary right, and secondly the introduction of a broader legal fiction in form of a country of origin principle.[105]

6.3.1 Introduction of a Unitary Copyright Title

A first intriguing thought is whether a unitary European copyright title would solve the multi-territorial licensing conundrum and cross-border

---

demand service in an EU country, Europeans outside the country can also pay to see it.' (Commission, 'Questions and answers – Digital Single Market Strategy.')

[101] Hugenholtz, 'Harmonization or Unification of EU Copyright Law', p. 194; also van Eechoud and others, p. 307.

[102] R. Ghafele, 'Europe's Lost Royalty Opportunity: a Comparison of Potential and Existing Digital Music Royalty Markets in Ten Different E.U. Member States', *Review of Economic Research on Copyright Issues*, 11 (2014) 60, 65.

[103] A. Katz, 'The Potential Demise of Another Natural Monopoly: New Technologies and the Administration of Performing Rights', *Journal of Competition Law and Economics*, 2 (2006), 262.

[104] Schovsbo, 'The Necessity to collectivize copyright – and dangers thereof', 18–20. Considering that EU countries were instrumental in creating the Berne Convention in the first place, one could assume that it is in the best position to propose brave solutions.

[105] R. M. Hilty and K. Köklü, 'Limitations and Exceptions to Copyright in the Digital Age' suggest four cornerstones of a future-proof legal framework in copyright law, which correlate with some of the measures discussed in the following. See also the economic analysis by Langus et al., commissioned by DG MARKT, which lays out different policy options, specifically the extension of the logic of *Premier League and Murphy* and a 'country of origin' principle. Interestingly, the study finds that the policy options would not yield benefits for consumers: see G. Langus, D. Neven and S. Pouken, *Economic Analysis of the Territoriality of the Making Available Right in the EU* (Report prepared for the European Commission, DG MARKT, 2014).

access issues in the Digital Single Market. From a United States–American perspective, Perlmutter notes that

Most fundamentally, the co-existence in the European Union of separate copyright rights in separate member states with the policy of promoting a single market produces complexities that the United States does not have to face. Our single national system means that consumers can access content anywhere in the country on identical terms, and carry it with them from state to state.[106]

Discussions around the introduction of a unitary copyright title are by no means novel.[107] Whereas it is sometimes perceived as radical,[108] Brinker and Holzmüller observe significant political impetus in this respect.[109] Towse asserts that 'the greatest barrier to competition is copyright law itself with its complexity of multiple rights, national laws and lengthy duration – hence the discussion proposing a Europe-wide copyright law'.[110] As pointed out in Chapter 1, in 2015 the European Commission (again) clearly articulated a single European copyright title as a long-term target. Also the European Parliament's report on the InfoSoc Directive considers the introduction of a single European copyright title.[111]

Hilty and Köklü, however, evaluate that the introduction of a unitary title '[a]t least in the new future (...) does not appear to be a very promising perspective'.[112] They offer a more restricted version, arguing that 'a comprehensive, entirely unified copyright system is not the precondition to establish a digital single market'.[113] Instead, it would in their

---

[106] S. Perlmutter, 'Making Copyright Work for a Global Market: Policy Revision on Both Sides of the Atlantic', *Columbia Journal of Law & the Arts*, 38 (2014), 49, 62.

[107] See, e.g., the proposal of the Wittem group. For a critical commentary, notably from an outside EU-perspective, see J. C. Ginsburg, '"European Copyright Code" – Back to First Principles (with Some Additional Detail)', Columbia Public Law & Legal Theory Working Papers 9193: http://lsr.nellco.org/columbia_pllt/9193

[108] R. Tryggvadóttir, 'Balancing of Interests and Cross-border Use. Room for Nordic Co-operation?', *Nordiskt Immateriellt Rättsskydd* [2015], 652, 654.

[109] I. Brinker and T. Holzmuller, 'Competition Law and Copyright – Observations from the World of Collecting Societies', *European Intellectual Property Review*, 32(11) (2010), 553, 554, with further evidence from former Commissioner Vivian Reding.

[110] R. Towse, 'Economics of collective management organisations in the creative industries' (WINIR conference, 4–6 April 2016), 7.

[111] See European Parliament, 'Report on the implementation of Directive 2001/29/EC of the European Parliament and of the Council of 22 May 2001 on the harmonisation of certain aspects of copyright and related rights in the information society (2014/2256 (INI))', 5. As was briefly touched upon in Chapter 3, a potential legal basis for this is provided for in Art. 118 TFEU, introduced by the Lisbon Treaty.

[112] Hilty and Köklü, 'Limitations and Exceptions to Copyright in the Digital Age', p. 295. Castets-Renard, 13, shares their pessimism, noting 'the ambition to create a Code is once again at the forefront of discussion but it is unlikely that these objectives will suffice to convince the Member States to go beyond the specificities of their national Laws'.

[113] Hilty and Köklü, 'Limitations and Exceptions to Copyright in the Digital Age', p. 295.

model be sufficient if 'at least certain – unified – exploitation rights can only be h[e]ld by a single individual or legal person'.[114] In this way, they argue, the fragmentation of rights could be mitigated.[115]

The question whether and how a copyright title would actually change the access scheme remains, however. Recalling the conceptual model from Section 2.1, it seems likely that the introduction of a unitary title alone would not be sufficient to secure cross-border access to content. Rights holders would still be able to determine the scope of their licences. Online service providers would still be free contractually to restrict access to specific territories, just as in the case of the facilitation of multi-territorial licensing. Thus, whereas some problems might be solved, notably in relation to the fragmentation of rights, it is likely that a unitary copyright tile would not transform the licensing and access practices in the short run.

6.3.2   A Country of Origin Principle for the Digital Content World

In a leaked draft of the White Paper *A copyright policy for creativity and Innovation in the European Union* from June 2014, the European Commission considered the cross-border dissemination of creative content in the single market and effective tools for a functioning marketplace and value-chain as two of three main areas for review. The Commission considered the obstacles of ubiquitous cross-border access to 'derive from both issues related to the definition and to the exercise of rights'.[116] In the internal draft it continues to consider the definition of the act of making available on the Internet and it suggests that this could be done by introducing a country of origin principle or localisation of the act in Member States towards which the activity is directed.[117]

As noted above, the extension of the SatCab-model to Internet uses had been considered earlier. Axhamn and Guibault, for example, have suggested a solution for the challenges of cultural-heritage organisations based on the country of transmission principle. They recognise, however, that this solution is 'quite far-reaching from the right holders' perspective as it takes away their legal and bargaining position in the

---

[114] Ibid. They continue to argue that this 'does not require a major intervention in the already existing legal framework. (…) The transfer of these exploitation rights to a new regulation implies a formal rather than a substantive amendment of the European copyright legislation'.

[115] Ibid., p. 294.

[116] Commission, 'A Copyright Policy for Creativity and Innovation in the European Union', 6.

[117] Ibid.

countries of reception. It could also be argued that it does not solve the problem of territorial delineation, as the right holder may still, through contractual provisions, limit the use of the content to certain territories'.[118]

Hugenholtz refers to the SatCab-model as 'both elegant and simple'[119] in a report commissioned by the consumer organisations' umbrella organisation BEUC. He argues that the 'only structural legislative solution to the problem of market fragmentation by territorial rights can be found' in the SatCab Directive.[120] Extending, or applying by analogy, the SatCab principles has been considered in the academic literature for some time.[121] But also the European Commission has turned towards the principle in several instances: it is already mentioned in its Green Paper from 1995, and also the AVMS Directive builds around a country of origin principle.[122] Also the Staff Working Document accompanying the Communication on *creative content online in the Single Market* contemplated this type of principle.[123] More recently, a country of origin principle was considered in relation to the CRM Directive: policy option B4 was based on the idea to combine extended collective licensing with a country of origin principle.[124] However, it was deemed that it would not ease the licensing process. Also, in a report prepared for the Commission from 2014, the broad introduction of a 'country of origin' principle was examined as to its impact on social welfare.[125] Most recently, a

[118] J. Axhamn and L. Guibault, *Cross-border Extended Collective Licensing: A Solution to Online Dissemination of Europe's Cultural Heritage?* (Final report prepared for EuropeanaConnect, 2011), 515–516.

[119] Hugenholtz, 'Extending the SatCab Model to the Internet', Study commissioned by BEUC (Brussels, 2015), 3.

[120] Hugenholtz, 'Harmonization or Unification of EU Copyright Law', p. 197. However, for more critical pieces on to the success of the SatCab model: van Eechoud and others, 314; Colomo, 'Copyright Licensing and the EU Digital Single Market Strategy', 7; Rognstad, 'The multiplicity of territorial IP rights and its impact on competition', p. 58.

[121] See, notably, Hugenholtz, 'Harmonization or Unification of EU Copyright Law', p. 202. See also Hugenholtz, Extending the SatCab Model to the Internet'.

[122] See, e.g., Recital 33, which reads: 'The country of origin principle should be regarded as the core of this Directive, as it is essential for the creation of an internal market.'

[123] See Commission, 'Document accompanying the Communication from the Commission to the European Parliament, the Council, the European Economic and Social Committee and the Committee of the Regions on creative content online in the Single Market' (Commission Staff Working Document) SEC/2007/1710 final, Brussels, 3 January 2008.

[124] See Commission, 'Impact Assessment accompanying the document Proposal for a Directive of the European Parliament and of the Council on collective management of copyright and related rights and multi-territorial licensing of rights in musical works for online uses in the internal market', 48.

[125] Langus, Neven and Pouken, *Economic Analysis of the Territoriality of the Making Available Right in the EU*, pp. 107 ff.

mechanism akin to the 'country of origin' approach in the SatCab Directive has been introduced with the Cross-border Portability Regulation (EU) 2017/1128 and suggested by the Commission in its proposal for a Regulation regarding ancillary online services of broadcasting organisations.[126] It seems a little less clear what the European Parliament's stance is. As noted in Section 2.1, the Committee on Legal Affairs of the European Parliament in its Report on the Implementation of the InfoSoc Directive of May 2015 emphasised 'that there is no contradiction between that principle and measures to ensure the portability of content'.[127] The question is, though, whether a 'country of origin' principle would be contradictory. Under the impression of the consideration of the introduction of a unitary copyright title, which seems to stretch territoriality even further, probably not. But the extension of the principle to certain ancillary online services of broadcasts is already controversial. Such issues would only increase with a broader application of the 'country of origin' principle to copyright-protected works. In a similar vein, Hilty and Köklü see as a major obstacle the 'political indecisiveness in the face of an army of lobbyists from the copyright industries who actually benefit from the current market fragmentation'.[128] Thus, a 'country of origin' principle does not come without drawbacks, either. Suffice it to note here that it seems to be incompatible with many of the currently existing business models (which, of course, is only one aspect of its desirability) and that the concept would have to comply with, e.g., the three-step test.

Still, the 'country of origin' principle has some appeal: thinking back to the conceptual model in Section 2.2, its effects, depending on how far reaching such legal fiction would be applied to the licensing agreements, are on both the licensing and access dimensions.[129] Yet again, the impact of such a principle could be rendered void if contractual freedom would allow service providers to divide the services into territories.[130]

---

[126] Commission, 'Proposal for a Regulation of the European Parliament and of the Council laying down rules on the exercise of copyright and related rights applicable to certain online transmissions of broadcasting organisations and retransmissions of television and radio programmes'.

[127] European Parliament, 'Report on the implementation of Directive 2001/29/EC of the European Parliament and of the Council of 22 May 2001 on the harmonisation of certain aspects of copyright and related rights in the information society (2014/2256 (INI))', Recital 6.

[128] Hilty and Köklü, 'Limitations and Exceptions to Copyright in the Digital Age', p. 292.

[129] However, for a more critical piece on the limited effect of the SatCab principle in practice, see, e.g., Colomo, 'Copyright Licensing and the EU Digital Single Market Strategy', 7.

[130] See also Langus, Neven and Pouken, *Economic Analysis of the Territoriality of the Making Available Right in the EU*, p. 107.

6.3.3   *Towards a Consumer Perspective in Access to Copyright-Protected Works*

As seen above, both the introduction of a unitary copyright title and a legal fiction akin to a 'country of origin' principle, in themselves, would be insufficient to ensure cross-border access. The same goes for the explored routes of multi-territorial licensing or territorial access-restrictions in licensing agreements. This also becomes visible from the conceptual model in Section 2.2. This leads me to a concluding consideration regarding limitations on contractual freedom.

For this, let me briefly touch upon one perspective that has been prevalent throughout the chapters of the book. Difficulties in rights clearance or copyright-related issues are not the only reasons for the territorial delineation in either licensing contracts or the service offerings of copyright-protected content. There exists a broad variety of reasons for territorial content services, which can be grouped roughly into autonomous commercial considerations and other legal factors, some of which are prevalent in all online activities, whereas others depend on the specific subject matter.[131] The 2010 Report by KEA and MINES for the European Commission, for example, concludes that the partitioning of the market in the audiovisual sector is 'primarily the consequence of a commercial decision to market copyright-protected content along territorial lines', as has been illustrated through competition investigations in Apple and iTunes.[132] Among costs of compliance with different national regulatory frameworks, aspects such as level of consumer protection, protection of minors, data protection, contract and tax law, film financing, VAT regime, national rating system and private copying regulations have been noted to play a role. Commercial considerations regarding the market have been articulated as regards consumer demand, linguistic differences and costs of contextualisation and versioning, release windows, demand, level of broadband access, accessibility of payment methods, level of piracy, cost of customer care, and divergent advertiser

---

[131] These factors are aggregated below and have been noted in, e.g., Commission, 'A Digital Single Market Strategy for Europe – Analysis and Evidence Accompanying the document Communication from the Commission to the European Parliament, the Council, the European Economic and Social Committee and the Committee of the Regions', 28; Commission, 'Impact Assessment accompanying the document proposal for a Regulation of the European Parliament and of the Council on adressing [*sic*] geo-blocking and other forms of discriminiation [*sic*] based on place of residence or establishment or nationality within the Single Market', 62; KEA European Affairs and Mines ParisTech, 158; Commission, 'Report on the responses to the Public Consultation on the Review of the EU Copyright Rules' (2014) DG MARKT, July 2014, 10–11.

[132] KEA European Affairs and Mines ParisTech, 158. See, more broadly, Mazziotti, 'Is geo-blocking a real cause for concern?', 370.

preferences. Suffice it to underline here that any regulatory intervention needs to consider and be balanced against these aspects. In fact, as Mazziotti points out, 'territoriality is also indirectly encouraged by EU media policy'.[133] He contemplates that towards the background of cultural diversity, 'an integration of markets for creative contents might never become a reality in Europe, at least not fully'.[134]

Coming back to the scope of this book, it becomes apparent that, in order to be effective, any measure must not only solve the underlying licensing problem but also address the access dimension – which, in the streaming age, is largely dictated by contractual arrangements, in both the licensor–licensee and licensee–consumer relationships. Thus, some kind of limitation on the contractual freedom in these relationships might be necessary to ensure access for consumers.[135] Otherwise, as Hilty and Köklü comment, rights holders would be free to oblige licensees to apply certain TPMs and geo-block the content.[136] They note that 'the scope of permitted uses can be defined more narrowly by contractual terms than it would be in light of the law makers' initial intention as reflected in the codified limitations and exceptions in traditional copyright laws'.

As Hilty and Köklü remark, contractual terms 'have the potential to significantly undermine the use of limitations and exceptions, and hence, to sustainably shatter the envisaged balance of involved interests in copyright law'.[137] In a similar vein, Guibault remarks that '[c]onsumers were in a much better position to access and use digital content distributed in a tangible format'.[138] In the analogue, tangible world, the exhaustion principle provided for an effective corrective, originally established by the Court of Justice in *Deutsche Grammophon*, before being enshrined in secondary legislation. It seems, though, that the Court has not given up its *Coditel II* line just yet.[139] For the digital world, outside copyright-

---

[133] Mazziotti, 'Is geo-blocking a real cause for concern?', 370, in particular pointing to Art. 13(1) of Audiovisual Media Services Directive.

[134] Mazziotti, 'Is geo-blocking a real cause for concern?', 375–376.

[135] Which would necessarily need to be balanced with, e.g., Art. 16 of the Charter of Fundamental Rights of the European Union 2012/C326/02 [2012] OJ C326/391. Then again, collective management is also limiting contractual freedom.

[136] Hilty and Köklü, 'Limitations and Exceptions to Copyright in the Digital Age', p. 293.

[137] Ibid., p. 290.

[138] L. Guibault, 'Individual Licensing Models and Consumer Protection', Amsterdam Law School, 13. 'Individual Licensing Models and Consumer Protection', Legal Studies Research Paper No. 2016–01 (2016): http://ssrn.com/abstract=2713765

[139] See also O.-A. Rognstad, 'The CJEU's Recent Findings on Digital Exhaustion and Linking and their Impact on Nordic Copyright Law', *Nordiskt Immateriellt Rättskydd* [2015], 624. Dusollier comments that the application of the exhaustion principle to digital good should be object to further research: see S. Dusollier, 'The relations between copyright law and consumers' rights from a European perspective' (2010) Directorate General for Internal Policies; Policy Department C: Citizens' Rights and

protected content, the European legislator has found another response partly in the Services Directive from 2006.[140]

Hilty and Köklü therefore suggest a further cornerstone, which centres around 'such obligations imposed by rightholders be declared void by the law (...) [because] if the digital single market is to become reality, any kind of geo-blocking is unacceptable'.[141]

Notably, with the Cross-border Portability Regulation, the European legislator introduced exactly that and addresses all three relations, namely between rights holders, online content service providers and consumers.

Considering both the 'passive sales' or 'additional obligation' rationale and the Portability Regulation, it is apparent that the 'consumer' is becoming more present as subject in copyright-related discussions on policy and regulatory levels. While that is essential to the exploitation of copyright, Dusollier notes that, in the analogue environment, the 'consumer has in principle no role to play in copyright'.[142] In a similar fashion, Hugenholtz and Helberger note that 'consumers remained largely off copyright law's radar screen'.[143] In a report for the European Commission, Dusollier concludes that '[t]he consideration of (...) the consumer as an end-user of copyrighted works has increasingly steeped into the copyright regulatory framework, which raises new issues (...)'.[144] In its Green Paper of 1995, the Commission had already recognised that 'the public at large, i.e. private users, professional users and institutional users will play an important role in the Information Society'.[145] As regards access arrangements in the digital content world, this role might slowly be manifesting itself.

The above-presented routes are just screws to adjust the system, which are additionally dependent on an intervention limiting contractual freedom. Also, the 2014 study for the Commission considered a

---

Constitutional Affairs, No PE 432.742, 27: http://ssrn.com/abstract=2127736. See also Mazziotti, 'Is geo-blocking a real cause for concern?', 367.

[140] Services Directive (2006/123/EC); see also Chapter 3.

[141] Hilty and Köklü, 'Limitations and Exceptions to Copyright in the Digital Age', p. 294. They continue: 'This does of course not mean that rightholders will lose control over the use of their works. Rather, they will not be allowed to discriminate against certain users based on their origin.'

[142] Dusollier, 'The relations between copyright law and consumers' rights from a European perspective', 8.

[143] Ibid., 10, citing B. Hugenholtz and N. Helberger, 'No Place Like Home for Making a Copy: Private Copying in European Copyright Law and Consumer Law', *Berkeley Technology Law Journal*, 22 (2007), 1061, 1077. See also Guibault, 'Individual Licensing Models and Consumer Protection', 1.

[144] Dusollier, 'The relations between copyright law and consumers' rights from a European perspective', 10.

[145] See Commission, 'Green Paper on Copyright and Related Rights in the Information Society', 26.

'country of origin' principle, which would either preclude contractual territorial restrictions by rights holders, or preclude such restrictions by both rights holders and service providers.[146] To what extent such solutions are desirable is yet another question. Notably, Langus et al., for example, point towards potential loss in social welfare in the event of free riding or when rights holders change their practice and refrain from licensing, thereby making less content available, as well as causing problems for rights holders in maintaining established mechanisms in the audiovisual sector such as pre-sales or the exploitation windows.[147] Thus, it remains to be seen what role consumers get to play in the Digital Single Market.

In this book, for the sake of clarity, a variety of areas have been left untouched. Licensing and ultimately the offering of services that exploit copyright-protected works online depend on the definition of the relevant rights and their interpretation, which have been outside the focus of this book. Another key aspect is the setting of licensing fees or royalties. As noted earlier, this research, with its emphasis on regulatory intervention, has centred on collective management, where the regulatory focus has been on CMOs. The workings of other important licensing relations remain a subject for future research (and future regulatory intervention). I have looked at the exploitation of copyright in a digital world, and that in the rather traditional domains of legacy rights holders. On a deeper, and in some ways more profound, level, the present changes in the landscape not only provide a great opportunity but also come with the need to revisit and possibly adjust some of the fundamental considerations upon which copyright is built. Many scholars notice the emergence of new ways of creating cultural goods, which operate outside the traditional exclusivity paradigm.[148] Ricolfi, for example, claims that '(. . .) in our legal systems the incentive provided by exclusivity is no longer always indispensable to generate the optimal rate of creativity'.[149] Untouched questions regard creative uses or remixes under the new regime or the immense popularity of new forms of user-generated content distributed, for example, via

---

[146] Langus, Neven and Pouken, *Economic Analysis of the Territoriality of the Making Available Right in the EU*, pp. 107ff.

[147] Ibid., p. 111. In referring, inter alia, to the introduction of a country of origin principle that limits contractual freedom, they find that 'policy changes to limit stakeholders' ability to exploit online content on a territory-by-territory basis are likely to impact social welfare through various mechanisms'.

[148] See, e.g., M. Ricolfi, 'The New Paradigm of Creativity and Innovation and its Corollaries for the Law of Obligations' in P. Drahos, G. Ghidini and H. Ullrich (eds.), *Kritika: Essays on Intellectual Property* (Edward Elgar, 2015), pp. 134 and 149.

[149] See ibid., p. 135.

YouTube channels.[150] It might well be that some of the measures are more feasible in these areas than regarding the exploitation of rights by legacy rights holders. Instead, this book has centred on the question of how it is proposed to reconcile more traditional models with the Internet.

6.4   Concluding Remarks

This book has explored some of the many ways in which the European institutions work on solving the problem of cross-border access to copyright-protected content in the Digital Single Market. I have touched upon a multitude of different, and in part highly specific, problems and questions, which are contained in the sub-conclusions in the respective chapters. This section provides concluding remarks on a more general level.

The first goal of this book was directed towards an expository analysis of the regulatory framework for licensing of – and, related to this – access to online music and audiovisual content in cross-border situations. As has been seen, this regulatory framework is highly complex. There exist major differences between cross-border licensing issues depending on both the subject matter and the different institutional arrangements. Given the different traditions of rights management and exploitation, the licensing arrangements regarding audiovisual works and musical works have naturally evolved in distinctive ways. Territoriality issues appear on different levels in the exploitation chain: territorial exclusive licences in the downstream relationship as regards audiovisual content, on the one hand, and territorial exploitation by intermediaries as regards music, on the other. Whereas repertoire aggregation is a much more prominent concern when it comes to music, territorial delineation and geo-blocking are much more topical as regards audiovisual works. This makes it difficult to impose a 'one-size-fits-all' regulatory approach and might restrict the transferability of findings. Yet, many of the underlying aspects relate to similar challenges, which might be tackled by similar solutions.

The second objective of this book was directed towards an analysis of the interaction between the different regulatory frameworks, potential inconsistencies and their solution. Competition law has always been applied as a (necessary) regulatory corrective to the monopolistic system that IP rights, and more specifically copyright, provide. This is no different in the case of online exploitation by rights holders involved in music or

---

[150] See, e.g., A, Fagerjord, 'After Convergence: YouTube and Remix Culture' in J. Hunsinger, L. Klastrup and M. Allen (eds.), *International Handbook of Internet Research* (Springer, 2010).

audiovisual works and their intermediaries. Competition law and sector regulation support each other to a certain extent, but there also exist areas of inconsistency. An example of the former is the apparent codification of case law, both from the Court's findings and from the Commission's competition proceedings, in Directive 2014/26/EU. An example of the latter is the exemption of audiovisual content from the Geo-blocking Regulation (EU) 2018/302, which otherwise likely could have been seen as being in line with the Court of Justice's findings in *Premier League and Murphy*.

In both industry verticals, but to varying degrees, the interplay between sector regulation and competition proceedings has been helpful in mitigating the effects of licences based on territoriality and thereby in enabling cross-border dissemination. In the case of music, the introduction of competition between intermediaries appears as the motor behind regulatory intervention, sometimes disguised as facilitation of licensing. For various reasons, the Commission refrained from proposing a system that would create a 'one-stop shop' in Europe. In the case of audiovisual content, it appears that the EU lawmaker has dropped its reluctance and, instead of relying on traditional regulatory mechanisms, chosen more ambitious legislative tools. However, there are many carve-outs, probably as a result of the limited political feasibility of more comprehensive measures, which make for several areas yet to be addressed by the lawmaker – or the Court, which has shown that it is willing to re-assess the fitness of the current legislative framework and its earlier findings inter alia in *Premier League and Murphy*.

Strikingly, in both areas, the competition law route seems to go beyond operating as a purely *ex post* corrective, though. Instead, competition proceedings appear to be used in a quasi-regulatory fashion, which not only eliminate vertical or horizontal anti-competitive practices but define the regulatory playing field for cross-border access and multi-territorial licensing.[151] At the heart of this stands the intra-institutional interplay within the European Commission between its different functions and Directorates-General. Evidence suggests that this interplay is conscious and points towards a somewhat systematic approach of the measures under different routes. Thus, what appears to be a piecemeal approach based on the Commission's gradual adjustment of the market resembles, to a certain degree, a refined interplay.

The actions by the European legislator are, however, not as homogenous as they appear at first and there remain many open issues in addition to the ones that I have addressed in the preceding chapters. Cross-border

---

[151] The judicial corrective via the courts comes into play, too.

access and licensing are related, and so should be the respective policies, in order to make for a coherent framework. This book suggests that more coherent measures are necessary in order to reduce frictions and to promote cross-border access. Regulatory interventions to date may have been largely driven by a competition and harmonisation agenda rather than a focus on consumers and service providers – which, irrespective of its merits, seems to be at odds with the current Commission's ambitious goals of the completion of the Digital Single Market. Under this vision, supported by political impetus, the complex task ahead seems to be to develop pan-European solutions that benefit all European consumers while safeguarding the interests of rights holders and softly guiding them into a commercial reality of a Digital Single Market. In this balancing exercise, benefits for society at large and the political goal of market integration have to be reconciled. In the last five years, many challenges have been addressed, but much is yet to be attended to. The market has, up to now, not come up with convincing solutions that correspond to a Digital Single Market, it seems.

In the analogue world, the free movement of (copyright-protected) goods has found its counterpart to a large extent in the exhaustion principle. The digital counterpart to the free movement of services in an online copyright-content world has yet to be found. Both the CRM Directive (including the different regulatory initiatives until then) and the *Premier League and Murphy* case, as well as its follow-up from DG COMP and, to some extent, the recent Regulations, indicate that competition law is the regulators' instrument of choice.

We are in the middle of exciting times, in which the fundamental freedoms find their digital counterparts on the way to the Digital Single Market – and it is a bumpy road for cross-border access to copyright-protected works.

References

Official documents

Bundesministerium der Justiz und für Verbraucherschutz, 'Referentenentwurf des Bundesministeriums der Justiz und für Verbraucherschutz Entwurf eines Gesetzes zur Umsetzung der Richtlinie 2014/26/EU über die kollektive Wahrnehmung von Urheber- und verwandten Schutzrechten und die Vergabe von Mehrgebietslizenzen für Rechte an Musikwerken für die Online-Nutzung im Binnenmarkt sowie zur Änderung des Verfahrens betreffend die Geräte- und Speichermedienvergütung (VG-Richtlinie-Umsetzungsgesetz)' (2015) 09 June 2015

Bundesrat, 'Beschluss des Bundesrates, Vorschlag für eine Verordnung des Europäischen Parlaments und des Rates zur Gewährleistung der grenzüberschreitenden Portabilität von Online-Inhaltediensten im Binnenmarkt' (2016) Drucksache 167/16, 22 April 2016

Bundesrat, 'Beschluss des Bundesrates, Vorschlag für eine Verordnung des Europäischen Parlaments und des Rates mit Vorschriften für die Wahrnehmung von Urheberrechten und verwandten Schutzrechten in Bezug auf bestimmte Online-Übertragungen von Rundfunkveranstaltern und die Weiterverbreitung von Fernseh- und Hörfunkprogrammen' (2016) Drucksache 566/16, 16 December 2016

Bundesregierung, 'Entwurf eines Gesetzes zur Umsetzung der Richtlinie 2014/26/EU über die kollektive Wahrnehmung von Urheber- und verwandten Schutzrechten und die Vergabe von Mehrgebietslizenzen für Rechte an Musikwerken für die Online-Nutzung im Binnenmarkt sowie zur Änderung des Verfahrens betreffend die Geräte- und Speichermedienvergütung (VG-Richtlinie-Umsetzungsgesetz)' (2015) RegE Gesetzentwurf der Bundesregierung, 11 November 2015

Commission, 'A Copyright Policy for Creativity and Innovation in the European Union' (2014) White Paper, Internal Draft

'A Digital Agenda for Europe' (Communication from the Commission to the European Parliament, the Council, The European Economic and Social Committee and the Committee of the Regions) COM(2010) 245 final/2, Brussels, 19 May 2010

'A Digital Single Market Strategy for Europe – Analysis and Evidence Accompanying the document Communication from the Commission to the European Parliament, the Council, the European Economic and Social

Committee and the Committee of the Regions' (Commission Staff Working Document) SWD(2015) 100 final, Brussels, 6 May 2015

'A Digital Single Market Strategy for Europe' (Communication) COM(2015) 192 final

'A Single Market for Intellectual Property Rights, Boosting creativity and innovation to provide economic growth, high quality jobs and first class products and services in Europe' (Communication from the Commission to the European Parliament, the Council, The European Economic and Social Committee and the Committee of the Regions) COM(2011) 287 final, Brussels, 24 May 2011

'Antitrust: Commission accepts commitments by Paramount on cross-border pay-TV services' (Press release) IP/16/2645, Brussels, 26 July 2016

'Antitrust: Commission investigates restrictions affecting cross border provision of pay TV services' (Press release) IP/14/15, Brussels, 13 January 2014

'Antitrust: European Commission welcomes Apple's announcement to equalise prices for music downloads from iTunes in Europe' (Press release) IP/08/22, Brussels, 9 January 2008

'Better regulation for better results – An EU Agenda' (Communication) COM(2015) 215 final

'Better Regulation Guidelines' (latest edition 19.5.2015) SWD(2015) 111 final, 'Commission opens proceedings into collective licensing of music copyrights for online use' (Press release) IP/04/586, Brussels, 3 May 2004

'Commission proposes new e-commerce rules to help consumers and companies reap full benefit of Single Market' (Press release) IP/16/1887, Brussels, 25 May 2016

'Commissioner Michel Barnier welcomes the trilogue agreement on collective rights management' (Press release) MEMO/13/955, Brussels, 5 November 2013

'Competition: European Commission confirms sending a Statement of Objections against alleged territorial restrictions in on-line music sales to major record companies and Apple' (Press release) MEMO/07/126, Brussels, 3 April 2007

'Content in the Digital Single Market' (Communication) COM(2012) 789 final

'Copyright: Commission urges industry to deliver innovative solutions for greater access to online content' (Press release) IP/12/1394, Brussels, 18 December 2012

'Creative Content, in a European Digital Single Market: Challenges for the Future' (A Reflection Document of DG INFSO and DG MARKT) 22 October 2009

'Creative Europe, Supporting Europe's cultural and creative sectors' (European Commission, 2016) https://ec.europa.eu/programmes/creative-europe/media/online-distribution_en

'Cross-border Access to Online Content, Report' (2015) Flash Eurobarometer 411, TNS Political & Social

'Digital Single Market' (*European Commission*, 25 February 2016) https://ec.europa.eu/digital-single-market/digital-single-market

'Document accompanying the Communication from the Commission to the European Parliament, the Council, the European Economic and Social Committee and the Committee of the Regions on creative content online in the Single Market' (Commission Staff Working Document) SEC/2007/1710 final, Brussels, 3 January 2008

'European governance – A white paper' (2002) White Paper, COM/2001/0428 final, OJ C287/1

'Geo-Blocking practices in e-commerce; Issues paper presenting initial findings of the e-commerce sector inquiry conducted by the Directorate-General for Competition' (Commission Staff Working Document) SWD(2016) 70 final, Brussels, 18 March 2016

'Green Paper on Copyright and Related Rights in the Information Society' COM(95) 382 final, Brussels, 19 July 1995

'Guidelines on the applicability of Article 101 of the Treaty on the Functioning of the European Union to horizontal co-operation agreements' (Communication – 2011/C 11/01) [2011] OJ C 11/1

'Guidelines on the application of Article 81(3) of the Treaty' (Communication – Notice 2004/ C101/08) [2004] OJ C101/97

'Guidelines on the application of Article 101 of the Treaty on the Functioning of the European Union to technology transfer agreements' (Communication) [2014] OJ C89/3

'Guidelines on Vertical Restraints' (Information) [2010] OJ C130/1

'Impact Assessment accompanying the document Proposal for a Directive of the European Parliament and of the Council on collective management of copyright and related rights and multi-territorial licensing of rights in musical works for online uses in the internal market' (Commission Staff Working Document) SWD(2012) 204/2

'Impact Assessment accompanying the document Proposal for a Regulation of the European Parliament and of the Council to ensure the cross-border portability of online content services in the internal market' (Commission Staff Working Document) SWD(2015) 270/final, Brussels, 9 December 2015

'Impact Assessment accompanying the document proposal for a Regulation of the European Parliament and of the Council on adressing [sic] geo-blocking and other forms of discriminiation [sic] based on place of residence or establishment or nationality within the Single Market' (Commission Staff Working Document) SWD(2016) 173 final, Brussels, 25 May 2016

'Impact Assessment reforming cross-border collective management of copyright and related rights for legitimate online music services' (Commission Staff Working Document) SEC(2005) 1254, Brussels, 11 October 2005

'The Juncker Commission: A strong and experienced team standing for change' (Press release) IP/14/984, Brussels, 10 September 2014

'Lack of choice driving demand for film downloads' (Press release) IP/14/120, Brussels, 6 February 2014

'The Management of Copyright and Related Rights in the Internal Market' (Communication from the Commission to the Council, the European Parliament and the European Economic and Social Committee) COM (2004) 261 final, Brussels, 16 April 2004

'Monitoring of the 2005 Music Online Recommendation' Brussels, 7 February 2008

'Online Platforms and the Digital Single Market, Opportunities and Challenges for Europe' (2016) Communication from the Commission, Draft

'Proposal for a Directive of the European Parliament and of the Council on collective management of copyright and related rights and multi-territorial licensing of rights in musical works for online uses in the internal market' COM(2012) 372/2, 2012/0180 (COD), Brussels, 11 July 2012

'Proposal for a Directive of the European Parliament and of the Council amending Directive 2010/13/EU on the coordination of certain provisions laid down by law, regulation or administrative action in Member States concerning the provision of audiovisual media services in view of changing market realities' COM(2016) 287 final, 2016/0151 (COD), Brussels, 25 May 2016

'Proposal for a Directive of the European Parliament and of the Council on copyright in the Digital Single Market' COM/2016/0593 final – 2016/0280 (COD), Brussels, 14 September 2016

'Proposal for a Regulation of the European Parliament and of the Council laying down rules on the exercise of copyright and related rights applicable to certain online transmissions of broadcasting organisations and retransmissions of television and radio programmes' COM/2016/0594 final – 2016/0284 (COD), Brussels, 14 September 2016

'Proposal for a Regulation on addressing geo-blocking and other forms of discrimination based on customers' nationality, place of residence or place of establishment within the internal market and amending Regulation (EC) No 2006/2004 and Directive 2009/22/EC' COM(2016) 289 final, 2016/0152 (COD), Brussels, 25 May 2016

'Proposal for a Regulation on ensuring the cross-border portability of online content services' COM(2015) 627 final, 2015/0284 (COD), Brussels, 9 December 2015

'Public Consultation on the review of the EU copyright rules' (2013) http://ec.europa.eu/internal_market/consultations/2013/copyright-rules/docs/consultation-document_en.pdf

'Public Consultation on the review of the EU copyright rules' (23 July 2014) http://ec.europa.eu/internal_market/consultations/2013/copyright-rules/index_en.htm

'Questions and answers – Digital Single Market Strategy' (Press release) MEMO15/4920, Brussels, 6 May 2015

'Report from the European Commission on the application of Council Directive 93/83/EEC on the coordination of certain rules concerning copyright and rights related to copyright applicable to satellite broadcasting and cable retransmission' COM(2002) 430 final, Brussels, 26 July 2002

'Report on the responses to the Public Consultation on the Review of the EU Copyright Rules' (2014) DG MARKT, July 2014

'State of the Union 2016: Commission proposes modern EU copyright rules for European culture to flourish and circulate' (Press release), IP/16/3010, Strasbourg, 14 September 2016

'Study on a Community Initiative on the Cross-Border Collective Management of Copyright' (Commission Staff Working Document) Brussels, 7 July 2005

'Synopsis Report on the Responses to the Public Consultation on the Review of the Satellite and Cable Directive', 4 May 2016

'Towards a modern, more European copyright framework' (Communication) COM(2015) 626 final

Council of the European Union, 'Proposal for a Directive of the European Parliament and of the Council on collective management of copyright and related rights and multi-territorial licensing of rights in musical works for online use in the internal market, Statements' ('I/A' Item Note 2014, 6434/14) Brussels, 17 February 2014

'Online cross-border TV and radio broadcasts: Council agrees negotiating stance' (Press release) 808/17, 15 December 2017

'Proposal for a Regulation of the European Parliament and of the Council laying down rules on the exercise of copyright and related rights applicable to certain online transmissions of broadcasting organisations and retransmissions of television and radio programmes – Final Presidency compromise proposal' (Note 2017, 15898/17), 2016/0284 (COD), Brussels, 19 December 2017

'Draft Regulation of the European Parliament and of the Council on addressing unjustified geo-blocking and other forms of discrimination based on customers' nationality, place of residence or place of establishment within the internal market and amending Regulations (EC) No 2006/2004 and (EU) 2017/2394 and Directive 2009/22/EC, Statements' ('I/A' Item Note 2018, 6054/18), 2016/0152 (COD), Brussels, 19 February 2018

'Geo-blocking: Council adopts regulation to remove barriers to e-commerce' (Press release) 95/18, 27 February 2018

European Parliament, 'Report on a Community framework for collecting societies for authors' rights (2002/2274(INI))' Committee on Legal Affairs and the Internal Market, Rapporteur: Raina A. Mercedes Echerer, A5-0478/2003 FINAL, 11 December 2003

'Resolution on a Community framework for collective management societies in the field of copyright and neighbouring rights (2002/2274(INI))' P5_TA (2004)0036 OJ C92 E/425

'Resolution of 13 March 2007 on the Commission Recommendation of 18 October 2005 on collective cross-border management of copyright and related rights for legitimate online music services (2005/737/EC) (2006/2008(INI))' P6_TA(2007)0064 OJ C301 E/64

'Resolution of 25 September 2008 on collective cross-border management of copyright and related rights for legitimate online music services' P6_TA (2008)0462 (2010/C 8 E/19) OJ 8 E/105

'Opinion of the Committee on International Trade for the Committee on Legal Affairs on the proposal for a directive of the European Parliament and of the Council on collective management of copyright and related rights and multi-territorial licensing of rights in musical works for online uses in the internal market (COM(2012)0372 – C7-0183/2012 – 2012/0180(COD))' Committee on International Trade, Rapporteur: Helmut Scholz, 2012/0180(COD), 20 June 2013

'Opinion of the European Economic and Social Committee on the 'Proposal for a Directive of the European Parliament and of the Council on collective management of copyright and related rights and multi-territorial licensing of rights in musical works for online uses in the internal market' COM(2012) 372 final – 2012/0180 (COD)' 2013/C 44/18 OJ C44/104

'Report on the proposal for a directive of the European Parliament and of the Council on collective management of copyright and related rights and multi-territorial licensing of rights in musical works for online uses in the internal market (COM(2012)0372 – C7-0183/2012 – 2012/0180(COD))' Committee on Legal Affairs, Rapporteur: Marielle Gallo, 2012/0180 (COD), 4 October 2013

'Opinion of the Committee on Industry, Research and Energy for the Committee on Legal Affairs on the implementation of Directive 2001/29/EC of the European Parliament and of the Council of 22 May 2001 on the harmonisation of certain aspects of copyright and related rights in the information society (2014/2256(INI))' Committee on Industry, Research and Energy, Rapporteur: José Blanco López, 20 April 2015

'Report on the implementation of Directive 2001/29/EC of the European Parliament and of the Council of 22 May 2001 on the harmonisation of certain aspects of copyright and related rights in the information society (2014/2256(INI))' Committee on Legal Affairs, Rapporteur: Julia Reda, PE 546.580v03-00, A8-0209/2015, 24 June 2015

'Draft Opinion of the Committee on the Internal Market and Consumer Protection for the Committee on Legal Affairs on the proposal for a regulation of the European Parliament and of the Council on ensuring the cross-border portability of online content services in the internal market (COM (2015)0627 – C8-0392/2015 – 2015/0284(COD))' Committee on the Internal Market and Consumer Protection, Rapporteur: Marco Zullo, PE583.879v01-00, 29 June 2016

'Draft Report on the proposal for a regulation of the European Parliament and of the Council on ensuring the cross-border portability of online content services in the internal market' Committee on Legal Affairs, Rapporteur: Jean-Marie Cavada, 2015/0284(COD), 21 June 2016

'Opinion of the Committee on Culture and Education for the Committee on Legal Affairs on the proposal for a regulation of the European Parliament and of the Council on ensuring the cross-border portability of online content services in the internal market (COM(2015)0627 – C8-0392/2015 – 2015/0284(COD))' Committee on Culture and Education, Rapporteur: Sabine Verheyen, 2015/0284(COD), 29 June 2016

'Report on the proposal for a regulation of the European Parliament and of the Council laying down rules on the exercise of copyright and related rights applicable to certain online transmissions of broadcasting organisations and retransmissions of television and radio programmes (COM(2016) 0594 – C8-0384/2016 – 2016/0284(COD))' Committee on Legal Affairs, Rapporteur: Tiemo Wölken, 27 November 2017

European Parliamentary Research Service, 'Regulating online TV and radio broadcasting' (Briefing, EU Legislation in Process), PE 620.217, April 2018

Folketinget, 'Political opinion on Commission proposal for reform of EU copyright rules (Erik Christensen, Orla Hav)' 11 May 2017

Intellectual Property Office, 'Collective rights management in the digital single market, Consultation on the implementation of the EU Directive on the collective management of copyright and multi-territorial licensing of online music rights in the internal market' [2015]

Joint Political Declaration of 28 September 2011 of Member States and the Commission on explanatory documents 2011/C 369/02 [2011] OJ C369/14

Kulturministeriet, 'Forslag til Lov om kollektiv forvaltning af ophavsret' (2015) Dok nr. 2772691

Licenses for Europe, 'Ten pledges to bring more content online' (13 November 2011) http://ec.europa.eu/internal_market/copyright/docs/licences-for-europe/131113_ten-pledges_en.pdf

Norden, 'Nordic Council: Digital television must be available to view throughout the Nordic Region' (*Nordic Council*, 2 November 2017) www.norden.org/en/news-and-events/news/nordic-council-digital-television-must-be-available-to-view-throughout-the-nordic-region

Praesidum of the European Convention, 'Explanations relating to the Charter of Fundamental Rights' (2007/C 303/02) [2007] OJ C303/17

Bibliography

Ackrill, R. and A. Kay, 'Multiple streams in EU policy-making: The case of the 2005 sugar reform', *Journal of European Public Policy*, 18 (2011), 72

Aguiar, L. and J. Waldfogel, 'Streaming Reaches Flood Stage: Does Spotify Stimulate or Depress Music Sales?' (2015) NBER Working Paper Series, Working Paper 21653: www.nber.org/papers/w21653

Ahlborn, C., D. S. Evens and A. J. Padila, 'The Logic & Limits of the "Exceptional Circumstances Test" in Magill and IMS Health', *Fordham International Law Journal*, 28 (2004), 1109

Andersen, M. B., *Ret og metode* (Gjellerup, 2002)

Ansip, Andrus C., 'Speech by Vice-President Ansip at the Creators Conference' (31 May 2016): https://ec.europa.eu/commission/2014–2019/ansip/announcements/speech-vice-president-ansip-creators-conference_en

Anthonis, E., 'Will the CRM-directive succeed re-aggregating the mechanical reproduction rights in the Anglo-American music repertoire?', *International Journal of Intellectual Property Management*, 7 (2014), 151

Aoki, R. and A. Schiff, 'Intellectual property clearinghouses: The effects of reduced transaction costs in licensing', *Information Economics and Policy*, 22 (2010), 218

Arezzo, E., 'Competition and intellectual property protection in the market for the provision of multi-territorial licensing of online rights in musical works – lights and shadows of the new European Directive 2014/26/EU', *International Review of Intellectual Property and Competition Law*, 46 (2015), 534

Axhamn, J., 'Nya normer för kollektiv rättighetsförvaltning på upphovsrättens område', *Nordiskt Immateriellt Rättskydd* (2015) 675

Axhamn, J. and J. Guibault, *Cross-border extended collective licensing: A solution to online dissemination of Europe's cultural heritage?* (Final report prepared for EuropeanaConnect, 2011)

Barbière, C., 'Geo-blocking attacked from all sides' (*EurActiv*, 2015): www.euractiv.com/section/digital/news/geo-blocking-attacked-from-all-sides/

Barker, G. R., 'Assessing the Economic Impact of Copyright Law: Evidence of the Effect of Free Music Downloads on the Purchase of Music CDs'. Centre for Law and Economics, ANU College of Law Working Paper No. 2 (2012)

Barnard, C. and P. Steve, *European Union Law* (Oxford University Press, 2014)

Batchelor, B. and T. Jenkins, 'FA Premier League: The broader implications for copyright licensing', *European Competition Law Review*, 33 (2012), 157

Batchelor, B. and L. Montani, 'Exhaustion, essential subject matter and other CJEU judicial tools to update copyright for an online economy', *Journal of Intellectual Property Law & Practice*, 10 (2015), 591

Batikas, M., E. Gomez-Herrera and B. Martens, 'Geographic Fragmentation in the EU Market for e-Books: The case of Amazon', Institute for Prospective Technological Studies, Digital Economy Working Paper 2015/13

Bently, L., 'Harmonization By Stealth: Copyright and the ECJ', (Fordham IP Conference, 2010): http://fordhamipconference.com/wp-content/uploads/2010/08/Bently_Harmonization.pdf

Besen, S. and S. N. Kirby, *Compensating Creators of Intellectual Property* (RAND Corp, 1989)

Besen, S. M., S. N. Kirby and S. C. Salop, 'An Economic Analysis of Copyright Collectives', *Virginia Law Review*, 78 (1992), 383

Black, J., 'Critical reflections on regulation', Centre for Analysis of Risk and Regulation, London School of Economics and Political Science (2002): eprints.lse.ac.uk/35985

Blomqvist, J., *Primer on International Copyright and Related Rights* (Edward Elgar, 2014)

Bonadio, E., 'Collective management of music copyright in the Internet age and the EU initiatives: From reciprocal representation agreements to open platforms' World Library and Information Congress, Helsinki, 2012: www.ifla.org/past-wlic/2012/148-bonadio-en.pdf

Brinker, I. and T. Holzmuller, 'Competition law and copyright – observations from the world of collecting societies', *European Intellectual Property Review*, 32 (2010) 553

Bundesverband Informationswirtschaft Telekommunikation und Neue Medien e.V. (bitkom), 'Stellungnahme zum Regierungsentwurf eines Verwertungsgesellschaftengesetzes (VGG)' (Berlin: 14 January 2016)

Bureau Européen des Unions de Consommateurs (BEUC), 'Collective Management of Copyright and Related Rights and Multi-territorial Licensing of Rights in Musical Works for Online, Proposal for a Directive', Ref.: X/2013/001 (Brussels, 08 January 2013): https://ameliaandersdotter .eu/sites/default/files/beuc_-_crm.pdf

Capobianco, A., 'Licensing of Music Rights: Media Convergence and EC Competition Law', *European Intellectual Property Review*, 26 (2004), 113

Caroll, M. W., 'A Realist Approach to Copyright Law's Formalities', *Berkeley Technology Law Journal*, 28 (2013), 1511

Castets-Renard, C., '"Digital Single Market": The European Commission presents its first measures in Copyright Law' (2016) *French Review: Recueil Dalloz*, 2016, n° 7, p. 388 (forthcoming): http://ssrn.com/ abstract=2802729

Chittenden, F., T. Abler and D. Xiao, 'Impact Assessment in the EU' in S. Weatherill (ed.), *Better Regulation: Studies of the Oxford Institute of European and Comparative Law*, vol. 6 (Hart Publishing, 2007)

Clark, R., 'Exhaustion, geographical licensing restrictions and transfer prohibitions: Two surprising decisions', *Journal of Intellectual Property Law & Practice*, 8 (2013), 460

Coase, R. H., 'The Nature of the Firm', *Economica* (1937), 386–405

Coase, R. H., 'The Problem of Social Cost', *Journal of Law and Economics*, 3 (1960), 1–44

Cole, M., 'PRSfM/STIM/GEMA/JV: Multijurisdictional Licencing for Music Streaming', *Journal of European Competition Law & Practice*, 7 (2016), 257

Colomo, P. I., 'The Commission Investigation into Pay TV Services: Open Questions', *Journal of European Competition Law & Practice*, 5 (2014), 531

'Copyright Licensing and the EU Digital Single Market Strategy' (2015) LSE Law, Society and Economy Working Papers 19/2015: http://ssrn.com/ abstract=2697178

'Copyright reform through competition law? The Commission's statement of objections in the pay TV investigation' (*Chillin'Competition*, 24 July 2015): https://chillingcompetition.com/2015/07/24/copyright-reform-through-com petition-law-the-commissions-statement-of-objections-in-the-pay-tv- investigation/

Crampes, C. and A. Hollander, 'The regulation of audiovisual content: Quotas and conflicting objectives', *Journal of Regulatory Economics*, 34 (2008), 195

Cryer, R., T. Hervey and B. Sokhi-Bulley, *Research Methodologies in EU and International Law* (Hart Publishing, 2011)

Danaher, B. and J. Waldfogel, 'Reel Piracy: The Effect of Online Film Piracy on International Box Office Sales', University of Minnesota and NBER (2012): http://ssrn.com/abstract=1986299

Dang Nguyen, G., S. Dejean and F. Moreau, 'Are Streaming and Other Music Consumption Modes Substitutes or Complements?': http://ssrn.com/ abstract=2025071

David, P. A., 'Why are institutions the "carriers of history"?: Path dependence and the evolution of conventions, organizations and institutions', *Structural Change and Economic Dynamics*, 5 (1994), 205

de Búrca, G. and Scott, J., 'New Governance, Law and Constitutionalism' (2006): www.ucl.ac.uk/laws/clge/docs/govlawconst.pdf

de Vries, S., 'Sport, TV and IP rights: Premier League and Karen Murphy', *Common Market Law Review*, 50 (2013), 591

Dehin, V., 'The Future of Legal Online Music Services in the European Union: A Review of the EU Commission's Recent Initiatives in Cross-Border Copyright Management', *European Intellectual Property Review*, 32 (2010), 220

Di Porto, F. and J. Drexl, 'Preface' in F. Di Porto and J. Drexl (eds.), *Competition Law as Regulation* (Edward Elgar, 2015)

Doukas, D., 'The Sky is not the (only) limit: Sports broadcasting without frontiers and the Court of Justice: Comment on Murphy', 37 *European Law Review* (2012), 605

Dreier, T., 'Regulating competition by way of copyright limitation and exceptions' in P. Torremans (ed.), *Copyright Law, A Handbook of Contemporary Research* (Edward Elgar, 2007)

'Online and Its Effect on the "Goods" versus "Services" Distinction', *International Review of Intellectual Property and Competition Law*, 44 (2013), 137

Drexl, J., 'Competition in the field of collective management: Preferring "creative competition" to allocative efficiency in European copyright law' in P. Torremans (ed.), *Copyright Law, A Handbook of Contemporary Research* (Edward Elgar, 2007)

'Collective Management of Copyrights and the EU Principle of Free Movement of Services after the OSA Judgment – In Favour of a More Balanced Approach' in K. Purnhagen and P. Rott (eds.), *Varieties of European Economic Law and Regulation, Liber Amicorum for Hans Micklitz*, vol. 3 (Springer, 2014)

Drexl, J. and others, 'Comments of the Max Planck Institute for Intellectual Property and Competition Law on the Proposal for a Directive of the European Parliament and of the Council on Collective Management of Copyright and Related Rights', Max Planck Institute for Intellectual Property and Competition Law Research Paper No. 13–04 (2012): http://ssrn.com/abstract=2208971

Dunne, N., *Competition Law and Economic Regulation, Making and Managing Markets* (Cambridge University Press, 2015)

Dusollier, S., 'The relations between copyright law and consumers' rights from a European perspective', Directorate General for Internal Policies; Policy Department C: Citizens' Rights and Constitutional Affairs, No PE 432.742 (2010): http://ssrn.com/abstract=2127736

Enser, J., 'Another consultation from Brussels- anyone for SatCab?' (*IP Kat*, 27 August 2015): http://the1709blog.blogspot.dk/2015/08/another-consulta tion-from-brussels.html

European Broadcasting Union (EBU), 'EBU Welcomes Steps to Update EU Cable and Satellite Directive for the Digital Age' (*EBU*, 26 August 2015): www.ebu.ch/news/2015/08/ebu-welcomes-steps-to-update-eu

'Satellite and Cable Licensing Solutions: The Key to Enhancing Cross-border Access to Online TV and Radio Content' *EBU* (9 December 2015): www.ebu.ch/news/2015/12/satellite-and-cable-directive-li

Fagerjord, A., 'After Convergence: YouTube and Remix Culture' in J. Hunsinger, L. Klastrup and M. Allen (eds.), *International Handbook of Internet Research* (Springer, 2010)

Fahey, E., 'Does the Emperor Have Financial Crisis Clothes? Reflections on the Legal Basis of the European Banking Authority', *Modern Law Review* (2011): ssrn.com/abstract=1715524

Farrand, B., *Networks of power in digital copyright law and policy* (Routledge, 2014)

'The EU Portability Regulation: One small step for cross-border access, one giant leap for Commission copyright policy?', *European Intellectual Property Review*, 38 (2016), 321

Favale, M., M. Kretschmer and P. C. Torremans, 'Is there an EU Copyright Jurisprudence? An Empirical Analysis of the Workings of the European Court of Justice', *Modern Law Review*, 79 (2016), 31–75: http://ssrn.com/abstract=2643699

Ficsor, M., 'Collective Management and Multi-territorial Licensing: Key Issues of the Transposition of Directive 2014/26/EU' in I. A. Stamatoudi (ed.), *New Developments in EU and International Copyright Law* (Kluwer Law International, 2016)

Gaster, J., 'Das urheberrechtliche Territorialitätsprinzip aus Sicht des Europäischen Gemeinschaftsrechts', *Zeitschrift für Urheber- und Medienrecht* (2016) 8

Geiger, C. (ed.), *The construction of intellectual property in the European Union: searching for coherence* (Edward Elgar, 2013)

Geiger, C. and others, 'Declaration, A Balanced Interpretation of the "Three-Step Test" in Copyright Law', *Journal of Intellectual Property, Information Technology and Electronic Commerce Law*, (2010) 119

'Moving out of the economic crisis: What role and shape for intellectual property rights in the European Union?' in H. Kalimo and M. S. Jansson (eds.), *EU Economic Law in a Time of Crisis* (Edward Elgar, 2016)

George, L. M. and C. Peukert, 'YouTube Decade: Cultural Convergence in Recorded Music', NET Institute, Working Paper #14–11 (2014): http://ssrn.com/abstract=2506357

Gervais, D., 'Collective Management: Theory and Practice in the Digital Age' in D. Gervais (ed.), *Collective Management of Copyright and Related Rights*, 2nd edn. (Wolters Kluwer, 2010)

'Keynote: The Landscape of Collective Management Schemes', *Columbia Journal of Law & the Arts*, 34 (2011), 423

Gervais, D. and A. Maurushat, 'Fragmented Copyright, Fragmented Management: Proposals to Defrag Copyright Management', *Canadian Journal of Law and Technology*, 2 (2003), 15

GESAC, 'Collective Rights Management in Europe – our thoughts on the road ahead' (Brussels, February 2013)

Ghafele, R., 'Europe's Lost Royalty Opportunity: A Comparison of Potential and Existing Digital Music Royalty Markets in Ten Different E.U. Member States', *Review of Economic Research on Copyright Issues*, 11 (2014), 60

Gilliéron, P., 'Collecting Societies and the Digital Environment', *International Review of Intellectual Property and Competition Law* (2006) 939

Ginsburg, J. C., 'From Having Copies to Experiencing Works: The Development of an Access Right in U.S. Copyright Law' (2000)

'"European Copyright Code" – Back to First Principles (with Some Additional Detail)' Columbia Public Law & Legal Theory Working Papers 9193: http://lsr.nellco.org/columbia_pllt/9193

'Authors' transfer and license contracts under U.S. copyright law' in J. de Werra (ed.), *Research Handbook on Intellectual Property Licensing*, ch. 1 (Edward Elgar, 2013)

Gómez, A. M. P. and M. A. E. Arcila, 'Collective administration of online rights in musical works: Analysing the economic efficiency of Directive 2014/26/EU', *International Journal of Intellectual Property Management*, 7 (2014), 103

Gomez-Herrera, E. and B. Martens, 'Language, Copyright and Geographic Segmentation in the EU Digital Single Market for Music and Films' (2015) Digital Economy Working Paper 2015–4

Graber, C. B., 'Collective rights management, competition policy and cultural diversity: EU lawmaking at a crossroads', *World Intellectual Property Organization Journal*, 4 (2012), 35

Greeley, K., 'Recommendations, Communications, and Directives, oh my: How the European Union isn't solving its licensing problem', *Georgetown Journal of International Law*, 44 (2013), 1523

Greenberg, J., 'For Netflix, Discontent over Blocked VPNs is Boiling' (*WIRED*, 3 July 2016): www.wired.com/2016/03/netflix-discontent-blocked-vpns-boiling/

Guibault, L., 'The Draft Collective Management Directive' in I. A. Stamatoudi and P. Torremans (eds.), *EU Copyright Law: A Commentary* (Edward Elgar, 2014)

'Individual Licensing Models and Consumer Protection', Amsterdam Law School Legal Studies Research Paper No. 2016–01 (2016): http://ssrn.com/abstract=2713765

Guibault, L. and J. P. Quintais, 'Copyright, technology and the exploitation of audiovisual works in the EU', (2014) Iris plus, 7

Guibault, L. and S. van Gompel, 'Collective Management in the European Union' in D. Gervais (ed.), *Collective Management of Copyright and Related Rights*, 2nd edn. (Kluwer Law International, 2010)

Gurry, Francis, '2013 Address by the Director General' *WIPO Assemblies* – September 23 to October 2, 2013: www.wipo.int/about-wipo/en/dgo/speeches/a_51_dg_speech.html

Gyertyánfy, P., 'Collective Management of Music Rights in Europe after the CISAC Decision', *International Review of Intellectual Property and Competition Law* (2010) 59

Handke, C., 'Collective administration' in R. Watt (ed.), *Handbook on the Economics of Copyright* (Edward Elgar, 2014)

'Joint Copyright Management by Collecting Societies and Online Platforms: An Economic Analysis': http://ssrn.com/abstract=2616442

Handke, C., J. P. Quintais and B. Balazs, 'The Economics of Copyright Compensation Systems for Digital Use' (SERCI Annual Congress 2013, Paris, July 2013)

Handke, C. and R. Towse, 'Economics of Copyright Collecting Societies' (2007): http://ssrn.com/abstract=1159085

Hansen, G. and A. Schmidt-Bischoffshausen, *Economic functions of collecting societies – Collective rights management in the light of transaction cost- and information economics* (2007)

Hilty, R. M., 'Individual, multiple and collective ownership: What impact on competition?' in J. Rosén (ed.), *Individualism and Collectiveness in Intellectual Property Law* (Edward Elgar, 2012)

Hilty, R. M. and K. Köklü, 'Limitations and Exceptions to Copyright in the Digital Age' in I. A. Stamatoudi (ed.), *New Developments in EU and International Copyright Law* (Kluwer Law International, 2016)

Hilty, R. M. and T. Li, 'Control Mechanisms for CRM Systems and Competition Law' (2016) Max Planck Institute for Innovation and Competition Research Paper No. 16–04 (Max Planck Institute for Innovation and Competition): http://ssrn.com/abstract=2772482

Hilty, R. M. and S. Nérisson, 'Collective Copyright Management and Digitization: The European Experience' (2013) Max Planck Institute for Intellectual Property and Competition Law Research Paper No. 13–09 (Max Planck Institute for Intellectual Property and Competition Law): http://ssrn.com/abstract=2247870

Hoeren, T., *Collecting societies and cultural diversity in the music sector* (2009)

Hoeren, T. and C. Altemark, 'Musikverwertungsgesellschaften und das Urheberrechtswahrnehmungsgesetz am Beispiel der CELAS' *Gewerblicher Rechtsschutz und Urheberrecht* (2010) 16

Hollander, A., 'Market structure and performance in intellectual property', *International Journal of Industrial Organization*, 2 (1984), 199

Hugenholtz, P. B., 'Harmonization or Unification of EU Copyright Law' in J. Axhamn (ed.), *Copyright in a Borderless Online Environment* (Norsteds Juriidik, 2012)

'Audiovisual Archives across Borders – Dealing with Territorially Restricted Copyright' *IRIS Special* 49 (2010)

'Harmonisation or Unification of European Union Copyright Law', *Monash University Law Review*, 38 (2012), 4

'Extending the SatCab Model to the Internet' Study commissioned by BEUC (Brussels, 2015)

Hunt, J. and J. Shaw, 'Fairy Tale of Luxembourg? Reflections on Law and Legal Scholarship in European Integration' in D. Phinnemore and A. Warleigh-Lack (eds.), *Reflections on European Integration, 50 Years of the Treaty of Rome* (Palgrave Macmillan, 2009)

Hviid, M., S. Schroff and J. Street, 'Regulating CMOs by competition: an incomplete answer to the licensing problem?' (2016) CREATe Working Paper 2016/03 (March 2016)

International Copyright Enterprise (ICE), 'Response, Global Repertoire Database Request for Information' (2010)

Kalimo, H., K. Olkkonen and J. Vaario, 'EU intellectual property rights law – driving innovation or stifling the Digital Single Market?' in H. Kalimo and M. S. Jansson (eds.), *EU Economic Law in a Time of Crisis* (Edward Elgar, 2016)

Katz, A., 'The potential demise of another natural monopoly: Rethinking the collective administration of performing rights', *Journal of Competition Law and Economics*, 1 (2005), 541

'The potential demise of another natural monopoly: New technologies and the administration of performing rights', *Journal of Competition Law and Economics*, 2 (2006), 245

Katz, B. G., 'Territorial Exclusivity in the Soft Drink Industry', *Journal of Industrial Economics*, 27 (1978), 85

Kautio, T., N. Lefever and M. Määttä, *Assessing the Operation of Copyright and Related Rights Systems, Methodology Framework* (Foundation for Cultural Policy Research (Cupore publication 26 2016)

Kay, A., 'A critique of the use of path dependency in policy studies', *Public Administration*, 83 (2005), 553

KEA European Affairs, *The Collective Management of Rights in Europe: The Quest for Efficiency* (Study commissioned by the European Commission, 2006)

Licensing music works and transaction costs in Europe (2012)

KEA European Affairs and Mines ParisTech, *Multi-Territory Licensing of Audiovisual Works in the European Union* (Final Report prepared for the European Commission, DG Information Society and Media, 2010)

Keller, P., 'Copyright Communication: The good, the bad, and the ugly' (*COMMUNIA Association*, 10 December 2015): www.communia-associa tion.org/2015/12/10/copyright-communication-commission-communiac tion-the-good-the-bad-and-the-ugly/

Kennedy, D., 'The Mystery of Global Governance' in J. L. Dunoff and J. P. Trachtman (eds.), *Ruling the World? Constitutionalism, International Law, and Global Governance* (Cambridge University Press, 2009)

Kivistö, M., 'Multi-territorial online licensing in the light of Title III of the Directive on collective rights management', *Nordiskt Immateriellt Rättskydd* (2015) 706

Klabbers, J., 'Law-making and Constitutionalism' in J. Klabbers, A. Peters and G. Ulfstein (eds.), *The Constitutionalization of International Law* (Oxford University Press, 2009)

KODA, 'Creative Commons nu i Danmark' KODA (Copenhagen, 24 January 2008)

KODA (Hüttel, Jakob), 'The CISAC Case & the 2005 Recommendation' *FEMR,* Sophienberg, 24 April 2009

Kretschmer, M., 'Access and Reward in the Information Society: Regulating the Collective Management of Copyright' (2007) CIPPM Working Paper 2007: http://dx.doi.org/10.2139/ssrn.2739837

'The Failure of Property Rules in Collective Administration: Rethinking Copyright Societies as Regulatory Instruments', *European Intellectual Property Review* (2002) 126

Kretschmer, T. and C. Peukert, 'Video Killed the Radio Star? Online Music Videos and Digital Music Sales' (2015): http://ssrn.com/abstract =2425386

Lamadrid, A., 'Breaking news: Pay-TV investigation- Paramount offers commitments' (*Chillin'Competition*, 22 April 2016): https://chillingcompetition.com/2016/04/22/breaking-news-pay-tv-investigation-paramount-offers-commitments/

Langenius, C., 'The ramifications of pan-European licensing for Nordic collective rights management', *Nordiskt Immateriellt Rättskydd* (2008) 29

Langus, G., D. Neven and S. Pouken, *Economic Analysis of the Territoriality of the Making Available Right in the EU* (Report prepared for the European Commission, DG MARKT, 2014)

Lessig, L., 'The New Chicago School', *Journal of Legal Studies*, XXVII (1998), 661

Liebowitz, S. J. and R. Watt, 'How to best ensure remuneration for creators in the market for music? Copyright and its alternatives', *Journal of Economic Surveys*, 20 (2006), 513

Lindholm, J. and A. Kaburakis, 'Cases C-403/08 and C-429/08 FA Premier League Ltd and Others v QC Leisure and Others; and Karen Murphy v Media Protection Services Ltd, 4 Oct 2011' in J. Andersen (ed.), *Leading Cases in Sports Law* (Springer, 2013)

Liu, W., 'Models for Collective Management of Copyright from an International Perspective: Potential Changes for Enhancing Performance', *Journal of Intellectual Property Rights*, 17 (2012), 46

Lüder, T., 'First experience with EU wide online music licensing', *Gewerblicher Rechtsschutz und Urheberrecht, Internationaler Teil* (2007), 649

Maasø, A., *User-centric settlement for music streaming; A report on the distribution of income from music streaming in Norway, based on streaming data from WiMP Music* (Clouds & Concerts research group, University of Oslo, 2014)

Marchegiani, L., 'Le licenze multiterritoriali per l'uso online di opere musicali nella disciplina comunitaria della gestione collettiva dei diritti d'autore e dei diritti connessi', *Osservatorio del diritto civile e commerciale*, 2 (2013), 293

Martin-Prat, M., 'The Future of Copyright in Europe', *Columbia Journal of Law & the Arts*, 38 (2014), 29

Matulionytė, R., 'Cross-Border Collective Management and Principle of Territoriality: Problems and Possible Solutions in the EU', *Journal of World Intellectual Property*, 11 (2009), 467

Max Planck Institute for Intellectual Property, Competition and Tax Law, 'Stellungnahme des Max-Planck-Instituts für Geistiges Eigentum, Wettbewerbs- und Steuerrecht zuhanden des Bundesministeriums der Justiz betreffend die Empfehlung der Europäischen Kommission über die Lizenzierung von Musik für das Internet vom 18. Oktober 2005 (2005/737/EG)' (2006): www.ip.mpg.de/fileadmin/ipmpg/content/stellungnahmen/stellungnahme-lizenzierungmusik1_01.pdf

Mazziotti, G., 'New Licensing Models for Online Music Services in the European Union: From Collective to Customized Management' Public Law & Legal

Theory Working Paper Group Paper Number 11–269, Columbia Law School: http://ssrn.com/abstract=1814264

'Is geo-blocking a real cause for concern?', *European Intellectual Property Review*, 38 (2016) 365

Merges, R. P., 'Contracting into Liability Rules: Intellectual Property Rights and Collective Rights Organizations', *California Law Review*, 84 (1996), 1293

Mestmäcker, E.-J., 'Collecting Societies' in C.-D. Ehlermann (ed.), *The Interaction between Competition Law and Intellectual Property Law*, European Competition Law Annual, 2nd edn. (Hart Publishing, 2005)

Metzger, A. and T. Heinemann, 'The Right of the Author to Grant Licenses for Non-Commercial Use: Creative Commons Licenses and the Directive on Collective Management', *Journal of Intellectual Property, Information Technology and Electronic Commerce Law*, 6 (2015), 11

Milosic, K., 'The Failure of the Global Repertoire Database' (*Hypebot*, 31 August 2015): www.hypebot.com/hypebot/2015/08/the-failure-of-the-global-repertoire-database-effort-draft.html

Morrison, A., 'European Commission's draft Geo-Blocking Regulation fails to clear the way' (*King & Wood Mallesons*), 21 June 2016: www.kwm.com/en/uk/knowledge/insights/european-commissions-draft-geo-blocking-regulation-fails-to-clear-the-way-20160621

Motta, M., P. Rey and N. Vettas, *Hardcore restrictions under the Block Exemption Regulation on vertical agreements: An economic view* (2009)

NCB, 'Buma/Stemra teams up with ICE and NMP for online administration services' *Press release* (Copenhagen, 3 December 2014)

Nérisson, S., 'Has Collective Management of Copyright Run Its Course? Not So Fast', *International Review of Intellectual Property and Competition Law* (2015), 505

Ohly, A., 'Geoblocking zwischen Wirtschafts-, Kultur-, Verbraucher- und Europapolitik', *Zeitschrift für Urheber-und Medienrecht* (2015) 942

Papadopoulos, Y., 'Problems of Democratic Accountability in Network and Multi-Level Governance', *European Law Journal*, 13 (2007), 469

Peczenik, A. (ed.), *Legal Doctrine and Legal Theory*, vol. 4, 'Scientia' (Springer, 2005)

Peifer, K.-N., 'Umsetzung der EU-Richtlinie für Verwertungsgesellschaften in deutsches Recht, Umsetzungsbedarf aus wissenschaftlicher Sicht', *Zeitschrift für Urheber-und Medienrecht* (2014) 453

Peitz, M. and P. Waelbroeck, 'An Economist's Guide to Digital Music' (2004) CESifo Working Paper No. 1333: cesifo.oxfordjournals.org/content/51/2–3/359.full.pdf

Perlmutter, S., 'Making Copyright Work for a Global Market: Policy Revision on Both Sides of the Atlantic', *Columbia Journal of Law & the Arts* (2014), 49, 49

Peters, A., 'Membership in the Global Constitutional Community' in J. Klabbers, A. Peters and G. Ulfstein (eds.), *The Constitutionalization of International Law* (Oxford University Press, 2009)

Petteri, G., 'Harmonising Collective Rights Management and Multi-Territorial Licensing of Music for Online Use in the European Union: A Review of the

Collective Rights Management Directive 2014/26/EU', *Nordiskt Immateriellt Rättskydd* (2015) 150

Peukert, A., 'Territoriality and Extraterritoriality in Intellectual Property Law' in G. Handl, J. Zekoll and P. Zumbansen (eds.), *Beyond Territoriality: Transnational Legal Authority in an Age of Globalization* (Brill Academic Publishing, 2012): http://ssrn.com/abstract=1592263

Pierre, J., 'Introduction: Understanding Governance' in J. Pierre (ed.), *Debating Governance* (Oxford University Press, 2000)

Plucinska, J., 'Leak: The Commission's latest geo-blocking plans' (*POLITICO*, 9 May 2016): www.politico.eu/pro/geoblocking-ecommerce-european-com mission-leak-eu/

POLARIS Nordic, 'Ground breaking initiative: Cross-border alliance lead the way for future rights management', *Press release* (3 February 2014)

Poll, G., 'CELAS, PEDL & Co.: Metamorphose oder Anfang vom Ende der kollektiven Wahrnehmung von Musik-Online-Rechten in Europa?', *Zeitschrift für Urheber-und Medienrecht* (2008) 500

Posner, R. A., 'Intellectual Property: The Law and Economics Approach', *Journal of Economics Perspectives*, 19 (2005), 57

'Transaction Costs and Antitrust Concerns in the Licensing of Intellectual Property', *John Marshall Review of Intellectual Property Law*, 4 (2005), 325

Quintais, J. P., 'The Empire Strikes Back: CISAC beats Commission in General Court', *Journal of Intellectual Property Law & Practice*, 8 (2013), 680

'Proposal for a Directive on collective rights management and (some) multi-territorial licensing', *European Intellectual Property Review*, 35 (2013), 65

Ramachandran, S., 'Netflix Says Push for Global Rights "Has Not Been an Easy Road"', *The Wall Street Journal* (7 December 2015): www.wsj.com/articles/netflix-says-push-for-global-rights-has-not-been-an-easy-road-1449508613

Reinbothe, J., 'Collective Rights Management in Germany' in D. Gervais (ed.), *Collective Management of Copyright and Related Rights*, 2nd edn. (Kluwer Law International, 2010)

Rethink Music, 'Fair Music: Transparency and Payment Flows in the Music Industry, Recommendations to Increase Transparency, Reduce Friction, and Promote Fairness in the Music Industry' (2015) Rethink Music, Berklee ICE, Boston: www.rethink-music.com/research/fair-music-transpar ency-and-payment-flows-in-the-music-industry

Riccio, G. M. and G. Codiglione, 'Copyright Collecting Societies, Monopolistic Positions and Competition in the EU Single Market', *Masaryk Journal of Law and Technology*, 7 (2013), 287

Ricolfi, M., 'Individual and collective management of copyright in a digital environment' in P. Torremans (ed.), *Copyright Law, A Handbook of Contemporary Research* (Edward Elgar, 2007)

'Collective Rights Management in a Digital Environment' in G. Ghidini and L. M. Genovesi (eds.), *Intellectual Property and Market Power, ATRIP Papers 2006–2007* (Eudeba, 2008)

'Consume and share: Making copyright fit for the digital agenda' in C. Geiger (ed.), *Constructing European Intellectual Property, Achievements and New Perspectives* (Edward Elgar, 2013)

'The new paradigm of creativity and innovation and its corollaries for the law of obligations' in P. Drahos, G. Ghidini and H. Ullrich (eds.), *Kritika: Essays on Intellectual Property* (Edward Elgar, 2015)

Riis, T., 'Collecting societies, competition, and the Services Directive', *Journal of Intellectual Property Law & Practice*, 6 (2011), 482

'Ophavsrettens fleksibilitet', *Nordiskt Immateriellt Rättskydd* (2012) 139

'User generated law: Re-constructing intellectual property law in a knowledge society' in T. Riis (ed.), *User Generated Law, Re-Constructing Intellectual Property Law in a Knowledge Society* (Edward Elgar, 2016)

Riis, T. and J. Schovsbo, 'Den grænseløse onlinebruger – geografisk opdeling af markedet for online- og streamingtjenester' in *Liber Amicorum Jan Rosén* (eddy.se 2016)

Rochelandet, F., 'Are copyright collecting societies efficient? An evaluation of collective administration of copyright in Europe' (The Society for Economic Research on Copyright Issues, Inaugural Annual Congress, Madrid, 2002)

Rognstad, O.-A., 'The multiplicity of territorial IP rights and its impact on competition' in J. Rosén (ed.), *Individualism and Collectiveness in Intellectual Property Law* (Edward Elgar, 2012)

'Legally Flawed but Politically Sound? Digital Exhaustion of Copyright in Europe after UsedSoft', *Oslo Law Review*, 3 (2014), 1

'The CJEU's Recent Findings on Digital Exhaustion and Linking and their Impact on Nordic Copyright Law', *Nordiskt Immateriellt Rättskydd* (2015) 624

'Restructuring the Economic Rights in Copyright – Some Reflections on an "Alternative Model"', *Journal of the Copyright Society of the USA*, 62 (2015), 503

Rosati, E., 'Online copyright exhaustion in a post-Allposters world' forthcoming in *Journal of Intellectual Property Law & Practice*: http://ssrn.com/abstract =2613608

'The Digital Single Market Strategy: Too many (strategic?) omissions' (*IPKat*, 7 May 2015): http://ipkitten.blogspot.dk/2015/05/the-digital-single-market-strategy-too.html

'Geoblocking: is the end in sight through ... competition law? Possibly not' (*IPKat*, 23 April 2016): http://ipkitten.blogspot.dk/2016/04/geoblocking-is-end-in-sight-through.html

'BREAKING: Report on responses to Public Consultation on EU copyright now available' (*IP Kat*, 23 July 2014): http://ipkitten.blogspot.dk/2014/07/breaking-report-on-responses-to-public.html

Ross, A., 'The new regulatory regime for collective rights management – the Government consults on how to implement', *Entertainment Law Review*, 26 (2015), 130

Rotondo, E., 'Three in One–Online: Collecting society joint venture cleared by the Commission', *Journal of Intellectual Property Law & Practice*, 11 (2016), 16

Samuelson, P., 'Should Economics Play a Role in Copyright Law and Policy?', *University of Ottawa Law & Technology Journal*, 1 (2004), 1

Savič, M., 'The CJEU AllPosters Case: Beginning of the End of Digital Exhaustion?' *European Intellectual Property Review*, 37 (2015), 389

Savin, A., 'The Commission's New Proposals on the Digital Single Market, May 2016' (*EU Internet Law & Policy Blog*, 25 March 2016): https://euinternetpo licy.wordpress.com/2016/05/25/the-commissions-new-proposals-on-the-di gital-single-market-may-2016/

Schovsbo, J., Grænsefladespørgsmål mellem immaterialretten og konkurrenceretten (Jurist- og Økonomforbundets Forlag, 1996)

'The Necessity to collectivize copyright – and dangers thereof' (2010): http://ssrn.com/abstract=1632753

Schwemer, S. F., 'The licensing of online music streaming services in Europe' in R. Watt (ed.), *Handbook on the Economics of Copyright* (Edward Elgar, 2014)

'Emerging models for cross-border online licensing' in T. Riis (ed.), *User Generated Law, Re-Constructing Intellectual Property Law in a Knowledge Society* (Edward Elgar, 2016)

'Geoblocking: im Visier der EU Kommission' (*HIIG Blog*, 13. November 2015): www.hiig.de/blog/geoblocking-im-visier-der-eu-kommission/

'The way forward to the Collective Rights Management Directive' (*The 1709 Blog*, 25 February 2014): http://the1709blog.blogspot.dk/2014/02/way-for ward-to-collective-rights.html

'Kollektiv forvaltning i informationssamfundet og det nye regime under direktivet 2014/26/EU i Danmark', *Nordiskt Immateriellt Rättskydd* (2015) 697

Senftleben, M. and others, 'The Recommendation on Measures to Safeguard Fundamental Rights and the Open Internet in the Framework of the EU Copyright Reform' (2017): https://ssrn.com/abstract=3054967

Shapiro, T., 'The proposed regulation on Portability – don't leave home without it', *Entertainment Law Review*, 27 (2016), 351

Simon, W. H., 'Toyota Jurisprudence: Legal Theory and Rolling Rule Regimes' in G. de Búrca and J. Scott (eds.), *Law and Governance in the EU and the US* (Hart Publishing, 2006)

Stalla-Bourdillon, S. and others, 'Open Letter to the European Commission – On the Importance of Preserving the Consistency and Integrity of the EU Acquis Relating to Content Monitoring within the Information Society' (2016): https://ssrn.com/abstract=2850483

Steyn, E., 'Collective rights management: Multi-territorial licensing and self-regulation', *Entertainment Law Review*, 25 (2014), 143

Stokkmo, O., 'The EU Collective Rights Management Directive and the RRO', *International Journal of Intellectual Property Management*, 7 (2014), 120

Street, J., D. Laing, and S. Schroff, 'Regulating for creativity and cultural diversity: The case of collective management organisations and the music industry', *International Journal of Cultural Policy*

Strowel, A. and B. Vanbrabant, "Copyright licensing: A European view" in J. de Werra (ed.), *Research Handbook on Intellectual Property Licensing* (Edward Elgar, 2013)

Stupp, C., 'Commission wants consumers to access digital content when they travel' (*EurActiv*, 9 December 2015): www.euractiv.com/section/digital/ne ws/commission-wants-consumers-to-access-digital-content-when-they-travel/

Szyszczak, E., 'Current Intelligence Karen Murphy: Decoding Licences and Territorial Exclusivity', *Journal of European Competition Law & Practice* (2011) 1

te Hacken, P., 'Terms and specialized vocabulary. Taming the prototype' in H. J. Kockaert and F. Steurs (eds.), *Handbook of Terminology*, vol. 1 (Jon Bejamins Publishing Co., 2015)

Thomes, T. P., 'An economic analysis of online streaming: How the music industry can generate revenues from cloud computing' (2011) ZEW-Centre for European Economic Research, Discussion Paper No. 11–039: http://ftp.zew.de/pub/zew-docs/dp/dp11039.pdf

Torremans, P., 'Questioning the principles of territoriality: The determination of territorial mechanisms of commercialisation' in P. Torremans (ed.), *Copyright Law, A Handbook of Contemporary Research* (Edward Elgar, 2007)
  'The Future Implications of the Usedsoft Decision' CREATe Working Paper 2014/2 (February 2014): www.create.ac.uk/publications/wp000012

Towse, R., 'Economics of collective management organisations in the creative industries' (WINIR conference, 4–6 April 2016)
  'Economics of copyright collecting societies and digital rights: Is there a case for a centralised digital copyright exchange?', *Review of Economic Research on Copyright Issues*, 9 (2012), 3

Towse, R., C. Handke and P. Stepan, 'The Economics of Copyright Law: A Stocktake of the Literature', *Review of Economic Research on Copyright Issues*, 5 (2008), 1

Train, K. E., *Optimal Regulation: The Economic Theory of Natural Monopoly*, 3rd edn. (MIT Press, 1994)

Trimble, M., 'The Territoriality Referendum', *World Intellectual Property Organization Journal* (2014) 89

Trubek, D. M., P. Cottrell and M. Nance, '"Soft Law", "Hard Law" and EU Integration' in G. de Búrca and J. Scott (eds.), *Law and Governance in the EU and the US* (Hart Publishing, 2006)

Tryggvadóttir, R., 'Balancing of Interests and Cross-border Use. Room for Nordic Co-operation?', *Nordiskt Immateriellt Rättskydd* (2015) 652

van Eechoud, M. and others, *Harmonizing European Copyright Law, The Challenges of Better Lawmaking*, vol. 19, Information Law Series (P. B. Hugenholtz (ed.), Wolters Kluwer, 2009)

van Gestel, R. and H.-W. Micklitz, 'Revitalizing Doctrinal Legal Research in Europe: What About Methodology?' in U. Neergaard, R. Nielsen and L. Roseberry (eds.), *European Legal Method – Pardoxes and Revitalisation* (DJØF Publishing, 2011)

van Gompel, S., 'Copyright Formalities in the Internet Age: Filters of Protection or Facilitators of Licensing', *Berkeley Technology Law Journal*, 28 (2013), 1425

Vestager, Margrethe, 'Competition policy for the Digital Single Market: Focus on e-commerce' (Bundeskartellamt International Conference on Competition, Berlin, 26 March 2015): http://europa.eu/rapid/press-release_SPEECH-15–4704_en.htm

'Intellectual property and competition' (19th IBA Competition Conference, Florence, 11 September 2015): http://ec.europa.eu/commission/2014–2019/vestager/announcements/intellectual-property-and-competition_en

von Albrecht, M., A. Mutschler-Siebert and T. Bosch, 'Die Murphy-Entscheidung und ihre Auswirkungen auf Sport- und Filmlizenzen im Online-Bereich, Die exklusive territoriale Rechtevergabe ist kein Modell der Vergangenheit!', *Zeitschrift für Urheber-und Medienrecht* (2012) 93

Vuckovic, R. M., 'Implementation of Directive 2014/26 on collective management and multi-territorial licensing of musical rights in regulating the tariff-setting systems in Central and Eastern Europe', *International Review of Intellectual Property and Competition Law*, 47 (2016), 28

Walker, N., 'EU Constitutionalism and New Governance' in G. de Búrca and J. Scott (eds.), *Law and New Governance in the EU and the US* (Hart Publishing, 2006)

Watt, R., *Copyright and economic theory: friends or foes?* (Edward Elgar, 2000)

'Copyright collectives: Some basic economic theory' in R. Watt (ed.), *Handbook on the Economics of Copyright* (Edward Elgar, 2014)

'Licensing of copyright works in a bargaining model' in R. Watt (ed.), *Handbook on the Economics of Copyright* (Edward Elgar, 2014)

'The Efficiencies of Aggregation: An Economic Theory Perspective on Collective Management of Copyright', *Review of Economic Research on Copyright Issues*, 12 (2015), 26

Weatherill, S., 'The Challenge of Better Regulation' in S. Weatherill (ed.), *Better Regulation* (Hart Publishing, 2007)

Whish, R. and D. Bailey, *Competition Law*, 8th edn. (Oxford University Press, 2015)

Williamson, O. E., *The Economic Institutions of Capitalism* (The Free Press, 1985)

Wolf, Alexander, 'Collecting societies as enablers for multiterritorial licensing of music', *EP Hearing on Collective Rights Management in the Digital Era*, 1 October 2012

Wood, A., 'The CJEU's ruling in the Premier League pub TV cases – the final whistle beckons: joined cases Football Association Premier League Ltd v QC Leisure (C-403/08) and Murphy v Media Protection Services Ltd (C-429/08)', *European Intellectual Property Review*, 34 (2012), 203

Yow, J. W. L., 'Creative Competition' with a Pan-European Licensing Body: Reconsidering the European Commission's Approach to Collecting Societies', *World Competition*, 34 (2011), 287

Index

Cambridge Intellectual Property and Information Law

Titles in the Series (formerly known as Cambridge Studies in Intellectual Property Rights)

Brad Sherman and Lionel Bently *The Making of Modern Intellectual Property Law*

Irini A. Stamatoudi *Copyright and Multimedia Products: A Comparative Analysis*

Pascal Kamina *Film Copyright in the European Union*

Huw Beverly-Smith *The Commercial Appropriation of Personality*

Mark J. Davison *The Legal Protection of Databases*

Robert Burrell and Allison Coleman *Copyright Exceptions: The Digital Impact*

Huw Beverly-Smith, Ansgar Ohly and Agnès Lucas-Schloetter *Privacy, Property and Personality: Civil Law Perspectives on Commercial Appropriation*

Catherine Seville *The Internationalisation of Copyright Law: Books, Buccaneers and the Black Flag in the Nineteenth Century*

Philip Leith *Software and Patents in Europe*

Edited by Geertrui van Overwalle *Gene Patents and Collaborative Licensing Models: Patent Pools, Clearinghouses, Open Source Models and Liability Regimes*

Edited by Lionel Bently, Jennifer Davis and Jane C. Ginsburg *Trade Marks and Brands: An Interdisciplinary Critique*

Jonathan Curci *The Protection of Biodiversity and Traditional Knowledge in International Law of Intellectual Property*

Edited by Lionel Bently, Jennifer Davis and Jane C. Ginsburg *Copyright and Piracy: An Interdisciplinary Critique*

Megan Richardson and Julian Thomas *Fashioning Intellectual Property: Exhibition, Advertising and the Press, 1789–1918*

Dev Gangjee *Relocating the Law of Geographical Indications*

Edited by Andrew T. Kenyon, Megan Richardson and Wee-Loon Ng-Loy *The Law of Reputation and Brands in the Asia Pacific*

Edson Beas Rodrigues, Jr *The General Exceptions Clauses of the TRIPS Agreements: Promoting Sustainable Development*

Edited by Annabelle Lever *New Frontiers in the Philosophy of Intellectual Property*

Sigrid Sterckx and Julian Cockbain *Exclusions from Patentability: How Far Has the European Patent Office Eroded Boundaries?*

Sebastian Haunss *Conflicts in the Knowledge Society: The Contentious Politics of Intellectual Property*

Edited by Helena R. Howe in consultation with Jonathon Griffiths *Concepts of Property in Intellectual Property Law*

Edited by Rochelle Cooper Dreyfuss and Jane C. Ginsburg *Intellectual Property at the Edge: The Contested Contours of IP*

Edited by Normann Witzleb, David Lindsay, Moira Paterson and Sharon Rodrick *Emerging Challenges in Privacy Law: Comparative Perspectives*

Paul Bernal *Internet Privacy Rights: Rights to Protect Autonomy*

Peter Drahos *Intellectual Property, Indigenous People and Their Knowledge*

For EU product safety concerns, contact us at Calle de José Abascal, 56–1°,
28003 Madrid, Spain or eugpsr@cambridge.org.